Tourism in Pacific Islands

Pacific Island Countries have been shown to be especially vulnerable to such external influences as natural disasters, political unrest and downturns in the global economy and their tourism industries have been notably affected. In particular, they typically have a narrow resource base and a fragile and often vulnerable natural environment. While there is some research on islands and small states, there is a dearth of information on the South Pacific and very little research is being undertaken in the region compared to other geographical regions in the world. This volume brings together current work in Pacific Island tourism.

In this collection, three main themes arise: Images of the South Pacific; Socioeconomic Impacts of Tourism; and Pacific Island Countries and the Outside World. The first focus is on the question of image, namely, stereotypes of a destination held by tourists and potential tourists, the extent to which residents, for their part, really welcome visitors, and the role tourism might play in changing pre-established images. The second theme is tourism's impacts, notably the economic and socio-cultural effects of international tourism's intrusion in the region which, though often hotly debated, have attracted relatively little empirical research. The third focus is on the challenges of how PICs articulate with their external geo-political and physical environment. These involve existing relations with formal colonial centres, geographical isolation, the need for greater air access to the outside world and for more tourists, and the continuing threat to several PICs of global warming, which increased air travel will inevitably exacerbate.

This text will be of interest to tourism students, researchers and academics in the fields of tourism, development studies and cultural studies.

Stephen Pratt is Assistant Professor at the School of Hospitality and Tourism Management, Hong Kong Polytechnic University, Hong Kong. His main research interests lie in the areas of economic impacts of tourism, tourism marketing, sustainable tourism and tourism in the South Pacific.

David Harrison was from 2008 until early 2014 Professor and Head of the School of Tourism and Hospitality Management, University of the South Pacific, Fiji. He is now Professor of Tourism at Middlesex University, London. His primary interests are the economic, social and cultural aspects of tourism in developing countries, and he has carried out research and written on tourism in the Eastern Caribbean, Southern Africa, Eastern Europe, South-East Asia and the South Pacific.

Contemporary Geographies of Leisure, Tourism and Mobility

Series Editor: C. Michael Hall, *Professor at the Department of Management, College of Business and Economics, University of Canterbury, Christchurch, New Zealand*

The aim of this series is to explore and communicate the intersections and relationships between leisure, tourism and human mobility within the social sciences.

It will incorporate both traditional and new perspectives on leisure and tourism from contemporary geography, e.g. notions of identity, representation and culture, while also providing for perspectives from cognate areas such as anthropology, cultural studies, gastronomy and food studies, marketing, policy studies and political economy, regional and urban planning, and sociology, within the development of an integrated field of leisure and tourism studies.

Also, increasingly, tourism and leisure are regarded as steps in a continuum of human mobility. Inclusion of mobility in the series offers the prospect to examine the relationship between tourism and migration, the sojourner, educational travel, and second home and retirement travel phenomena.

The series comprises two strands:

Contemporary Geographies of Leisure, Tourism and Mobility aims to address the needs of students and academics, and the titles will be published in hardback and paperback. Titles include:

1. **The Moralisation of Tourism**
   Sun, sand ... and saving the world?
   Jim Butcher

2. **The Ethics of Tourism Development**
   Mick Smith and Rosaleen Duffy

3. **Tourism in the Caribbean**
   Trends, development, prospects
   Edited by David Timothy Duval

4. **Qualitative Research in Tourism**
   Ontologies, epistemologies and methodologies
   Edited by Jenny Phillimore and Lisa Goodson

5. **The Media and the Tourist Imagination**
   Converging cultures
   Edited by David Crouch, Rhona Jackson and Felix Thompson

6. **Tourism and Global Environmental Change**
   Ecological, social, economic and political interrelationships
   Edited by Stefan Gössling and C. Michael Hall

7. **Cultural Heritage of Tourism in the Developing World**
   Edited by Dallen J. Timothy and Gyan Nyaupane

Routledge Studies in Contemporary Geographies of Leisure, Tourism and Mobility is a forum for innovative new research intended for research students and academics, and the titles will be available in hardback only. Titles include:

47. A Hospitable World?
Organising work and workers
in hotels and tourist resorts
*Edited by David Jordhus-Lier
and Anders Underthun*

48. Tourism in Pacific Islands
Current issues and future
challenges
*Edited by Stephen Pratt and
David Harrison*

Forthcoming:

**Social Memory and Heritage
Tourism**
*Edited by David L. Butler,
Perry Carter, Stephen P. Hanna,
Arnold Modlin and Amy E. Potter*

**International Tourism and
Cooperation and the Gulf
Cooperation Council States**
Warwick Frost and Jennifer Laing

Affective Tourism
Dark routes in conflict
Dorina Maria Buda

Volunteer Tourism and Development
Jim Butcher and Peter Smith

The Business of Sustainable Tourism
*Edited by Michael Hughes,
David Weaver and Christof Pforr*

**Imagining the West through Film
and Tourism**
*Marcus Stephenson and
Ala Al-Hamarneh*

Scientific and Research Tourism
*Edited by Susan L. Slocum,
Carol Kline and Andrew Holden*

**Tourism and Development in
Sub-Sahara Africa**
Marina Novelli

Mountaineering Tourism
*Edited by Ghazali Musa,
Anna Thompson and James Higham*

Research Volunteer Tourism
Angela M. Benson

Tourism and the Anthropocene
*Edited by Martin Gren and
Edward H. Huijbens*

**Women and Sex Tourism
Landscapes**
Erin Sanders-McDonagh

**The Politics and Power of Tourism
in the 'Holy Land'**
*Edited by Rami K. Isaac,
Freya Higgins-Desbiolles and
C. Michael Hall*

Tourism in Pacific Islands
Current issues and future challenges

Edited by
Stephen Pratt and David Harrison

Routledge
Taylor & Francis Group

LONDON AND NEW YORK

First published 2015
by Routledge

2 Park Square, Milton Park, Abingdon, Oxon OX14 4RN
711 Third Avenue, New York, NY 10017, USA

Routledge is an imprint of the Taylor & Francis Group, an informa business

First issued in paperback 2017

British Library Cataloguing in Publication Data
A catalogue record for this book is available from the British Library

Library of Congress Cataloging in Publication Data
   Tourism in Pacific Islands : current issues and future challenges / edited by Stephen Pratt and David Harrison.
      pages cm. – (Contemporary geographies of leisure, tourism and mobility)
   Includes bibliographical references and index.
   1. Tourism–Oceania. 2. Tourism–Social aspects–Oceania. 3. Oceania–Social conditions. 4. Oceania–Economic conditions. I. Pratt, Stephen (Assistant professor)
   G155.O25T68 2015
   338.4'7919504–dc23
                     2014030577

ISBN: 978-1-138-77535-0 (hbk)
ISBN: 978-1-138-08383-7 (pbk)

Typeset in Times New Roman
by Taylor & Francis Books

Contents

List of illustrations

Figures

Tables

List of contributors

Emma Calgaro is a member of the Asia-Pacific Natural Hazards Group, University of Sydney, Australia. She is a human geographer specialising in disaster risk reduction, vulnerability and resilience. Her research explores the drivers of vulnerability and resilience in the coupled human-environment system with a regional focus on South-East Asia and Australia and the South Pacific. Specifically, she focuses on understanding the complex set of contextual factors (socio-cultural, political, economic and biophysical) that impede and/or improve resilience and vulnerability levels to risk, with a strong focus on contextual vulnerability in tourism destinations. Her research aims to advance the theoretical underpinnings of vulnerability research and sustainability science and apply these theoretical advances to the tourism context.

Anand Chand is an Associate Professor in Management and Public Administration in the Faculty of Business and Economics at the University of the South Pacific in Fiji Islands. His major research focus is the areas of supply chain management, human resource, employment relations and agri-business. He has published more than 50 articles in international journals, and a book: *Global Supply Chains in the South Pacific Region: A Study of Fiji's Garment Industry* (Nova Science Publishers) and (with S. Naidu) *Best Human Resource Management and Firm Performance in the Pacific Island Countries* (Nova Science Publishers).

Dr **Joseph M. Cheer** is Lecturer and Associate Director of the Australia and International Tourism Research Unit (AITRU) at the National Centre for Australian Studies, Monash University. His research examining issues of development, socio-economic and cultural change and postcolonial legacies (especially in the South Pacific) has been published in *Annals of Tourism Research, Tourism Analysis, Pacific Economic Bulletin, Journal of Heritage Tourism* and *Tourism Planning and Development*. Joseph is finalising a sole-authored book stemming from his doctoral research examining the tourism and traditional culture nexus. As a practitioner, Joseph has held senior and advisory roles in the international hotel industry, in international development and in corporate finance.

Terry DeLacy is a Professor in Sustainable Tourism and Environmental Policy at Victoria University, Australia. He was previously the director of the Australian government-established national Sustainable Tourism Cooperative Research Centre (STCRC). Terry has recently published two books on the transformation of the tourism sector into the emerging green economy.

Associate Professor **Dale Dominey-Howes** is Director of the Asia-Pacific Natural Hazards Research Lab, University of Sydney, Australia. His expertise is in natural hazards, hazard, risk and vulnerability assessment, disaster and emergency management.

Dr **Sebastian Filep**, PhD, specialises in tourism and well-being research. Apart from the key research interest in well-being, Sebastian has contributed to government-level research projects in the Pacific on sustainability and climate change. He is a co-author of *Tourists, Tourism and the Good Life* (Routledge, 2011) and the lead editor of *Tourist Experience and Fulfilment: Insights from Positive Psychology* (Routledge, 2013). Dr Filep is a Lecturer at the University of Otago in New Zealand and Honorary Fellow at Victoria University in Melbourne, Australia.

Dawn Gibson is a Senior Lecturer at the School of Tourism and Hospitality Management, Faculty of Business and Economics, University of the South Pacific, Suva, Fiji. Her PhD research was on the cultural challenges of indigenous community tourism operations in Fiji. Her research interests include sustainable tourism development, impacts of tourism, community/indigenous tourism, backpacker and volunteer tourism, employee empowerment, service quality, retail tourism, strata title ownership in multinational corporations, hospitality, and increasing local agricultural linkages to tourism through farm-to-table initiatives with hotels/resorts and local communities.

David Harrison is a sociologist/anthropologist with a special interest in tourism as a development tool. Formerly Head of School of Tourism and Hospitality Management at the University of the South Pacific (2008–14), he is now Professor of Tourism at Middlesex University, London, and Visiting Senior Research Fellow in the Department of Geography, King's College London. Author of *The Sociology of Modernisation and Development* (Routledge, 1988), editor of several books, including *Pacific Island Tourism* (2001), and many book chapters and peer-reviewed journal articles, he is a Fellow of the International Institute for the Study of Tourism and a member of several editorial boards of tourism journals, including *Annals of Tourism Research*. He has researched the role of tourism in the Caribbean, Eastern Europe, Southern Africa, South-East Asia and the South Pacific, and is currently focusing on globalisation and the role of mass tourism in developed and developing countries.

Anne-Marie d'Hauteserre is Tourism Programme Convenor in the School of Social Sciences at the University of Waikato, Aotearoa New Zealand. Her research investigates issues linked to tourism development from a critical social science perspective. Her main areas of interest have been indigenous tourism development in the French Pacific and at Foxwoods Casino Resort, CT, USA; urbanisation and tourism in the Eastern Paris Basin in France and in the Principality of Monaco. She has had numerous publications on these topics in both English and French scholarly journals and books.

Emma Hughes is a PhD student in the Institute of Development Studies at Massey University. Her research looks at the impact of corporate community development in the tourism sector from community perspectives. It is part of a larger study into private sector-led development in mining and tourism in the Pacific, led by Regina Scheyvens and Glenn Banks. Emma's previous research has focused on indigenous activism and development, with co-author Sita Venkateswar, *The Politics of Indigeneity: Dialogues and Reflections on Indigenous Activism* (Zed Books, 2011).

Dr **John S. Hull** is an Associate Professor of Tourism Management at Thompson Rivers University in British Columbia, Canada. He is also a Visiting Professor at Buskerud and Westfold University College in Norway and at the Harz University of Applied Sciences, Wernigerode, Germany. His research addresses the sustainability of tourism in peripheral regions, focusing on creative tourism, cruise tourism, agri-tourism, geotourism, Arctic tourism, mountain tourism and wellness tourism. John has consulted for numerous agencies in the Asia-Pacific as a member of the New Zealand Tourism Research Institute (NZTRI), including the UN Convention on Biological Diversity, the South Pacific Tourism Organisation and the NZSerivceIQ. He is also a member of the International Tourism Studies Association (ITSA).

Dr **Min Jiang** is a Senior Research Fellow at College of Business, Victoria University and an Honorary Research Associate at the University of Sydney, Australia. As an environmental lawyer by training, Min has published internationally in academic journals and books in the areas of tourism vulnerability, resilience, adaptation to climate change, and water governance. She has led and coordinated a number of research and industry consultancy projects on climate change adaptation, sustainable tourism and the green economy in Australia, China and the South Pacific. Min is the sole author of the commissioned book *Towards Tradable Water Rights: Water Law and Policy Reform in China* (Springer).

Yoko Kanemasu is a Senior Lecturer in Sociology at the University of the South Pacific. Her research areas include the politics of representation, tourism, identity, sport and rural development. Her recent publications include: (with G. Molnar) 'Life after Rugby: Issues of Being an "Ex" in

Fiji Rugby', *International Journal of the History of Sport* 31(11) (2014): 1389–405; (with G. Molnar) 'Pride of the People: Fijian Rugby Labour Migration and Collective Identity', *International Review for the Sociology of Sport* 48(6) (2013): 720–35; 'Social Construction of Touristic Imagery: Case of Fiji', *Annals of Tourism Research* 43 (2013): 456–81; and 'A National Pride or a Colonial Construct? Touristic Representation and the Politics of Fijian Identity Construction', *Social Identities* 19(1) (2013): 71–89. She was a key convenor of the Fiji Rugby Centenary Conference held at the University of the South Pacific in 2013.

Dr **Uwe Kaufmann** is Trade and Economic Analyst and Lecturer at the Institute for International Trade (IIT) at the University of Adelaide, Australia. Uwe's areas of expertise include applied services trade, goods trade, data and economic research and analysis, and trade negotiation-related preparation required for trade negotiations. He has worked on a wide range of projects including the Organisation for Economic Co-operation and Development (OECD) Services Restrictiveness Index, several Pacific Island trade impact studies, a study on the Canada–Australia bilateral trade, investment and services relationship, and he is one of the key facilitators in IIT's Pacific and African trade training programmes, which focus on capacity building and enhancing trade policy knowledge and skills of the participants. Uwe holds a PhD in Economics from the University of Adelaide and a Master's degree in Commerce in Economics from the University of the South Pacific.

Dr **Louise Munk Klint** is currently a Tourism Development Officer for Moira Shire Council, Australia, responsible for developing and implementing their new tourism strategy. Louise specialises in tourism and climate change research, with a particular focus on vulnerability assessments and the Pacific.

Dr **Barbara Koth** completed this work as a Senior Lecturer with the School of Natural and Built Environments at the University of South Australia (Adelaide). She is currently an Adjunct Lecturer with the Barbara Hardy Institute (sustainability) at UniSA, and a consultant in ecotourism, destination management, park planning, sustainability and behaviour change in individuals and organisations, community engagement and conscious capitalism. Previously she held positions with the University of Minnesota (USA), the Scenic Byways Program with the US Federal Highway Administration, and with overseas aid development projects (World Bank, USAID, FINNIDA, private sector) in South-East Asia, Africa and the Middle East. Recent research publications focus on food waste composting at tourism businesses, management of wildlife tourism, tourism mobility, cycle tourism, water-sensitive urban design and the dynamics of local food production. Koth is an avid sailor, cyclist and Pacific traveller.

Dr **Jennifer H. Laing** is a Senior Lecturer in the Department of Marketing and Tourism and Hospitality at La Trobe University. Her research interests include travel narratives, the role of events in society, heritage tourism and adventure travel. Jennifer is a foundation co-editor of the Routledge Advances in Events Research series and has co-written three books: *Books and Travel: Inspiration, Quests and Transformation* (Channel View, 2012), *Commemorative Events: Memory, Identities, Conflict* (Routledge, 2013), and *Explorer Travellers and Adventure Tourism* (Channel View, 2014).

Simon Milne is Professor of Tourism at Auckland University of Technology, where he directs the New Zealand Tourism Research Institute (www.nztri. org). Simon's current research focuses on the links between tourism, ICT and sustainable community development, and he also undertakes tourism strategy development work in the Pacific Islands and around the world. Simon has worked as a consultant to a number of international agencies including the UN Economic and Social Commission for Asia and the Pacific, the UN Development Programme, European Union and the Organization of American States.

Apisalome Movono has an undergraduate background in marine affairs and tourism, and gained his MA from the School of Tourism and Hospitality Management, University of the South Pacific, Fiji. He is particularly interested in the socio-economic impacts of tourism on indigenous Fijian communities, and has a passion for understanding issues of sustainability and sustainable livelihoods. He has co-authored a number of papers and has published in the *Asia Pacific Journal of Tourism Research*, and a book chapter on 'Slow Tourism: Travel and Mobilities' (Channel View Publications). He was recently an Assistant Lecturer with the School of Tourism and Hospitality Management at the University of the South Pacific, and is now a PhD candidate with the Griffith Institute for Tourism, Department of International Business and Asian Studies, Griffith University, Australia.

Suwastika Naidu is an Assistant Lecturer in the School of Management and Public Administration in the Faculty of Business and Economics at the University of the South Pacific in Fiji Islands. Her major research focus is the area of human resource and agri-business. She has published more than 20 articles in international journals, and co-authored a book (with A. Chand) *Best Human Resource Management and Firm Performance in the Pacific Island Countries* (Nova Science Publishers).

Dr **Haruo Nakagawa** is Fellow at the School of Government, Development and International Affairs, Faculty of Business and Economics at the University of the South Pacific (USP), Suva, Fiji. Haruo's main interests are goods and services trade, public economics and economic growth particularly in the Pacific island region. He holds a PhD in Economics from the Australian National University (ANU) in 2004 and joined the faculty of the USP in 2005. He also has Master's degrees in Development Economics

(ANU) and International Affairs (Columbia University, New York). Before starting his academic career, he worked for 14 years for the Customs Service and the Ministry of Finance of Japan.

Steve Noakes is Adjunct Professor at the Griffith Institute for Tourism, Griffith University, Australia. He has an extensive industry, academic and non-governmental organisation background throughout the Asia-Pacific region, with expertise in sustainable tourism, international development, and tourism and destination management.

Dr **Stephen Pratt** is currently Assistant Professor at the School of Hotel and Tourism Management, Hong Kong Polytechnic University. He has been there since January 2013. He was previously Senior Lecturer at the University of the South Pacific. Stephen completed his PhD at the University of Nottingham, United Kingdom, under the supervision of Professors Thea Sinclair and Adam Blake. Prior to undertaking his PhD, he was a Research Director for several marketing consultancies both in Hawaii and Australia. His research interests include the economic, socio-cultural and environmental impacts of tourism, destination marketing, cruise tourism and film tourism.

Professor **Keir J. Reeves** holds a chair in regional engagement at Federation University Australia. Previously he has held roles as a Senior Monash Research Fellow and Director of the Australian and International Tourism Research Unit, Monash University, and lecturer and Australian Research Council Post-doctoral Research Fellow at the University of Melbourne. His current research concentrates on Asia and the Pacific cultural heritage, tourism studies, regional development and history. In 2013 he was a Visiting Fellow at Clare Hall Cambridge and a Visiting Researcher at the McDonald Institute for Archaeological Research, University of Cambridge. Keir has also co-edited four books: *Island of War, Islands of Memory* (Cambridge University Press, 2015), *Anzac Journeys: Walking the Battlefields of World War Two* (Cambridge University Press, 2013), *Places of Pain and Shame: Dealing with 'Difficult' Heritage* (Routledge, 2009), and *Deeper Leads: New Approaches in Victorian Gold Fields History* (BHS Publishing, 2007).

Regina Scheyvens heads Development Studies at Massey University, where she combines a passion for teaching about international development with research on tourism and development. Two books have emerged from this research: *Tourism for Development: Empowering Communities* (Pearson, 2002), and *Tourism and Poverty* (Routledge, 2011), along with articles on themes such as backpacker tourism, ecotourism, empowerment and sustainable tourism. Her current research (with co-author Emma Hughes) examines the contributions of multinational tourism resorts to community development in Fiji.

Theo Simos is an Associate Researcher in the Faculty of Professions, University of Adelaide in Australia. His major research focus is agri-business and marketing of pearls in the South Pacific region. He specialises in doing primary research and has written a number of reports.

Evangeline Singh is a Senior Research and Evaluation Analyst, Strategy and Governance at the Ministry of Business, Innovation and Employment, Government of New Zealand (www.mbie.govt.nz). Evangeline has a PhD from Auckland University of Technology and her current research and evaluation focus on stakeholder feedback, quality of policy advice, performance measures and effectiveness in the public sector, local economic development, South Pacific regional issues, economic contribution and development of Pacific people in New Zealand, and tourism and agriculture links.

Paul C. Southgate is Professor in Tropical Aquaculture at James Cook University's Centre for Sustainable Tropical Fisheries and Aquaculture in Australia. His major research focus is the biology and culture of pearl oysters and of particular interest is the potential for pearl culture to support livelihood opportunities in coastal communities throughout the developing world. He has published more than 70 articles in scientific journals dealing with pearl oysters and co-edited the only monograph on this topic, which is the 'go-to' source for researchers in this field: (ed. with J. Lucas) *The Pearl Oyster* (Elsevier, 2008).

Semisi Taumoepeau is a Senior Lecturer and the Head of the Tourism Management Department (2003–present), Auckland Institute of Studies in Auckland, New Zealand. He is also an Associate Director of the New Zealand Tourism Research Institute, Auckland University of Technology. Previous positions include the Directorship of Tourism for the government of Tonga (1979–2003), CEO of the Tonga national airline (1999–2002), and Chairman of the South Pacific Tourism Organisation (SPTO), Suva, Fiji for two terms during the 1980s and the 1990s. He has published several publications in the field of Pacific tourism and aviation and is currently a tourism consultant for several regional and national tourism projects in the South Pacific. Semisi holds a BSc degree (Auckland), MSc degree (Surrey) and a DBA (University of the Sunshine Coast), with his thesis on the economic sustainability of Pacific airlines. His research interests include economic sustainability of Pacific airlines, tourism planning and development, human resource development tourism and hospitality training across the South Pacific.

Acknowledgements

Both editors wish to acknowledge the support received from former collea-gues at the University of the South Pacific, especially the School of Tourism and Hospitality Management, as well as others in the Business School. Although we no longer work at USP, our commitment to the region and the friendships remain. Both editors would like to thank the authors of the indi-vidual chapters for their contributions. We hope that our review and editing process helped polish and refine your contributions and our suggested revi-sions and edits improved your chapters. Thank you for your patience in dealing with us. We would both like to thank the publishing staff at Taylor & Francis for their patience and professionalism.

I would like to thank my wife, Rebecca Pratt, for her continued support while working on this book. I would also like to thank my children, Micah, Zoe and Zedekiah. While spending their formative years in Fiji, they can all say they have some personal insights into the current issues and future chal-lenges of tourism in Pacific islands. Lastly, I would like to thank my co-editor, one-time boss and (still) friend, David Harrison. I have enjoyed working with you, learning from you and discussing and debating tourism in developing countries, particularly in the Pacific.

Stephen Pratt

I am especially grateful to Senimili Kamikamica for her support, which now continues in the UK.

David Harrison

List of abbreviations

ADF	Augmented Dicky Fuller
AFC	Asian financial crisis
AGBOM	Australian Government Bureau of Meteorology
AGDCCEE	Australian Government Department of Climate Change and Energy Efficiency
ANZ	Australia and New Zealand
ARDL	Autoregressive Distributed Lag
ASA	air services agreement
ASMPG	average seat mile per gallon
CBE	community-based ecotourism
CBT	community-based tourism
CBTI	community-based tourism initiative
CRMD	Chief Roi Mata's Domain
CSIRO	Commonwealth Scientific and Industrial Research Organization, Australia
CSR	corporate social responsibility
DSF	Destination Sustainability Framework
EC	error correction
ECM	Error Correction Modelling
ENSO	El Niño Southern Oscillation
FAO	Food and Agriculture Organization
FAR	Fourth Assessment Report
FGD	focus group discussion
FMOLS	Phillips and Hansen Fully Modified OLS
FSA	full-service airline
FVB	Fiji Visitors Bureau
GDP	gross domestic product
GETS	General to Specific
GFC	global financial crisis
GHGs	greenhouse gases
GNP	gross national product

GSTC	Global Sustainable Tourism Council
ICAO	International Civil Aviation Organization
IPCC	Intergovernmental Panel on Climate Change
JAL	Japan Airlines
JML	Johansen Maximum Likelihood
LCC	low-cost carrier
LDC	least developed countries
MDGs	Millennium Development Goals
ME	maximum eigenvalue
MIRAB	migration remittances aid bureaucracy
MOP	mother-of-pearl
NGO	non-governmental organisation
NIWAR	National Institute of Water and Atmospheric Research
NLTB	Native Land Trust Board
PARDI	Pacific Agriculture Research Development Initiative
PIASA	Pacific Islands Air Services Agreement
PIC	Pacific island country
PICTs	Pacific island countries and territories
PPT	pro-poor tourism
REER	real effective exchange rate
RESET	Regression Equation Specification Error Test
RGDI	real gross domestic income
RGDP	real gross domestic product
SARS	severe acute respiratory syndrome
SIC	Schwarz Information Criterion
SIDS	small island developing states
SIDSNET	Small Island Developing States Network
SIDSTs	small island developing states and territories
SITE	small island tourism economy
SMTEs	small and medium-sized tourism enterprises
SPC	Secretariat of the Pacific Community
SPTO	South Pacific Tourism Organisation
SSC	South Seas Cruises
STD	sustainable tourism development
TDA	tourism development areas
TLTB	*iTaukei* Land Trust Board
TNC	transnational company
TW REER	trade-weighted real effective exchange rate
TWRGDP	trade-weighted real gross domestic product
UN	United Nations
UNEP	United Nations Environment Programme
UNESCAP	United Nations Economic and Social Commission for Asia and the Pacific
UNESCO	United Nations Educational, Scientific and Cultural Organization

UN-OHRLLS	UN Office of the High Representative of the Least Developed Countries, Landlocked Developing Countries and Small Island Developing States
UNWTO	United Nations World Tourism Organisation
USP	University of the South Pacific
VAR	Vector Autoregression
WHTC	World Heritage Tourism Committee
WTTC	World Travel and Tourism Council

Part I
Background

1 Tourism in Pacific island countries
Current issues and future challenges

David Harrison and Stephen Pratt

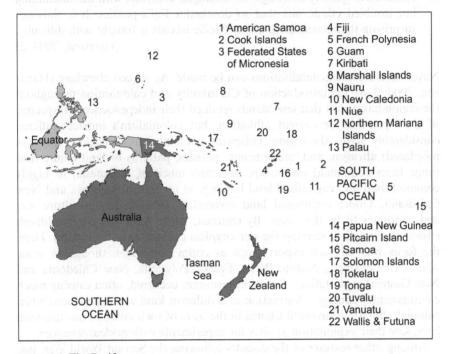

1 American Samoa	4 Fiji
2 Cook Islands	5 French Polynesia
3 Federated States	6 Guam
of Micronesia	7 Kiribati
	8 Marshall Islands
	9 Nauru
	10 New Caledonia
	11 Niue
	12 Northern Mariana
	Islands
	13 Palau
	14 Papua New Guinea
	15 Pitcairn Island
	16 Samoa
	17 Solomon Islands
	18 Tokelau
	19 Tonga
	20 Tuvalu
	21 Vanuatu
	22 Wallis & Futuna

Figure 1.1 The Pacific
Source: www.lonelyplanet.com/maps/pacific/

Background

Islands in the developing world are often said to share similar characteristics. Prominent among these are isolation, smallness of scale and weak economies, all of which affect the cost of 'development, access to markets and expertise', and result in a limited resource base, small domestic markets, 'limited infrastructure and institutional mechanisms, and dependency on external forces' (Carlsen and Butler, 2011: 1–2). However, regions defined as 'islands' also differ in numerous physical, economic or social characteristics, and (conversely) some landlocked territories may, in fact, evidence 'island' features (Butler, Harrison and Filho, 1996: 1). With regard to Pacific island countries (PICs), it is certainly the case that they come in all shapes and sizes:

> Coral atolls are common in Polynesia, where a total population of some half a million is widely dispersed, but the more populous Melanesian islands tend to be volcanic and more densely populated, and two thirds of their six million people are in Papua New Guinea. Even within Pacific island national societies, there are considerable differences. The relative ethnic homogeneity of Tonga, for example, contrasts with the fascinating but troubled ethnic mix that so dominates Fiji's politics. It is thus not surprising that generalising about Pacific islands is fraught with difficulty.
>
> (Harrison, 2004: 2)

Nevertheless, some generalisations can be made. As argued elsewhere (Harrison, 2004: 2–4), the introduction of Christianity and colonisation throughout the region has meant that few islands retained their independence, irrespective of their previous or current affiliation, but colonialism's impacts differed considerably across the region. Following combinations of neglect, (perhaps misplaced) altruism, and 'modernising' policies, patterns of land tenure now range from communal ownership, as across much of Melanesia, to highly commoditised and capitalised land holding, as in French Polynesia and New Caledonia. Under communal land ownership, subsistence agriculture was and continues to be the norm. By contrast, where land was commoditised, efforts were made to develop the stereotypical colonial export economy. Here, the focus was on such export crops as copra and sugar, though in some islands (for example, Nauru, Palau, French Polynesia, New Caledonia and New Guinea) exploitation of mineral resources occurred, often causing much environmental damage. Destruction of a different kind was experienced when colonial affiliations involved islands in the wars of their colonial masters and, later, saw their exploitation as sites for experiments with nuclear weapons.

Among other features of the decades following the Second World War, two are especially relevant in the present context, and they are connected. First, it was a period of formal decolonisation. In 1962, Samoa became the first PIC to obtain independence, self-government in the Cook Islands followed in 1965, and over the next decade other colonies either achieved formal independence from or developed some form of association with former colonial powers: Nauru, 1968; Fiji and Tonga (formerly a British Protectorate), 1970; Niue, in association with New Zealand, 1974; Papua New Guinea, 1975; Solomon Islands and Tuvalu, 1978; Kiribati, 1979; and Vanuatu, 1980. In 1986 the Federated States of Micronesia and the Marshall Islands became independent in association with the USA, with Palau following in 1994. At least officially, the problems of 'development' in these 'new nations' were in local hands (Crocombe, 2008: 403–22). Here, we come to the second common feature of the post 1945 period: as in developing countries elsewhere, their leaders increasingly felt that tourism would be their 'passport to development' (de Kadt, 1979).

Tourist arrivals to Pacific island countries

As indicated elsewhere (Harrison and Prasad, 2013), tourism is a key driver in the economies of several PICs and it is becoming increasingly important in others. However, the *growth* of tourism in PICs has been consistently less than in the world as a whole or in the Asia-Pacific region, as indicated in Table 1.1. Since 2015, global tourism has grown by 29.5%, that of Asia/Pacific 52%, and that of PICs by only 10.5%. When one examines the fortunes over the same period of different PICs, they are variable. Such PICs as Niue, Tuvalu, the Federated States of Micronesia, Palau and Kiribati are so small, and start from such a small base, that almost any variation in arrivals has a drastic impact on the statistics. Others, which continue to be administratively linked to former colonial powers, have struggled to maintain momentum. In 2012, French Polynesia, for example, actually received 18.8% fewer tourists than in 2005, and over the same period numbers visiting the Marshall Islands plummeted by 50%. Guam managed only an 8.3% increase and Palau a more respectable 38.2%, primarily because of the introduction of Saipan Airline in 2012. Except for Papua New Guinea and Solomon Islands, both in some respects special cases, the most obvious success stories among PICs are Cook Islands, Vanuatu and Samoa. Tiny fish in the massive Pacific pool, with small or relatively small populations (about 15,000, 255,000 and 190,000, respectively), they epitomise how a few tourists can make a huge difference to small societies. Since 2008, tourism in all three has increased by well over the regional average (but only in Vanuatu at a greater pace than the rest of the Asia/Pacific region). Tourism to Fiji, too, increased over the period, but its tourism has been consistently undermined by a series of coups since the mid-1980s (Harrison and Pratt, 2012).

Most PICs are primarily holiday destinations (Table 1.2), whose attractions are primarily sun, sea and (sometimes) sand. Exceptions are Papua New Guinea and Solomon Islands, in particular, which possess considerable economic potential and attract a high percentage of business tourists, as do Kiribati, Marshall Islands, New Caledonia and Niue, while many visitors to Tonga, Samoa, Niue and Kiribati are migrants returning to visit friends and relatives. Often dismissed as 'only locals', their impact on the economy is nevertheless considerable, even though their patterns of expenditure differ from that of other international visitors (Tauatofua and Craig-Smith, 2010).

Geographical propinquity and previous metropolitan affiliation help determine tourists' destination choice. As discussed elsewhere (Harrison and Pratt, 2013: 7–8), Australians make up the majority of visitors to 'Melanesian' Fiji, Papua New Guinea, Solomon Islands and Vanuatu; the 'Polynesian' Cook Islands, Niue and Tonga, especially, attract New Zealanders, and a high

Table 1.1 Tourist arrivals to PICs: selected years, 2000–12

Country	2000	2005	2010	2011	2012	% market share of PICs 2012	% increase 2005–12
Cook Islands	72,994	88,405	104,265	112,643	121,757	3.59	37.7
FSM	20,501	18,958	20,580	18,986	20,141	0.59	6.2
Fiji	294,070	545,145	631,868	675,050	660,590	19.50	21.2
French Polynesia	233,326	208,067	153,919	162,776	168,978	4.99	-18.8
Guam	1,279,243	1,184,928	1,170,857	1,122,921	1,283,000	37.88	8.3
Kiribati	4,829	4,693	3,490	2,194	4,907	0.14	4.6
Marshall Islands	5,246	9,173	4,563	4,559	4,590	0.14	-50.0
New Caledonia	109,587	100,651	98,562	111,875	112,204	3.34	11.5
Niue	1,939	2,793	6,214	6,000	5,048	0.15	80.7
Northern Marianas	526,111	529,557	379,091	340,957	400,296	11.82	24.4
Palau	57,732	86,124	85,593	109,057	119,000	3.51	38.2
Papua New Guinea	58,448	69,251	148,943	164,993	169,975	5.02	145.4
Samoa	87,688	101,807	129,500	127,604	134,662	3.98	32.3
Solomon Islands	10,134	9,400	20,521	24,497	23,925	0.71	154.5
Tonga	34,694	43,380	48,740	46,005	49,010	1.45	13.0
Tuvalu	1,079	1,085	1,657	1,232	1,019	0.03	-6.1
Vanuatu	57,591	62,123	97,180	93,960	108,145	3.19	74.1
Total PICs	2,855,212	3,065,540	3,105,543	3,125,309	3,387,245	100	10.5
Asia/Pacific ('000,000)	110.1	153.6	204.4	217.0	233.5		52
World ('000,000)	674	799	940	983	1,035		29.5
PICs as % of Asia-Pacific	2.6	2.0	1.5	1.4	1.5		
PICs as % of world	0.4	0.4	0.3	0.3	0.3		

Source: Harrison and Pratt, 2013: 6; UNWTO, 2014: 4; www.sboc.fm

Table 1.2 Pacific destinations by purpose of trip

Country	Holiday	Business	VFR	Other	Year
Cook Islands	86%	4%	8%	2%	2013
Federated States of Micronesia	70%	24%	3%	3%	2006
Fiji	75%	6%	8%	11%	2012
French Polynesia	81%	6%	11%	2%	2011
Guam	85%	7%	2%	6%	2011
Kiribati	11%	49%	28%	13%	2008
Marshall Islands	33%	33%	10%	27%	2005
New Caledonia	46%	17%	22%	15%	2011
Niue	50%	20%	30%	0%	2009
Palau	89%	6%		5%	2013
Papua New Guinea	22%	73%	4%	1%	2011
Samoa	30%	12%	36%	22%	1996
Solomon Islands	22%	67%	9%	3%	2007
Tonga	39%	11%	43%	7%	2011
Tuvalu	22%	58%	11%	9%	2010
Vanuatu	83%	9%	8%	1%	2013

percentage of visitors to the Federated States of Micronesia and the Marshall Islands are from the USA, to which they are affiliated, or (like Guam and the Northern Marianas) from Asia, especially Japan. By contrast, however, French Polynesia, commonly considered a mature and somewhat expensive destination, is highly reliant on tourists from Europe (mainly France) and North America (Cottom, 2006).

Finally, as indicated earlier, small numbers of tourists can be economically important to Pacific island countries. Unfortunately, precise figures on economic benefits are hard to find. Current estimates of tourism's benefits to Fiji, an established destination, for example, are projected from data obtained in the early 1990s (Tourism Council of the South Pacific, 1992), and even then they were problematic. Now, when tourism in Fiji is more extensive and structurally different, it is a very rough yardstick against which to measure tourism's importance. The direct contribution of travel and tourism to gross domestic product (GDP) in 2013 was FJ$1,055.1 million (13.8% of GDP), and this was forecast to increase by 7.9% in 2014 (World Travel and Tourism Council, 2014). Travel and tourism in Fiji also generated 43,000 jobs directly in 2013 (12.4% of total employment), and this was forecast to grow by 6.4% in 2014 (World Travel and Tourism Council, 2014). Nevertheless, it is obvious that tourism has a substantial impact on the overall economies of several PICs, as seen in its contribution to GDP, foreign exchange and employment.

As noted by Harrison and Prasad (2013), for Pacific island developing economies as a group, the share of tourism in their GDP averaged 11.9%. There is a large degree of variation between PICs. Palau and Cook Islands, where tourism's economic contribution is 67.1% and 50.0% of GDP, respectively, could be classified as small island tourism economies (SITEs). In other PICs, tourism is less important. Solomon Islands and Papua New Guinea, for example, where tourism's economic contribution to GDP is 1.7% and 0.1%, respectively, are resource rich and hence do not prioritise tourism. Alternatively, several Pacific island countries lack the resources, among other factors, for tourism to provide significant economic benefits. Marshall Islands, Tonga and Federated States of Micronesia can be classified as MIRAB (migration remittances aid bureaucracy) states (Bertram and Watters, 1985). Here, tourism contributes 2.9%, 6.0% and 7.3% of GDP, respectively. Somewhere in between MIRAB states and SITEs can be found such economies as Fiji, Vanuatu, Samoa and French Polynesia, where tourism contributes 10%–30% of GDP. Compared to MIRAB states, small island tourism economies exhibit more favourable characteristics on a range of economic, social and demographic indicators (McElroy and Hamma, 2010; McSorley and McElroy, 2007).

Issues and challenges

This book is an introduction to international tourism in PICs. As editors, we are mindful of the dangers inherent in generalising about relatively small island nations and dependencies scattered in the vast expanse of the Pacific Ocean. We are also conscious of an unevenness in our coverage of PICs, which reflects the patchy nature of research into Pacific island tourism (and, in all likelihood, our own limitations). At the same time, there are many common features, aspirations and constraints in PIC attempts to develop their tourism sectors and these are addressed in the following chapters.

The second chapter is d'Hauteserre's introduction to tourism in PICs most closely associated with France. Because of their continued reliance on the former colonial power, and the subsidies it provides, the *intrusion*[1] of tourism into these PICs is somewhat different from that of many other PICs. In Tahiti, transnational corporations dominate the accommodation sector and emphasis is on the higher end of the market, while in other islands poor planning, a lack of regional cooperation, distance from France and difficulties in air access, environmental pollution, and competition from other PICs and islands further afield, together ensure that tourism in these French territories is languishing. D'Hauteserre suggests that the islands' arts and crafts, though already noteworthy, have potential for further development, as does the culture of the region, and she correlates a *lack* of attention to culture as a tourism resource to the pervasive but negative portrayals of indigenous people, arguing that 'varieties of Polynesian culture, especially Chinese and French, could be more effective in distinguishing the French Pacific from its competitors than non-existent beaches and seductive *vahines* [women of Polynesian descent]'. Readers requiring evidence for her assertions need only glance at online publicity for the region, for example, the official website of Tahiti Tourisme (www.tahiti-tourisme.com), to discover that images presented of French Polynesia differ but little from those of Fiji and other PICs: sun, sea, sand, sunsets, scenery and beautiful, welcoming islanders, while searching online for '*vahine*' and 'Tahiti' will soon confirm the longevity of the image of the Tahitienne as the erotic and exotic 'other'.

Several themes raised by d'Hauteserre are picked up in the following chapters, which are broadly divided into three sections. The first focus is on the question of *image*, namely, stereotypes of a destination held by tourists and potential tourists, the extent to which residents, for their part, really welcome visitors, and the role tourism might play in changing pre-established images. The second theme is tourism's impacts, notably the economic and socio-cultural effects of international tourism's intrusion in the region which, though often hotly debated, have attracted relatively little empirical research (Harrison, 2003: 11–14). Yet, when apparently sacrosanct traditions are confronted by international tourism and its attendant economic, social and cultural imperatives, the internal challenges are considerable and far-reaching. The third focus is on the (sometimes contradictory) challenges of how PICs articulate with their external geo-political and physical environment. These involve, *inter alia*, existing relations with formal colonial centres, geographical isolation, the need for greater air access to the outside world and for more tourists, and the continuing threat to several PICs of global warming, which increased air travel will inevitably exacerbate.

Images of Pacific island countries

Both editors have spent time working at the University of the South Pacific in Fiji, an admission that frequently prompted an envious response. The dominant image of PICs continues to be positive and highly romantic, even if it bears only a passing resemblance to (another?) reality. Such stereotyping, where tropical islands are often portrayed as a welcoming 'paradise' or a latter-day Garden of Eden, dates back to the earliest years of colonisation (Harrison, 2001b). In the third chapter of this book, Harrison explores how long-held images of Fiji (and, by extension, other PICs) were reinforced and perpetuated by the picture postcards that were so ubiquitous in the first three decades of the twentieth century. Produced by and for people of European origin, they generally presented prettified nature, largely without human presence, colonial towns and the economy and, to a lesser extent, ceremonial activities or the 'picturesque' military or police. When ethnic Fijians were portrayed, men were usually in traditional dress, and women were often Fijian versions of their Edwardian counterparts, of ethnographic interest or – perhaps less so than 'Polynesian' Samoan women – examples of the undressed and erotic 'other'. Many such themes are reproduced in current tourist brochures and online advertising, not only in Fiji, but also throughout the South Pacific. Worthy of note, too, is that Fijians of Indian descent were almost totally absent from the postcards, just as they are in contemporary tourism brochures (Harrison, 1998: 134).

Natives of PICs do not necessarily conform to their stereotype. As Kanemasu suggests in the fourth chapter, tourism's benefits to Fiji have been contested, and the welcome to tourists is not always guaranteed. Indeed, from the 1960s to the 1980s, tourism was often viewed with ambivalence and some scepticism, and it took a vigorous campaign by the media and the increasingly powerful Hotel Association in the 1990s to turn public opinion around. Even in 1996, it was alleged indigenous Fijians received only 'crumbs from the table' (Samy, 1996), and had to 'make do with the leftovers' from Pacific tourism (Le Fevre, 1996). While she accepts that Fiji tourism currently has extensive public support, Kanemasu cites numerous recent conflicts with landowners and argues that resentment still surfaces, fuelled by foreign ownership and control in the hotel sector, low wages, the poor representation of locals in management positions and, especially, inequalities in the distribution of monies paid for the lease of customary owned native land.

Legislation enacted in 2013 might reduce this problem in Fiji, where customary owned land is 88% of the total land area,[2] but in Fiji and many other PICs, where customary land tenure is as extensive as, but less institutionalised than Fiji, conflicts between traditional landowners and the tourism sector have undoubtedly been common and virulent (Harrison, 1997: 173–76;

Sofield, 2003: 225–58; Slatter, 2006; Commonwealth of Australia, 2008: 3–8; Boydell and Baya, 2014).

Landowners appear in a very different guise in the chapter by Cheer, Reeves and Laing. They examine the significance of Chief Roi Mata's Domain, in Vanuatu, which in 2008 became Vanuatu's first World Heritage Site. In fact, there are three associated sites. One contains the tomb of Roi Mata, the last holder of the title of Paramount Chief, who was buried in about 1600 along with 50 or so of his domestic entourage. Their remains in a mass grave suggest that some, at least, did not go willingly to their deaths. Roi Mata is now revered as a peacemaker, and Cheer and his co-authors see this example of dark tourism as a useful and quite *deliberate* corrective to the prevailing touristic image of Vanuatu as yet another island paradise. In effect, the World Heritage Site (also discussed later in this chapter) presents a darker (and more realistic?) image of Vanuatu than tourist brochures and, at the same time, enables the empowered landowners to gain a livelihood from tourism while revering Roi Mata as a peacemaker, role model and symbol of national unity, even though his achievements may, in fact, have been an historical amalgam of several chiefs rather than of one man.

The socio-economic context

Critics of tourism in developing countries tend to assess tourism's impact on indigenous culture and tradition as negative, though value judgements and ideologies tend to overwhelm empirical evidence (Harrison, 2001c: 256–60). In fact, the intrusion of tourism is tempered by pre-existing geo-political and structural conditions (Harrison, 2001d: 28–33). Furthermore, as Simpson has noted, community-based tourism initiatives (CBTIs) and resident participation take many forms, and speculation on the optimum type of community participation may be less important than the extent of benefits actually received by residents (Simpson, 2008). Two chapters in this book, by Movono and his co-authors and by Dawn Gibson, are especially relevant to this debate, as both examine indigenous Fijian involvement in the tourism sector.

The two villages studied by Movono, Pratt and Harrison have been exposed to tourism for more than three decades and employment at two transnational-operated hotels nearby is the major source of cash income for both villages. In addition, some villagers 'piggy back' on the success of tourism in the area by running their own businesses – for example, village stays and nature tours, massage parlours and jet skis. Overall, the material benefits brought by tourism were highly appreciated and there was general agreement that standards of living had improved, to the extent that the villages were among the most highly developed in Fiji. Certainly, Vatuolalai and Votua should not be cited as epitomising the downside of tourism. However, while villagers showed no resentment towards foreign-owned hotels and the unequal income distribution at the hotels that had been previously reported in Fiji (Burns, 2003: 86–87), some believed the wage economy had led to reduced time spent on subsistence farming and fishing, and that young people and women had become less dependent on traditional village authorities. Importantly, too, young people in the landowning *mataqalis* (clans), who had priority in jobs at the hotels, were leaving school early to take up low-paying positions rather than staying on to further their education. Clearly, tourism was seen as a mixed blessing, but no one in these villages wanted to turn the clock back.

The participation in tourism of residents of Vatuolalai and Votua was primarily through their employment in hotels. By contrast, Gibson studied *i-Taukei* landowner entrepreneurs in Wayalailai, a backpacker resort in the Yasawa chain of islands, Fiji, recording the challenges they face and the extent the community's priorities were met through the resort's operations. As Gibson and others also indicate elsewhere (Rodman, 1987; de Burlo, 2003; Gibson, 2013a, 2013b), indigenous entrepreneurs must balance traditional obligations and business imperatives, and at the same time continue to live in the community. For them, profit is not the only or even the major criterion. Rather, what matters is being able to contribute to village development and meet their traditional obligations to church and community.

Most employment opportunities for villagers from Votua and Vatuolalai are provided by the Naviti and the Warwick International Resort and Spa, two of four hotels in Fiji owned by Warwick International Hotels. In Fiji, transnational companies (TNCs) operate more than half the rooms in the premium and high categories in Fiji, and they also dominate the tourism sector in French Polynesia, Vanuatu, Guam and Palau (Harrison and Pratt, 2013: 17). As a rule of thumb, except for the special case of the Cook Islands,[3] the more developed the tourism industry in a PIC, the greater the role of TNCs. This overall *structure* of international tourism in PICs was outlined more than two decades ago by Britton (1982, 1987, 1989; Britton and Clarke, 1987), who followed a classic dependency line in arguing that when TNCs were so strongly present, 'local elites and foreign interests were the primary beneficiaries of tourism (Britton, 1982: 335). Britton's preference was the type of small-scale, indigenous-owned tourism found in the 'rigid monarchic structure of Tonga', where the Tongan elite 'sheltered the country from outside forces' (Britton, 1982: 349), a view somewhat puzzling in the light of his assertion that Tonga also suffered as a result of *not* being colonised (Britton, 1987: 131).

One of several difficulties with Britton's position is that, for no apparent good reason, he supported local against foreign capital, a stance common among *dependistas* (Phillips, 1977: 19). Not only this, but it is unclear why he does oppose foreign capital, except perhaps because it *is* foreign. An alternative argument is that large-scale tourism, concentrated as it is both within and across PICs, is easier to control and more sustainable than small-scale tourism. Furthermore, what evidence there is suggests that TNCs pay more, have better training schemes, offer better career prospects than their local counterparts and, in many cases, engage more in corporate social responsibility (CSR) (Harrison and Prasad, 2013: 750–55).

Building on previous research (Scheyvens and Russell, 2010), Scheyvens and Hughes note the increasing importance attributed to CSR. They cite examples from PICs, most notably Vanuatu and Fiji, where CSR in tourism plays a significant role, both in the companies' pursuance of their core business (for example, in food procurement) and in their charitable donations. At first sight, the list of CSR initiatives is impressive, but Scheyvens and Hughes conclude that, on a scale ranging from minimalist activities, through philanthropy, long-term partnerships ('encompassing') and comprehensive social activism, most tourism companies engage in CSR at the lower levels. The potential is there, but at present CSR in PICs is somewhat ad hoc. Much remains to be done.

The involvement of local farmers and producers of other goods in mainstream tourism, and the more general development of backward linkages to tourism, has long been advocated for small island developing states (SIDS) (Bélisle, 1983; Momsen, 1986; Meyer, 2006; Hampton and Jeyacheya, 2013: 23–28, 54–65), and in recent years, analysis of value chains by proponents of pro-poor tourism (PPT) has shown it can make a considerable difference to local incomes (Mitchell and Ashley, 2006; Weiermair, 2006; Van der Duim, 2008). Clearly, the idea has merit, and isolated advances can be reported, as in Jamaica (Hampton and Jeyacheya, 2013: 24–25), but overall progress has been slow, which is probably why the recommendation is recycled decade after decade, outlining the same constraints and challenges, often accompanied by the observation that the agricultural sector in SIDS is declining (Gomez, 1993; Dodman and Rhiney, 2008: 116–18; UNWTO, 2012).

Such difficulties are apparent in the chapter by Singh and her co-authors, on Niue, a tiny PIC with a (declining) population of about 1,300 (although 20,000 Niueans live in New Zealand) and about 5,000 annual visitors. She finds minimal linkages of agriculture and tourism, and suggests even most food consumed by the local population is imported. The small commercial agriculture sector produces crops for export, farmers cultivate subsistence crops, hotels rely on imports for good-quality foodstuffs and reliable supply, and tourists are perceived to have no interest in local cuisine, about which, in any case, they know little. In an economy that is already barely viable, the links between tourism and agriculture remain negligible.

The story is similar in more developed PICs. Reporting on the results of a value chain analysis of agriculture and tourism in Samoa, Sofield and Tamasese estimate that 'linkages [of agriculture] with tourism are weak ... [T] here is a high leakage factor in terms of food and beverages (F and B). Commercial accommodation properties import almost 70% of their F and B requirements' (Sofield and Tamasese, 2011: 6). This is especially noteworthy because in Samoa, where most accommodation units and restaurants are small-scale and locally owned, we should expect a higher propensity to buy local.

In more 'developed' Fiji, where larger, TNC-operated hotels are common, hotel demand for some fruit can be met locally, and there is potential for considerably more import substitution in other fruits and vegetables (Young and Vinning, 2007). However, an as yet unpublished value chain analysis of hotel purchases of food and beverages in the Mamanuca chain of islands, carried out in 2011 by Sofield, Harrison and Pratt, indicates that more than 67% of their food and beverages were imported. Some food crops are undoubtedly difficult to produce in Fiji, and much of the tourist demand for alcoholic drinks has to be met by imports, but considerable potential remains. At present, though, the agricultural sector is simply not structured to cater for tourist demand, *i-Taukei* farmers focus primarily on subsistence crops and know little of the crops or cuisine favoured by visiting tourists, and hoteliers of international-standard hotels turn to imports to ensure consistency in both quantity and quality. Mere tinkering with menus and attempting to make local foodstuffs more palatable to international visitors will not bring about lasting change. The problems involved in linking tourism and agriculture are *structural* and *cultural* and can be solved *only* by structural and cultural change.

In their chapter, Anand and his co-authors show how pearl and mother of pearl jewellery industries in Fiji bring in foreign exchange and provide incomes and employment, including work outside the main island of Viti Levu. Second, they show that – as in the Cook Islands and Tahiti – these industries can have a genuinely mutually beneficial relationship with tourism. A wide range of tourists already purchase their products, and further development is clearly possible. Third, members of several ethnic groups in Fiji, including *i-Taukei*, are among the entrepreneurs. This is important, because it is often argued that *i-Taukei* are somehow culturally unsuited to take entrepreneurial roles (Rao, 2004). Fourth, the industry has been developed with government support, though such assistance will be a tiny proportion of the $25 million a year the government allocates to Tourism Fiji to market the country to holidaymakers. Finally, not only are pearls and mother of pearl products valued as souvenirs by a wide range of tourists, but also the pearl farms themselves are an additional secondary attraction and thus a useful (and culturally interesting) supplement to the more stereotypical appeal of sun, sea and sand.

Like other sections of the tourism 'industry', the pearl and mother of pearl jewellery industries take a natural resource, commoditise it, and then use it as a tool for development. More contentious, perhaps, is the extent to which PIC *culture* can or should be packaged and sold by tourism marketing agencies to increase tourist numbers. The issue has been debated since social scientists first started studying tourism and was highlighted by Greenwood's (later modified) attack on Spanish tourism authorities for selling 'culture by the pound' (Greenwood, 1978, 1989; Harrison, 2001d: 28–33). In PICs, too, the commoditisation of local culture and tradition has long been disputed (Tupouniua, Crocombe and Slatter, 1975; Rajotte and Crocombe, 1980), and again emerged when the town of Levuka, the first colonial capital of Fiji, was mooted as a World Heritage Site (Harrison, 2005), finally being placed on the list in 2013 (whc.unesco.org/en/list/1399/). It is noteworthy that the significance of Levuka was contested, as some *i-Taukei* insisted it was an example of 'half-caste' history, a history chequered with tribal conflict, and not a site with which indigenous Fijians could identify.

By contrast, in their chapter on Chief Roi Mata's Domain in Vanuatu, the World Heritage Site discussed earlier, Cheer and his co-authors suggest that commoditisation of this site serves several positive functions: it assists in the 'debunking' of the image of Vanuatu as 'paradise'; it is *specifically* set up to provide work in tourism for local people and to reduce the rate of urbanisation, and it establishes Chief Roi Mata, a peacemaker, as a national role model, culture hero and moderniser. According to this view, commoditisation is a process to be welcomed and developed. Culture by the dollar or the pound? Please sir, I'd like some more.

PICs and the outside world

If they are to increase tourist numbers, PICs must ensure that tourists can actually make the trip, and that it is affordable, and two chapters in this book discuss the challenges and constraints experienced by PICs in relation to air transport. For Taumoepeau, small is not beautiful. Economic growth in most PICs is limited by smallness in size and population, geographical isolation, a lack of natural resources, and small domestic markets. Consequently, airlines cannot make economies of scale, and low load factors make their operations even more economically unsustainable. Problems are compounded because in developed countries, the source of most PIC tourists, airport charges are high, as are costs of fuel, spare parts and replacement aircraft, whether leased or purchased. In view of such constraints, PIC options are limited. Partnerships with regional airlines are one possibility, and another is to operate their own national airline, alone or bilaterally with other partners, which may have nationalistic appeal but inevitably raises financial problems. At the management level, governments are often unable to define airline objectives or exert adequate financial control, and are be committed to heavy financial outlay for aircraft and ongoing government operational subsidies. Another option for governments is to deregulate, increase the competition (which will then affect the viability of their own airlines) and encourage low-cost carriers (LCCs) to enter the market, a policy Taumoepeau suggests has led to substantially increased tourist numbers in some PICs.

Kaufmann and Nakagawa examine changes in demand for tourism in Fiji over the period 1979 to 2009. Despite coups and attempted coups, tourism in Fiji increased, assisted by such internal factors as the 2004 decision to deregulate air transport and encourage competition from LCCs. Arguably, though, external factors are more important. The global financial crisis (GFC) that began in 2008, for example, had huge negative effects worldwide, as well as in Fiji, where its impacts were exacerbated early in 2009 by floods in Nadi. However, its impacts on Fiji tourism were cushioned by the resilience of the

Australian economy (thus sustaining tourism demand), substantial discounting by hotels and the national airline, and the 20% devaluation of the Fiji dollar in 2009. As a consequence, tourist *numbers* did not decline catastrophically, although *earnings* from tourism were reduced (Harrison and Prasad, 2013: 745).

According to Kaufmann and Nakagawa, other decisions made elsewhere in the world also affected Fiji. In 2000, the discontinuation by Japan Airlines of direct flights to Fiji (apparently prompted by the attempted coup that year) had an untoward affect. On the positive side, continued direct flights to Fiji by Korean Airlines from Seoul, an international hub of importance to Fiji for its connections with East Asia, works to Fiji's advantage and opens up the possibility of developing new markets, for example, in India and China, both of which have been targeted by the Fiji government.

While air travel is the main method of transporting tourists to PIC destinations, it is not the only one, and India and China are not the only new markets that might be targeted by PICs. Bluewater sailors, who are discussed in Koth's chapter, are a distinct niche market, and for them the journey itself is intrinsic to their long-term holiday experience. Unlike most other tourists, they do not require accommodation or other specialised infrastructure. Their main needs are safety and security for their boats and themselves, supplies of potable water and fresh fruit and vegetables (in quantities that locals should be able to provide), skilled workers to help them repair and maintain their boats, and opportunities to socialise with one another and with local residents, whom they may often assist with community projects. Koth's recommendations to policy makers interested in attracting bluewater sailors, a category of tourist that might be especially appropriate to small PICs, are simple and few: at a time when other parts of the world are becoming dangerous, consider the needs of these sailors, provide separate facilities from other marine traffic, and in so doing you can reap the benefits of a small-scale, low-impact and sustainable form of tourism development which can bring several social and economic benefits to host communities.

In fact, sustainable tourism development (STD) in PICs is honoured much in rhetoric but little in practice. Reviewers of Fiji's *Tourism Development Plan 1998–2005* (Ministry of Transport and Tourism, 1997) criticised its advocacy of tourism development areas (TDAs) and large-scale tourism, and suggested, instead, the prioritisation of smaller-scale and more appropriate forms of tourism (Levett and McNally, 2003: xi–xv). This did not happen. Instead, the following plan (Ministry of Tourism and Environment, 2007), completed during the 2006 coup, *retained* TDAs and discussed three possible scenarios ('managed growth', 'low growth' and 'aggressive growth'), all of which envisaged a much greater increase in tourist numbers than, in fact, was to occur (Ministry of Tourism and Environment, 2007: 28).

Samoa's experience is similarly instructive. Most of its accommodation is locally owned and operated (Harrison and Prasad, 2013: 749), and it received many plaudits when it adopted a coherent series of sustainable tourism indicators (Twining-Ward, 2003). Within a few years, though, hoteliers were admitting they were too complex to implement, and the *Samoa Tourism Development Plan: 2009–2013* ambitiously aimed to increase tourist numbers by 40% and visitor nights to more than 1 million (Samoa Tourism Authority, 2009: 2), assisted by an increasing emphasis on overseas investment. It remains to be seen if Samoa's claims for sustainability can continue, following recently announced cooperation with the Global Sustainable Tourism Council (GSTC).[4]

Clearly, there are internal challenges to achieve sustainable tourism development but, by contrast, climate change is an externally generated threat to tropical islands, including PICs, and their tourism industries (Becken, 2004; Becken and Hay, 2007: 45–58; Bueno, Herzfeld, Stanton and Ackerman, 2008). Ironically, the threat would be increased if PICs were able to attract more flights and bring in more tourists. By and large, though, climate change results from factors outside the control of PIC governments. They cannot stop it, but they can try to reduce their vulnerability and adapt.

The last two chapters in this book deal with the external challenge of climate change and the need of PICs to counter its impacts. Klint and her co-authors first discuss the general implications of increases in sea levels, beach erosion, and the frequency and intensity of cyclones, all of which have knock-on effects on tourism. They then focus specifically on Kiribati, Samoa and Vanuatu, elaborate on changes to the natural resources that are so vital in attracting tourists, and suggest a variety of adaptation measures that might be implemented. These include coastal protection, desalination plants, rainwater tanks, relocation of tourism infrastructure, higher building standards, and attempts to redirect tourist demand to a wider range of tourism products.

By contrast, Min Jiang and her colleagues focus specifically on Samoa and outline its vulnerability to climate change – a task perhaps made both easier and more urgent as a result of the 2009 tsunami. They identify community perceptions of where Samoan tourism is most vulnerable to climate change and where it is most resilient when faced with external climate shocks. For their informants, limited marketing resources, limited access to finance capital and insurance, insecurities in employment, poor infrastructure and transport, inadequate support from and communication with government, weakness in disaster preparedness, and lack of local finance to aid recovery are all factors that make enterprises vulnerable to climate change. Importantly, they note the tendency for government and the private sector to rebuild on land previously devastated by the tsunami. However, vulnerability can be balanced by resilience, and informants also indicate where they believe Samoan enterprises are resilient, identifying: strong family and kinship ties; multi-occupations (including access to productive land); consistent arrivals throughout the year; remittance support from Samoans resident overseas; and strong (and hierarchical) local governance. They also see evidence that some communities and tourism enterprises are attempting to guard against future disaster by building sea walls, moving inland and constructing more durable buildings.

Both these chapters indicate challenges presented by climate change to PICs, and outline how they might be met by governments, but if threats are to be successfully countered, they will need international support and understanding. This is already happening, though clearly more aid is required. PIC governments not only need the awareness of what should be done, but also the commitment to implement policies that are so obviously required. Whether or not the necessary aid will be forthcoming, and commitment exists, remains to be seen.

In the following chapters, the issues and challenges summarised in this introduction will be discussed in some detail. They include the origin and role of a destination's *image*, the *impacts* of international tourism on economies and cultures of PICs, and the internal and external challenges with which PICs must contend. There are, of course, other challenges: huge disparities in income exist within the tourism sector, especially between locals and expatriates; indigenisation of higher levels of management has advanced but little; education and training institutions in tourism and hospitality in the region are stretched to meet the demands of employers and governments (who often undervalue education in favour of training), and there is a sound case for making the career structure in tourism and hospitality throughout PICs more attractive. Put simply, while there are attempts to address these problems (New Zealand Tourism Research Institute, 2013), meeting the human resource needs of the travel and tourism sector in PICs is a major challenge for governments and the private sector.

Finally, perhaps the greatest challenge is to ensure that tourism *is* a passport to development. More than increasing tourist numbers (a priority too little questioned) and GDP, governments of PICs need to ensure economic benefits from tourism are used for progressing the common good, and not only that of an economic elite. That would certainly give residents of destination areas something to smile about.

Notes

1 The term 'intrusion' is borrowed from geology, where it refers to liquid rock that forms under the earth's surface and then pushes upwards, thus producing new formations in the overlying strata. It seems a useful analogy, in that tourism is a new phenomenon, inserted into established socio-cultural and economic structures, which thus take on a different appearance and suffer varying degrees of displacement and topographical change.

2 In 2013, the Bainamarama government issued Decree 61 of 2010 (Native Land Trust (Leases and Licenses) Amendment Regulations 2010), allocating lease monies equally among owners of customary land and thus overturning the previous system, in which chiefs had received a disproportionate share of such lease payments (Boydell and Baya, 2014: 8–9). As Kanemasu notes, at the time of writing it was too early to assess how far the legislation had succeeded in creating a more equal system of distribution and satisfying the critics.

3 The Cook Islands is clearly a special case. Accommodation in this country is small scale and, at least in theory, owned and operated by Cook Islands citizens. However, it is hardly a typical PIC: it has a per capita income of about NZ $25,000,

mainly because of its situation as a freely associated state of New Zealand, from which it receives considerable overseas aid. Its citizens are *also* citizens of New Zealand, to which they can freely travel without restriction. Tourism accounts for about 75% of GDP, and some 63% of its visitors come from New Zealand, while 15% and 12%, respectively, come from Australia and Europe (Cook Islands Statistics Office, 2014; Ministry of Foreign Affairs and Trade, 2014).

4 In March 2014, Samoa became the first PIC to complete the Global Sustainable Tourism Council's Early Adopter Program. According to the press release, 'The Early Adopter Program is overseen by GSTC's Destination Working Group and implemented by NGO [non-governmental organisation] partner Sustainable Travel International. It applies the recently developed GSTC Destination criteria in assessing current sustainability levels and providing direction for future improvements. These guidelines complement the existing GSTC Criteria for Hotels and Tour Operators, which is the worldwide sustainability standard for tourism businesses' (www.gstccouncil.org/blog/1215/samoa, accessed 7 July 2014). This seems impressive but at the time of writing it was too early to assess how far Samoa would be able to benchmark its sustainable tourism practices against international criteria.

References

Barkham, P. (2001) 'Paradise Lost Awaits Asylum Seekers.' *The Guardian* 11 September: 3.

Becken, S. (2004) *Climate Change and Tourism in Fiji: Vulnerability, Adaptation and Mitigation.* Suva: University of the South Pacific.

Becken, S. and Hay, J. (2007) *Tourism and Climate Change: Risks and Opportunities.* Clevedon: Channel View.

Bélisle, F. (1983) 'Tourism and Food Production in the Caribbean.' *Annals of Tourism Research* 10(4): 497–513.

Bertram, G. and Watters, R.F. (1985) 'The Mirab Economy in South Pacific Microstates.' *Pacific Viewpoint* 26(3): 497–519.

Boydell, S. and Baya, U. (2014) *Using Trust Structures to Manage Customary Land in Melanesia: What Lessons can be Learnt from the iTaukei Land Trust Board in Fiji?* Paper prepared for presentation at 2014 world Bank conference on Land and Poverty, The World Bank, Washington, DC, 24–27 March 2014.

Britton, S. (1982) 'The Political Economy of Tourism in the Third World.' *Annals of Tourism Research* 9(3): 331–58.

——(1987) 'Tourism in Pacific Island States: Constraints and Opportunities.' In S. Britton and W. Clarke (eds) *Ambiguous Alternatives: Tourism in Small Developing Countries.* Suva: University of the South Pacific, 113–39.

——(1989) 'Tourism, Dependency and Development: A Mode of Analysis.' In T.V. Singh, H.L. Theuns and F.M. Go (eds) *Towards Appropriate Tourism: The Case of Developing Countries.* Frankfurt and Berne: Lang, 93–110.

Britton, S. and Clarke, W. (eds) (1987) *Ambiguous Alternatives: Tourism in Small Developing Countries.* Suva: University of the South Pacific.

Bueno, R., Herzfeld, C., Stanton, E. and Ackerman, F. (2008) *The Caribbean and Climate Change: The Costs of Inaction.* sei-us.org/Publications_PDF/SEI-Caribbean AndClimateChange-08.pdf (accessed 5 July 2014).

Burns, L. (2003) 'Indigenous Responses to Tourism in Fiji: What is Happening?' In D. Harrison (ed.) *Pacific Island Tourism.* New York: Cognizant, 82–93.

Butler, R., Harrison, D. and Filho, W.L. (1996) 'Introduction.' In L. Briguglio, R. Butler, D. Harrison and W.L. Filho (eds) *Sustainable Tourism in Islands and Small States: Case Studies.* London: Pinter, 1–10.

Carlsen, J. and Butler, R. (2011) 'Introducing Sustainable Perspectives of Island Tourism.' In J. Carlsen and R. Butler (eds) *Island Tourism: Sustainable Perspectives.* Wallingford: CAB International, 1–7.

Commonwealth of Australia (2008) *Making Land Work: Volume 1: Reconciling Customary Land and Development in the Pacific.* Canberra: AusAID.

Cook Islands Statistics Office (2014) *Tourism Statistics.* www.spc.int/prism/country/ck/stats/statistics/tourism (accessed 29 June 2014).

Cottom, S. (2006) *French Polynesia, Investor's Paradise?* Sydney: HVS International.

Crocombe, R. (2008) *The South Pacific.* Suva: University of the South Pacific.

de Burlo, C. (2003) 'Tourism, Conservation, and the Cultural Environment in Rural Vanuatu.' In D. Harrison (ed.) *Pacific Island Tourism.* New York: Cognizant, 69–81.

de Kadt, E. (ed.) (1979) *Tourism: Passport to Development?* Oxford: Oxford University Press.

Dodman, D. and Rhiney, K. (2008) '"We Nyammin?" Food Supply, Authenticity, and the Tourist Experience in Negril, Jamaica.' In M. Daye, D. Chambers and S. Roberts (eds) *New Perspectives in Caribbean Tourism.* New York and London: Routledge, 115–32.

Gibson, D. (2013a) 'The Cultural Challenges Faced by Indigenous-owned Small Medium Tourism Enterprises (SMTEs) in Fiji: Case Studies from the Yasawa Islands.' *The Journal of Pacific Studies* 32: 106–31.

——(2013b) *Living in the Moment: Cultural Challenges Faced by Indigenous-owned Budget Resorts in Fiji – Case Studies from Wayalailai, Yasawa Island Group.* Unpublished PhD thesis. Suva: University of the South Pacific.

Gomez, A. (1993) 'Integrating Tourism and Agricultural Development.' In D. Gayle and J. Goodrich, *Tourism Marketing and Management in the Caribbean.* London and New York: Routledge, 155–66.

Greenwood, D. (1978) 'Culture by the Pound: An Anthropological Perspective on Tourism as Cultural Commoditization.' In V. Smith (ed.) *Hosts and Guests: The Anthropology of Tourism.* First edition. Oxford: Basil Blackwell, 129–38.

——(1989) 'Culture by the Pound: An Anthropological Perspective on Tourism as Cultural Commoditization.' In V. Smith (ed.) *Hosts and Guests: the Anthropology of Tourism.* Second edition. Oxford: Basil Blackwell, 171–85.

Hampton, M. and Jeyacheya, J. (2013) *Tourism and Inclusive Growth in Small Island Developing States.* London: Commonwealth Secretariat.

Harrison, D. (1992) 'International Tourism and the Less Developed Countries: The Background.' In D. Harrison (ed.) *Tourism and the Less Developed Countries.* London: Belhaven, 1–18.

——(1997) 'Globalization and Tourism: Some Themes from Fiji.' In M. Oppermann (ed.) *Pacific Rim Tourism.* Wallingford: CAB International, 167–83.

——(1998) 'The World Comes to Fiji: Who Communicates What, and to Whom?' *Tourism Culture and Communication* 1: 129–38.

——(2001a) 'Less Developed Countries and Tourism: The Overall Pattern.' In D. Harrison (ed.) *Tourism and the Less Developed World: Issues and Case Studies.* Wallingford: CAB International, 1–22.

——(2001b) 'Islands, Images and Tourism.' *Tourism Recreation Research* 26(3): 9–14.

——(2001c) 'Afterword.' In D. Harrison (ed.) *Tourism and the Less Developed World: Issues and Case Studies*. Wallingford: CAB International, 251–63.

——(2001d) 'Tourism and Less Developed Countries: Key Issues.' In D. Harrison (ed.) *Tourism and the Less Developed World: Issues and Case Studies*. Wallingford: CAB International, 23–46.

——(2003) 'Themes in Pacific Island Tourism.' In D. Harrison (ed.) *Pacific Island Tourism*. New York: Cognizant, 1–23.

——(2004) 'Tourism in Pacific Islands.' *Journal of Pacific Studies* 26(1–2): 2.

——(2005) 'Levuka, Fiji: Contested Heritage?' In D. Harrison and M. Hitchcock (eds) *The Politics of World Heritage: Negotiating Tourism and World Heritage*. Clevedon: Channel View, 66–89.

Harrison, D. and Prasad, B.C. (2013) 'The Contribution of Tourism to the Development of Fiji and Other Pacific Island Countries.' In C. Tisdell (ed.) *Handbook of Tourism Economics: Analysis, New Applications and Case Studies*. New Jersey: World Scientific, 741–62.

Harrison, D. and Pratt, S. (2012) 'Political Change and Tourism: Coups in Fiji.' In R. Butler and W. Suntikul (eds) *Tourism and Political Change*. Oxford: Goodfellow, 160–74.

——(2013) *Tourism in Pacific Island Countries*. Contemporary Tourism Reviews. Oxford: Goodfellow.

Le Fevre, T. (1996) 'Making Do with the Leftovers from Pacific Tourism.' In S. Tupouniua, R. Crocombe and C. Slatter (eds) *The Pacific Way: Social Issues in National Development*. Suva: South Pacific Social Sciences Association, 215–21.

Levett, R. and McNally, R. (2003) *A Strategic Environmental Assessment of Fiji's Tourism Development Plan*. Report prepared by the South Pacific Programme, Worldwide Fund for Nature, Godalming, UK.

McElroy, J.L. and Hamma, P.E. (2010) 'Sites Revisited: Socioeconomic and Demographic Contours of Small Tourist Economies.' *Asia Pacific Viewpoint* 51(1): 36–46.

McSorley, K. and McElroy, J.L. (2007) 'Small Island Economic Strategies: Aid-remittances Versus Tourism Dependence.' *e-Review of Tourism Research* 5(6): 140–48.

Meyer, D. (2006) 'Caribbean Tourism, Local Sourcing and Enterprise Development: Review of the Literature.' *PPT Working Paper No. 18*. London: Overseas Development Institute.

Ministry of Foreign Affairs and Trade (2014) *Cook Islands*. www.mfat.govt.nz/Countries/Pacific/Cook-Islands (accessed 29 June 2014).

Ministry of Tourism and Environment (2007) *Fiji Tourism Development Plan: 2007–2016*. Suva: Department of Tourism.

Ministry of Transport and Tourism (1997) *Fiji Tourism Development Plan: 1998–2005*. Suva: Ministry of Transport and Tourism.

Mitchell, J. and Ashley, C. (2006) 'Tourism Business and the Local Economy: Increasing Impact through a Linkage Approach.' *ODI Briefing Paper*, March.

Momsen, J.H. (1986) *Linkages between Tourism and Agriculture: Problems for the Smaller Caribbean Communities*. Newcastle-upon-Tyne, Seminar paper no. 45, Department of Geography.

New Zealand Tourism Research Institute (2013) *Pacific Regional Tourism and Hospitality Human Resources Development Plan*. Suva: Auckland University of Technology and South Pacific Tourism Organisation.

Phillips, A. (1977) 'The Concept of Development.' *Review of African Political Economy* 18: January–April: 7–20.

Rajotte, F. and Crocombe, R. (eds) (1980) *Pacific Tourism as Islanders See It*. Suva: Institute of Pacific Studies, University of the South Pacific.

Rao, D.R. (2004) *Culture and Entrepreneurship in Fiji's Small Tourism Business Sector*. Unpublished PhD thesis. Melbourne: Victoria University of Technology.

Rodman, M. (1987) 'Constraining Capitalism: Contradictions of Self-reliance in Vanuatu Fisheries Development.' *American Ethnologist* 14(4): 712–26.

Samoa Tourism Authority (2009) *Samoa Tourism Development Plan: 2009–13*. Apia: Samoa Tourism Authority.

Samy, J. (1996) 'Crumbs from the Table? The Workers' Share in Tourism.' In S. Tupouniua, R. Crocombe and C. Slatter (eds) *The Pacific Way: Social Issues in National Development*. Suva: South Pacific Social Sciences Association, 205–14.

Scheyvens, R. and Russell, M. (2010) *Sharing the Riches of Tourism: Summary Report*. Palmerston North: Massey University.

Simpson, M. (2008) 'Community Benefit Tourism Initiatives – A Conceptual Oxymoron?' *Tourism Management* 29: 1–18.

Slatter, C. (2006) *The Con/Dominion of Vanuatu? Paying the Price of Investment and Land Liberalisation – A Case Study of Vanuatu's Tourism Industry*. New Zealand: Oxfam.

Sofield, T. (2003) *Empowerment for Sustainable Tourism Development*. Oxford: Pergamon.

Sofield, T. and Tamasese, E. (2011) *Samoa: Tourism-led Poverty Reduction Programme*. Geneva: International Trade Centre.

Tauatofua, R.G. and Craig-Smith, S. (2010) 'The Socio-cultural Impacts of Visiting Friends and Relatives on Hosts: A Samoan Study.' *WIT Transactions on Ecology and the Environment* 130: 89–100.

Tourism Council of the South Pacific (1992) *Economic Impact of Tourism in Fiji*. Suva: Tourism Council of the South Pacific.

Tupouniua, S., Crocombe, R. and Slatter, C. (eds) (1975) *The Pacific Way: Social Issues in National Development*. Suva: South Pacific Social Sciences Association.

Twining-Ward, L. (2003) *Indicator Handbook: A Guide to the Development and Use of Samoa's Sustainable Tourism Indicators*. Apia, Samoa: South Pacific Regional Environment Facility and Samoa Tourism Authority.

UNWTO (United Nations World Tourism Organization) (2012) *Challenges and Opportunities for Tourism Development in Small Island Developing States*. Madrid: UNWTO.

——(2013) *UNWTO Tourism Highlights: 2013 Edition*. Madrid: UNWTO.

——(2014) *UNWTO Tourism Highlights: 2014 Edition*. Madrid: UNWTO.

Van der Duim, V.R. (2008) 'Tourism Chains and Pro-poor Tourism Development: An Actor-network Analysis of a Pilot Project in Costa Rica.' *Current Issues in Tourism* 11(2): 109–23.

Weiermair, K. (2006) 'Prospects for Innovation in Tourism: Analysing the Innovation Potential throughout the Tourism Value Chain.' *Journal of Quality Assurance in Hospitality* 6(3–4): 59–72.

Young, J. and Vinning, G. (2007) *Fiji: Commodity Chain Study: Outcomes from the Investigations Implemented to Assess Import Substitution Potentials of Selected Horticultural Products*. Apia, Samoa: Food and Agriculture Organization for the United Nations

World Travel and Tourism Council (2014) *Travel and Tourism Economic Impact 2014 Fiji*. www.wttc.org/site_media/uploads/downloads/fiji2014.pdf (accessed 17 July 2014).

2   Tourism in the French Pacific

Anne-Marie d'Hauteserre

Introduction

This chapter discusses French Pacific territories, their political economy, and the extent they have used tourism as a development tool, focusing especially on its low rates of growth over the past 20 years, even though many destinations elsewhere have recorded increases. I use a postcolonial paradigm to emphasise sensitivity to the political and economic consequences of tourism development. It is an approach that demands the consideration of alternative solutions that represent a break from the unequal relations neo-liberalism has imposed in many areas.

Colonialism has introduced modernity and incorporated inhabitants of many small islands into numerous international networks. Such incorporation has made them realise they must participate in globalisation, including tourism, to survive economically, and they need to protect what is left of their customary culture in their quest for identity and respectful recognition (n.a., 1998). For this to occur, indigenous aspirations, experiences and realities must guide the type, size and location of destinations if they are to 'maintain their lifestyle', as underlined by Logologofalau, a past president of the territorial assembly of Wallis and Futuna, when he endorsed the idea of tourism development (cited in Angleviel *et al.*, 1994: 8).

After a brief description of the French Pacific, this chapter will examine recent political evolutions, noting how subsidies and specific economic benefits prevent most French territories from seeking total independence, and then discuss tourism's role in the region's development.

What is the French Pacific?

Several territories make up this entity and they are widely spread across the South Pacific. French Polynesia covers about 118 small islands, only 76 of which are inhabited, and they are either high volcanic (up to 2,240 metres at Mount Orohena in Tahiti) or atolls. Global warming could erase these coral formations from world maps if the ocean rises faster than they can develop, and increased heat and storms can cause them major structural damage. All these islands are scattered through 5.5 million square kilometres of ocean, an area equal to that of Europe. However, while they thus offer a variety of tropical backdrops for tourism development, handicaps remain, including their remoteness for Western outbound markets, the physical separation of the various territories, and great distances within islands in the same territory. Polynesia is inhabited by 270,000 people, some 70% of whom live in Tahiti, in the Society Islands. Ethnically, 84% are Polynesian, while the Chinese represent 12%, the French or whites (*Farani* or *Popa'a*) 3%, and others 1% (Institut de la Statistique de Polynésie française, 2008).

New Caledonia is essentially an outcrop of nickel, chrome, copper and a few other minerals, and includes several islands besides la Grande Terre or *le caillou* (the rock). A drifting piece of Gondwanaland, when compared to other island destinations in the South Pacific it offers a very different landscape for the tourist gaze, even from the Loyalty Islands, which are raised coral formations (not really low atolls or high islands). It currently has a total population of 250,000. The largest single ethnic group is the Kanak, who in 1996 constituted 45% of the population but by 2009 had declined to 40%. By contrast, Europeans, a category including both settlers or *Caldoches* (18.5%) and *Metropolitans* (officials sent by the French government or private-sector employees, or simply people wanting a change from life in France) constituted 34% of the population in 1996 but only 29% in 2009. At the earlier date, too, there were Wallisians and Futunans (9%), Tahitians (2.6%), Indonesians (2.5%) and others (7%) (Institut de la Statistique de Nouvelle Calédonie, 2006). In 2009, more than 8% of the population considered themselves of mixed blood, a new category (David, 2011).

Wallis and Futuna, one of the least known entities of the South Pacific, comprises 13,500 Polynesians and a scattering of French (teachers, administrators, trades people), but another 21,300 live overseas, mostly in New Caledonia (IEOM, 2008). The territory is made up of three islands: Wallis and Futuna, which are two hours apart by airplane and are inhabited, and Alofi, which is used solely for cultivation by residents of Futuna and is visible from Futuna. Wallis has an outer reef used for diving and a lagoon that has been depleted by fishing with explosives, while Futuna suffers from earthquakes and has only two small beaches.

Modernisation has not by-passed these islands. Indeed, the French state and local territorial governments have invested heavily in modern telecommunication and transport systems. Most residents own a mobile phone, many islands have a concrete landing strip, and some – notably Wallis, the New Caledonia mainland, Tahiti, Hao and Rangiroa – can accommodate jet aircraft. Such infrastructure is essential to maintain local residents in their archipelagos and to satisfy tourist demand, though it is perhaps contrary to the expectations of tourists visiting these remote peripheries, as shown in the TV series *Survivors*, one of which was filmed in the Marquesas in 2001.

Colonisation in the French Pacific

The French presence in the region has been contested. Australasians and North Americans, for example, want the French state to relinquish its 'colonial' possessions in the South Pacific, as noted in a geography textbook used in the USA (de Blij and Muller, 2000: 75). In fact, most Pacific islands have experienced some form of colonial rule, which has led to forced contact, and often friction, in the global economy and world politics. Such results include nuclear testing and inflated revenues in French Polynesia and nickel exploitation in New Caledonia, and have served to erode customary ties without providing other forms of social bonding (Faberon and Postic, 2004; Doumenge, 2002).

In the 1800s, the French state took possession of land not claimed by Polynesians, but since then has returned most of it to the territorial government (d'Hauteserre, 2005; Bambridge, 2011). Nevertheless, in French Polynesia the main problem is the impossibility to subdivide, as land is held by extended families. Tourism development has often required long negotiations with multiple owners, sometimes successfully, as in the case of the Kia Ora resort on Rangiroa (which had 27 owners), but at other times resorts have closed because some owners have demanded outrageous rents (Club Med in Moorea). In Fakarava, it was discovered that the amount of land 'owned' was greater than the total land area of the atoll (d'Hauteserre, 2008)!

In New Caledonia, the Kanak suffered the worst forms of colonial administration. They were interned into reservations, the area of which shrank consistently over decades, and the land they lost was redistributed by the French government to the French. In 1878, a Kanak rebellion was brutally put down, but demands for independence have periodically re-emerged. Although a referendum for independence was scheduled for 2014 (Faberon and Postic, 2004), no date has actually been set. The territorial Congress elected in May was supposed to set a date between now and 2018.

In Wallis and Futuna, little land remains to be distributed, as most is already in the hands of local families, the Catholic Church or the French administration. Most is still held customarily, but this form of tenure is considered a barrier to outside investment. Indigenous customs survive, despite opposition from Marist missionaries. Nevertheless, much money continues to be spent on elaborate churches and chapels, which are possible tourist attractions, and many Catholics visit the tomb of the sainted Pierre Chanel, a Marist missionary killed in 1834 in Futuna.

Economic development

Economically, the French Pacific is very different from other Pacific island countries. Some residents enjoy high incomes, thanks to the generosity of the French state, and public administration (much of it subsidised by the French) provides around 20% of the territories' gross domestic product (GDP). While poverty exists, it is considerably less than elsewhere in Pacific (Abbott and Pollard, 2005). However, French support is under review and could be reduced, which is likely to create problems. As Poirine notes, 'a sudden end to metropolitan subsidies would create catastrophic conditions, considering the demise of the primary sector and the predictable concurrent collapse of the commercial sector' (Poirine, 1995: 121). In such circumstances, tourism – previously not considered a tool for development – might carry new appeal.

The main economic product of New Caledonia continues to be nickel mining and processing. The Nouméa Accord (*Accord de Nouméa*; n.a., 1998) forced redistribution of mineral rights and took mines away from white monopoly, so the Northern Province now owns both a mine and a smelter, which provides wealth but relatively few jobs (6.4% of the labour force). Consequently, tourism is seen as a means of employment and 'a source of social progress', as – following the Nouméa Accord (n.a., 1998) – the jobs it provides should lead to social development, more equity between Nouméa and the rest of the territory, and an increased standard of living of Kanak who live mostly in rural areas. Tourism development is of particular importance in the Loyalty Islands, where presently there is no potential mining activity (n.a., 2002; Descombels, 2007; Guiart, 2004; Perret, 2002; interviews, 2010).

In Wallis and Futuna, the local government is in charge of areas of economic development other than major infrastructural projects, but the formal sector of the economy is weak and 60% of the population practises subsistence living. Again, tourism is considered attractive by the Department of Cultural Affairs because it promises to protect the islands' cultural heritage and environment. However, while the continued survival of culture would be a definite asset in ecotourism, tourism development in any form depends on local political will, and to date there has been no real political response to President Logologofalau's 1986 call for democratic progress via tourism:

> The frequency of air service and telephone connections that need not transit via New Caledonia, have ended our isolation. We will attract tourists, but we want to maintain our identity, and our warm welcome is the guarantee. Our way of life, the way we respect visitors and our enchanting sites are the basic elements that enable us to trust in a future development of tourism.
>
> (cited in Angleviel *et al.*, 1994: 8)

Since 1993, when it signed a pact with the French government, French Polynesia has sought to increase its economic autonomy and move towards political independence. However, 70% of its economy remains dependent on transfers from France, and over the last few years the economy has shrunk despite (or because of) these subsidies (*DIXIT*, 2011; *Fenua-Economie*, 2011). Problems are compounded by the need to curtail migration from the outer archipelagos to Tahiti, where employment is hard to obtain and migrants simply join the ranks of the unemployed. Viable solutions to these problems have been prevented by political wrangling (du Prel, 2012: 5) and tourism's potential for development has been ignored as the government has neither created development plans nor reduced the misuse of transfers from the French state.

The situation is no more promising elsewhere. It has even been declared that, for Wallis and Futuna, 'economic development is impossible' (*Tahiti Pacifique*, 2012b: 20), and the author adds that Wallis, a mere hour away by plane from Fiji, cannot hope to attract many tourists. This is probably why the territory insists on maintaining its status of *Territoire d'Outre-Mer* (Overseas Territory) and seeks no further autonomy. By contrast, in New Caledonia, the French state (n.a., 1998) has encouraged Kanak to participate in diversifying the territory's economy, even though, until then, such participation was practically prohibited by the local Caldoche government (Faberon and Postic, 2004).

France's South Pacific dependencies cost Paris billions of dollars annually and monetary transfers from France are expected to continue beyond 2015, decreasing, but at less than the anticipated growth of the economy. Ideally, such transfers should promote sustainable economic development; in fact, economic autonomy is but a dream. The dilemma for the French State is that it can contribute but not manage, as to do so would run counter to decentralisation policies and the need to encourage the voluntary participation of local authorities and residents.

Tourism development in the French Pacific

It is common now to recognise that for many developing countries tourism has considerable potential as a tool for development. Its economic consequences are generally (albeit not always) considered positive. There has also been considerable discussion as to the social and cultural consequences of international tourism, both generally (Harrison, 1992a, 1992b), and with specific reference to Pacific island countries (Harrison, 2003).

Because tourism has been considered a means of reducing inequalities, consolidating citizenship rights, and a generator of employment for the relatively unskilled and uneducated, it has been encouraged in all three territories of the French Pacific. Such efforts have not been hugely successful. Along with 11 other Pacific island countries, French Polynesia and New Caledonia are members of the Fiji-based South Pacific Tourism Organisation (SPTO), but their international arrivals, when compared with other selected members of that organisation, and to the overall increase for all members, are unimpressive (Table 2.1).

Tourism in French Polynesia is based on luxury resorts run by international corporations. In 1999, it provided 11% of the gross national product' (GNP), up from 8% in 1993, but faced a reduction of 18% between 2008 and 2009, when the territory welcomed no more than 160,447 tourists (see Gay, 2009,

Table 2.1 Visitor arrivals for selected Pacific island countries, 2007–12

	2007	2008	2009	2010	2011	2012	% 2007–12
Cook Islands	97,019	94,776	101,229	104,265	113,114	121,757	25.5
Fiji	539,881	585,031	542,186	631,868	675,050	660,590	22.4
French Polynesia	218,241	196,496	160,447	153,919	162,776	168,978	-22.6
New Caledonia	103,363	103,672	99,379	98,562	111,875	112,204	8.6
Samoa	122,356	122,163	129,305	129,500	127,420	134,660	10.0
Tonga	43,344	50,462	45,711	47,081	46,005	49,010	13.1
Vanuatu	81,345	90,654	100,675	97,180	93,824	108,145	32.9
Total of all SPTO countries	1,339,903	1,395,857	1,338,234	1,446,964	1,533,296	1,564,808	16.8

Source: personal communication, South Pacific Tourism Organisation (SPTO), July 2013

for more details). In 2010, the number of visitors to Tahiti plummeted further and this led to the cancellation of air links by Air Tahiti Nui to New York and to Sydney. Indeed, over the period 2007 to 2012, arrivals to French Polynesia *declined* by more than 22%.

The decline in recent years might be partly attributed to the global financial crisis, which led to reduced outward travel by the French and Americans, who make up the bulk of the French Polynesia market. However, the figures from 2001 (when there were 228,000 arrivals) show a similar trend (UNWTO, 2007: 70), prompting one commentator of tourism in French Polynesia to describe the region as a 'tourist wasteland', littered with abandoned hotels (Bachimon, 2012).

Some comfort might be taken from the fact that the occupancy rate of luxury resort hotels rose from 48.4% in 2009 to 54% in 2010, though this was because several closed, and it fell again to 48% in 2012 (*Fenua-Economie*, 2011; *DIXIT*, 2012). In any case, the decline in French Polynesia was not restricted to the big hotels. Even though the government depicted the home-stays and bed and breakfast accommodation in the outer archipelagos as 'unique in the world' (*Te Fenua*, 2001: 2), in part because they directly benefit Polynesian families, they too suffered a 45% decline in visitor numbers between 2008 and 2010. This included a reduction in domestic travellers, who had been relied upon to make ends meet.

In 2010, attempts were made to create a strategy for the development of tourism in French Polynesia, but constant changes of government doomed those efforts to failure (interviews, 2010). The cruise market, which had suffered heavy losses in 2008 and 2009, was revived with some success (*Hitu News*, 2009: 4–10), but an enormous amount of work remains if tourism is to be developed. Tahiti and its islands expected rich visitors but never developed the services required. While most tourists are interested in ecotourism, biodiversity and culture, and come as couples, tourism promotion still focuses on the myth of the beautiful and seductive Tahitian *vahine* who lives in paradise, as described by Bougainville and prolonged by Paul Gauguin's paintings (Fayaud, 2011). It seems the territory still believes it is a privilege to visit its islands but most visitors first encounter a city that is noisy and unclean, suffers from traffic jams, has no cultural markers, and completely shuts down on Sundays.

The story of tourism in New Caledonia is a little more positive. Since 2001 there has been a period of steady if unspectacular growth (UNWTO, 2007: 133), and – apart from the slight decline in 2009 and 2010 – this continued up to 2012. Over the period 2008 to 2012 there was a modest increase of slightly less than 9% (Table 2.1) but, again, compared to other Pacific island countries, the performance was disappointing. Indeed, despite 12 years of cooperation among the provinces in tourism marketing, fewer tourists visited New Caledonia in 2012 than in 1986 (UNWTO, 1990: 109)! Tourism still provides less than 5% of the jobs in the territory (mostly in the Southern Province) and 4% of GDP.

There have been some attempts at planning. The *Plan de Développement Touristique* was to be implemented in three phases over 12 years from 2006 (interviews, 2007, 2010). By 2018, the end of the third phase of the plan, New Caledonia was to attract 180,000 international visitors (three times today's number, excluding cruise ship visitors). It was hoped that tourism would bring benefits to the Kanak community, hitherto denied access to economic well-being. Efforts are being made to encourage grass-roots forms of development, including tourism, but tourism development remains embryonic, providing activities for only a small proportion of Kanak in the Northern Province, while in the Loyalty Islands a few have managed to make a living as employees or entrepreneurs.

As the overall economic development plan for New Caledonia has been only partially implemented, and tourism development delayed, the government of the Northern Province has encouraged tourism development on its own. It has focused mainly on resort-type hotels located at beautiful sites – for example, the former Club Med in Hienghène – and on a few three-star hotels, most of which are owned by SOFINOR, a provincial government organisation. Two others (in Kone and in Koumac) are privately owned, but the province has provided subsidies for their upgrade.

The province has also tried to develop ecotourism and several attractions to complement accommodation in the Northern Province. The latter include a Museum of Coffee (situated on tribal land), a heart-shaped mangrove (made famous by the photographer Yann Arthus-Bertrand), visits to the Tiébaghi chrome mine and a ghost miners' village, and trips to tribal villages for meals and/or overnight stays. These enable visitors to discover local biodiversity and the culture of local residents. In addition, training for guides has also encouraged the creation of nature treks. However, only a small percentage of all such activities are likely to emerge as major income earners and attractions (d'Hauteserre, 2010).

In general, tourism development in French Polynesia and New Caledonia has been sketchy. Mass tourism is hardly on the horizon, and plans laid more than a decade ago to increase visits to the former in 2015 to 600,000 (Mission d'Evaluation et de Prospective, 2000b), and the latter to 180,000 (interviews, 2010) are highly unlikely to be achieved.

Finally, there have been some attempts to develop tourism in the islands of Wallis and Futuna. While the French state instigates such large projects as hospitals, schools, access to running water and roads, the local government is responsible for other areas of economic development, including tourism, which is based on the surviving local Polynesian culture, including the manufacture of tapa cloth and coconut oil perfumed with local flowers. Tourism has been included in the plan for the strategic sustainable development of the territory (Ministry of Foreign Affairs, 2002), signed by the local authorities and the French state, but so far its recommendations have not been implemented. Meanwhile, despite requests over several years from the local Chamber of Commerce for a tourism information centre, one has not yet been provided.

Within the French Pacific, there is a small niche market for (mainly) local and some international religious tourism. This involves home visits and attendance at congresses, for example, the March 1997 bicentenary celebration of the Evangelical Church's presence in Tahiti. Wallis and Futuna attracts between 40 and 70 tourists per year (interviews, 2009). Many come to visit the tomb of St Chanel, the island's patron saint, while other visitors, coming on yachts, are attracted by the islands' remoteness. As one Italian couple noted, 'we came here because it was such an unknown part of the South Pacific' (interviews, 2009). Personal observation suggests that remoteness can certainly be found: there is no welcoming infrastructure, tourists are left to find their own accommodation and design their own itinerary, and they may not find their hosts when they land (personal observation, 2005, 2009).

Constraints to tourism development in the French Pacific

There are numerous constraints to tourism development in the French Pacific, some of which are general throughout the region, while others are more specific. First, the region is not – and has never been – organised as a single tourism destination (Sigogne, 1922; ESCAP, 2001) and within the region there are several different tourism organisations (including three in French Polynesia and New Caledonia, besides provincial ones). Indeed, although governments in the French Pacific have provided such services as education and health, transport and communications, along with logistical and financial support to jumpstart enterprises that utilise or process local resources (Etat-Territoire, 1994; Pacte de Progrès, 1993; Laventure, 1997), even within the French Pacific there is little coordination among hotels, transportation services and local entrepreneurs.

Second, international air transport remains the Achilles heel of the territories. Flight frequency and seat allocation, and the distribution of airport slots in Paris, London, Los Angeles, Tokyo or Osaka (the region's main outbound markets), are considered insufficient by elected officials and tourism professionals. Consequently, they have invested in Air Tahiti Nui and Air Calin, locally owned international airlines, to avoid being at the mercy of decisions taken elsewhere about flight frequency or service. The decision has merit, as research confirms their analysis (Vellas and Cauet, 1997: 86), but the ability of these companies to make a profit is much reduced by cronyism (*Tahiti Pacifique*, 2010, 2012a; *Fenua-Economie*, 2011).

Another general factor is that substitutes exist even for remote destinations, and these are not restricted to other Pacific islands. Increasing numbers of culturally fascinating destinations can be found in Asia or closer to the main global outbound markets, even on the doorsteps of Europe and North America (veilletourisme.ca/2011/02/16/des-offres-touristiques-importees-dailleurs/, accessed 17 February 2011). It is questionable how much substitutability the market can absorb: for most consumers from the developed world, islands are consumable, glossy and generic – 'islands' means 'tropical islands', irrespective of their particular characteristics (King and Connell, 1999).

More specific to the French Pacific, the physical environment has been much degraded, greatly reducing its attraction for tourists. The extraction of coral to construct roads and the in-filling of shallow lagoon areas are the main causes of the degraded seashore, affecting an estimated 7% to 11% of all reefs in French Polynesia (Mission d'Evaluation et de Prospective, 2000a: 140). At the time of writing, 50% of the seashore in Moorea was considered 'dead'. In addition, soil erosion and material displaced by residential construction or mining on hillsides create major problems of sedimentation in the lagoons, and walls in Tahiti cut off any view of the seashore along the main road even when it is close to the edge of the lagoon. In Wallis, too, sand has been removed to construct retaining walls and houses and decorate gardens; as a consequence, the only remaining beaches are around small *motus* (small islets) of its outer reef.

Opportunities for tourism development in the French Pacific

The existence of traditional cultures provides a major opportunity for tourism development in the French Pacific but it is a problematic issue. Some cultural tourists, perhaps initially few in number, could have an interest in the architecture and ceremonies associated, for example, with churches in New Caledonia, Tongan forts in Wallis and Futuna, and Marae ceremonies in Tahiti. Such an appeal is reflected in publicity brochures: 'You cannot possibly be farther from civilisation than in Manihi'; 'Marquesas islands, the most isolated islands in the world. Know that no other land lies as far removed from any continent'.

In New Caledonia, cultural tourism development seems reserved for provinces populated by Kanak, as it focuses on their Melanesian traits (d'Hauteserre, 2010). Despite the emphasis in the Matignon Accord (Connell, 1988) on 'rebalancing' geographic and ethnic inequities, images of the authentic, traditional Kanak way of life are used to lure domestic tourists searching for 'exotica' or 'ecstasies of experience'. Later, the Nouméa Accord (n.a., 1998) claimed to have 'opened a new era, marked by the full recognition of Kanak identity' (Faberon and Postic, 2004: 15). As Lefebvre (1991 [1974]: 84) earlier remarked, 'if the maps and guides are to be believed a veritable feast of authenticity awaits the tourist'. However, maps and guides may *not* be believed, for the culture of display (exhibition, staging) is shaped by complex relations of colonisation, modernity and neo-colonialism.

Visitors indeed come from wealthier parts of the world to experience traditional culture but promotional campaigns resort to belittling images of Kanak that emphasise their difference, their 'natural' state and their primitiveness. Publicity for New Caledonia as a tourism destination has long downplayed the presence of the Kanak, their culture, and their ownership of the land on which the resorts are built. They were either erased from the New Caledonia landscape or assimilated into nature, from which civilisation would rescue them (Wilmer, 1993; d'Hauteserre, 2011). However, the success of such campaigns has been minimal; as indicated earlier, the number of tourists has remained static (d'Hauteserre, 2011; Gay, 2009). Today, Kanak culture is exploited for tourism development by outside investors and 'subjugation continues as an insidious process because it silences constituencies even as it gives voice and face to their culture and histories' (Farred, 1995: 22).

It is a moot point as to whether or not tourism's promotion of indigenous culture means it will inevitably be appropriated by visitors, even if only fragments can be displayed (McCarthy, 2007). An associated concern is how far indigenous people can be empowered to guarantee and defend their cultural expression, for tourism is part of a process of global hegemony that, arguably, marginalises and oppresses colonised people. Nevertheless, despite such reservations, as Jean-Marie Tjibaou (2005: 93) has said of tourism and souvenirs, 'It would be good for *Pokens* (foreigners) to see the artefacts too. They see it as a tourist visit but for us it's a chance to gain their respect by explaining who we are, since they don't know us'.

Irrespective of the arguments for and against indigenous tourism, however, traditional arts and crafts – suitably adapted for tourism – have been promoted throughout the French Pacific, especially in French Polynesia, because of the profits they can generate. Production and sales are supported by several agencies, notably Service de la Culture et du Patrimoine, and Maison de la Culture et Centre des Metiers d'Art (which aims to teach the skills required to adapt culture to contemporary demands). Two academies, modelled on the Académie Française, which regulates the evolution of the French language, safeguard Marquisian and Tahitian languages. The Museum of Tahiti and its Islands (*Te Fare Manaha*) collects, preserves and displays cultural heritage, mostly of French Polynesia, while the Museum of New Caledonia carries out a similar function for that territory.

Arts and crafts provide an income for many families in the French Pacific. Using surpluses of primary products (*pandanus*, shells and mother of pearl shells discarded after pearls have been harvested), they support indigenous culture and maintain social cohesion, especially in the outside archipelagos, where they facilitate intergenerational exchange and enable residents to earn cash without leaving their islands. Although the local and international tourist market is small, it represents a major outlet for such production.

In Tahiti, the *Heiva* is a yearly competition of traditional arts and practices, carried out during July by all Polynesians of French Polynesia for their own benefit. It started in 1882, under the name of *Tiurai*, as a celebration of Bastille Day, which enabled residents to perform certain cultural practices, e.g. traditional dances that had previously been prohibited by missionaries (Durban, 2005). Focused on Polynesian culture, artisans exhibit such skills as weaving, sewing and sculpture, and performers compete in traditional sports and perform songs and dances. The *Heiva* asserts the cultural values of the winners of the competitions. Its events are not staged for tourists, though they are welcome, and most ticket holders are local residents. A short translation in English and French summarises the theme of every presentation, but the *Orero* (the story as it unfolds of the dance spectacle) and the texts of the songs for the competition remain in Tahitian (personal observations over several decades; *Hiro'a Magazine*, 2012: 11–17; Durban, 2005; Fayn, 2007).

The above examples indicate a level of indigenous production for tourism. What often fall between the cracks in discourses on economic and social development in New Caledonia are the realities and cultures of several minorities (Javanese, Japanese, Khabil, Wallisian or Tahitian, for example). Arguably, an expansion of such production would counteract the neo-colonial tendencies of global tourism and might eliminate the need to question the authenticity of the experiences offered. Indeed, Polynesian and Melanesian cultures, alongside other ethnicities such as Chinese, French and others cited above, could be more effective in distinguishing the French Pacific from its competitors than non-existent beaches and seductive *vahines*.

Conclusion

Even though French Polynesia, New Caledonia and Wallis and Futuna are financially costly for France, it does not seem that France will cease to maintain them. At the same time, the French Pacific cannot wean its economy from dependence on French subsidies because the productive capacities of the territories can neither maintain nor develop the infrastructure of transport, health or education to which they have become accustomed. Numerous development plans remain 'works in progress' and most residents are unconcerned by the demands such a situation puts on them as hosts. As a result of French nuclear tests and mining operations, there is an expectation of continued financial assistance, and most residents are convinced that the territories are major strategic and emotional assets for France. Monetary transfers from France are expected to continue beyond 2015, even though the total amount will continue to decrease from its 2004 peak.

In such circumstances, it is not surprising that there is a focus on 'development', though this is a discourse often enunciated for the benefit of those who *provide* the development (for example, employees of aid agencies, non-governmental organisations (NGOs), multinationals and government officials), rather than those who receive it. Equally unsurprisingly, tourism is seen by many as a *tool* for development, an economic driver that provides employment for people with few skills, and in this chapter it has been suggested that tourism's potential in the region is far from being met. However, if France could invest its largesse in a policy for the sustainable use of local resources and improved economic returns for the residents of all South Pacific island nations, French prestige would increase and the French presence would be more acceptable.

References

Abbott, D. and Pollard, S. (2005) *Hardship & Poverty in the Pacific*. Manila: Asian Development Bank.

Angleviel, F. *et al.* (1994) *Wallis et Futuna. Hommes et espaces.* Nouméa: CTRDP.

Bachimon, P. (2012) 'Tourist Wastelands in French Polynesia – Examination of a Destination in Crisis and Manner of Resistance to International Tourism', *Via@*, Varia, 1. Posted on 28 September (accessed 21 July 2013).

Bambridge, T. (2011) *Le foncier en Polynésie française*. Papeete: Editions Univers Polynésiens.

Connell, J. (1988) *New Caledonia: The Matignon Accord and the Colonial Future*. Sydney: Research Institute for Asia and the Pacific.

David, C. (2011) 'Le recensement ethnique.' In J.Y. Faberon, V. Fayaud and J.-M. Regnault (eds) *Destins des Collectivités politiques d'Océanie*. Aix-Marseille: Presses Universitaires, 675–86.

de Blij, H.J. and Muller, P. (2000) *Geography: Realms, Regions and Concepts*. New York: John Wiley & Sons.

Descombels, A. (2007) *Quelle économie pour la Nouvelle Calédonie*. Nouméa: private publication.

d'Hautesserre, A.-M. (2005) 'Customary Practices and Tourism Development in the French Pacific.' In C. Cooper and M. Hall (eds) *Handbook on Oceania*. New York: Channel View Publications, 308–20.

——(2008) 'Paradis extrêmes: restructuration économique ou perte de culture? Les Tuamotu et le tourisme.' In O. Dehoorne and P. Saffache (eds) *Mondes insulaires tropicaux*. Paris: Ellipses, 127–46.

——(2010) 'Government Policies and Indigenous Tourism in New Caledonia.' *Asia Pacific Journal of Tourism Research* 15(3): 285–303.

——(2011) 'Politics of Imaging in New Caledonia.' *Annals of Tourism Research* 38(2): 380–402.

DIXIT (2011) Vol. 19. Papeete: Compagnie Océanienne de Gestion.

——(2012) Vol. 20. Papeete: Compagnie Océanienne de Gestion.

Doumenge, J.-P. (2002) 'Pluralité ethno-culturelle dans les territoires d'outre-mer français.' *Hermès* 32–33: 141–55.

du Prel, A. (2012) 'Quand on refuse de voir la réalité.' *Tahiti-Pacifique Magazine*, June/July : 5.

Durban, J.-F. (2005) *Les acteurs de la tradition en Polynésie française.* Paris: L'Harmattan.

ESCAP (Economic and Social Commission for Asia and the Pacific) (2001) *Promotion of Investment in Tourism Infrastructure.* New York: United Nations, ST/ESCAP/ 2133.

Etat-Territoire (1994) 'Contrat de développement Etat-Territoire 1994–98.' Papeete: *Journal Officiel de la Polynésie Française* 143(1): 2–51.

Faberon, J.-Y. and Postic, J.R. (2004) *L'accord de Nouméa, la loi organique et autres documents juridiques et politiques de la Nouvelle Calédonie.* Nouméa: Ile de Lumière.

Farred, G. (1995) 'Untitled Contribution to Race and Racism: A Symposium.' *Social Text* 42: 21–26.

Fayaud, V. (2011) *Le paradis autour de Paul Gauguin.* Paris: CNRS Editions.

Fayn, D. (2007) *Ori Tahiti, la danse a Tahiti.* Papeete: Ile des Vents.

Fenua-Economie (2011) Vol. 8. Papeete: La Dépêche.

Gay, J.C. (2009) *Les cocotiers de la France.* Paris: Belin.

Guiart, J. (2004) *Les Mélanésiens devant l'économie de marché.* Nouméa: Le Rocher-à-la-Voile.

Harrison, D. (1992a) 'International Tourism and the Less Developed Countries: The Background.' In D. Harrison (ed.) *Tourism and the Less Developed Countries.* Chichester: Wiley, 1–18.

——(1992b) 'Tourism to Less Developed Countries: The Social Consequences.' In D. Harrison (ed.) *Tourism and the Less Developed Countries.* Chichester: Wiley, 34.

——(2003) 'Themes in Pacific Island Tourism.' In D. Harrison (ed.) *Pacific Island Tourism.* New York: Cognizant, 1–23.

Hiro'a Magazine (2012) Special edition on *Heiva*, July.

Hitu News (2009) 19/25 February edn.

IEOM (Institut d'Emission d'Outremer) (2008) *Rapport.* Wallis.

Institut de la Statistique de Nouvelle Calédonie (2006) *Tableaux de l'économie calédonienne.* Nouméa, New Caledonia.

Institut de la Statistique de Polynésie française (2008) *Tableaux de l'Economie de Polynésie française.* Papeete: Institut.

King, R. and Connell, J. (eds) (1999) *Small Worlds, Global Lives. Islands and Migration.* London: Pinter.

Laventure, M. (1997) *Le tourisme, facteur de développement de l'outre-mer français.* Paris: Direction des journaux officiels.

Lefebvre, H. (1991 [1974]) *The Production of Space.* Translated by Donald Nicholson-Smith. Oxford: Blackwell.

McCarthy, C. (2007) *Exhibiting Maori. A History of Colonial Cultures of Display.* New York: Berg.

Ministry of Foreign Affairs (2002) *Plan de Stratégie de Développement Durable de Wallis et Futuna.* Paris: Ministry of Foreign Affairs.

Mission d'Evaluation et de Prospective (2000a) *Rapport d'évaluation.* Papeete: Présidence du Gouvernement de la Polynésie Française.

——(2000b) *Rapport de prospective.* Papeete: Présidence du Gouvernement de la Polynésie Française.

n.a. (1998) *Accord de Nouméa* (Nouméa Accord). Paris: Ministry of Foreign Affairs.

n.a. (2002) *Actes du Séminaire: Foncier et Développement en Nouvelle Calédonie*. Nouméa, Centre Culturel Tjibaou.

Pacte de Progrès (1993) *Propositions de la Délégation Polynésienne*. Papeete: Editions Charte du Développement.

Perret, C. (ed.) (2002) *Perspectives de Développement pour la Nouvelle-Calédonie*. Grenoble: Presses Universitaires de Grenoble.

Poirine, B. (1995) *Les petites économies insulaires: théorie et stratégies de développement*. Paris: L'Harmattan.

Sigogne, L. (1922) 'Le tourisme en Océanie.' *Bulletin de la Société d'Etudes Océaniennes* 6: 52–54.

Tahiti Pacifique (2010) Various short commentaries.

——(2011) Various short commentaries.

——(2012a) Various short commentaries.

——(2012b) May edn: 20.

Te Fenua (2001) Bi-monthly publication of the territorial government of French Polynesia, November edn.

Tjibaou, J.-M. (2005) *Kanaky*. Translators Helen Fraser and John Trotter. Canberra, ANU: Pandanus Books.

UNWTO (United Nations World Tourism Organization) (1990) *Compendium of Tourism Statistics: 1985–1989*. Madrid: UNWTO.

——(2007) *Compendium of Tourism Statistics: Data 2001–2005*. Madrid: UNWTO.

Vellas, F. and Cauet, J.-M. (1997) *Le tourisme et les îles*. Paris: l'Harmattan.

Wilmer, F. (1993) *The Indigenous Voice in World Politics*. London: Zed Books.

Part II
Images of the South Pacific

.

3 Tourism and postcards from the colonial periphery

Vintage postcards from Fiji

David Harrison

Introduction: from exploration to colonialism

Tourism makes a substantial contribution to many Pacific island countries (PICs) (Harrison and Prasad, 2013), and their current appeal as sun, sea and sand destinations has been carefully fostered by traditional brochures and, more recently, internet sites. Historically, though, Western perceptions of such island states have been ambivalent, vacillating from idyllic scenes of pre-Fall Paradise, inhabited by men and women of innate nobility and unparalleled beauty, to regions of threat and danger, whose peoples display almost proto-human primitive characteristics (Harrison, 2001).

Such conflicting perceptions are certainly not new (Grove, 1995: 23–24; Mackay, 1999; Sturma, 2002; Reidy, Kroll and Conway, 2007; Lay, 2008). Rather, they have been perpetuated by generations of novelists (Defoe, 1976 [1719]; Loxley, 1990; Marryat, 2011 [1841]; Melville, 1996 [1846]; Wyss, 1993 [1812]; and Ballantyne, 1995 [1858]), some of whom wrote specifically for children. As Edmond notes:

> The South Pacific was also a perfect setting in which new mid-century concepts of boyhood could be dramatised and elaborated. The Victorian invention of boyhood was signalled, among other things, by the emergence of the boys' adventure story in the 1840s.
>
> (Edmond, 1997: 142)

Artists also contributed to the image of Pacific islands (Day, 1987; Lay, 2008). Gauguin 'was only the last in a long line of French artists to portray Oceania' (Fayaud, 2006: 12.1), and the development of photography merely added impetus to the exoticisation of tropical islands in the European mind. Late in the nineteenth century, photographs of Melanesia encouraged travel to Papua New Guinea, New Hebrides (Vanuatu) and Solomon Islands, prompting Burns Philp and Co. Ltd to introduce the first cruise ship to New Guinea in 1884 (Douglas, 1996: 44–50), and the photographs of Walter Spies and Beryl de Zoete helped transform Bali's image for Western visitors (Hitchcock and Norris, 1995).

The colonisation of Pacific islands from the mid-nineteenth century heightened interest in tropical islands. World fairs and exhibitions (Benedict, 1983; Geppert, Coffey and Lau, 2000) frequently exhibited 'natives' from the colonies, implicitly portraying the civilisation of Europe and North America as superior, and 'alternately filtering out or emphasising the disturbing and exotic qualities of the "Other"' (Cohen and Manspeizer, 2009: 85). When Fijians appeared, public interest in their cannibalistic past continued, despite the colonial authorities' intentions (Johnston, 2005), but, more generally, such exhibitions have been held responsible for actually *creating* the image of 'the savage' and relegating colonised peoples to a human zoo (Thuram, Blachnard, Boëtsch and Jacomijn Snoep, 2012). In 1910, for example, an Arcadian version of Samoa was portrayed at an anthropological exhibition, *Die Samoaner* (The Samoans), which was actually held in Cologne Zoological Gardens:

> Staged according to evolutionary prejudices, next to animals in the zoo, those displays were less scientific explorations than sensationalist sideshows designed to attract and entertain crowds whose curiosity was piqued by the increase in colonial activity.
>
> (Weinstein, 1993: 185)

Tourist images and the portrayal of 'native' people

In the twentieth century, long-established stereotypes of tropical islands continued to be circulated throughout the developed world by travel writers, story tellers, anthropologists, artists, photographers and film makers (Harrison, 2001, 2004; Stephen, 1993; and Geiger, 2007).[1] Most prominently, Michener's *Tales of the Pacific* (1947) formed the basis for *South Pacific*, perhaps the most influential of numerous feature films that brought the eroticised and exotic Pacific islands to a mass twentieth-century audience (Harrison, 2001: 12–13; Jolly, 1997: 111–22).

From the 1950s, stereotypical images of tropical islands were adopted as tourism marketing tools (Cohen, 1982) and 'paradise' remains one of the most hackneyed descriptions of island destinations in tourist brochures (Cohen and Manspeizer, 2009: 86; Whittaker, 2009).[2] At the same time, scholarly studies of the role of destination image have increased, using content analysis or through semiotics (Albers and James, 1988). Many commentators have noted how 'realities' of destinations have been distorted to attract tourists (Britton, 1979, Adams, 1984; Mohamed, 1988; Cohen, 1989; Reimer, 1990; Silver, 1993; Buzinde, Santos and Smith, 2006; and Hunter, 2008). Selwyn (1993) sees tourist brochures as purveyors of well-established myths of South-East Asia; Wilson (1994) relates changes in tourism advertising to political change in the Seychelles; and Thurot and Thurot (1983) and Moeran (1983) link changes in tourism advertising to changing features of life in tourist-sending societies.

Dann, in particular, analyses how residents are portrayed in tourism brochures and other tourism literature (Dann, 1996a, 1996b, 1996c), implying that the images are manipulated for tourism purposes. Similar views are expressed by Cohen (1995) for the British Virgin Islands, and Mason (1995) for Hawai'i. More generally, Graburn (1983) argues that, at least in some countries, tourism is akin to prostitution. Such portrayals of the South Pacific re-present a colonial image of the destination which, in fact, may be unacceptable to those being so represented. According to Ide Gde Ing. Bagus, a Balinese historian, for example, 'the Dutch wanted us to be a living museum', and so 'Balinese tradition became something that could be served to Western tourists' (in Yamashita, 2003: 33).

Specifically referring to the South Pacific, d'Hauteserre (2010) notes how New Caledonia continues to be promoted for tourism as a French enclave, and Harrison (1998) suggests that in the Fiji of tourist brochures primacy has consistently been accorded to indigenous Fijian peoples and their culture, while those of Indian origin, a substantial proportion of the population, are virtually absent.

The emergence and analysis of the picture postcard

Like other photographs, picture postcards involve a 'framing' of the world, both literally and metaphorically (MacCannell, 1976: 43–45; Robinson and Picard, 2009: 13), and producers both select and orchestrate the subject(s), staging and taking the best picture, according to their cultural assumptions about the *nature* of the subject and the context and their expectations of the picture's potential audience (Robinson and Picard, 2009: 13–24).

Unlike commercial photographs, however, the mass-produced picture postcard was a cheap and relatively rapid method of communication. Coincidentally, it emerged soon after Pacific island colonialism began and the first two decades of the twentieth century were a 'golden age' for postcards in North America, Europe and Australasia. By the year ending June 1908, for example, more than 700 million were posted in the USA alone (Bassett, 2012: 1), and postcards continued as a highly popular form of communication until the 1930s when, with the introduction of the telephone, a relative decline started. However, until the recent emergence of the internet and social networking media, for people away from home, on holiday or business, the postcard remained a highly popular method of communicating with family and friends.

In the heyday of the picture postcard, there was a deliberate effort to exchange cards and develop collections. More recently, collectors and scholars have recognised that they are an important source of social history, and deltiology (postcard collecting) has become an increasingly popular hobby (Willoughby, 1992; Staff, 1996; Phillips, 2000; Beukers, 2007). Online databases are becoming common, and these include several in university library collections (www.natlib.govt.nz/collections/types-of-items/ephemera/?

searchterm=postcards, accessed 17 June 2012), though information on museum collections suggests that (in so far as they include postcards at all) they have had little public exposure.[3] With specific reference to Pacific islands, valuable databases of published postcards for such Pacific islands as Hawai'i (Steiner, 2001) and Fiji (Stephenson, 1997; Dear, 2008) are now available.

Social scientists studying tourism now make use of such resources. Edwards (1996) suggests that behind their apparent ethnographic objectivity, postcards exoticise the 'Other', conveying images of authenticity and giving a false impression of universalism. Burns (2004), too, emphasises the 'Otherness' conveyed in postcards from North Africa and the Eastern Mediterranean, and Mellinger (1994) notes the unfavourable stereotypes of African Americans in postcards depicting the Deep South. By contrast, Mamiya shows how postcards reveal 'a highly exoticised and romanticised image of Hawaiian culture' (Mamiya, 1992: 89), marginalising Hawaiians and (literally and metaphorically) stripping them of their ethnic identity' (Mamiya, 1992: 97), while Markwick's study of Maltese postcards indicates a shift from images of sun-and-sea-and-sex to a focus on culture and everyday authenticity, albeit with a veneer of domestic simplicity (Markwick, 2001). Other studies, focusing on how ethnic images have been portrayed in postcards, include the stereotype of the Argentine gaucho as an epitome of national identity (Norrild, 2001), the privileging of the city of Cardiff in modern postcards of Wales (Pritchard and Morgan, 2003), and *contrasting* images and varieties of staged authenticity of Zulus, the Sámi and the Welsh (Thurlow, Jaworski and Ylänne-McEwen, 2005: 99).

Fiji and the picture postcards: the 1890s to 1920s

Fiji was first settled by Europeans[4] in the 1920s. Initially, they settled mainly on the island of Ovalau, at Levuka, which became the country's first capital in 1874, when Fiji became a British colony. Eight years later, because of Levuka's geographical position and its inability to expand, the capital was subsequently moved to Suva, on the main island of Viti Levu.

Like other tropical islands, Fiji was developed as a sugar colony. From 1879 until 1916, indentured labourers were imported from India to work on sugar plantations. By contrast, indigenous Fijians (*i-taukei*) were largely subsistence farmers on communally held land, which comprised more than 80% of the area of Fiji. Indeed, only early in the twenty-first century did as many Fijian citizens live in urban as rural areas (Fiji Islands Bureau of Statistics, 2009: 10). Despite major outbreaks of disease – measles in 1875, which killed 25% of the population, and Spanish influenza in 1918, which killed 14% – the population increased from 121,180 in 1891 (when less than 3% were European or part-European and 6% were Indian) to 588,068 in 1976, six years after Fiji had obtained its independence. Of this number, 50% were of Indian origin and 44% *i-taukei*, with the remainder mainly comprising Europeans (0.8%), part-Europeans (1.7%), Chinese and part-Chinese (0.8%), and

Rotumans and other Pacific islanders (2.4%). Later political developments, primarily two coups in 1987, an attempted coup in 2000 and a further coup in 2006, led to continuous emigration of the Indo-Fijian population, and by 2007 indigenous Fijians were nearly 57% of a population of 837,271, while Indo-Fijians were only 38% (Fiji Islands Bureau of Statistics, 2009: 3).

The period covered in this content analysis of postcards of Fiji is from the 1890s to the 1930s, when British colonialism was being established. During this period, the heyday of the postcard, postcards of Fiji were overwhelmingly produced by 'Europeans', though several were overseas migrants who had taken up residence in Fiji (Stephenson, 1997: 47–52, 75–76). Most card producers were from Australia, but some came from North America, the United Kingdom and other parts of Europe (Stephenson, 1997: 37–146).

It was therefore with a European gaze that producers selected their scenes. They were then purchased by and sent to people of European origin. Coincidentally, 1923 saw the formation of the Suva Tourist Bureau, the forerunner of the Fiji Visitors Bureau. Itself an offshoot of the White Settlement League, in 1926 it entertained some 3,000 overseas visitors, along with 'several thousands who were passengers or crew aboard ships in transit' (Scott, 1970: 42). These people, along with the 3,000 European residents, were probably the primary consumers of the Fiji picture postcard, which thus served as a quick method of communication, a personal souvenir and an early advertisement for tourists.

Content analysis of Fiji postcards

At the outset, three caveats should be recorded concerning the sample of nearly 2,000 cards on which this content analysis is based.[5] First, it is difficult to estimate the *popularity* of any one card. However, the regularity of types of cards appearing on the market today, and their prices, tend to reflect the findings of the content analysis. River and coastal scenes, for example, are common and cheap, whereas the more scarce 'cannibal' pictures, 'erotica' and scenes of special events in the life of the colony are considerably more expensive.

Second, many photographs and prints were initially sold individually or published in books and only afterwards were reproduced as postcards. Once published in card form, they were often reproduced by other publishers, perhaps if a company was sold or merged, or if rights to the picture changed hands. Many 1930s cards, for example, are reproductions of earlier cards, including those reproduced by Christian missions operating in Fiji and throughout the South Pacific. However, no estimate was made of cards reproduced *later* in the period. The focus is on *themes* rather than absolute numbers.

Finally, it is impossible to estimate how many postcards were produced over the period. It has been suggested that by 1925, Carl Meyer alone had taken 'about 7,000 post card photos', including 'beautiful views of Suva, its people, customs and its many beauties, of Fiji industries, of sea and land views, of natives with their glorious "busbies" [hair style] and other subjects' (Stephenson, 1997: 68–69). However, it is believed the sample is sufficiently large to give an accurate indication of the overall themes depicted in cards over this period.

In all, 1,904 postcards of Fiji were analysed. Most were commercially produced and issued approximately between 1895 and the early 1920s by 22 publishers, but 292 (15.3%) were published anonymously. When analysed for their content, they were initially placed into one of 16 distinct categories, along with several sub-categories, as indicated in Table 3.1.

Cards focusing primarily on nature comprised 20.8% of the collection. Landscapes, seascapes, lakes, waterfalls and riverscapes without any sign of human settlement made up 8.4% of all the cards (Figure 3.1), and a further 12.4% gave some small indication of human settlement, e.g. a canoe or a few

Table 3.1 Fiji postcards by category

Category		Total	%
Transport		73	3.9
Landscape	with social	55	2.9
	without social	44	2.3
Seascape, lake or waterfall	with social	86	4.5
	without social	90	4.7
Riverscape	with social	96	5.0
	without social	26	1.4
Material culture	villages	117	6.1
	native housing	98	5.1
	colonial building	157	8.2
	towns	255	13.4
	economy	138	7.2
Culture	religion	17	0.9
	ceremonial	133	7.0
Food/fruit/cooking		32	1.7
Men	primitive	20	1.0
	dignified	83	4.4
Women	voyeuristic	88	4.6
	dignified	65	3.4
Family/group		11	0.6
Social occasions	private	8	0.4
	public	44	2.3
	special occasions	24	1.3
Police/military		33	1.8
Children		22	1.2
Indian		18	0.9
Humour/bizarre		5	0.3
Re-enactment		17	0.9
Other		49	2.6
Total		1,904	100.0

No. 6. Day break. Fiji.

I hope I han't sent one like this before.
Please send an actress or any name with actresses

Figure 3.1 Coastal scene: Fiji
Source: Publisher unknown: undivided back, posted 1902 from Fiji to Sydney, New South Wales

small human figures, which was not, though, a central feature of the picture. Together, such cards might be categorised as *Arcadian*, or examples of the *picturesque*. An exception, though, is the type of card specifically focusing on native canoes, either singly (as in Figure 3.2) or in groups, where the canoe itself is the subject of the card and is thus of interest to the ethnographer or historian (Stephenson, 1997: 222–27).

Another popular category is made up of cards that together illustrate features of modernity introduced through colonialism. This group makes up 21.6% of the collection. It is a broad category and includes many early panoramic views of Levuka and Suva, both municipal areas that were a direct result of colonialism (Figure 3.3). It also includes buildings symbolic of colonial 'progress', and health, learning, religion, communications and governance are all represented in such cards. The development of civil society is seen in the construction in 1904 of the Queen Victoria Memorial Hall, a civic centre popularly known as the Town Hall (Figure 3.4), which initially housed the museum, and improvements in communications are epitomised in the General Post Office and Cable Office. Religious development is seen in Anglican, Roman Catholic and Presbyterian churches, constructed in 1886, 1902 and 1883, respectively, while learning is represented in pictures of the Masonic Lodge (in Fiji since the mid-nineteenth century), and the Carnegie library of 1909. Improvements in health were depicted in pictures of the Colonial War Memorial Hospital (built in 1923) and cards issued by several

CANOE UNDER SAIL.
Series 43—Fiji.   *Kerry (Copyright) Sydney*

You asked me to let you know
what series I had. I have some
if not all of 1, 7, 8, 9, 11, 16, 17, 18, 19, 24,
25, 28, 30, 32, 35, 36, 39, 40, 41, 43, 45, 47,
48. Love to Granny & yourself. Lorna.

Figure 3.2 Canoe under sail
Source: Published by Kerry (Sydney) and posted in New South Wales, 1906

missionary organisations.[6] Townscapes were also an early subject (Figure 3.5)
and street scenes became common in the early 1920s, especially in the work of
Harry Gardiner and the prolific Carl Meyer (Stephenson, 1997: 47–52, 68–71).

Some 7.2% of the cards focused on the colony's economy. About half portrayed the formal agricultural sector, illustrating relatively unsuccessful early
crops such as tea, as well as the more successful bananas and sugar, which for
decades were Fiji's main source of foreign exchange. Arguably, these cards, as
elsewhere, showed 'the orderliness of production and the fortuitously happy
deployment of colonial labour' (Whittaker, 2009: 132) and, with photographs
of modern buildings and developing townscapes, demonstrated the progress
of the new colony to recipients of cards in Australasia, North America and
Europe. By contrast, other cards focus on the traditional sector of the

Figure 3.3 Suva
Source: Publisher unknown; undivided back, posted from Fiji to Victoria, Australia, c.1905

Figure 3.4 Queen Victoria Memorial Hall, Suva
Source: Publisher unknown: undivided back, c.1904

Figure 3.5 Street scene, Suva
Source: Published by Gus Arnold, Suva: posted from Suva to British Columbia, 1908

economy, often with a more explicit (but not necessarily unambiguous) ethnographic content, as in basket making (Figure 3.6).[7]

Many cards have native housing or villages as subjects and thus also have an ethnographic interest. In all, 117 cards (6.1%) depict Fijian villages, while another 98 (5.1%) portray Fijian houses and their construction. Some pictures of villages and houses tend to prettify them, aestheticising poverty, as in the 1930s reproduction of Namosi village, an early photographic subject (Figure 3.7), but others have a more realistic aspect and remain of educational and ethnographic value, as in the case of the house in Figure 3.8 (though the Fijians in the former had clearly put on their best clothes for the occasion).

Cards featuring men (5.4%) and women (8%) as single subjects, and in groups (0.6%) made up 14% of the cards analysed. A key interest here is how far their portrayal can be linked to the noble-savage continuum so common in Western perceptions of island societies, especially of Fiji, considered by many, including Beatrice Grimshaw, as intersecting the divide between the 'lotus-eating' Polynesia and cannibalistic Melanesia (Jolly, 1997: 105–11; Johnston, 2005). This, in turn, creates problems at the evaluative level, especially in examining the portrayals of women in Fiji.

Pictures of men (nearly always indigenous Fijians and *very* rarely Indian) were initially categorised as either 'dignified' or 'primitive', but of 103 cards, only 20 were considered in the latter category. An obvious case of the 'primitive', even the 'savage', is Cannibal Tom, a known Suva 'character' who features in several early cards (Figure 3.9), and whom Stephenson (1997: 260–61)

Figure 3.6 Making baskets, Fiji
Source: Published by J.W. Waters, Suva, undivided back, c.1905

Figure 3.7 Early morn, Namosi, Fiji
Source: Published by Co-operative, early 1930s (from an earlier photograph)

50 *David Harrison*

Figure 3.8 Fiji Island
Source: Publisher unknown, c.1910

Figure 3.9 An old cannibal
Source: Publisher unknown, undivided back, c.1905

claims to have been 'much in demand by Suva photographers'. There is undoubtedly an element of primitiveness (but not savagery) in some of the village pictures. More typical, though, is 'Fijian and Club' (Figure 3.10), and many such cards, of considerable ethnographic value as records of dress, war clubs and hair styles (Stephenson, 1997: 209–15) were issued, along with others of Fijian men who had converted to Christianity, and of Cakobau, under whose chieftancy Fiji was ceded to the British. In all these cases, while the element of 'the Other' is frequently present, it is the dignity of the men photographed, rather than primitiveness or savagery, that comes through.

As indicated earlier, and again reflected in Grimshaw's writing in the early twentieth century, *Polynesian* island women, especially, have often been portrayed as both beautiful and available (Jolly, 1997: 105–11). *Some* evidence that this perception was held among postcard producers is available, but it is far from definitive. Of 153 cards showing Fijian women, 65 (45%) portrayed them as dignified and, in some cases, as almost stereotypically Edwardian. This was especially the case for pictures of women from chiefly families – for example, Adi (Princess) Cakobau and her cousin, Adi Kuila, whose pictures frequently appeared on early postcards.

Figure 3.10 Fijian and Club
Source: Published by J.W. Waters, Suva: undivided back but postmarked Fiji, 1914

Nevertheless, if cards showing naked or bare-breasted women in an obviously posed and non-work environment are defined as voyeuristic,[8] 55% of the cards of women in Fiji cards (some of whom were clearly described as Samoan) fell into this category. 'A Fijian Beauty' (Figure 3.11) is an example, and many cards were issued of bare-breasted women posing at waterfalls, on mats, or languidly resting by the sea. Others, though, are more ambiguous, as in pictures of women fishing or returning from fishing, making baskets (as in Figure 3.6), or posing as fan dancers, where although there may well have been a voyeuristic element for Edwardian recipients, there is *also* an informative, ethnographic element. Finally in this category, there are arguably voyeuristic pictures of bare-breasted native women that might *also* be considered 'quasi-ethnographic', as in Figure 3.12, a photograph later reproduced as a postcard, which features a man with two young women (his daughters?), all of whom seem at ease in front of the camera.

What does this tell us about the differential portrayal of Fijian and Polynesian women? Alone, not a great deal, but other facts are instructive. In this

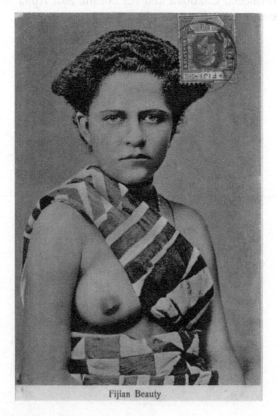

Fijian Beauty

Figure 3.11 A Fijian Beauty
Source: Published by A.M. Brodziak: Fiji postmark, c.1910

Figure 3.12 Real photograph, c.1920

collection of Fijian postcards, those of women made up 8% of the total and, of these, 55% might be described as voyeuristic. By contrast, an analysis of 535 postcards of Samoa, in the same collection, indicates that 33% of all cards were women, of which half were clearly in the 'voyeuristic' category, while most of the others, where women were fully clothed, were portraits of a 'glamorous' nature. None was shown in working circumstances. In short, assuming equal representativeness in the collections, women were deemed far more important as *subjects* of cards in 'Polynesian' Samoa than in 'Melanesian' Fiji, and in the former context were more likely to be portrayed in a voyeuristic/glamorous manner.

Two important categories of cards remain to be discussed: those focusing on religion and ceremonial activities (including the police and the military), and those dealing with special occasions. Interestingly, the former category (amounting to 10.5% of the collection) includes very few cards on traditional religion; although there are occasional pictures of Fijian graves, those of Protestant and Catholic missions are more common (and could be considered as further examples of modernity). Most ceremonial activities portrayed involve men and women participating in *mekes* (dances), e.g. as warriors or fan dancers, or sitting around the kava bowl, drinking a mildly intoxicating drink derived from the root of the shrub *piper methysticum* (Figure 3.13), or Fijian men beating the *lali* (drum) or firewalking – all scenes commonly found in modern tourist brochures, as are pictures of the Fiji military and the police, in their scalloped white *sulus*.

The final category of any importance is where social occasions are illustrated, and this became more significant as the colony was established. By the 1920s, photographic records of events on important dates in the colonial calendar were being circulated in the work of Harry Gardiner and Carl Meyer (along with pictures taken by many amateur photographers), and included celebrations of the king's birthday, visits by important personages and/or the British Navy (along with cricket games against teams from the ships), and souvenirs of such colonial social occasions as picnics at Nukulau, a small island off Suva (Figure 3.14).

Discussion

Several interpretive themes thus emerge in picture postcards of Fiji published from approximately 1900 until the late 1920s:

- *The picturesque*, where nature, tamed and prettified, is a key feature, and the presence of people – where it occurs – is as a backdrop, another part of the scenery, and not a central feature.

Figure 3.13 Kava making, Fiji
Source: Published by Gus Arnold, Suva: undivided back, c.1905

PICNICERS AT NUKULAU FIJI.   Harry Gardiner.

Figure 3.14 Picnic[k]ers at Nukulau Fiji
Source: Published by Harry Gardiner: early 1920s

- *Colonial modernity*, mainly towns (overwhelmingly Levuka and Suva), townscapes and prominent buildings relating to health, governance, education and formal religion.
- *Material culture*, implicitly contrasting the formal and informal, traditional (often of ethnographic interest) and modern (mainly the export economy).
- *Native villages and housing*, again of ethnographic interest, often contrasting (sometimes prettified) native poverty and backwardness with the perceived advantages of colonialism.
- *The natives*, with men normally the dignified yet primitive 'other', less often cannibals or converts, with occasional staged depictions of the cannibalistic past.[9] Women, sometimes depicted as Edwardian matrons, are more likely the stereotyped South Pacific 'maidens', and thus subject to a voyeuristic male gaze (though perhaps less so than in 'Polynesian' Samoa).
- *Ceremonial and religious activities*, including native dances, *masi* (bark cloth) production kava consumption, and the police and the military (with an occasional Indian).
- *Records of social occasions*, formal and informal, showing visiting dignitaries and special formal occasions, as well as more common features of everyday (settler) social life in the developing colony.

As indicated earlier, the picture postcards analysed here were nearly all photographed, published and consumed by expatriates, many of whom were avid postcard collectors. Some were clearly produced by Christian missions for their propaganda value. However, in most cases it is unlikely the 'natives' had much choice in how they were photographed and 'framed', and they seem ill at ease in many cards.

Evaluating such cards is inevitably subjective, but often there are distinct implications of the exotic 'Other' and, in some pictures of women, the 'erotic Other'. However, there was much less overt racism than anticipated. It was not entirely absent, as seen in the unpleasant 'Civilized Fiji' (Figure 3.15), sent to a child in the UK with the message 'Early learning to ride, with love to my little girl from Dada', but such cards were rare. Rather, as today, cards featuring natural scenes, colonial modernity in its different forms, and showing Fijians and Fijian ceremonies in a dignified light were far more common, and many early cards continue to have an ethnographic value.

A final caveat is necessary: the collection on which this content analysis is based is primarily of *commercially produced* cards. By the 1920s, such photographers as Carl Meyer and Harry Griffiths were increasingly choosing topics that reflected the social and political life of the colony (Stephenson, 1997: 141–43), and thousands of other pictures were produced by unknown amateurs. Like the 'must see' sights recorded in today's social media, some topics were more or less universal, but others – especially those sent by residents to friends and relatives abroad – were more reflective of individual experience. Indeed, in this author's own collection there are examples of cards sent by visiting sailors recording their visits to villages, pictures and accounts of galas

Figure 3.15 Civilized Fiji
Source: Publisher unknown: undivided back, c.1905

held in Levuka to raise funds for soldiers wounded during the First World War, and photographs of official visits to the colony. They are but the tip of another rich vein of social history depicted in picture postcards that is yet to be seriously explored.

The publishers detailed in Table 3.2 were not the only publishers of cards on Fiji over the period, but they are the majority and they are representative.

Another topic that deserves further research is the continuity of the images of Fiji (and indeed of South Pacific islands in general) from the early twentieth century until today. It is remarkable how many of these early (albeit highly selective) themes continue to be reproduced in today's postcards, on the internet, in tourist brochures and across the mass media. Those that predominate are picturesque seascapes and riverscapes, men and women in 'traditional' dress (now devoid of eroticism), *yaqona* ceremonies, and (now extremely rare) traditional thatched housing and villages. In many respects, of course, it is a world that has largely been lost, but for the tourism industry, and for some Fijian traditionalists, such images continue to resonate (Harrison, 1998). The past might indeed be a foreign country, but it continues to serve the needs of the present.

Table 3.2 Publishers of the cards analysed

Publisher	Date operating	No. of cards
Anderson, L.N.	1904–11	67
Anon 1900–20s	1900–20s	292
Arnold, Gus	1904–08	72
Brodziak	1904–11	107
Caine, F.W.	1914–30s	192
Cooper, W.H.	1904–14	18
Co-operative	1930 forwards	130
Gardiner, Harry	1918–28	148
Griffiths, G.L.	1902–08	40
Hedemann	1902–14	28
Hussey-Gillingham	1890s–1911	62
Imperial Institute	1930s	7
Kerry	1890s–1913	20
Kodak (indep)	1914–30s	91
Le Faivre	1904–14	14
Marks, Henry	1906–21	33
Meyer, Carl	1923–30s	197
Michelmore	1925–30s	34
Mills, Arthur	1905–10	57
Morris Hedstrom	1903–11	37
NSW Bookstall	1906 forwards	31
Robbie and Co	1906–11	30
Waters	1903–13	197
Total cards		1,904

Source: Stephenson, 1997: 36–146

Notes

1 The process described here was not unique to islands. Bandyopadhyay and Nascimento (2010), for example, assert that Brazil's reputation as a sexual playground for tourists is but a continuation of its image under colonialism.
2 Yet tensions remain: in October 2011, a German tourist visiting Nuku Hiva, the largest of the Marquesas islands (and site of Melville's South Seas *Typee*) was reportedly killed and eaten by a local resident (*Daily Mail* Reporter, 2012). Paradise continues to be flawed.
3 This is the case for the Fiji Museum, in Suva, which has several hundred uncategorised cards.
4 'European' here refers to everyone of European *origin*, including citizens of New Zealand, Australia and the USA (a local usage that continues to the present).
5 The cards analysed are the Fiji component of a much wider collection of vintage postcards owned by Mr Max Shekleton of New Caledonia, who has one of the largest private collections in the world of commercially produced postcards of the region, as well as many cards produced by individuals and printed and sent on a non-commercial basis. Most of the cards analysed were produced and sold commercially. Thanks are due to Mr Shekleton for his willingness to share his collection and for his hospitality.
6 Numerous postcards were issued by Christian missionary organisations operating in Fiji. They tended to show mission stations and illustrate missionary involvement in education and health, e.g. that of the Marist Order serving lepers on the island of Makogai, but they also reproduced photographs of general scenes of Fijian life (Stephenson, 1997: 122–24).
7 This card, for example, was clearly considered unacceptable in some circles. When the Society for the Propagation of the Gospel reproduced this card a few years later, the breasts had been painlessly removed.
8 This was basically the criterion used for categorising a card as 'voyeuristic'. Glimpses of female flesh were regarded as immoral (at least by legislators) in the late Victorian and Edwardian periods (Martin and Skinner, 2007), but there is ample evidence from press reports that in the early 1900s, upholders of the law in Australia, New Zealand, the USA and the UK were hard-pressed to control what some described as a 'plague of indecent postcards' (Timespanner, 2011; *Star*, 1906; NZ Truth 1906).
9 In general, *i-taukei* (indigenous Fijians) remain silent on the issue of cannibalism in Fiji's history, and it is studiously avoided in tourism advertising material which otherwise emphasises the strength and importance of Fiji tradition.

References

Adams, K.M. (1984) 'Come to Tana Toraja, Land of the Heavenly Kings.' *Annals of Tourism Research* 11(3): 469–85.
Albers, P.C. and James, W.R. (1983) 'Tourism and the Changing Photographic Image of the Great Lakes Indians.' *Annals of Tourism Research* 10(1): 122–48.
——(1988) 'Travel Photography: A Methodological Approach.' *Annals of Tourism Research* 15(1): 134–58.
Ballantyne, R.M. (1995 [1858]) *The Coral Island*. London: Penguin.
Bandyopadhyay, R. and Nascimento, K. (2010) 'Where Fantasy becomes Reality: How Tourism Forces made Brazil a Sexual Playground.' *Journal of Sustainable Tourism* 18(8): 933–49.
Bassett, F. (2012) 'Wish You Were Here! The Story of the Golden Age of Picture Postcards.' www.nysl.nysed.gov/msscfa/qc16510ess.htm (accessed 17 June 2012).

Benedict, B. (1983) *The Anthropology of the World's Fairs: San Francisco's Panama Pacific International Exposition of 1915.* London: Scholar Press.

Beukers, A. (2007) *Exotic Postcards: The Lure of Distant Lands.* London: Thames and Hudson.

Britton, R. (1979) 'The Image of the Third World in Tourism Marketing.' *Annals of Tourism Research* 6(3): 318–29.

Burns, P. (2004) 'Six Postcards from Arabia: A Visual Discourse of Colonial Travels in the Orient.' *Tourist Studies* 4(3): 255–75.

Buzinde, C.N., Santos, C.A. and Smith, S.L.J. (2006) 'Ethnic Representations: Destination Imagery.' *Annals of Tourism Research* 33(3): 707–28.

Cohen, B. and Manspeizer, I. (2009) 'The Accidental Tourist: NGOs, Photography and the Idea of Africa.' In M. Robinson and D. Picard (eds) *The Framed World: Tourism, Tourists and Photography.* Aldershot: Ashgate, 79–94.

Cohen, C.B. (1995) 'Marketing Paradise: Making Nation.' *Annals of Tourism Research* 22(2): 404–21.

Cohen, E. (1982) *The Pacific Islands from Utopian Myth to Consumer Product: The Disenchantment of Paradise.* Aix-en-Provence: Centre des Hautes Etudes Touristiques.

——(1989) 'Primitive and Remote: Hill Tribe Trekking in Thailand.' *Annals of Tourism Research* 16(1): 30–61.

Daily Mail Reporter (2012) www.dailymail.co.uk/news/article-2051431/Henri-Haiti-suspected-eating-Stefan-Ramin-tattoo-cannibal-tribe.html (accessed 30 August 2012).

Dann, G.M.S. (1996a) 'Images of Destination People in Travelogues.' In R. Butler and T. Hinch (eds) *Tourism and Indigenous Peoples.* London: Thomson, 349–75.

——(1996b) 'The People of Tourist Brochures.' In T. Selwyn (ed.) *The Tourist Image: Myths and Myth Making in Tourism.* Chichester: John Wiley and Sons, 61–81.

——(1996c) *The Language of Tourism: A Sociolinguistic Perspective.* Wallingford: CAB International.

Day, A.G. (1987) *Mad About Islands.* Honolulu: Mutual Publishing Co.

Dear, J. (2008) *The Picture Postcards of Fiji.* Second edn. London: The Pacific Islands Study Circle.

Defoe, D. (1976 [1719]) *Robinson Crusoe.* London and Oxford: Oxford University Press.

d'Hauteserre, A.-M. (2010) 'Politics of Imaging New Caledonia.' *Annals of Tourism Research* 38(2): 380–402.

Douglas, N. (1996) *They Came for Savages: 100 Years of Tourism in Melanesia.* Lismore, NSW: Southern Cross University Press.

Edmond, R. (1997) *Representing the South Pacific: Colonial Discourse from Cook to Gauguin.* Cambridge: Cambridge University Press.

Edwards, E. (1996) 'Postcards – Greetings from Another World.' In T. Selwyn (ed.) *The Tourist Image: Myths and Myth Making in Tourism.* Chichester: John Wiley and Sons, 197–221.

Fayaud, V. (2006) 'A Tahitian Woman in Majesty: French Images of Queen Pomare.' *History Australia* 3(1): 12.1–12.6.

Fiji Islands Bureau of Statistics (2009) *Key Statistics, June 2009.* Suva: Fiji Islands Bureau of Statistics.

Geiger, J. (2007) *Facing the Pacific: Polynesia and the U.S. Imperial Imagination.* Honolulu: University of Hawai'i Press.

Geppert, A.T., Coffey, J. and Lau, T. (2000) *International Exhibitions, Expositions Universelles and World's Fairs, 1851–2005. A Bibliography.* www.tu-cottbus.de/theo

riederarchitektur/Wolke/eng/Bibliography/ExpoBibliography.htm (accessed 17 June
2012).
Graburn, N. (1983) 'Tourism and Prostitution.' *Annals of Tourism Research* 10(3): 437–42.
Grove, R.H. (1995) *Green Imperialism: Colonial Expansion, Tropical Island Edens and the Origins of Environmentalism, 1600–1860.* Cambridge: Cambridge University Press.
Harrison, D. (1998) 'Tourism in Fiji: Who Communicates What, to Whom?' *Tourism, Culture and Communication* 1(2): 129–38.
——(2001) 'Islands, Image and Tourism.' *Tourism Recreation Research* 26(3): 3–8.
——(2004) 'Tourism in Pacific Islands.' *The Journal of Pacific Studies* 26(1 and 2): 1–28.
Harrison, D. and Prasad, B. (2013) 'The Contribution of Tourism to the Development of Fiji Islands and Other Pacific Island Countries.' In C. Tisdell (ed.) *A Handbook of Tourism Economics.* Singapore: World Scientific Publishing Company, 741–61.
Hitchcock, M. and Norris, L. (1995) *Bali: The Imaginary Museum: The Photographs of Walter Spies and Beryl de Zoet.* Kuala Lumpur: Oxford University Press.
Hunter, W.C. (2008) 'A Typology of Photographic Representations for Tourism: Depictions of Groomed Spaces.' *Tourism Management* 29: 354–65.
Johnston, E. (2005) 'Reinventing Fiji at 19th-Century and Early 20th-Century Exhibitions.' *The Journal of Pacific History* 10(1): 23–44.
Jolly, M. (1997) 'From Point Venus to Bali Ha'i: Eroticism and Exoticism in Representations of the Pacific.' In L. Manderson and M. Jolly, *Sites of Desire, Economies of Pleasure.* Chicago and London: University of Chicago Press, 99–122.
Lay, G. (2008) *In Search of Paradise: Artists and Writers in the Colonial South Pacific.* Auckland, New Zealand: Random House.
Loxley, D. (1990) *Problematic Shores: The Literature of Islands.* New York: St Martin's Press.
MacCannell, D. (1976) *The Tourist: A New Theory of the Leisure Class.* New York: Schocken Books.
Mackay, D. (1999) 'Myth, Science and the British Construction of the Pacific.' In A. Calder, J. Lamb and B. Orr (eds) *Voyages and Beaches: Pacific Encounters, 1769–1840.* Honolulu: University of Hawai'i Press, 100–13.
Mamiya, C.J. (1992) 'Greetings from Paradise: The Representation of Haiwaiian Culture in Postcards.' *Journal of Communication Inquiry* 16(2): 86–101.
Markwick, M. (2001) 'Postcards from Malta: Image, Consumption, Context.' *Annals of Tourism Research* 28(2): 417–38.
Marryat, F. (2011 [1841]) *Masterman Ready.* London: Dent and Co.
Martin, M.L. and Skinner, T. (2007) *Naughty Victorians and Edwardians.* Lancaster, PA: Schiffer.
Mason, G. (1995) 'Cinder Eyes and Chocolate Thighs: Packaging the Exotic for Visitor Consumption.' In P. Burns (ed.) *Tourism and Minorities' Heritage: Impacts and Prospects.* London: University of North London Press, 70–82.
Mellinger, W.M. (1994) 'Towards a Critical Analysis of Tourism Representations.' *Annals of Tourism Research* 2(4): 756–79.
Melville, H. (1996 [1846]) *Typee.* Edited with an introduction by Ruth Blair. Oxford: Oxford University Press.
Michener, J. (1947) *Tales of the South Pacific.* London: Macmillan.
Moeran, B. (1983) 'The Language of Japanese Tourism.' *Annals of Tourism Research* 10(1): 93–108.

Mohamed, M. (1988) 'Moroccan Tourism Image in France.' *Annals of Tourism Research* 15(4): 558–61.

Norrild, J.A. (2001) 'Postcards as Creators of Images of Destinations.' *Studies and Perspectives in Tourism* 10: 131–51.

NZ Truth (1906) paperspast.natlib.govt.cgi-bin/ (accessed 16 June 2006).

Phillips, T. (2000) *The Postcard Century.* London: Thames and Hudson.

Pritchard, A. and Morgan, N. (2003) 'Mythic Geographies of Representation and Identity: Contemporary Postcards of Wales.' *Tourism and Cultural Change* 1(2): 111–30.

Reidy, M.S., Kroll, G. and Conway, E.M. (2007) *Explorations and Science: Social Impact and Interaction.* California: ABC Clio.

Reimer, G.D. (1990) 'Packaging Dreams: Canadian Tour Operators at Work.' *Annals of Tourism Research* 17(4): 501–12.

Robinson, M. and Picard, D. (2009) 'Moments, Magic and Memories: Photographing Tourists, Tourist Photographs and Making Worlds.' In M. Robinson and D. Picard (eds) *The Framed World: Tourism, Tourists and Photography.* Aldershot: Ashgate, 1–37.

Scott, R.J. (1970) 'The Development of Tourism in Fiji since 1923.' *Transactions and Proceedings of the Fiji Society* 12: 40–50.

Selwyn, T. (ed.) (1993) *The Tourist Image: Myths and Myth Making in Tourism.* Chichester: Wiley.

Silver, I. (1993) 'Marketing Authenticity in Third World Countries.' *Annals of Tourism Research* 20(2): 302–18.

Staff, F. (1996) *The Picture Postcard and its Origin.* New York: Praeger Publishers.

Star (1906) *Putanga 8658, 26 Pipiri:3: Alleged Indecent Postcards.* paperspast.natlib. govt.cgi-bin/ (accessed 16 June 2012).

Steiner, K. (2001) *Hawai'i's Early Territorial Days: Viewed from Vintage Postcards by Island Curio.* Honolulu: Mutual Publishing.

Stephen, A. (ed.) (1993) *Pirating the Pacific: Images of Travel, Trade and Tourism.* Haymarket, NSW: Powerhouse Publishing.

Stephenson, E. (1997) *Fiji's Past on Picture Postcards.* Suva: Caines Jannif.

Stevenson, R.L. (1994 [1883]) *Treasure Island.* London: Penguin.

Sturma, M. 2002) *South Sea Maidens: Western Fantasy and Sexual Politics in the South Pacific.* Westport, CT: Greenwood Press.

Thuram, L., Blachnard, P., Boëtsch, G. and Jacomijn Snoep, N. (2012) *Exhibitions: L'invention du Sauvage.* Musée du quai Branly: Actes Sud.

Thurlow, C., Jaworski, A. and Ylänne-McEwen, V. (2005) 'Half-hearted Tokens of Transparent Love? "Ethnic" Postcards and the Visual Mediation of Host-tourist Communication.' *Tourism, Culture and Communication* 5: 93–104.

Thurot, J. and Thurot, G. (1983) 'The Ideology of Class and Tourism: Confronting the Discourse of Advertising.' *Annals of Tourism Research* 10(1): 173–89.

Timespanner (2011) *A Plague of Indecent Postcards.* timespanner.blogspot.com/2011/03/plague-of-indecent postcards.html (accessed 16 June 2012).

Weinstein, J. (1993) 'Review of Jill Lloyd, German Expressionism, Primitivism and Modernity.' *The Art Bulletin* 75(1): 183–87.

Whittaker, E. (2009) 'Photographing Race: The Discourse and Performance of Tourist Stereotypes.' In M. Robinson and D. Picard (eds) *The Framed World: Tourism Tourists and Photography.* Farnham, Surrey: Ashgate, 117–38.

Willoughby, M. (1992) *A History of Postcards.* New Jersey: The Wellfleet Press.

Wilson, D. (1994) 'Probably as Close as you can get to Paradise: Tourism and the Changing Image of Seychelles.' In A.V. Seaton *et al.* (eds) *Tourism: The State of the Art.* London: Wiley, 765–74.

Wyss, J. (1993 [1812]) *The Swiss Family Robinson.* Ware, Hertfordshire: Wordsworth.

Yamashita, S. (2003) *Bali and Beyond: Explorations in the Anthropology of Tourism.* Translated and with an introduction by J.S. Eades. New York and Oxford: Berghahn Books.

4 Fiji tourism half a century on
Tracing the trajectory of local responses
Yoko Kanemasu

Introduction

Modern tourism in its current institutionalised form and structure emerged in Fiji in the 1960s. Since then, the industry has grown, despite a number of setbacks and challenges, into nothing less than the country's economic mainstay. In the 1980s tourism overtook sugar to become the country's principal foreign exchange earner (Ministry of Transport and Tourism et al., 1997b) and has since retained this position. In 2012, the total economic contribution of the travel and tourism industry was estimated at F$2,508.6 million, accounting for 35.8% of gross domestic product (GDP), and 108,500 jobs or 32.3% of the total employment (World Travel and Tourism Council, 2013). With the sugar and garment industries continuing to face challenges, tourism is today widely regarded as the fundamental basis of the country's economic growth and development. Its importance is expected to grow even further in the future; by 2023 the travel and tourism industry is estimated to be responsible for over 41% of the total employment and over 45% of GDP (World Travel and Tourism Council, 2013).

Notably, this vital industry relies heavily on the cooperation of the local populations. Needless to say, successful tourism in any society presupposes favourable attitudes and responses of host communities, but tourism in Fiji has a particular emphasis that makes them simply indispensable for survival. While the industry from its infancy capitalised on the islands' tropical climate and natural environment as an ideal setting for 'sun, sand and sea' tourism, from the late 1960s onwards the reputation of the Fiji Islanders as a 'naturally' hospitable and amiable people developed into an essential 'part of the commodity package' (Samy, 1980: 81), and indeed a key competitive advantage of the tourism product (Kanemasu, 2013). That is, as stakeholders searched for a unique advantage to compete with other tropical destinations, the image and reputation of the smiling, friendly (especially indigenous) Fijians came to take centre stage as 'the icon of Fiji' (Fiji Times, 2000a), providing an effective selling point. The industry thus depends critically on the active support and cooperation from the local populations both as hospitality workers and as a host population who embody the treasured image.

This renders the Fiji Islanders' perceptions of and responses to tourism a subject worthy of research attention, given the scarcity of relevant literature. In contrast to the large body of existing work in this area undertaken in various other socio-cultural settings (see e.g., Burns, 2003; Dunn and Dunn, 2002; Johnson, Snepenger and Akis, 1994; Milman and Pizam, 1988), previous tourism research in Fiji has focused predominantly on the economic, socio-cultural and environmental effects and potential of the industry (see e.g., Britton, 1983; Farrell, 1977; Harrison and Prasad, 2013; Narayan, 2004; Rajotte and Crocombe, 1980). Few studies have closely examined the ways in which the people of Fiji – both residents and governments – have perceived and responded to tourism development. Notable exceptions include the questionnaire survey studies by Plange (1985), and King, Pizam and Milman (1993), which provide a valuable basis for further research by capturing the host community attitudes and perceptions of the mid-1980s and early 1990s, respectively. What may be usefully added to this emergent literature is an overview of the historical changes and transitions in local responses to tourism. In addition, to gain an insight into the dynamics of the interaction between tourism and local communities, it is worthwhile to examine how the industry and stakeholders have engaged with these responses.

Consequently, this chapter traces the contours of the historical trajectory of local responses to tourism development in Fiji, as well as some of the key factors that may have influenced and steered this process, with special attention to the industry stakeholders' role. Although a comprehensive survey (especially of popular responses) is not possible due to the limited availability of relevant documentation, broad trends can be suggested through a review of official and academic literature, mass media contents and other documents. It is shown that the industry, which appears to enjoy nation-wide support, has previously faced a considerable amount of uncertain and even oppositional responses from the local communities. The shift in their perceptions and reactions occurred in parallel with tourism's rising economic significance and, at least in part, as a result of the vigorous and continuous efforts by the Fiji Visitors Bureau (FVB, rebranded as Tourism Fiji in 2009) and stakeholders, and later by the national government and the mass media, to induce favourable public opinion and accommodation of the industry needs. The chapter also observes that despite such relentless public relations campaigns and the conspicuously positive public opinion of the industry today, remnants of the former ambivalence and discontent linger on, and that this has been consistently linked, *inter alia*, to the perceived inequity of the structure of mass tourism. This discussion pays particular attention to a series of disputes that have taken place between indigenous landowners and tourism owners/operators since the late 1980s.

Early beginnings of tourism

The earliest origin of touristic activities in Fiji can be traced back to at least as early as the second half of the nineteenth century. Most European visitors at the time had purposes other than leisure for their visits, but occasionally took time to experience for pleasure the exotic and the novel in the islands (Kanemasu, 2005). Since today's popular image of 'friendly Fijians' was still in the making, it was largely the islands' botanical and scenic beauty that most delighted the visitors. Aspects of indigenous culture were also beginning to attract touristic attention. Indigenous firewalkers, for example, participated in the Christchurch Exhibition in 1906 as 'one of its principal attractions' (Allen, 1984 [1907]: 190). Thus, by the early 1900s, foundations had been laid for institutionalised tourism.

Further development was facilitated by the British colony's growing importance as a focal point of trans-Pacific shipping and trade (Plange, 1985). From the end of the nineteenth century to the 1930s, Suva was established as a port of call for scheduled steamships (Douglas and Douglas, 1996). In 1923, the White Settlement League set up the Suva Tourist Board (which was replaced by the Fiji Publicity Board two years later), the main activity of which was to distribute a tourist gazette to overseas travel agencies and shipping companies to attract European immigrants and tourists (Scott, 1970).

The Second World War disrupted the tourist flow but also paved the way for post-war tourism development. In the 1940s and 1950s, Fiji became a key aircraft refuelling stopover (Plange, 1996), which led to the establishment of hotel accommodation and tourist-oriented businesses in Nadi and elsewhere. In 1953, the Fiji Publicity Board became the Fiji Visitors Bureau, a statutory body with a mandate to promote Fiji as a tourist destination. Although the post-war development was gradual, the number of visitors rose from 5,600 in 1952 to 12,600 in 1959 (Legislative Council of Fiji, 1965). While most of these were official or business travellers, there was also a significant number of pleasure seekers.

It is difficult to assess the local people's reaction to tourism during these years, as there is little relevant documentation. However, the limited scale of the earliest touristic operation suggests that its impact was felt only by a small minority of settlers and local people, and that there was little systematic reaction. It was not until the 1960s, when mass tourism emerged and rapidly expanded, that its presence and impact began to be regularly felt, commented on and responded to by larger sections of society.

The tourism boom of the 1960s and early 1970s: ambivalence and scepticism

The introduction of jet aircraft prompted global tourism expansion, which led to a great tourism boom in Fiji, with Nadi as a key destination, from 1961 to 1973 (Coopers & Lybrand, 1989). During this period, the arrivals figure grew at an average rate of 29.3%[1] (Fiji Visitors Bureau, 1998), reaching 186,323 in 1973 (Fiji Visitors Bureau, n.d.). This coincided with the vast expansion of hotel accommodation, establishment of organised tourist activities, and vigorous marketing initiatives by the FVB (Kanemasu, 2005). The massive growth was due primarily to large-scale foreign investment in the accommodation, transport and other sectors, which created a hierarchy of industry ownership. This was topped by foreign/multinational hotel chains and other tourism corporations, followed by local owners of European origin, then by part-European and Indo-Fijian business interests, with marginal participation by indigenous Fijians (Plange, 1996). It also established mass tourism, centred on large-scale accommodation and services, as the basis of the industry.

The government approach towards tourism during this period was ambivalent. While the industry's economic potential was highlighted by the *Checchi Report*, the first comprehensive tourism survey (Checchi & Co., 1961), some sections of the colonial administration expressed apprehension over its socio-cultural and economic implications.[2] Among the official critics, the most prominent was Ratu Kamisese Mara, who publicly spoke of his misgivings about tourism development and called for its control in the late 1960s and 1970s. On many occasions, in his capacity as the chief minister and later as the first prime minister of independent Fiji, Mara expressed critical views on various aspects of the emerging industry, such as the low level of local ownership, the industry's potentially detrimental socio-cultural impact, and the threat that he felt it represented to the country's autonomous control over development.

In 1969, Mara discussed the 'appalling state' Fijians were reduced to in tourism, and cited cases of 'exploitation' of local woodcarvers and cruise operators (*Fiji Times*, 1969b). In 1972, he addressed the Pacific Asia Travel Association Conference as the country's first prime minister, strongly suggesting that foreign tourism operators 'could not care less what happens to the culture and customs of the people in Fiji' (quoted in Fox, 1977: 33). In 1973, in an evident attempt to exercise some state control, the Native Land Trust Board (NLTB, renamed iTaukei Land Trust Board in 2011),[3] revised the land lease procedures for tourism development, with protective provisions concerning the lease period, share participation by landowners, rental assessment and employment of landowners (Britton, 1983).

On the other hand, as Mara himself noted as early as 1964 (*Fiji Times*, 1964), Fiji was heavily dependent on the primary industries of sugar and copra, and faced a vital need for export diversification and employment generation (Britton, 1983). The government therefore somewhat paradoxically committed itself to the industry by encouraging and even subsidising its development. The colonial government introduced the Hotels Aid Ordinance (first enforced in 1958 and re-written in 1964), which provided considerable concessions for investment in the accommodation sector (Belt Collins & Associates, 1973). A 1962 Act allowing duty-free shopping provided further investment incentive and particularly encouraged Indo-Fijian participation (Britton, 1983). In addition, the government made a significant increase in its annual grant to the FVB (Kanemasu, 2005); as private-sector contributions to the Bureau were minimal, this effectively subsidised the private sector. Indeed, shouldering the cost of tourism promotion became a routine government responsibility that continues until today. As Britton was to note, during this period (and over the following years), state policy consisted of '*ad hoc* measures that appear neither to fully support, nor adequately guide the industry' (Britton, 1983: 201).

Because documentary evidence is limited, popular views on tourism at the time are difficult to ascertain. However, local newspaper contents suggest that popular and media perceptions of tourism were similarly mixed. Some citizens wrote to the *Fiji Times* protesting against the discriminatory treatment they received from tourism businesses.[4] The newspaper editorial commended Mara for expressing 'the disquiet felt by some Fiji Islanders about the tourism boom' (*Fiji Times*, 1969a), and presented its own criticisms.[5] Critical views were also voiced by non-governmental organisations (NGOs) and social scientists, who vigorously debated and warned of a range of detrimental effects of foreign-owned mass tourism (Fong, 1973; Qionibaravi, 1973; Slatter, 1973). However, there were also strong expressions of support. Some citizens, in their letters to the *Fiji Times*, criticised local stall keepers and taxi drivers for their aggressive business approaches, arguing that they might undermine Fiji's tourist reputation.[6] Photographs of happy tourists and Fijians entertaining them, and stories of various tourist complaints were also regularly printed by the newspaper to attract the attention of general readers and the industry.

Such mixed – and often clearly critical – local views soon became a major concern of the industry, especially because the reputation of (especially indigenous) Fijian amiability was becoming a major attraction of Fiji's tourism. While much tourism promotion/advertising had previously lacked distinctive characterisation, a new advertising approach was placing indigenous Fijians and their image at its centre, alongside the 'sun, sand and sea'. By the mid-twentieth century, the dominant European image of indigenous Fijians had become closely associated with smiles and amiability (Kanemasu, 2013). This image was actively adopted in tourism promotion/advertising from the late 1960s onwards, in conspicuous contrast to the under-representation of Indo-Fijians and other ethnic groups (Harrison, 1998; Kanemasu, 2013).

Such an emphasis became evident not only in tourism promotion/advertising but also in the ethnic division of labour in tourist businesses. By this time, hotels/resorts had come to routinely place indigenous Fijians in positions involving direct contact with visitors while keeping Indo-Fijians 'behind the scenes' in the accounts, maintenance, gardens and kitchens (Samy, 1980), a tendency that would continue in the following decades (Harrison, 1998). Indigenous Fijians were thus incorporated into tourism not only to provide a popular selling image, but also as hospitality workers who lived up to this reputation and sustained its attraction.

This meant that ensuring (especially indigenous Fijian) popular support for and commitment to tourism was paramount for the growing industry. Accordingly, the scepticism and ambivalence prevalent at the time prompted a series of public relations activities by the FVB and stakeholders. These were perhaps also motivated by the cases of the Caribbean destinations and Hawaii, where local resentment towards mass tourism took overt and sometimes violent forms (Young, 1973; Turner and Ash, 1975). An equivalent of what Turner (1976: 20) described as 'smile-campaigns' in the Caribbean was in existence in Fiji at least as early as in 1961, when the FVB conducted a weekly radio programme on tourism (Checchi & Co., 1961).

In 1969, the Bureau launched a major public relations campaign with a poster titled *Keep them Smiling* (Figure 4.1), accompanied by the message:

> If you are happy in your work then you make visitors happy too. They tell their friends to come to Fiji. Fiji needs the money visitors bring with them. We all need it! So work well. Be happy. Smile. YOUR SMILE HELPS FIJI.

In addition, a booklet in English, Fijian and Hindustani (Figure 4.2) was produced for those involved in tourism. Like the poster, the booklet, titled *The Tide is Coming In*, appealed for cooperation with the industry by emphasising its economic significance:

Figure 4.1 Your smile helps Fiji

Figure 4.2 The Tide is Coming In

Fiji has visitors, and they PAY to come and see us. If you realise the importance of visitors to Fiji, if you help make Fiji attractive to visitors, you will help yourself too.

(Fiji Visitors Bureau, 1969: 1–3)

In 1971, the Bureau appointed an education representative to 'travel throughout Fiji explaining the economic and social values of tourism to local groups' (*Pacific Travel News*, August 1971: 28). The importance of local reception was highlighted by Fiji's first large-scale official tourism study, *Tourism Development Programme for Fiji*, in 1973 (Belt Collins & Associates, 1973: 57): 'Fiji is well known for its warm, friendly and hospitable people. This courteous and hospitable attitude needs to be maintained for ... the success of tourism.' Citing the case of the Caribbean, the report urged the government to take steps to prevent the development of popular resentment. Thus, as Fijians assumed an increasingly important role in the industry, ensuring their accommodation of this role and containing any potential opposition became an ongoing concern of the industry.

Growth decline from 1974 to the 1987 coups: persisting doubts

Shortly after the national independence of 1970 and the global energy crisis of 1973, Fiji's tourism plunged into a slump, which continued until the late

1980s. In 1987, it was greatly damaged by two military coups, which caused a 26% decline in visitor arrivals (Fiji Visitors Bureau, 1998). Although tourism development never halted and indeed saw Fiji become established as a major island destination in the region, the growth clearly slowed down.

With the industry in stagnation, the government approach was characterised by uncertainty and reservation. In 1975, the government launched its *Seventh Development Plan* (Central Planning Office, 1975: 167–73), which, while acknowledging the economic significance of tourism, expressed 'great concern' over its high profit leakage and perceived negative socio-cultural impact, concluding that the 'Government is responsive to the effects of social change and … will not hesitate to introduce measures to ensure long-run social harmony within the nation'. Around the same year, the government grant to the FVB was reduced by 20% (Dakuvula, 1977). In 1979, Prime Minister Mara once again made his apprehensions clear at the Fiji Tourism Convention, describing tourism as 'the last colonialism' and arguing that it must be made secondary to other industries (*Fiji Times*, 1979a). While disappointed stakeholders reacted to this remark, some citizens expressed their support in letters to the *Fiji Times*.[7] The newspaper editorial summarised the national atmosphere as 'ambivalent' (*Fiji Times*, 1979b).

Government apprehensions persisted in the first half of the 1980s.[8] In 1980, the *Eighth Development Plan* (Central Planning Office, 1980: 194–98) expressed a mixture of support and concern and indicated interest in smaller-scale and localised 'alternative tourism'. In the same year, the NLTB (1980) formulated a new policy to concentrate tourism development in such areas as the Mamanucas, Nadi, the Coral Coast, Deuba and Suva, and reserve others as the Visitor Interest Areas, where no resort accommodation was permitted. Popular views in the mid-1980s were captured by Plange's (1985) study, which reported that while many respondents acknowledged tourism's significance as a source of employment, over 66% felt that it was controlled by foreigners and over 85% agreed that the locals were left out of higher-paid professional jobs. Academic appraisal of tourism similarly remained predominantly critical (Vusoniwailala, 1980; Samy, 1980; Britton, 1983).

Amid the general ambivalence and criticism, the FVB continued its public relations efforts. Favourable public opinion was made even more urgent by the industry's further reliance on the image and reputation of Fijian amiability. A smile came to be highlighted as a trademark of Fijians (see Figure 4.3), and advertising/promotional materials began almost invariably to present Fiji as 'a world where a warm friendly smile is not an ornament for a visitor, but a way of life' (FVB advertisement, *Pacific Travel News*, May 1982: 31). Consequently, it became a matter of utmost importance that the local population demonstrated this quality. In the early 1970s, the Bureau produced a booklet titled *What is Tourism?* (Figure 4.4), a revised version of *The Tide is Coming In*, to encourage public cooperation and to dispel concerns over tourism's socio-cultural impact.

Figure 4.3 The friendly face of Fiji
Source: Fiji Airways (former Air Pacific, www.fijiairways.com) advertisement, Pacific
Islands Monthly, July 1988

The Bureau also continued actively to organise school talks and lectures
(Fiji Visitors Bureau, 1982). The objective of these efforts was plainly
explained:

> Fiji has often been referred to as an island destination inhabited by the
> friendliest group of people in the world. Whilst the Bureau has been
> capitalizing on this positive appeal ... we are also very much aware of the
> potential danger that any change in attitude may bring.
>
> (Fiji Visitors Bureau, 1984: 13)

Stakeholders were more than ever aware of the risks that the critical local
views presented and sought vigorously to turn them round.

Coups, recovery and steady growth: from scepticism to celebration

The late 1980s were significant in the history of Fiji tourism as there was a
positive shift in both the industry performance and local perceptions, which

72   *Yoko Kanemasu*

Figure 4.4 What is Tourism?

set the tone for development in the following two decades. The military coups of 1987 severely undermined tourism, yet recovery was rapid and pre-coup arrival figures were regained and surpassed in 1990 (Harrison and Pratt, 2010). Subsequent arrivals indicated relatively steady, though gradual, growth. This was even more evident in tourism earnings: the 1987 figure more than doubled in five years and tripled in a decade (Fiji Visitors Bureau, 1998). The industry's foreign exchange earnings exceeded those of sugar in the 1980s, and by 1997 it directly or indirectly generated almost a third of formal employment (Ministry of Transport and Tourism *et al.*, 1997a).

This sustained growth was upset by an attempted coup in 2000, which led to a 28% decrease in visitor arrivals and a 21% decrease in tourism earnings for that year (Fiji Visitors Bureau, 2000). However, the industry again recovered quickly and pre-coup figures were surpassed in three years (Fiji Bureau of Statistics, 2013). Indeed, in the midst of political and economic uncertainty, the early recovery rendered tourism something of a 'lifeline' for the reeling nation. The durability of the industry was yet again demonstrated in 2006, when another military coup resulted in less than a 2% decline in visitor arrivals (Fiji Bureau of Statistics, 2013). As observed by Harrison and Pratt (2010), whilst the domestic political instabilities, as well as natural disasters and external economic/political/environmental factors, did have a major negative impact, tourism sustained its position as a key source of foreign exchange and employment in the 2000s, and the country's reliance on the industry became more pronounced than ever.

In this context, the government's approach turned markedly positive. Tourism came to be approved of as an essential and promising component of the national economy. In 1985, the *Ninth Development Plan* was launched with a noteworthy approval of the economic potential of tourism: 'In the short-to-medium term, the tourism sector appears best placed to contribute most towards economic growth and employment generation' (Central Planning Office, 1985: 87). Mara himself publicly adjusted his views at the Fiji Tourism Convention in 1991:

> I will confess that at first my own appraisal was extremely cautious and wary ... Those of us in Government who were at first reluctant travellers on tourism's highway now look upon the industry as one which has proved its worth a thousand times. It is a permanent and crucial part of the economy which will continue to provide ever-increasing benefits to the country ... I have to say at this point that my early fears ... have been largely unfounded.
>
> (Fiji Tourism Convention, 1991: 4–8)

The government approach indicated a further swing in 1992, as Sitiveni Rabuka, the leader of the 1987 military coups, was elected as prime minister. Soon after taking office, he addressed the Fiji Tourism Convention with strong support for tourism, calling it 'a bread and butter industry in Fiji' (Fiji Tourism Convention, 1992: 2). Large-scale foreign investment was encouraged and the 1996 Hotels Aid (Amendment) Act offered several concessions, including a 20-year income tax holiday. The government also more than doubled its FVB grant from F\$4.5 million to F\$11 million (Fiji Visitors Bureau, 1997). Although concern over the low level of Fijian ownership continued to be heard from some Cabinet members,[9] this became Fiji's first government officially to embrace mass tourism development supported by large-scale foreign investment.

Consequently, state policy on tourism development on Native Land underwent liberalisation. The former policy of concentrating development in the designated areas was relaxed, and the new 1990 policy removed the category of the Visitor Interest Area, where no tourism development had been permitted, on the grounds that it 'raises the issue of "compensation" to landowners for opportunities to earn revenue from tourism forgone' (NLTB, 1990: 8). The NLTB's concern clearly shifted from containing tourism development to '[e]nsuring a more equitable spread of development opportunities and revenues from the tourism industry' (NLTB, 1990: 10).

In 1999 an incoming government planned several policy changes, but the Mahendra Chaudhry regime was toppled by the attempted coup of 2000 before seeing them through. Shortly afterwards, Laisenia Qarase's interim government allocated F\$4 million to the FVB for recovery plans (*Fiji Times*,

2000b). Under the subsequent Qarase government that came into power following the 2001 general election, the annual grant to the FVB was further increased to $13 million, and funds were allocated for ecotourism projects as well as for infrastructural support for the country's largest resort project, in Natadola (Government of Fiji, 2003). At the same time, the Qarase government, in line with its openly ethno-nationalist agenda, attempted to introduce a controversial Qoliqoli Bill designed to transfer the proprietary rights to and interests in *qoliqoli* (marine) areas to indigenous landowners, which would have significantly affected tourism operations (although this did not eventuate, as the 2006 coup forced yet another change of government) (Lal, 2009).

At the time of writing (May 2014), the post-coup caretaker government has provided Tourism Fiji (the successor to the FVB) with the largest FVB grant to date, amounting to F$23.5 million (Bainimarama, 2013), and has indicated interest in, among other things, the development of the country's first casino resort (*Sydney Morning Herald*, 2010). Voreqe Bainimarama, the interim prime minister and coup leader, has publicly pledged his commitment to the industry: 'My government recognises the importance of the tourism industry for the sustained economic growth of Fiji and its ability to create a sustained livelihood' (Wilkinson, 2011). Similarly, the iTaukei Land Trust Board (TLTB, formerly the NLTB) continues to promote tourism development, with its goal 'to explore the best way forward of how tourism on native land could be expanded to generate more commercial wealth for landowners' (*Fiji Times*, 2009). While successive governments have shown varying degrees of support for alternative and/or locally owned tourism, the predominance of foreign investment-led mass tourism as the main driver of the industry has not changed over the decades (Scheyvens and Russell, 2010). It seems probable today that regardless of changes of government, as long as mass tourism maintains its economic significance, a certain level of state support will remain a matter of necessity.

It is not only the national government, but also the local media that came to express taken-for-granted support. Tourism was now seen by the media as the country's economic hope, and the issue of public debate shifted from its acceptability, to the maximisation of its economic opportunity. A *Fiji Times* editorial wrote:

> [W]ith the tremendous potential we have as a tourist destination … a lot
> could be gained if this opportunity to develop and expand the industry is
> fully exploited. Government, which must be prepared to commit a higher
> level of involvement in the industry, has to lead the way. All others,
> especially the private sector, must follow with the same objectives,
> direction and purpose.
>
> (*Fiji Times*, 1996)

The national newspapers had thus become ardent supporters, criticising the government for insufficient assistance for the industry. Following the 2000 political crisis, their support became even more prominent. A *Fiji Times* editorial called on the public to cooperate with industry leaders in recovery efforts: 'Let's all rally behind them because it's in the best interest of the nation' (*Fiji Times*, 2000d); and it applauded their success in the following year: 'The whole industry deserves the nation's thanks' (*Fiji Times*, 2001).

It is easy to conclude from the above that the nation today wholeheartedly embraces tourism. Since the 1980s, there have been relatively few public expressions of scepticism or apprehension. In 1993, for example, King, Pizam and Milman (1993) found that the residents of Nadi had markedly favourable views of the industry and its social and economic impacts (despite some reservation in the area of law and order). Tourism's growing presence in the national economy, the vigorous and relentless public relations campaigns, and perhaps the similar shift in public opinion that was observed in the wider Pacific region in the 1990s (Hall, 1994) are all likely to have contributed to this conspicuously positive turn. Notably, however, while tourism itself seems to have come to be welcomed and affirmed by most local communities, there have been grassroots (and controversial) expressions of discontent with its present form and structure throughout the current period of positive appraisal.

Since the late 1980s, the country has witnessed a series of disputes between indigenous landowners and tourism business operators/owners. Most stemmed from landowners' claims to greater financial returns or compensation for the lease/use of their land/fishing grounds, or disputes concerning employment in tourism businesses. Many of these escalated into drastic and/or unlawful actions by landowners, such as strikes, demonstrations and occupation of, and blockage of access to, hotels/resort premises. Publicised cases include (but are not limited to) the Denarau Island demonstration in 1989,[10] the Club Naitasi Resort occupation in 1990,[11] the Man Friday Resort access blockage in 1990,[12] the Blue Lagoon Cruise strike[13] and Fijian Resort access blockage in 1992,[14] the Paradise Island Resort occupation in 1995,[15] the Turtle Island Resort occupation[16] and the Buca Bay Resort occupation in 2000,[17] the Sonaisali Island Resort water supply dispute in 2004,[18] the Fantasy Island access blockage in 2007,[19] the Tiliva Resort dispute in 2006,[20] the Natadola Resort disputes in 2006–07,[21] the Namale Resort dispute in 2008,[22] the Cloud 9 dispute and the Paradise Cove Resort dispute in 2013,[23] and the Sheraton Fiji Resort and Westin Denarau Island Resort and Spa strike in 2014.[24]

The government, FVB and stakeholders regarded these as a serious threat to the industry.[25] In 1997, the Ministry of Fijian Affairs (renamed the Ministry of iTaukei Affairs in 2011) responded by creating a new position of *Roko Tui Saravanua*, with the responsibility (until its removal in 2005) to engage in a 'year-round programme of visits and meetings with landowning units and villages, particularly in tourist areas', with the aim of 'increasing landowners' and plant stakeholders' understanding of each others' rights and responsibilities' (Fiji Visitors Bureau, 1999: 2). Following the political crisis of 2000, the FVB launched a campaign 'aimed at the local indigenous community for their help, assurance and hard work to rebuild the friendly Fiji Islands atmosphere', with advertisements on local television featuring tourism workers and landowners who spoke of the importance of the industry and called for public cooperation (*Fiji Times*, 2000c). The FVB launched another television/radio campaign in the following year, calling on the public to 'show them [tourists] that *bula*[26] spirit; show them that *bula* smile' (Kanemasu, 2013: 475).

Landowner disputes: persisting grassroots ambivalence and discontent

As the above disputes demonstrate, the positive appraisal and support that generally dominate public discourse on tourism cannot be taken for granted. The grassroots opposition, which has been strongly condemned by the state and the industry, has also been identified by tourism researchers (Narayan and Prasad, 2003; Singh, 2012) as a serious disincentive to investment, along with the requirements for tourism operators to provide landowners with first preference in employment and extra rent. In particular, landowners' actions 'seeking hefty compensations from operators' (Narayan and Prasad, 2003: 11) have been denounced as untenable demands stemming from a lack of sufficient knowledge of, and capacity to engage competently with, the institutional protocols, provisions and requirements of the industry.

A lack of primary data does not allow analysis of landowner motivations in these disputes, but some factors are worthy of consideration. First, the national political climate, and especially the rise of ethno-nationalism among indigenous Fijians, appears to constitute a key societal context for the recurrence of protest actions. The available documentation suggests that such incidents originate roughly from the late 1980s, shortly after the 1987 ethno-nationalist coups. The *Taukei* (indigenous landowners') Movement, which emerged at the time to advocate the paramountcy of indigenous rights, prompted 'marches, road blocks and fire-bombing of offices and businesses' by indigenous Fijians to agitate against what they perceived to be a threat to this supremacy (Naidu, 2009: 240). The 2000 coup led to a revival of the movement, with protest marches against what was seen as an Indo-Fijian-dominated government, as well as looting and vandalism in Suva (Naidu, 2007). It is not clear if these ethno-nationalist sentiments and outbursts indeed 'created a false impression in the minds of some indigenous Fijians about the taking of laws into their hands' in their dealings with tourism businesses (Waqaisavou, 2001: 5), but the political ideology popularised by these events, which centred on alleged threats to indigenous rights and control over the country, probably induced among landowners a heightened sense of ownership of *vanua* (land, people and tradition), and resentment at what they perceived to be their politico-economic marginalisation.

Second, such opposition cannot be simply reduced to cases of ill-informed masses taking the law into their own hands or politically fuelled acts of aggression. Despite the recent shift in public opinion, institutionalised tourism has consistently faced scepticism and criticism from the local population.

Popular critiques have highlighted, above all, the existing structure of mass tourism and the position it allocates to local people. Although forms of alternative tourism, such as ecotourism, began to receive some policy attention from the late 1980s onwards (Harrison, 1999; Korth, 2000), they have remained a decidedly minor component of the industry. As the *Fiji Tourism Development Plan: 1998–2005* stated, 'for the foreseeable future, resort tourism will continue to be the overwhelming fount of Fiji's tourism' (Ministry of Transport and Tourism *et al.*, 1997a: 43–44). Similarly, the latest *Fiji Tourism Development Plan 2007–2016* retains an emphasis on foreign investment alongside community participation and ecotourism (Ministry of Tourism and Transport, 2007). Narayan and Prasad (2003) show that of 132 tourism projects implemented between 1988 and 2000, 94% were foreign owned. Despite increased local ownership of mass tourism recently witnessed in cases such as the InterContinental Fiji Golf Resort & Spa Hotel owned by the Fiji National Provident Fund, the Hideaway Resort by the Fiji Teachers Union, and several hotels (in Fiji, Samoa and New Zealand) by the Tanoa Hotel Group, the fundamental structure of tourism, which is dominated by foreign or large local corporations, remains unchanged.

Clearly, masses of indigenous Fijians own or control a minimal share of this industry whilst they are expected to supply its key competitive advantage of Fijian hospitality. They are the largest beneficiaries of hotel employment (as well as corporate social responsibility initiatives and related benefits) (Harrison and Prasad, 2013), but jobs in hotels and related businesses are routinely allocated on ethnic lines, with indigenous Fijians placed mostly in lower-paid, direct-service positions. Although the scarcity of alternative employment renders hotel jobs a vital source of income for many, they are keenly aware of the structure of the distribution of industry profit and the relative exiguity of their allocation. It is thus not surprising that most protests by landowners are directly linked to their discontent with such disparity and their claims to a greater share of tourism development.

Third, landowner discontent also appears, at least in part, to arise from the way land lease income has been distributed. Until 2010, 15% of the rental income from Native Land lease was deducted by the TLTB as administration costs, with 30% of the remaining amount allocated to the heads (chiefs) of official indigenous landowning social units[27] and 70% to the members of the units. Consequently, only 59.5% of the gross rental was distributed among a large number of ordinary members of the units, a fact noted by many landowners (*Fiji Times*, 2007). However, as a result of a major reform introduced by the interim Bainimarama regime, rents must now be distributed to all members of landowning units in equal proportion (Government of Fiji, 2013). At the time of writing, however, this did not seem to have prevented landowner disputes and conflicts.

Landowner protests are a complex phenomenon embedded in multiple politico-economic relations and further analysis is beyond the scope of the present discussion. However, what emerges from this chapter is the desire of landowners to maximise their share of tourism's economic benefits and their frustration and resentment at their marginalisation by such dominant stakeholders as foreign (and large local) corporations and state/statutory organisations. Arguably, the widespread ethno-nationalist sentiments may have shaped the expression of these grievances in a drastic and sometimes violent manner. While much of the public discourse on landowner protests focuses solely on the illegitimacy of the acts of aggression, it is also instructive to consider the continuity of local ambivalence and discontent with the industry in its present form and structure that such protests also represent. These incidents allow a glimpse of grassroots perspectives that do not always find their way into mainstream forums of discussion.

Conclusions

The history of Fiji Islanders' responses to tourism development indicates both significant change and continuity. The arrival of mass tourism in the 1960s and the ensuing industry boom until the early 1970s were met by ambivalence and criticisms from government officials, the local media, NGOs, social scientists and the general public. The industry's foreign domination and sociocultural impacts were vigorously debated, while the government somewhat paradoxically also facilitated its development through investment incentives and financial assistance to the FVB. The end of the boom in the 1970s and the stalemate until the late 1980s did not improve public opinion, and tourism was further challenged by the military coups of 1987. These challenging circumstances made it a major concern of the FVB and stakeholders to secure local accommodation of the industry needs through public relations campaigns. Tourism's increasing reliance on the Fijian reputation for friendliness as its key competitive advantage made it an even more urgent task.

Once recovery from the coups started, tourism experienced relatively steady growth in the 1990s. Although this was disrupted by more coups in 2000 and 2006, the industry made a relatively swift recovery and emerged as the country's economic mainstay. As the national economy depended progressively on tourism for foreign exchange and employment, the government and media positions turned wholly and conspicuously affirmative, evident in vast increases in the FVB grant, foreign investment-oriented policies and positive media coverage. At the time of writing, public discourse on tourism was dominated by near-automatic support for and celebration of the industry. Along with the growing economic importance of tourism, the role of the FVB (now Tourism Fiji) in steering this trajectory is noteworthy. The statutory body has consistently and resolutely acted to induce local people's accommodation of the industry and their role in it – which is perhaps indicative of how keenly the industry has recognised the vital importance of Fijian amiability towards tourism/tourists as a requisite for its existence and success.

However, the near-absence of criticism in the public sphere cannot be equated with the absence of popular discontent or ambivalence. Since the

1980s, a series of controversial disputes have erupted between indigenous landowners and tourism business owners/operators. Notably, there is an underlying continuity between these landowners' grievances, the criticisms faced by the industry over previous decades, and the rise of ethno-nationalism as a key political context that may have prompted drastic and sometimes violent manifestations of discontent. Despite the positive shift in public opinion, there is a continuing critique of the structure of the industry, which is felt by many to deny local people both access to ownership and control, and an equitable distribution of economic benefits.

Tourism in Fiji has come a long way. Since the early years of uncertainty, it has acquired an unquestioned status as the nation's economic foundation and hope. Yet, absent from public forums of discussion, the discontent and ambivalence of a potentially significant section of the local communities is articulated in a sporadic, highly politicised and/or violent manner. An industry that relies critically on the smiles of the local populations needs to heed such protests and address them by more than public relations exercises. Sustainable tourism development necessitates a process of collective exploration, owned and engaged by diverse communities of interest, with an acknowledgement of their highly differential capacities to shape this process. Towards this end, there is an urgent need for further academic research, especially supported by primary data, to represent the perspectives of the communities who, after all, make the most indispensable contribution of sustaining the industry as the 'icon of Fiji'.

Notes

1 Some studies (Coopers & Lybrand, 1989; Plange, 1996) consider the 'boom' to be from the mid-1960s to 1973, with the average growth rate of 21% in visitor arrivals. However, in view of the currently available statistics, the first half of the 1960s is included in the boom period in the present discussion.

2 This paralleled the regional and worldwide trend towards critical appraisal of tourism during this period (Hall, 1994).

3 About 87% of land in Fiji is owned collectively by indigenous Fijians, and the management and negotiation of its lease is vested with the iTaukei Land Trust Board, a statutory organisation.

4 'Tourist Operations', *Fiji Times*, 6 November 1969; 'Hotel Incident', *Fiji Times*, 22 October 1970.

5 'Must it Happen Here?' *Fiji Times*, 8 January 1966; 'Creeping Uniformity', *Fiji Times*, 10 July 1969; 'Tourism Expansion', *Fiji Times*, 11 October 1969; 'Tourism Spectre', *Fiji Times*, 20 March 1970; and 'Sharing Tourism', *Fiji Times*, 18 September 1970.

6 'Seller's Conduct', letter to the editor, *Fiji Times*, 18 August 1966.

7 'Keynote Speech', letter to the editor, *Fiji Times*, 12 June 1979; and 'Support for PM', letter to the editor, *Fiji Times*, 14 June 1979.

8 1986 Fiji Tourism Convention proceedings, 'Tourism's Effects on Traditions', *Fiji Times*, 4 April 1974; 'Tourism Effects Raise Doubts', *Fiji Times*, 4 April 1974; and '$78m. Leakage from Tourism', *Fiji Times*, 5 October 1983.

9 'Fijian Employment in Tourism Worried Govt', *Fiji Times*, 27 February 1995; and 'Give Landowners a Land Deal Chance', *Fiji Times*, 22 April 1995.
10 'Villagers Resume Denarau Protest', *Fiji Times*, 13 September 1989.
11 'Landowners in Hotel Closure', *Fiji Times*, 12 January 1990; and 'NLTB Condemns Takeover', *Fiji Times*, 13 January 1990.
12 'Serua Villagers Cut off Access to Resort', *Fiji Times*, 6 October 1990.
13 'More Blue Lagoon Workers Join Strike', *Fiji Times*, 23 September 1992.
14 'Cuvu's Fires of Anger', *Fiji Times*, 5 November 1992.
15 'Namoli Villagers Take Over Bekana Beach', *Fiji Times*, 4 April 1995.
16 'Group Grabs Posh Hotel', *Fiji Times*, 12, 17 July 2000.
17 'Police at Troubled Hotel', *Fiji Times*, 15 August 2000.
18 'NLTB Moves to End Row', *Fiji Times*, 3 March 2004.
19 'Landowners Halt Project, Demand 11,000 Shares', *Fiji Times*, 12 July 2007.
20 'Hotels Hurt by Rise in Landowner Ransom Demands', *Fiji Times*, 20 November 2006.
21 'Fiji Landowners Protest Sale of Coral Coast Island', *Fiji Times*, 12 July 2006, cited in East West Centre, 2006; 'Keep Out, NBRL Tells Gavidi', *Fiji Times*, 3 November 2007; and 'Natandola Case', *Fiji Times*, 9 February 2008.
22 'Tribe Backs Resort Strike', *Fiji Times*, 15 August 2008; and 'Pay $200,000 or Move Out, Resort Told', *Fiji Times*, 26 August 2008.
23 *Time World*, 2013; 'Police Deployed to Village', *Fiji Times*, 22 May 2013.
24 'Hotel Strike', *Fiji Times*, 1 January 2014.
25 Coopers & Lybrand, 1989; Fiji Visitors Bureau, 1999; 'Tourism Obstacle Identified in Report', *Fiji Times*, 25 June 2003; 'Hoteliers Want Urgent Redress', *Fiji Times*, 27 March 2004; and 'Stop Harassing Visitors: Tourism Minister Warns Attackers', *Fiji Times*, 21 November 2006.
26 *Bula* is an indigenous Fijian word that denotes 'hello' and 'welcome'.
27 Some 5% of the remaining rental income went to *Turaga i Taukei* (head of the *Vanua*, official indigenous Fijian social unit consisting of several Yavusa of a particular locality), 10% to *Turaga ni Yavusa* (head of the *Yavusa*, official indigenous Fijian social unit consisting of several *Mataqali*), and 15% to *Turaga ni Mataqali* (head of the *Mataqali*, the official landowning unit) (Boydell and Baya, 2014).

References

Allen, P.S. (1984 [1907]) *The Cyclopedia of Fiji*. Suva: Fiji Museum.
Bainimarama, V. (2013) *Fiji Budget Speech 2013: Investing in Our Future*. www.fiji village.com/eventpages/2012/NationalBudget/documents/PM-Budget-Address-2013. pdf (accessed 27 February 2014).
Belt Collins & Associates (1973) *Tourism Development Programme for Fiji*. Washington, DC: Tourism Project Department, International Bank for Reconstruction and Development.
Boydell, S. and Baya, U. (2014) *Using Trust Structures to Manage Customary Land in Melanesia: What Lessons Can Be Learnt from the iTaukei Land Trust Board in Fiji*. Paper presented at Integrating Land Governance into the Post-2015 Agenda: Annual World Bank Conference on Land and Poverty, Washington, DC, 24–27 March 2014.
Britton, S.G. (1983) *Tourism and Underdevelopment in Fiji*. Canberra: Australian National University.
Burns, P.M. (2003) 'Local Perceptions of Tourism Planning: the Case of Cuéllar, Spain.' *Tourism Management* 24: 331–39.

Central Planning Office (1975) *Fiji's Seventh Development Plan 1976–1980.* Suva.
——(1980) *Fiji's Eighth Development Plan 1981–1985.* Suva.
——(1985) *Fiji's Ninth Development Plan 1986–1990: Policies, Strategies and Programmes for National Development.* Suva.
Checchi & Co. (1961) *The Future of Tourism in the Pacific and Far East.* Washington: US Department of Commerce.
Coopers & Lybrand (1989) *Fiji Tourism Masterplan Project Draft Final Report.* Report prepared for Asian Development Bank and the Government of Fiji, n.p.
Dakuvula, J. (1977) 'Disappointing Returns of Tourism in Fiji.' In B.H. Farrell (ed.) *The Social and Economic Impact of Tourism on Pacific Communities.* Santa Cruz: University of California, 60–62.
Douglas, N. and Douglas, N. (1996) 'Tourism in the Pacific: Historical Factors.' In C. M. Hall and S.J. Page (eds) *Tourism in the Pacific: Issues and Cases.* London: International Thompson Business Press, 19–35.
Dunn, H.S. and Dunn, L.L. (2002) 'Tourism and Popular Perceptions: Mapping Jamaican Attitudes.' *Social and Economic Studies* 51: 25–45.
East West Centre (2006) *Pacific Islands Report.* pidp.org/archive/2006/July/07-12-10. htm (accessed 15 March 2014).
Farrell, B.H. (ed.) (1977) *The Social and Economic Impact of Tourism on Pacific Communities.* Santa Cruz: University of California.
Fiji Bureau of Statistics (2013) *Visitor Arrivals Statistics.* www.statsfiji.gov.fj/index. php/migration-a-tourism/10-migration-statistics/migration-a-tourism/115-visitor-arri vals-statistics (accessed 10 February 2014).
Fiji Times (1964) 'Tourism Brings Many Benefits to Islands.' 19 October.
——(1969a) 'Accepting Criticism.' 25 October.
——(1969b) 'Fijians in Tourism.' 18 December.
——(1979a) 'Tourism Growth Must be Limited.' 5 June.
——(1979b) 'What We Should Do about Tourism.' 28 June.
——(1996) 'Looking up to Tourism.' 1 April.
——(2000a) 'The Free-Fall of Tourism.' *Fiji Times,* 18 June.
——(2000b) 'Tourism Shortfall to Cost State up to $146 million.' 28 July.
——(2000c) 'Efforts to Revive Tourism.' 12 August.
——(2000d) 'Saving Tourism.' 2 September.
——(2001) 'A Sign of Hope.' 27 April.
——(2007) 'Gavidi: $40m Misleading.' 24 November.
——(2009) 'Native Land Income Boosts Tourism.' 1 May.
Fiji Tourism Convention (1991) *Proceedings.*
——(1992) *Proceedings.*
Fiji Visitors Bureau (1969) *The Tide is Coming In.* Suva.
——(1973) *Fiji Visitors Bureau Annual Marketing Review for 1973.* Suva.
——(1982) *1979–1981 Annual Report.* Suva.
——(1984) *1982/1983 Annual Report.* Suva.
——(1997) *1998 Marketing Plan.* Suva.
——(1998) *1999 Marketing Plan.* Suva.
——(1999) *1998 Annual Report.* Suva.
——(2000) *2000 Annual Report.* Suva.
——(n.d.) *What is Tourism?* Suva.
Fong, A. (1973) 'Tourism: A Case Study.' In A. Rokotuivuna *et al., Fiji: A Developing Australian Colony.* Melbourne: International Development Action, 26–38.

Fox, M. (1977) 'The Social Impact of Tourism – A Challenge to Researchers and Planners.' In B.R. Finney and K.A. Watson (eds) *A New Kind of Sugar: Tourism in the Pacific*. Honolulu: University of Hawaii Press, 27–47.

Government of Fiji (2003) *Fiji Government Online*. www.fiji.gov.fj/index.html (accessed 18 December 2003).

——(2013) *Government to Ensure Equal Benefit for Landowners*. www.fiji.gov.fj/Media-Center/Press-Releases/GOVERNMENT-TO-ENSURE-EEQUA-BENEFIT-FOR-LANDOWNERS.aspx?feed=news (accessed 20 May 2014).

Hall, C.M. (1994) *Tourism in the Pacific Rim: Development, Impacts and Markets*. Melbourne: Longman Cheshire.

Harrison, D. (1998) 'The World Comes to Fiji: Who Communicates What, and to Whom?' *Tourism, Culture and Communication* 1: 129–38.

——(ed.) (1999) *Ecotourism and Village-based Tourism: A Policy and Strategy for Fiji*. Unpublished policy paper. Ministry of Tourism and Transport, Department of Tourism.

Harrison, D. and Prasad, B. (2013) 'The Contribution of Tourism to the Development of Fiji and Other Pacific Island Countries.' In *Handbook of Tourism Economics, Analysis, Applications, Case Study*. Singapore: World Scientific Publishing, 741–61.

Harrison, D. and Pratt, S. (2010) 'Political Change and Tourism – Coups in Fiji.' In R. Butler and W. Suntikul (eds) *Tourism and Political Change*. Oxford: Goodfellow Publishers, 160–74.

Johnson, J.D., Snepenger, D.J. and Akis, S. (1994) 'Residents' Perception of Tourism Development.' *Annals of Tourism Research* 21: 629–42.

Kanemasu, Y. (2005) *From the Cannibal Isles to the Way the World Should Be: A Study of Ideology, Hegemony and Resistance*. Unpublished doctoral dissertation, University of New South Wales, Australia.

——(2013) 'Social Construction of Touristic Imagery: Case of Fiji.' *Annals of Tourism Research* 43: 456–81.

King, B., Pizam, A. and Milman, A. (1993) 'Social Impacts of Tourism: Host Perceptions.' *Annals of Tourism Research* 20: 650–65.

Korth, H. (2000) 'Ecotourism and the Politics of Representation in Fiji.' In A.H. Akram-Lodhi (ed.) *Confronting Fiji Futures*. Asia Pacific Press, 249–68.

Lal, B. (2009) 'Anxiety, Uncertainty and Fear in Our Land: Fiji's Road to Military Coup, 2006.' In J. Fraenkel, S. Firth and B.V. Lal (eds) *The 2006 Military Takeover in Fiji: A Coup to End All Coups?* Canberra: ANU E Press, 21–41.

Legislative Council of Fiji (1965) *Report on a Study of the Travel and Tourist Industry of Fiji*. Council Paper 32, Suva: Government Press.

Milman, A. and Pizam, A. (1988) 'Social Impacts of Tourism on Central Florida.' *Annals of Tourism Research* 15: 191–204.

Ministry of Tourism and Transport (2007) *Fiji Tourism Development Plan 2007–2016*. Suva, Fiji.

Ministry of Transport and Tourism, Deloitte and Touche and Tourism Council of the South Pacific (1997a) *Fiji Tourism Development Plan: 1998–2005*. Suva.

——(1997b) *Fiji Tourism Development Plan Draft Final Report, Appendices*, 3 vols. Suva: in conjunction with Tourism Council of the South Pacific.

Naidu, V. (2007) 'Coups in Fiji: Seesawing Democratic Multiracialism and Ethno-nationalist Extremism.' *Devforum* 26: 24–33.

——(2009) 'Heading for the Scrap Heap of History? The Consequences of the Coup for the Fiji Labour Movement.' In J. Fraenkel, S. Firth and B.V. Lal (eds) *The 2006 Military Takeover in Fiji: A Coup to End All Coups?* Canberra, ANU E Press, 237–51.

Narayan, P.K. (2004) 'Economic Impact of Tourism on Fiji's Economy: Empirical Evidence from the Computable General Equilibrium Model.' *Tourism Economics* 10: 419–33.

Narayan, P.K. and Prasad, B.C. (2003) 'Fiji's Sugar, Tourism and Garment Industries: A Survey of Performance, Problems and Potentials.' *Fijian Studies* 1: 3–27.

NLTB (Native Land Trust Board) (1980) *A Policy Towards Tourist Oriented Development on Native Land.* Suva.

——(1990) *A Policy for Tourism Development on Native Land 1990–1995.* Suva.

Plange, N. (1985) *Tourism in Fiji: How People See it and what they Think of It.* Suva: Fiji Visitor Education Council.

——(1996) 'Fiji.' In C.M. Hall and S.J. Page (eds) *Tourism in the Pacific: Issues and Cases.* London: International Thompson Business Press, 205–18.

Qionibaravi, M. (1973) 'The Social Impact of Tourism.' In *Tourism in Fiji: The Ray Parkinson Memorial Lectures.* Suva: University of the South Pacific, 37–51.

Rajotte, F. and Crocombe, R. (eds) (1980) *Pacific Tourism: As Islanders See It.* Suva: University of the South Pacific.

Samy, J. (1980) 'Crumbs from the Table: The Workers Share in Tourism.' In F. Rajotte (ed.) *Pacific Tourism: As Islanders See It.* Suva: University of the South Pacific, 67–82.

Scheyvens, R. and Russell, M. (2010) *Sharing the Riches of Tourism: Summary Report – Fiji.* Palmerston North, New Zealand: Massey University.

Scott, R. (1970) *The Development of Tourism in Fiji since 1923.* Unpublished paper prepared for Fiji Visitors Bureau, Suva.

Singh, G. (2012) 'Political Environment and its Impact on Tourism Marketing: A Case Study of Fiji.' *Journal of Marketing, Financial Services & Management Research* 1: 1–13.

Slatter, C. (1973) 'The Tourist Industry in Fiji.' In A. Rokotuivuna *et al.*, *Fiji: A Developing Australian Colony.* Melbourne: International Development Action, 18–25.

Sydney Morning Herald (2010) 'Fiji Invites Tenders for First Casino.' news.smh.com. au/breaking-news-business/fiji-invites-tenders-for-first-casino-20101029-176vd.html (accessed 10 February 2014).

Time World (2013) 'In Fiji, Machete-Wielding Locals Spook Tourists and Investors.' 28 August. world.time.com/2013/08/28/in-fiji-machete-wielding-locals-spook-touris ts-and-investors/ (accessed 3 March 2014).

Turner, L. (1976) 'The International Division of Leisure: Tourism and the Third World.' *Annals of Tourism Research* 4: 12–24.

Turner, L. and Ash, J. (1975) *The Golden Hordes: International Tourism and Pleasure Periphery.* London: Constable.

Vusoniwailala, L. (1980) 'Tourism and Fijian Hospitality.' In F. Rajotte and R. Cro-combe (eds) *Pacific Tourism: As Islanders See It.* Suva: University of the South Pacific, 101–6.

Waqaisavou, T. (2001) *Tourism in Fiji: Native Land Owner Attitude and Involvement.* Paper presented at Pacific Rim Real Estate Society Annual Conference, Adelaide, Australia, 21–24 January 2001.

Wilkinson, J. (2011) *Exclusive Video: Fijian PM Frank Bainimarama Talks Tourism.* www.hotelmanagement.com.au/2011/11/09/exclusive-video-fijian-pm-frank-bainimar ama-talks-tourism/ (accessed 11 February 2014).

World Travel and Tourism Council (2013) *Travel & Tourism Economic Impact 2013 Fiji.* n.p.

Young, G. (1973) *Tourism: Blessing or Blight?* Harmondsworth: Penguin Books.

5 Debunking Pacific utopias
Chief Roi Mata's Domain and the re-imagining of people and place in Vanuatu
Joseph M. Cheer, Keir J. Reeves and Jennifer H. Laing

Introduction

The view of Pacific island countries (PICs) as paradise has persisted since the arrival of Europeans over two centuries ago (Daws, 1980; Connell, 2003). Juxtaposed against utopian ideals is the reality that island countries in the region labour under a multiplicity of serious threats including climate change, economic vulnerability, political upheaval and persistent underdevelopment. Yet the paradise narrative endures in the imaginings of people and place, most notably through tourism destination marketing that constructs and manipulates place image. Associated with this has been the attendant fetishising of islanders as stereotypical noble or ignoble savages (Campbell, 1980; Fry, 1996), or their infantilisation as congenial, subaltern hosts, reinforcing notions of Pacific island communities as a latter-day Shangri-La in the Pacific (Douglas, 1997). In stark contrast, PIC prehistory suggests that islanders had enormous resilience, ingenuity, fierce warrior cultures and a reputation as seafarers of enormous competence and sophistication – attributes far removed from the docile and indigent exemplifications of recent times.

Crocombe (2001) and Denoon *et al.* (1997) allude to the paradoxical nature of PIC conceptualisations, highlighting that in fact pre-colonial, colonial and postcolonial historiography suggests that islanders have always endured a vexed, fickle and challenging space. For example, the practice of cannibalism and the waging of inter-island warfare are thought to have been common prior to the arrival of Europeans and the ensuing Christian missions (Matsuda, 2012; Oliver 1989). This was followed by a prolonged period of colonial dominance and native subjugation, where indigenous islander cultures and symbols were decried as antithetical to Christianity and civilisation (Campbell, 1989). The independence era of the 1960s to the 1980s ensued, promising self-determination and emancipation (Denoon, 1997). Yet decades later, islanders face precarious futures – beset by natural and man-made encumbrances (Crocombe, 2001; Connell, 2010). As Samoan scholar Sina Va'ai (2005) argued, so-called 'Pacific utopias' are dissonant and far removed from the realities of contemporary island life.

This chapter adopts Va'ai's stance and explores the paradox of the imaginings of people and place, using the case study of Chief Roi Mata's Domain (CRMD) (Figures 5.1 and 5.2) –Vanuatu's only United Nations Educational, Scientific and Cultural Organization (UNESCO) World Heritage Site, designated a 'continuing cultural landscape' (Wilson, Ballard and Kalotiti, 2011: 5). Vanuatu's historiography is imbued with themes of hurricanes, sorcery, warfare and cannibalism (Spriggs, 1986) and the mythology of CRMD is an archetypal narrative of the harsh and distinctive Melanesian socialities predating the arrival of Europeans. CRMD is a mass burial site for the legendary Chief Roi Mata and his people, and symbolic of a dark and disturbing side to the country's past (Garanger, 1982). CRMD is examined in this chapter to illustrate how the utilisation of such cultural heritage can serve to replace hackneyed and patronising imaginings of people and place with a more reflective understanding of a sophisticated and nuanced historical and extant milieu. This chapter sets out to achieve this by connecting dark tourism and archaeotourism, as reflected in CRMD, to the construction of people and place conceptions. This argument complements Trau's (2012b: 4) assertion that:

> Given that it is the local Indigenous community – and not the state – that is primarily responsible for World Heritage in Vanuatu, it is vital that this glocalised brand of CRMD's *Wol Heritij* (with all of its complexity, fluidity and unpredictability) is seriously recognized and adequately supported.

The invocation of CRMD is used to argue that an urgent re-imagining of PICs and islanders is pressing if they are to be accurately portrayed within the wider global gaze. In scholarly tourism parlance, CRMD aligns with what is defined as dark tourism – tourism that leverages aspects of death and disaster (Lennon and Foley, 2000). CRMD is also a rare case of archaeotourism at work in PICs – visitation to sites of archaeological value (Giraudo and Porter, 2010). Together, dark tourism and archaeotourism mechanisms, as exemplified in CRMD, are arguably the antithesis of contemporary PIC imaginings, and may serve to moderate tourist expectations and in turn lead to a more productive and fulfilling exchange between ni-Vanuatu (indigenous people of Vanuatu) and their guests. Thus, collectively, they may well enforce more expansive and erudite conceptions of people and place.

Context: New Hebrides to Vanuatu

The island nation that makes up the Republic of Vanuatu is a curiosity given that it holds the unique distinction of being the only PIC that was subject to dual colonial powers – the condominium of France and Britain. The condominium was formerly known as the New Hebrides or *Nouvelles Hebrides* until it gained political independence in 1980. For the most part, Vanuatu's

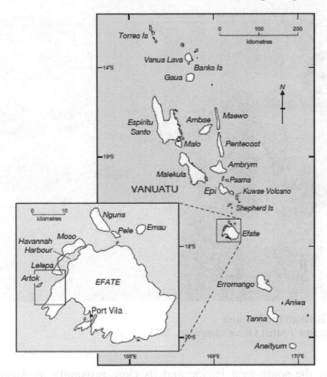

Figure 5.1 CRMD in relation to Vanuatu
Source: Republic of Vanuatu, 2007

Figure 5.2 CRMD signage for proposed World Heritage listing
Source: Photo by Cheer, 2008

Figure 5.3 Beneath the Volcano
Source: Vanuatu Tourist Office campaign, 2011

location in the south-west Pacific and its close proximity to Australia has been beneficial, enabling the countries to develop close trading and diplomatic ties. Tourism has become a cornerstone of the country's economy, with sector activity predominantly limited to leisure tourism. Vanuatu's natural landscapes have arguably been its biggest draw for visitors to the country (Figure 5.3). However, a renewed emphasis by tourism authorities to showcase its unique cultural heritage for tourism development has started to take place. This heritage includes the inimitable land diving or *naghol* in the southern area of Pentecost Island, the John Frumm and Prince Philip cargo cults on the island of Tanna, Second World War heritage sites and the wreckage of the SS *Coolidge* on Espiritu Santo, and the historic cannibal sites and caves on Malekula island.

Vanuatu is typical of small island developing states (SIDS) in the region in that its population is widely dispersed with the greater majority considered to be residing in rural and outer island locations. The country's economy labours under the weight of a narrow set of exploitable sectors including tourism, fisheries, copra and offshore banking. In the main, Vanuatu is considered a less developed country, meaning that it is subject to underdevelopment, poverty and its vulnerability to internal and external economic and climate-related shocks is high. Vanuatu's political milieu is notoriously fickle and volatile with effective governance considered its major impediment to economic growth and development.

Chief Roi Mata's Domain: semiotics, masculinities and place making

Chief Roi Mata's Domain is associated with the life and death of the last holder of the title Paramount Chief, or Roi Mata, who lived around 1600 AD (Garanger, 1982). CRMD was listed as UNESCO Site 1280 and officially ratified in 2008 after its initial tentative listing in 2004 (Garanger, 1982). It is made up of sites on Efate and Lelepa Island, the whole of Artok Island and the body of water that separates them. The tiny islands of Lelepa and Artok are located off the north-west coast of Efate (Figure 5.4). These three sites are recognised as part of the last Roi Mata's domain as Paramount Chief of Efate and the surrounding locale, as imbued in collective memory and substantiated through the path-finding archaeological works of Jose Garanger. Garanger's excavations commenced in 1967, whereupon he uncovered the burial site of men, women and children – all assumed to be part of the last Roi Mata's familial and domestic entourage.

Wilson, Ballard and Kalotiti (2011: 6) point out that 'Roi Mata appears to have been one of the more senior titles associated with the arrival on Efate of new chiefs and a system of "court" positions between about 800–1000 AD. The legendary Roi Mata thus probably represents the conflation of several

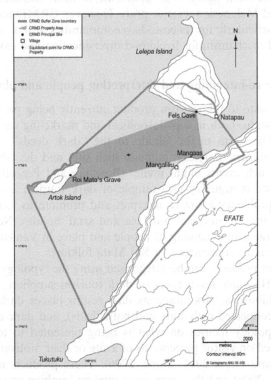

Figure 5.4 Boundaries of World Heritage property and buffer zone of CRMD
Source: Republic of Vanuatu, 2007

centuries of deeds associated with successive holders of the Roi Mata title'. Garanger (1982) expounds that Chief Roi Mata had a profound impact on islander sociality and that his legacy endures in the present day as a talisman for the moral values he advocated, including the social reforms central to conflict resolution and the cessation of inter-tribal warfare. According to Chief David Richard, patriarch of the *Malvatumauri* (National Council of Custom Chiefs of the Republic of Vanuatu), the Roi Mata legend is steeped in the sanctity of traditional culture and inextricably linked to ancestor veneration (Richard, 2011).

In adding to the Roi Mata legend, Garanger (1982: 15) wilfully conflates the past with the present, arguing that 'there is great unease in these Melanesian Islands where the past was brutally thrust aside and where the present is marking time between the wish to oppose and the attempt to adapt to religious ideas, principles of authority and foreign socioeconomic systems'. Garanger's sentiments argue that the spirit of Roi Mata was also imbued in the struggle for independence and autonomy, and is now observable in the drive for economic development. As well as the immense folkloric semiotics that permeate CRMD at a local level, nationally this spirit bolsters the country's cultural heritage and sense of pride, given that Roi Mata is the archetypal patriarchal figure – so dominant in local socialities – inspiring masculinity and Melanesian warrior pride. However, CRMD today represents much more, particularly for its custodian communities; it has the potential to serve as a vital mechanism for livelihood diversification and cash income.

Dark tourism: re-imagining and interpreting people and place

The polar opposite to the tourism product currently being promoted in connection to Vanuatu, both in a philosophical and marketing sense, is the *dark tourism* site. This term might 'allude to the "dark deeds" (e.g. genocide, assassination, murder, war) that animate such sites and the "dark mood" or morose tones such events might invite' (Bowman and Pezzullo, 2009: 188). The CRMD site is arguably an example of dark tourism and represents a complex and problematic site to interpret and promote to tourists, in comparison to the more traditional 'sun, sea and sand' holiday. Nevertheless, its potential to forge a re-imagining of people and place in Vanuatu is profound given the muscular pervasiveness of Roi Mata folklore.

Dark tourism products can be categorised using the typology developed by Stone (2006). He notes seven types of dark tourism suppliers: dark fun factories, dark exhibitions, dark dungeons, dark resting places, dark shrines, dark conflict sites (connected with wars and battlefields), and dark camps of genocide. This typology focuses on what is being presented to tourists, rather than being based on visitor perceptions of a site or their motivations to visit it (Biran, Poria and Oren, 2011; Stone, 2006). These products may be multi-layered (Stone, 2006) and thus may cross over or combine several categories. CRMD might be conceptualised as a dark resting place (although it is not a formal cemetery) as it marks the graves of over 50 men and women along with the remains of Chief Roi Mata. It might also be labelled a 'dark camp of genocide', given that many of the family and court members were buried alive with the Chief and it is not clear whether all the deaths were voluntary.

CRMD therefore falls at the darker end of the dark tourism spectrum (Stone, 2006), in that it is a site *of* death and suffering, rather than merely associated with these things, and its presentation for tourism is oriented towards education rather than entertainment. This is a place of deep spirituality and sober contemplation, with a highly authentic product and location. There is little tourism infrastructure at present and thus a lack of commodification, other than the presence of a local guide. In terms of Sharpley's (2005) 'continuum of purpose', this site might also be categorised as a form of *grey tourism supply*, in that the site can be experienced in a variety of ways, both for its connection with death but also as a place of contemplation, which is replete with intangible heritage.

While a long period of time has elapsed since the occurrence of the event (the deaths occurred about 1600 AD; see Wilson, 2006), this has not diminished the sense of immediacy with respect to what happened. As Wilson (2006: 36) notes, 'Many members of the local community are reluctant to visit Fels Cave, for fear of the power of Roi Mata and also the spirit beings that are currently said to inhabit the place'. Thus, Lennon and Foley's (2000) view that dark tourism only relates to events that have occurred within the lifetime or living memory of visitors does not apply in this instance. Their conceptualisation of dark tourism as a postmodern phenomenon disregards the handing down of narratives in traditional cultures, which can avoid 'chronological distance' and keep the sense of darkness alive across successive generations.

In the context of CRMD, these legends resulted in the site being declared *tabu*, or forbidden. While the stories are told less frequently today, there are strident moves by the *Malvatumauri* to revive this history (Wilson, 2006). Those who visit CRMD (locals as well as tourists) are either aware or told of the background to and significance of the site. The sacred banyan tree at Mwalasayen is supposed to embody the 'chiefly power' of Roi Mata, and it is said that 'those who venture near the tree speak softly, and many will not come within 15 metres of its base'. This supports Seaton's (1996) contention that a 'thanatoptic tradition', exemplified by a fascination with places of death and suffering, can be traced back far beyond the current era. Stone and Sharpley (2008) note that this tradition may be a way of dealing with our own mortality and making sense of death, which contributes to our health and well-being. In this way, dark tourism might have more to do with 'life and the living, rather than the dead and dying' (Stone and Sharpley, 2008: 590).

Visits to sites such as CRMD are more than likely understood as a form of heritage tourism, albeit contested or dissonant in nature (Tunbridge and Ashworth, 1996). In the case of CRMD, what is being developed for tourism appears to be a 'profound heritage experience' (Biran, Poria and Oren, 2011:

822). Those who visit CRMD might not be interested in its connection with death, but instead simply see it as an important historical site that represents some of the complex cultural heritage of Vanuatu and is emblematic of similar contexts in PICs. Interpretation must therefore tread a careful path between the macabre elements of the story and a more nuanced approach, where this heritage is framed in terms of ni-Vanuatu *kastom* (a term in Bislama, the home-grown pidgin language of Vanuatu, analogous with Tok Pisin in Papua New Guinea connoting the abiding framework of custom and tradition) and identity, with visitors being educated and enriched by the experience. The narrative of suffering provides one of the many layers of this cultural landscape, but it is not the only one that needs to be or indeed can be presented to tourists.

Archaeotourism: empowering and re-imagining people and place

The significance of archaeotourism in enabling what Giraudo and Porter (2010: 7) regard as 'authentic encounters with the past' is a departure from the ubiquity of the reproduction of culture seen in *kastom* villages (replicas of traditional villages) so prevalent in Vanuatu. Giraudo and Porter argue that archaeotourism sites can be linked to economic development as sites of cultural consumption and indigenous enterprise in developing countries. The notion of archaeological sites as a mechanism for archaeotourism-led development is also argued by Babalola and Ajekigbe (2007) to have a duality of purpose at a local level: economic and socio-cultural enrichment.

In 2006, the World Heritage Tourism Committee (WHTC), pertaining to custodian groups of CRMD, drafted an inaugural strategy deliberately seeking to leverage its livelihood's potential. The *Cultural Tourism Strategy for Chief Roi Mata's Domain*, arguably an archaeotourism initiative, explicitly includes 'starting a successful and profitable local community business' as a key objective (Greig, 2006: 4). In recognition of the site's intrinsic vulnerability, especially in light of its World Heritage listing and impending development for tourism, a *Plan of Management for Chief Roi Mata's Domain* was finalised, 'to provide management guidelines for the individuals responsible' (Wilson, 2006: 6). Moves for the development of CRMD are a growing response to the need for cash incomes at the grassroots (Wilson, Ballard and Kalotiti, 2011), where subsistence living has always predominated.

Recent pioneering analysis of CRMD by Adam Trau (2012b) suggests that enhancing the capacity for bottom-up local forces to preside over the presentation and operations of CRMD is critical if such heritage is to endure and provide financial recompense and, by implication, socio-cultural empowerment at a local level. By extension, Trau (2012a) draws a link between tourism-centred development and poverty alleviation for the traditional custodians of CRMD. The terms 'glocalisation' and 'grassroots globalisation' are conflated by Trau (2012b: 4) to draw attention to the tensions inherent when 'local *kastom* and global commerce' are necessarily conjoined.

Trau (2012b: 13) makes the point that 'financial and regulatory scaffolding for glocalised business models such as Roi Mata Cultural Tours must be engineered if the benefits of tourism are to be realised by rural ni-Vanuatu communities'.

The socio-cultural and political empowerment that Babalola and Ajekigbe (2007) maintain is a critical component of archaeotourism is also acknowledged by Garanger (1982) with regards to CRMD. Garanger (1982: 15) argues that in the case of Vanuatu, 'the beginning of the historical period hardly more than a century and a half ago was often so painful that the wounds of the first traumas are not all healed despite the efforts of some men of calibre, missionaries, colonists or administrators, anxious to maintain a balance between the frequently opposed forces, while at the same time giving the people the economic and cultural benefits of our society'. In a sense, Garanger makes the case that the semiotics and masculinities that underpin the Roi Mata legend may well be critical in nation building and identity formation for ni-Vanuatus and, if this is so, CRMD can meet the dual purpose (Babalola and Ajekigbe, 2007) of providing for both economic and socio-cultural and political strengthening.

Conclusions

Like most, if not all, PICs, the utopian thematic predominates place making in Vanuatu. CRMD is a counter-discourse to this and is arguably an example of dark tourism (defined broadly as tourism predicated on dissonant heritage), which by its very nature represents a complex and problematic site to interpret and promote to tourists in comparison to the more traditional 'sun, sea and sand' holiday. At another level CRMD is a demonstration of layered and deep cultural heritage, symbolic of a rich past to which local tourism gives little attention. In concert with dark tourism, the potential for archaeotourism has been neglected hitherto in Vanuatu. A second counter-discourse to utopian imaginings is the mobilisation of archaeotourism: as Babalola and Ajekigbe (2007: 240) argue, 'the development and improvement of tourism should look towards developing archaeological recourses to cater for the participation of local population in the tourism industry to curb the influx of youths to the urban centres'. Babalola and Ajekigbe also point to archaeotourism as a means of bolstering national pride, cultural heritage revival and self-sufficiency. Similarly, as Trau (2012a) argues, here lies the potential for CRMD to enhance economic, socio-cultural and political empowerment.

What is currently being offered to tourists is low-key and low-impact; there are no gift shops selling souvenir T-shirts (Strange and Kempa, 2003). Keeping tours of the site small-scale and respectful will maintain not only the perceived authenticity of the site, but also the 'darker' image. This provides atmosphere and a sense of place, but also a means by which to provide a more rounded and multifaceted picture of Vanuatu as a nation, including its history and likely future. As Bowman and Pezzullo (2009: 194) observe,

'Death is not merely an event in our past'. While hyping up the narrative may make it more marketable (Strange and Kempa, 2003; Tunbridge and Ashworth, 1996), it might also be the means of destroying the intrinsic value of the site.

Part of CRMD's importance as a narrative lies in its ability to change the way the landscape is read by visitors. Rather than understanding the site simply as an undisturbed utopia with pristine and palm-fringed beaches, it takes on a more disturbing and disquieting image, as well as sacred or spiritual qualities. The interpretation of CRMD that tells the unsettling story of the site might lead into a more complex presentation of local history, with implications for shaping people's place identity. According to Wilson (2006: 29), 'Many ni-Vanuatu now identify the male figure in Vanuatu's coat of arms as Roi Mata, in his new guise as a national culture hero'. Unlike American dark tourism sites such as Alcatraz Island or the site of the shooting of President John F. Kennedy in Dallas, there are no blockbuster films or books that have placed the Roi Mata story on the 'mental map' of tourists (Strange and Kempa, 2003). As most international visitors will not have heard about the site, and may have no 'personal attachment' or connection to it (Biran, Poria and Oren, 2011), an opportunity is provided to present the narrative without overlays of over-simplification, prejudice, bias or hyperbole. Instead, unlike Evergreen Tours' Mele Cascades attraction (a nature-based tourism product just outside the capital, Port Vila), visiting the inscribed section of Roi Mata's site involves a loosely guided, technically oriented heritage experience that takes place against a backdrop of dramatic tropical maritime beauty. Such an approach abides by what Trau (2012a: 4) argues are 'local reconfigurations of tourism that better represent and utilise *kastom*'.

Interpretation must therefore tread a careful path between the macabre elements of the story and a more nuanced approach where this heritage is framed in terms of ni-Vanuatu cultural heritage and identity, so that visitors become privy to a more sophisticated and enriching experience. Part of its importance as a narrative for people and place making lies in its ability to change the way the cultural landscape is read by visitors. Rather than understanding the site simply as an undisturbed piece of 'paradise', visitors can be encouraged to interpret it as a more nuanced, thought-provoking and disquieting image, which would include recognition of its sacred or spiritual qualities. Logan and Reeves's (2008: 2) assertions that 'an effective management plan for such places must be based on an analysis of the way in which such heritage sites are said to be significant and remembered', is a salient reminder to ensure that optimum participation of custodian groups or traditional owners are central to initiatives focused on the protection, presentation and commercialisation of such sites.

The duality of reconceptualising people and place through dark tourism and archaeotourism using CRMD is rare in PIC contexts. Thus, the case to invoke cultural heritage such as CRMD holds a strong position. Va'ai (2005: 2) argues that debunking Pacific utopias is an overdue undertaking and the 'quest by Pacific islanders for new postcolonial cultural identities and liberalisation from the past' ought to be sustained. In a sense, Va'ai is advocating that islander conceptualisations should be based on their cultural and historical terms, no longer couched in exogenous expressions developed in the colonial past and perpetuated in the present. Both dark tourism and archaeotourism may potentially satisfy Va'ai's calls and in so doing work towards what Trau (2012b) argues is the need for more nuanced and mutually beneficial 'global-local interactions'. Trau (2012b: 9) promotes the notion of 'supreme power and agency of locality' advocating that 'it is vital that such naturally non-constant, unpredictable, unceasing, even occasionally unstable, reconfigurations of glocality be recognised, supported and sustained'. If indeed the calls of both Va'ai and Trau are to be heeded, heritage such as CRMD must serve a multiplicity of purposes: strengthening the articulation of customary cultural heritage, aiding livelihood diversification and making way for a more empowering and reverential invocation of islander imaginings.

Acknowledgements

The authors would like to thank Chief David Richard 'Fandanumata' and Vanuatu MP Abel David (coordinator of the Vanuatu Indigenous Descendants Association) for their deep and intimate insights that provided the inspiration for this and other research undertakings. Special thanks are also due to Mrs Jocelyn Mete for her warm friendship and expert advice, and to Mr Kirk Huffman, former director of the Vanuatu Kaljoral Senta, for his erudite and enduring support. *Tank yu tumas olgeta.*

References

Babalola, A. and Ajekigbe, P. (2007) 'Poverty Alleviation in Nigeria: Need for the Development of Archaeo-Tourism.' *Anatolia* 18(2): 223–42.

Biran, A., Poria, Y. and Oren, G. (2011) 'Sought Experiences at (Dark) Heritage Sites.' *Annals of Tourism Research* 38(3): 820–41.

Bowman, M.S. and Pezzullo, P.C. (2009) 'What's So "Dark" about "Dark Tourism"? Death, Tours and Performance.' *Tourist Studies* 9(3): 187–202.

Campbell, I.C. (1980) 'Savages Noble and Ignoble: The Preconceptions of Early European Voyagers in Polynesia.' *Pacific Studies* 4(1): 45–59.

——(1989) *A History of the Pacific Islands,* University of California Press.

Connell, J. (2003) 'Island Dreaming: The Contemplation of Polynesian Paradise.' *Journal of Historical Geography* 29(4): 554–81.

——(2010) 'Pacific Islands in the Global Economy: Paradoxes of Migration and Culture.' *Singapore Journal of Tropical Geography* 31(1): 115–29.

Crocombe, R. (2001) *The South Pacific.* Suva: USP Institute of Pacific Studies.

Daws, G. (1980) *A Dream of Islands: Voyages of Self-discovery in the South Seas.* New York and London: W.W. Norton & Co.

Denoon, D. (1997) 'Pacific Edens? Myths and Realities of Primitive Affluence.' In D. Denoon, S. Firth, J. Linnekin, M. Meleisea and K. Nero (eds) *The Cambridge History of the Pacific Islands.* Cambridge: Cambridge University Press, 80–96.

Denoon, D., Firth, S., Linnekin, J., Meleisea, M. and Nero, K. (eds) (1997) *The Cambridge History of the Pacific Islands.* Cambridge: Cambridge University Press.

Douglas, N. (1997) 'Melanesians as Observers, Entrepreneurs and Administrators of Tourism.' *Journal of Travel & Tourism Marketing* 6(1): 85–92.

Fry, G. (1996) *Framing the Islands: Knowledge and Power in Changing Australian Images of the South Pacific.* Canberra: Department of Industrial Relations, Australian National University.

Garanger, J. (1982) *Archaeology of the New Hebrides: Contribution to the Knowledge of the Central Islands.* Sydney: Oceania Publications.

Giraudo, R.F. and Porter, B.W. (2010) 'Archaeotourism and the Crux of Development.' *Anthropology News* 51(8): 7–8.

Greig, C. (2006) *Cultural Tourism Strategy for Chief Roi Mata's Domain (Northwest Efate, Vanuatu).* Port Vila: World Heritage and Tourism Committee (WHTC) and the Lelepa region community.

Lennon, J.J. and Foley, M. (2000) *Dark Tourism: [The Attraction of Death and Disaster].* Cengage Learning EMEA.

Logan, W. and Reeves, K. (2008) *Places of Pain and Shame: Dealing with 'Difficult Heritage'.* Abingdon, UK: Routledge.

Matsuda, M.K. (2012) *Pacific Worlds: A History of Seas, Peoples, and Cultures.* Cambridge: Cambridge University Press.

Oliver, D.L. (1989) *The Pacific Islands.* University of Hawaii Press.

Republic of Vanuatu (2007) *Chief Roi Mata's Domain: Nomination by the Republic of Vanuatu for Inscription on the World Heritage List.* Port Vila, Vanuatu: Vanuatu Kaljoral Senta.

Richard, D. (2011) *Vanuatu Tourism, Cultural Landscapes & Livelihoods Project – Fatumaru Bay Hotel* (in-depth interview ed.). Port Vila.

Seaton, A.V. (1996) 'Guided by the Dark: From Thanatopsis to Thanatourism.' *Journal of Heritage Studies* 2(4): 234–44.

Sharpley, R. (2005) 'Travels to the Edge of Darkness: Towards a Typology of Dark Tourism.' In C. Ryan, S. Page and M. Aitken (eds) *Taking Tourism to the Limits: Issues, Concepts and Managerial Perspectives.* Oxford: Elsevier, 217–28.

Spriggs, M. (1986) 'Landscape, Landuse and Political Transformation in Southern Melanesia.' In P.V. Kirch (ed.) *Island Societies: Archaeological Approaches to Evolution and Transformation.* Cambridge: Cambridge University Press, 6–19.

Stone, P.R. (2006) 'A Dark Tourism Spectrum: Towards a Typology of Death and Macabre Related Tourist Sites, Attractions and Exhibitions.' *Tourism* 54(2): 145–60.

Stone, P. and Sharpley, R. (2008) 'Consuming Dark Tourism: A Thanatological Perspective.' *Annals of Tourism Research* 35(2): 574–95.

Strange, C. and Kempa, M. (2003) 'Shades of Dark Tourism: Alcatraz and Robben Island.' *Annals of Tourism Research* 30(2): 386–405.

Trau, A. (2012a) 'Beyond Pro-poor Tourism: (Re)interpreting Tourism-based Approaches to Poverty Alleviation in Vanuatu.' *Tourism Planning & Development* 9(2): 149–64.

——(2012b) 'The Glocalisation of World Heritage at Chief Roi Mata's Domain, Vanuatu.' *Historic Environment* 24: 4–11.

Tunbridge, J. and Ashworth, G. (1996) *Dissonant Heritage: The Management of the Past as a Resource in Conflict*. Chichester: Wiley.

Va'ai, S. (2005) 'Pacific Utopias and National Identities in the Twenty-first Century.' *Portal Journal of Multidisciplinary International Studies* 2(2): 1–23.

Wilson, M. (2006) *Plan of Management for Chief Roi Mata's Domain*. Lelepa Region: World Heritage & Tourism Committee.

Wilson, M., Ballard, C. and Kalotiti, D. (2011) 'Chief Roi Mata's Domain: Challenges for a World Heritage Property in Vanuatu.' *Historic Environment* 23(2): 5–11.

Part III

Socio-economic impacts of tourism

6 Adapting and reacting to tourism development

A tale of two villages on Fiji's Coral Coast

Apisalome Movono, Stephen Pratt and David Harrison

Tourism and development: a summary

There has been much discussion over the extent to which theories of development are at an 'impasse' (Sharpley, 2009: 39; Payne and Phillips, 2010: 3), leading to calls for a return 'to the intellectual project of political economy and the diverse theoretical traditions associated with it' (Payne and Phillips, 2010: 181). Not surprisingly, such uncertainties have been reflected in changing perspectives over tourism's role in 'development', and Jafari might indeed be correct in suggesting that general attitudes to tourism, at least, have moved from positions of advocacy and caution, through adaptation, to a greater (and less ideological) focus on knowledge and research (Jafari, 2003). However, as he notes, 'the text and position of one platform led to the formation of the next; and indeed all four platforms exist today' (Jafari, 2003: 9).

The emergence of theories of sustainable development in the 1980s, and their subsequent linking with sustainable *tourism* development, while ostensibly attractive, in effect served only to tie one set of fuzzy concepts to another (Harrison, 1996), and despite recent attempts to clarify the theoretical confusion over the role of tourism in development (Sharpley, 2000, 2009; Sharpley and Telfer, 2002), consensus remains as elusive as ever. Mowforth and Munt (2009), for example, consider all tourism 'alternative', and otherwise to be ultimately and distressingly linked to capitalism, while serious attention has only recently centred on the role of mass tourism (Aramberri, 2010). The prevailing ambivalence is amply demonstrated by Sharpley, who accepts that mass tourism brings benefits but nevertheless contends the structure of international tourism reflects the inequalities posited by dependency theorists while those who implement tourism development focus primarily on economic growth and (consciously or otherwise) follow the tenets of modernisation theory. Consequently, they are intrinsically at odds with 'the principles and objectives embodied in the concept of sustainable development' (Sharpley, 2000: 14).

At the conceptual level it might be best to perceive international tourism development from a non-prescriptive globalisation perspective (Harrison, 2014), but there can be little doubt about the current distrust of grandiose statements about tourism development. As with development generally, however, this need not cause dismay. Instead, we should stand again on the 'knowledge platform', carry out empirical research and pay attention to the findings that emerge. As with the proverbial angels dancing on a pin, there is no substitute for empirically examining what is happening on the ground – or, to be more precise, at the end of the pin!

Tourism in Fiji

The Republic of Fiji is an archipelago with more than 300 islands. With a combined land mass of about 18,274 square km, it is 16° south of the equator and just west of the international dateline. Most of its 830,000 people live on the two main islands of Viti Levu and Vanua Levu, and Suva, the nation's capital, is in Viti Levu, the most populated and developed island. Indeed, more than 25% of the population is concentrated in and around Suva and the environs of Lautoka, Nadi and Ba, all of which are on Viti Levu (Fiji Bureau of Statistics, 2010).

Tourism in Fiji first began in Suva in 1920, with the establishment of the White Settlers League, a body comprising white settlers who marketed Fiji to passengers disembarking there while crossing the Pacific (Scott, 1970: 1). This organisation developed into the Suva Tourism Board and, later, the Fiji Tourist Board, and then Tourism Fiji, currently the national tourism organisation. However, despite its early beginnings, tourism really developed only as a major economic force after the Second World War, prompted by the rise of disposable incomes in Australia, New Zealand and the USA (Fiji's main sources of tourists) and by developments in air transport that made Fiji more accessible. Its potential was recognised by the colonial government (Harris, Kerr, Foster and Co., 1965) but it was not until three years after independence that the first serious moves to establish tourism were made (Belt Collins and Associates Ltd, 1973) and it took until 1982 for tourism to replace sugar as the main source of foreign exchange (Narayan, 2000: 15). From then onwards, though, tourism developed quickly and by 2008 receipts from tourism were more than 50% higher than the combined totals of receipts from Fiji's next five major sources of foreign exchange – notably, sugar, garment manufacture, gold, timber and fishing (Fiji Bureau of Statistics, 2014).

Measurements of tourism's contribution to national economies are subject to considerable variation, depending on their source. However, while its methods have been queried (UNWTO, 2008: 2–3), according to the World Travel and Tourism Council (WTTC), in 2012 tourism directly contributed 13% to Fiji's gross domestic product (GDP) (and overall 36%), and directly contributed 12% to employment (overall 32%). There can be no doubt that tourism's role in Fiji's development is substantial, but the benefits are unequally spread (WTTC, 2013). As noted in Harrison and Prasad (2013: 747), accommodation is concentrated in four parts of Fiji: Sigatoka/Nadroga (the Coral Coast), Nadi (in the west, where the only fully international airport is located), and the Mamanuca and Yasawa Islands, to the north-west of Nadi, where some of the best beaches in Fiji are situated. As they note, 'These four regions account for 90% of all beds in Fiji, and 60% of all the beds are on the main island of Viti Levu' (Harrison and Prasad, 2013: 747). More specifically, the Coral Coast, where the two villages that are the focus of the case studies below are situated, accounts for some 18% of all international visitors to Fiji (Fiji Ministry of Tourism, 2009).

Lists of tourism's alleged negative and positive impacts on developing societies, in particular, have been extensively produced (Smith, 1978: 3–13; de Kadt, 1979: 1–76) and reproduced (Harrison, 1992a, 11–18; Harrison, 1992b, 2001, 2010; Richardson and Fluker, 2004). Its impacts on Pacific island countries have been less detailed, but nevertheless follow the general pattern and have been discussed at length elsewhere (Harrison, 2003: 11–18). Britton, for example, followed an underdevelopment perspective and in an influential series of papers criticised the way tourism in the region both demonstrated and perpetuated dependency and social inequalities and enhanced the role of transnational companies (Britton, 1982, 1987a, 1987b), although his support for what many have regarded as the near-feudal Tongan monarchy might seem a contradiction (Britton, 1982: 349). Similarly, Samy (1980) criticised tourism for providing most of the population only with 'crumbs from the master's table'.

Others focused more on social and cultural impacts. Douglas and Douglas (1996), for example, point to stresses when there are differences in host and guest culture, unfavourable ratios of visitors to residents, and the problems of rapid tourism development, while Bolabola (1980) noted the unfavourable impact on tradition that arises from commoditisation in satisfying tourist demand for arts and crafts. In her study of tourism's impact in Fiji, she showed that the commoditisation of woodcarvings led to alterations in the motifs and design and changed the manufacturing process. Following increased tourist demand, carvers produced items from readily available wood, rather than the rare Vesi hardwood traditionally used. They also adopted Polynesian motifs and carved masks, animals and other items which, although not 'traditionally' Fijian, appealed to tourists (Bolabola, 1980; Niukula, 1980: 94).

By contrast, Burns (2003) looked at the impact of tourism on the women of Beqa (a small island south of Viti Levu). When entering hotel work, many women became the main breadwinners of the family, and thus no longer remained in the traditionally subordinate role of Fijian women, a situation with much potential for domestic and community conflict (Burns, 2003: 85). The newly found independence also provided them with avenues for social mobility, again taking them away from their traditional position in the home (Niukula, 1980).

Such changes need not be considered negative. Ravuvu, known for his strong Fijian nationalism, nevertheless recognises that the introduction of the cash economy and new economic activity were major forces for change and inevitably influenced the modernisation of Fijian culture and communities

(Ravuvu, 1988: 32–48). Host communities can be selective, at least to some extent, in which elements of modernisation they accept. Certainly, they should not be seen as hapless or passive when faced with pressures to change. Even three decades ago, MacNaught (1982: 365–66) argued against the 'fatal impact' thesis, suggesting that cultures of Pacific island countries vary in their resilience when confronted by pressures to change when interacting with tourists. Nevertheless, he and Douglas (1996) agree that interaction with tourists, relative to their numbers and the intensity of contact, can have important social consequences in tourist-receiving communities.

In short, such issues as cultural imperialism, 'demonstration effects', commoditisation, authenticity and socio-cultural change *may* be related to tourism but the *extent* such changes will occur cannot be stipulated in advance. Rather, specific circumstances need to be studied and assessed, which is where case studies become valuable. In this chapter, there is an examination of two indigenous Fijian (*i-Taukei*) villages, which have been exposed to tourism over a long period, and then a reflection on how they have reacted and adapted to tourism development and a discussion on the lessons that might be learned from their experiences.

The case study villages

During the mid-1900s, the southern Coral Coast underwent a series of developments. The first, in 1942, was the construction of the Queen's Highway by the US Army, and this in turn prompted further development, which

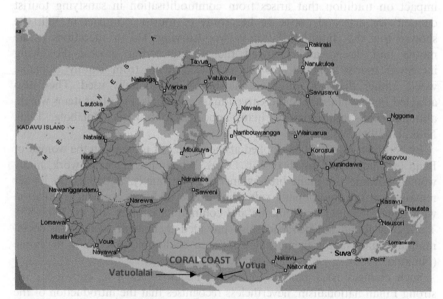

Figure 6.1 Location of Votua and Vatuolalai villages in Fiji
Source: Source: www.mapia.com

led to the opening of the area to tourism. In 1952, Fiji's first resort hotel was constructed in Korolevu, next to the village of Votua (one of the case study villages), and this was followed in 1972 by the Warwick Resort (also near Votua) and in 1974 by the Naviti Resort, adjacent to the village of Vatuolalai (the second case study village). Later, in the late 1970s and early 1980s, the Tambua Sands and Hideaway resorts were built (Ravonoloa, 2009), and other, small-scale operations soon emerged, including backpacker resorts, ecotourism ventures, dive centres and homestays.

By 2011, the Coral Coast was Fiji's second largest tourism destination, with over 40 licensed establishments accounting for more than 150,000 international visitors annually (Fiji Ministry of Tourism, 2009). Indeed, tourism has been perceived as the lifeblood of the Coral Coast, contributing to the development of the various communities mainly through employment, land lease benefits and other tourism-related activities (Fong, 2006; Kado, 2007; Sofer, 1990).

Votua and Vatuolalai, the two villages selected as case studies for examining the impacts of tourism, are respectively 43 km and 48 km from Suva, Fiji's capital, and 56 km and 51 km from Nadi, where Fiji's main international airport is situated. They are several minutes' drive apart and in the district of Korolevu-i-wai. Vatuolalai consists of 32 households and a population of about 185–200 people. Immediately adjacent to the Naviti Resort, it is one of the most well-developed villages in the country and has modern housing and amenities. In the 1970s, landowners agreed to lease their land to the hotel provided work was given to the people of Vatuolalai, and they were among the first Fijians to gain employment in tourism when the resort opened in 1974.

Votua village, with some 44 households and a population of about 200, is located a few minutes' drive from the Warwick Resort and is near the site of Korolevu Resort (which closed in 1983). Votua is the chiefly village of the district of Korolevu-i-wai, home of Tui Davutukia, the district chief.[1] Because of this association, the village is often the venue of important meetings, where decisions concerning the district are made. The people of Votua have been engaged in tourism since the 1950s and many villagers continue to be involved in tourism.

Both villages are located at the heart of the tourist belt, on the Queen's Highway that links Suva with Nadi and Lautoka. They are typical of other villages in the district in geographical features, distance from markets, access to various services and links to the tourist industry (Sofer, 1990: 109). As indicated below, over the years the people of Votua and Vatuolalai have adapted and reacted to environmental, social and economic changes brought by tourism.

Methods

The value of case studies is well established. They enable us to interpret social phenomena and the ways social change impacts on communities, assist us in isolating specific aspects of community development, and reflect and reflect *back* on theoretical orientations (Veal, 2006).

As Stake notes, a case study approach enables the researcher to put boundaries on the investigation, select relevant themes or issues, isolate patterns of data, triangulate observation, structure alternative interpretations, and 'develop assertions or generalisations about the case' (Stake, 2000: 448).

In examining and interpreting tourism's social and economic impacts on Votua and Vatuolalai, a mixed methodology was employed, using both quantitative and qualitative approaches. These included formal and informal interviews, participant observation and a quantitative questionnaire. Data were collected from May to September in 2010. Recognising the value of in-depth interviews (Walsh, 1996), a total of 16 were conducted with key informants, usually people who had extensive knowledge on issues being researched, for example, the *Turaga ni koro* (village headman), *Turaga ni mataqali* (clan head), heads of social committees, village elders and retirees. Topics raised included village histories and informants' perceptions, experiences and ideas of evidence of economic and social impacts of tourism in both Votua and Vatuolalai.

In addition, over 20 informal interviews and casual discussions about tourism were held with many community members, and information was obtained as and when opportunities arose – for example, when watching afternoon volleyball matches, at informal meetings, over kava[2] sessions, and at formal and informal family gatherings. As found elsewhere, in the village setting, where most communication is conducted orally and at a more personal level, such informal interviews and discussions were a key source of data (Bouma and Ling, 2004).

Participant observation, an established approach in obtaining data (Waddington, 1994), was also invaluable. The lead author of this research, an indigenous Fijian, lived in the communities for two weeks and actively participated in village life. As a young Fijian male, he participated in such typical village activities as gardening, fishing and other communal work – for example, village clean-ups – and attended village meetings and other functions. Participation in village affairs was essential, and allowed the researcher to blend into the community and develop favourable relationships. A key factor that influenced the ease of access into these communities and the relatively smooth data collection is the traditional relationship that exists between the lead author and the members of the two communities. This is the '*dreu*' system whereby people from the villages are traditionally obliged to be genuinely hospitable (Movono, 2012). This facilitated a favourable rapport from both communities as well as relatively good and open exchanges during the course of the research.

Finally, questionnaires were administered by the researcher to 76 households in both villages. They sought information on economic activities, the number of villagers working in tourism, energy requirements for cooking, and the perceived benefits and disadvantages of tourism. Because questionnaires were directly administered, on-the-spot clarification could be given to inter-viewees, and because villagers were asked by the district chief to cooperate, the completion rate was 100%.

Inevitably, problems were encountered, especially when sensitive issues were raised. Fijian culture is highly stratified and traditional roles are observed in both villages. As a consequence, when discussions were in groups of family or clan members, members of low-ranked clans, women and youth were reluc-tant to comment on village conflicts, or on the distribution of financial bene-fits arising from land leases. In such circumstances, later and more private discussions normally led to more open information being provided.

There were also ethical considerations. The protocols of the villages had to be respected, respondents were assured of anonymity, and the researcher had to be as non-intrusive and as objective as possible. This was not always easy, as participant observation included involvement in such social functions as evening kava sessions (a common form of entertainment), church, village and family meetings, and drinking alcohol with younger members of the villages. However, villagers in both communities were advised that the interviews and questionnaires were being undertaken only for research purposes, and were assured that confidentiality would be respected and that no one would be identified in the findings of this research.

Findings

The research findings can be categorised under the following headings: housing and education; income and livelihoods; health; and women and youth.

Housing and education

Both communities are relatively well endowed in housing and amenities. All homes have corrugated iron roofs, and 90% of houses in both villages are constructed from brick and concrete. In addition, everyone has flush toilets. There was also a high incidence of ownership of such luxury items as suites of furniture, television sets, DVD players, refrigerators and gas stoves, with 85% of all households in both villages having access to at least five of them. This suggests a relatively high standard of living in the cohort when compared to other parts of Fiji. According to the Ministry of Fijian Affairs (2009), 78% of indigenous Fijians live below the poverty line and more than 70% who live in indigenous Fijian villages lack access to basic infrastructure and sanitation, and have little means to access the items described above. A similar study conducted by Kado (2007) further reinforces the notion that because of tourism, communities on the Coral Coast, especially Vatuolalai, have gained immensely in terms of improved housing and raised standards.

As a 32-year-old male respondent from Vatuolalai stated, 'because we have jobs at the hotels, we can easily buy TV sets, gas stoves, sofas and other items on easy weekly instalments through hire purchase'. A 45-year-old female respondent from Vatuolalai said: 'when mobile phones first came to Fiji, people in my village were the first to buy phones, even without reception in the village.' In fact, 82% of respondents from both villages agree that their sound financial position, good housing and raised living standards can be attributed, directly or indirectly, to tourism. Such comments demonstrate that villagers are fully aware of their relative prosperity because of their involvement in tourism.

By contrast, however, tourism was perceived to have a negative effect on the educational achievement of children. Because villagers are guaranteed employment in the resorts, there is little incentive for children to stay on at school. In Vatuolalai, especially, this was especially noticeable. As a male respondent noted:

> [M]ost people in our village know how easy it is to get jobs at the resort, so they don't really care too much about education. Because work is guaranteed, children just give up after failing form four. I mean, why should they worry when they have their own land, own homes, steady incomes? At least that's how they think; there is little need for formal education.

A retired deacon of the Methodist church said:

> In the history of our village, only 6 people have graduated from tertiary institutions with diplomas and degrees. Most children just finish form 4 or 5 and go straight into the hotels. It seems that people here do not care too much about education because work is guaranteed. I have served in different parts of Fiji, and to come back and witness this kind of attitude in my own village, it is worrisome; people are not looking for other, better opportunities.

On the other hand, Votua villagers place a slightly higher emphasis on education when compared to Vatuolalai. This was reflected by a 39-year-old female respondent from Votua, who stated: 'we know that work at the hotels is not stable; in the slack periods we get laid off, and this is not good.' Overall, Votua villagers are more reserved and mature when asked about tourism because they have had the longest involvement in tourism, know its volatility, and have experienced the impact on tourism of three devastating cyclones and three coups over their 60-year exposure to the industry. Nevertheless, employment in tourism has provided both communities with the funds to pay for school fees, textbooks and other materials. In total, six families from both villages have also been able to send their children to private schools in Suva.

Income and livelihoods

Work in the hotels and other tourism-related businesses are the major source of income in both villages. In Vatuolalai, 92% are employed either directly or indirectly in tourism compared to 84% of villagers in Votua. Income for people in both communities is obtained in several distinct ways. First, it accrues to villages through regular payments by the hotels for leasing land, which go through the *i-Taukei* Land Trust Board (TLTB, formerly the Native Land Trust Board). In Fiji, 87% of land is owned by *mataqali*, clans that are also indigenous landowning units. The TLTB arranges lease agreements, administers lease arrangements and works in promoting the interests of both the tenant and landlord.

In Vatuolalai, lease money is paid to only three of the four clans in the village. Every clan member receives close to FJ$5,000 a year, amounting to an annual total for the clan of FJ$250,000.[3] In Votua it is different, as the lease monies are received by only one family because the actual land is owned by a sub-clan that consists of only one nuclear family. This also equates to around FJ$300,000 a year. In both cases, clan members receive direct payments and much of the money is spread in the villages through contributions to village development projects and church levies, along with payments made to village funds. The remaining clan in Vatuolalai that does not receive land lease payments is also the only clan with members who have pursued further education, gained bachelor's degrees and diplomas and have moved on to professional work in urban areas around Fiji.

Second, more than half the working population in both villages is employed directly by the resorts. Some 71% of the respondents in Vatuolalai agree that they have steady jobs at the hotels, compared to 64% in Votua. In both communities, more than 36% of workers are women, which further suggests the role of tourism in empowering women. In Votua, villagers work in different hotels along the Coral Coast, but mainly in the Warwick Resort, Naviti Resort and Tambua Sands, some 20 minutes' bus ride away. By contrast, most of those employed in tourism from Vatuolalai work at the Naviti Resort.

As a result of working at the resorts, both villages have obtained considerable economic benefit and there are also indirect benefits. In Vatuolalai and Votua, a further 15% of villagers generate income through tourism-related businesses. These include village stays, village tours, nature tours, hair braiding salons, massage parlours, sales of handicrafts and a jet ski business. It is estimated that on average around FJ$60,000 per annum is injected into the village economy of each village through income derived from such activities.

While tourism employment is vital to both villages, it has differentially affected their traditional economies, especially subsistence agriculture and fishing. Before hotels were built, farming and fishing were primarily conducted for subsistence and any surplus was sold. At the time of the research, however, more villagers from Votua (the village with less tourism impact) fish and/or collect seafood than people in Vatuolalai. Although fishing and farming were for subsistence, more people would sell the surplus catch and crops to those who worked at the resorts. This is reflected in 30% of respondents in Votua stating that they fished and farmed on a weekly basis, compared to only 5% of respondents in Vatuolalai. Most of those surveyed in both communities agree that tourism has led to seafood collection being less frequent, primarily because those employed in tourism have less time to fish and collect seafood and, because they have more disposable income, they can purchase fish or meat from within the village or elsewhere. As one respondent, a young man aged 26, remarked, 'I consider fishing a hassle because I work at the bar. When I come home I am too tired to go out and fish. It is easier to just buy it and store it in the 'fridge'. Like fishing, subsistence farming is another traditional village activity, but respondents indicate that a substantial majority of the population in both communities no longer or only infrequently engage in agricultural activity. Like farming, fishing has become a 'hassle', especially for villagers engaged in shift work at the resorts.

Health

Because of tourism, and the decline in fishing and subsistence agriculture, the diets of the villagers have changed. There has been an increased preference for such items as chicken, tinned fish and meat. As a 54-year-old female respondent noted, 'people are going for easy and faster food options and now prefer to buy food from the supermarkets, such as, rice, noodles and potatoes and [do] not prepare and eat cassava, dalo or yams regularly'. Generally, the Vatuolalai cohort believe that diets have changed for the following reasons: there is less engagement in farming (32%), less fishing (35%), more time is spent working at the hotels (38%), and a there is preference for purchased food (27%). Similar responses were found in Votua, where it was agreed that diets were changing because less time was being spent on subsistence farming (32%), fishing and seafood collection (27%), that more time was spent working at the hotels (27%), and that preference for purchasing processed food was increasing (18%). For both villages, these figures indicate a general shift away from subsistence living, less reliance on locally sourced food, and evidence of how the diets of villagers have changed as a result of involvement in tourism.

Nevertheless, most respondents from both villages felt their health situation had improved as a result of tourism. About 68% of respondents of Vatuolalai rated it 'much better', while 26% agreed it had become 'better', and only 6% considered there had been 'no change'. Similarly, in Votua, 79% of respondents rated their health situation 'much better', 14% agreed that the health situation had become 'better', and only 7% felt there had been 'no change'. Most respondents also agreed that the communities had better health-care services. In Vatuolalai, 62% of respondents took this view, while 64% of respondents in Votua were similarly positive. In this context, it should be noted that by 'health-care services', villagers mean medical services as well as general village health and sanitation. In Fijian, *tiko bulabula* refers to medical health as well as the overall well-being of the community, inclusive of such things as village cleanliness and sanitation.

The data suggest respondents recognise their village health committees and village nurses as key authorities on village health issues. Both villages have a health committee, which oversees general village health issues. It comprises about 12 individuals, who are tasked with monitoring and managing village cleanliness, drainage, sanitation and health. The committee is also responsible for disseminating information on communicable and non-communicable diseases as well as other health matters. It liaises with such groups as the government health department, non-governmental organisations (NGOs) and specific interest groups, and is expected to oversee issues pertaining to village health. One 57-year-old male respondent from Votua said: 'We are lucky to have a very active health committee which provides the relevant health services to the community. They regularly attend meetings and workshops and come and implement what they learn in the village.' A 32-year-old woman from Vatuolalai commented:

> In our village, we have our own health committee that oversees issues pertaining to our health and wellbeing. When we have any issues like a recent outbreak of scabies, our health committee was quick to get help and medicines from the health authorities, so we just went straight to them.

In support of such views, respondents cited the ability to access better health-care services, either in the community or elsewhere, to access potable water, better sanitation and toilets, and an efficient drainage system and a cleaner and healthier environment.

Villagers' perceptions are supported by objective evidence. Vatuolalai receives its water supply directly from the resort, while Votua has its own reservoir which, at the time of the research, had recently been upgraded with aid from New Zealand and money raised by the villagers themselves. As an elderly male noted:

> When we started working in the hotels and developing our communities, we first wanted good houses with good toilets. Having flush toilets elevates our standards. This is modern, and it is good that we no longer have the unhygienic pit or water sealed toilets in the village. This is a sign of progress.

Women and youth

The development of tourism has led to changing roles, particularly among the women and youth in the villages. A significant proportion of those employed at the resorts and in tourism businesses, women and young people now earn their own income and, as a result, want more say in how it is spent. This conflicts with traditional Fijian protocols and customs; for example, women are expected to behave conservatively, and are frowned upon if they engage in alcohol consumption. As a 29-year-old female respondent from Votua commented, 'it is our culture to submit to men, but times are changing and we want our voices to be heard as well. We also work and earn money for our families'. In some instances, women were the sole breadwinners. Another respondent, the 37-year-old village headman from Vatuolalai, remarked:

> Women are better with money. They can save and manage money wisely. This can be witnessed through women's projects in the village, which include village hall equipment such as crockery and plates for hosting village events, as well as a village education fund, set up by women in the respective communities.

A 46-year-old woman from Votua remarked: 'women are becoming more recognised for their contributions to our community, yet at home they remain in their roles as mothers and the "second boss" in the household.'

Fijian culture emphasises the need for young people to obey their elders, and expects them to take care of the land and promote their culture (Ravuvu, 1987). Youths must 'take their place' as young members of the community and conform to the decisions made by village elders. Women assume special obligations: for example, at village functions they focus on food preparation, whereas men participate in such ceremonies as the *i sevusevu*, a traditional welcoming ceremony. This is a reciprocal protocol performed by guests when entering a community. They seek blessing and approval for entering the village, normally presenting kava as a gift, with a ceremonial exchange of words announcing their arrival, their place of origin and reasons for the visit. Villagers, in turn, respond in an appropriately formal manner and offer them hospitality.

According to villagers in both communities, young people are increasingly unable to carry out these ceremonial roles satisfactorily, and sacrifice community obligations for earning money and individual advancement. There were reports from both communities of 'quarrels', 'talking back', general disobedience and fading moral values among the youth of the both villages, and 87% respondents from both communities attributed wage work at the hotels as the key driver of such changes. Significantly, perceptions that young people were misbehaving were more pronounced in Vatuolalai, where 65% of respondents held this view. By contrast, in Votua this criticism was voiced by only 22%. At the same time, however, 90% of respondents in both communities recognised that tourism had brought considerable employment and other opportunities for young people. Those in Votua, for instance, valued tourism not only for its economic benefits, but also for the resorts' contribution to youth projects, including a fully equipped rugby gymnasium, and rugby teams from both villages receive sponsorship and uniforms from the resorts. As a young 19-year-old male respondent remarked, 'youths have more opportunities now to work and earn money. With money comes freedom and the tourism industry can give this freedom!'

Conclusions and recommendations

In the Pacific, and specifically in Fiji, tourism is continually promoted for its economic benefits and as a means whereby indigenous communities can be advanced (Harrison and Pratt, 2010; Rao, 2002). This study is an attempt to understand its impacts in two *i-Taukei* (indigenous Fijian) communities, the villages of Votua and Vatuolalai on the Coral Coast of Fiji. Among the first in Fiji to have been involved with tourism, they reveal the complexities of tourism's role as an agent of socio-economic and cultural change.

As the previous discussion has shown, villagers appreciate the material benefits – especially better-quality housing, sanitation and health facilities – that tourism has brought to Votua and Vatuolalai. There was widespread agreement that their standard of living had improved. Respondents also noted the diminishing value placed by many villagers on education. They also felt that reliance on tourism employment had led to a decline in subsistence agriculture and fishing, and contributed to tensions arising from the changing status of women and village youth. However, such conflicts should not be overplayed: communities were generally positive towards tourism, although it was recognised that it had both positive and negative socio-economic and cultural consequences.

This research is not without its limitations. The lead author spent a month in the two villages, and a longer period might have produced additional insights. At the same time, though, it is felt he was welcomed and integrated into the villages because of existing traditional links, and subsequent experience during regular visits to the villages by all authors suggest that the findings are valid.

There is a clear need, however, for more specific studies of tourism's impacts on indigenous communities and their culture. The impacts of tourism in the two villages discussed in this chapter might not occur elsewhere, although the findings may be generalisable to other *i-Taukei* villages. At the same time, there is much to recommend more dialogue and closer relations with the resorts, and data elsewhere from Fiji suggest that corporate social responsibility is on the increase (Scheyvens and Hughes, in this book; Harrison and Prasad, 2013: 752–55). It is evident from this research that when circumstances are favourable, *i-Taukei* communities are able to operate their own businesses and develop closer linkages with resorts. Indeed, local businesses already 'piggy-back' on larger resorts by offering their guests additional services, and closer links would enable further entrepreneurial development at a local level.

Government could encourage greater local participation in business by providing technical and financial support to existing or potential businesses in these communities. Although villagers in both communities have some experience and understanding of owning and operating tourism business operations, they lack expertise in marketing and strategic product development. Government could facilitate training in business planning and management, book-keeping and marketing, and initiate microfinance schemes to help establish small-scale businesses. This would increase participation by locals, encourage them to be better organised, and improve the way they market their products. There is a need, too, for closer linkages of resorts and surrounding local communities in producing food, beverages and other items for tourist consumption – not just in Fiji, but in many developing societies (Momsen, 1986; McBain, 2007; Young and Vinning, 2007; Torres and Momsen, 2011). In addition, despite the low soil fertility in the district, there is huge potential to breed organic livestock and grow pineapples, watermelons, corn and other crops consumed by tourists (Ministry of Agriculture, 2009).

The findings of this empirical study fill a significant void in the literature. They provide clear evidence of the economic and socio-cultural impacts of tourism in Fiji and thus reinforce the research of others who have shown how tourism can bring economic benefits, develop entrepreneurial activities and improve the quality of life of 'host' communities (Sofer, 1990; Weaver and Oppermann, 2000). This research also demonstrates tourism's links to changing traditions more widely – for example, in gender roles, youth empowerment and traditional cultures – and thus again reinforces the findings of research in other communities (Burns, 2003; Cohen, 1988; de Burlo, 2003; Douglas and Douglas, 1996; Harrison, 2004). However, two case studies are nowhere near sufficient fully to understand tourism's impacts in Fiji, let alone elsewhere. Much yet remains to be done.

Notes

1 Fiji is divided into 14 provinces which consists of various districts. Every district comprises a collection of villages, and district chiefs are often regarded as 'high chiefs' of the various villages that make up the district.
2 A traditional drink made from the dried pounded roots of the piper methisticum plant.
3 Equivalent to US$128,456.

References

Aramberri, J. (2010) *Modern Mass Tourism*. Bingley: Emerald.
Belt Collins and Associates Ltd (1973) *Tourism Development Program for Fiji*. Washington: United Nations Development Program/International Bank for Reconstruction and Development.
Bolabola, C.A.B. (1980) 'The Impact of Tourism on Wood Carving.' *Pacific Tourism: As Islanders See It*. Suva: The Institute of Pacific Studies, 93–98.
Bouma, G.D. and Ling, R. (2004) *The Research Process*. New York: Oxford University Press.
Britton, S. (1982) 'The Political Economy of Tourism in the Third World.' *Annals of Tourism Research* 9(3): 331–58.
——(1987a) 'Tourism in Pacific Island States: Constraints and Opportunities.' In S. Britton and W. Clarke (eds) *Ambiguous Alternatives: Tourism in Small Developing Countries*. Suva: University of the South Pacific, 113–39.

——(1987b) 'Tourism in Small Developing Countries: Development Issues and Research Needs.' In S. Britton and W. Clarke (eds) *Ambiguous Alternatives: Tourism in Small Developing Countries.* Suva: University of the South Pacific, 167–87.

Burns, G.L. (2003) 'Indigenous Response to Tourism in Fiji. What is Happening?' In D. Harrison (ed.) *Pacific Island Tourism.* New York: Cognizant Communication Corporation, 82–93.

Cohen, E. (1988) 'Authenticity and Commoditization.' *Annals of Tourism Research* 15 (3): 371–86.

de Burlo, C.R. (2003) 'Tourism, Conservation and the Cultural Environment in Rural Vanuatu.' In D. Harrison (ed.) *Pacific Island Tourism.* New York: Cognizant Communication Corporation, 69–81.

de Kadt, E. (ed.) (1979) *Tourism: Passport to Development.* Oxford: Oxford University Press.

Douglas, N. (1996) *Transport. They Came for Savages: 100 Years of Tourism in Melanesia.* Lismore, Australia: Southern Cross University Press.

Douglas, N. and Douglas, N. (1996) 'Social and Cultural Impacts of Tourism in the Pacific.' In C.M. Hall and S. Page (eds) *Tourism in the Pacific: Issues and Cases.* London: International Thompson Business Press, 49–64.

Fiji Bureau of Statistics (2010) *Key Statistics.* Suva: Fiji Bureau of Statistics.

——(2014) *Key Statistics.* Suva: Fiji Bureau of Statistics.

Fiji Ministry of Tourism (2009) *Fiji International Visitor Survey Report.* Suva: Fiji Ministry of Tourism.

Fong, S. (2006) *Community based Coastal Resource Management in the Fiji Islands: A Case Study of Korolevuiwai District, Nadroga.* Suva: University of the South Pacific.

Harris, Kerr, Foster and Co. (1965) *Report on a Study of the Travel and Tourist Industry of Fiji.* Legislative Council of Fiji, Council Paper No. 32. Suva: Government Printer.

Harrison, D. (1992a) 'International Tourism and the Less Developed Countries: The Background.' In D. Harrison (ed.) *Tourism and the Less Developed Countries.* Chichester: John Wiley & Sons, 1–18.

——(1992b) 'Tourism to Less Developed Countries: The Social Consequences.' In D. Harrison (ed.) *Tourism and the Less Developed Countries.* Chichester: John Wiley & Sons, 19–34.

——(1996) 'Sustainability and Tourism: Reflections from a Muddy Pool.' In L. Briguglio, B. Archer, J. Jafari and G. Wall (eds) *Sustainable Tourism in Islands and Small States: Issues and Policies.* London: Pinter Press, 69–89.

——(2001) 'Less Developed Countries and Tourism: The Overall Pattern.' In D. Harrison (ed.) *Tourism and the Less Developed World: Issues and Case Studies.* Wallingford: CABI Publishing, 1–19.

——(2003) 'Themes in Pacific Island Tourism.' In D. Harrison (ed.) *Pacific Island Tourism.* New York: Cognizant, 1–23.

——(2004) 'Tourism in Pacific Islands.' *The Journal of Pacific Studies* 26(1 & 2): 1–28.

——(2010) 'Tourism and Development: Looking Back and Looking Ahead – More of the Same? In *Tourism Research: A 20-20 Vision.* Woodeaton, Oxford: Goodfellow Publishers Limited, 40–52.

——(2014, forthcoming) 'Tourism and Development: From Development Theory to Globalisation.' In M. Hall, A. Lew and A. Williams (eds) *The Wiley-Blackwell Companion to Tourism.*

Harrison, D. and Prasad, B.C. (2013) 'The Contribution of Tourism to the Development of Fiji and other Pacific Island Countries.' In C. Tisdell (ed.) *Handbook of Tourism Economics: Analysis, New Applications and Case Studies*. Singapore: World Scientific, 741–69.

Harrison, D. and Pratt, S. (2010) 'Political Change and Tourism: Coups in Fiji.' In R. Butler and W. Suntikul (eds) *Tourism and Political Change*. Oxford: Goodfellow Publishers, 160–74.

Jafari, J. (2003) 'Research and Scholarship: The Basis of Tourism Education.' *Journal of Tourism Studies* 14(1): 6–16.

Kado, M. (2007) *Tourism and Poverty Alleviation in Fiji: Examining the Impact of Coral Coast Tourism on Village Livelihoods, the Case of the Villages of Namatakula and Vatuolalai*. Suva: University of the South Pacific.

MacNaught, T.J. (1982) 'Mass Tourism and the Dilemmas of Modernisation in Pacific Island Communities.' *Annals of Tourism Research* 9(3): 359–81.

McBain, H. (2007) *Caribbean Tourism and Agriculture: Linkages to Enhance Development and Competitiveness*. Port of Spain: United National Commission for Latin America and the Caribbean (ECLAC).

Ministry of Agriculture (2009) *Annual Report*. Suva, Fiji: Ministry of Agriculture Forestry and Fisheries.

Ministry of Fijian Affairs (2009) *Fiji Provincial Profiles*. Suva, Fiji: Ministry of Fijian Affairs

Momsen, J.H. (1986) *Linkages between Tourism and Agriculture: Problems for the Smaller Caribbean Economies*. Seminar paper no. 45, University of Newcastle upon Tyne, Department of Geography.

Movono, A. (2012) *Tourism's Impact on Communal Development in Fiji: A Case Study of the Socio-economic Impacts of The Warwick Resort and Spa and The Naviti Resort on the Indigenous Fijian Villages of Votua and Vatuolalai*. Unpublished Master's thesis, School of Tourism and Hospitality Management, the University of the South Pacific, Suva.

Mowforth, M. and Munt, I. (2009) *Tourism and Sustainability: Development, Globalisation and New Tourism in the Third World*. Third edn. London: Routledge.

Narayan, P. (2000) 'Fiji's Tourism Industry: A SWOT Analysis.' *Journal of Tourism Studies* 11(2): 15–24.

Niukula, P. (1980) 'The Impact of Tourism on Suvavou Village.' *Pacific Tourism: As Islanders See It*. Suva: Institute of Pacific Studies, 83–86.

Oppermann, M. and Chon, K. (1997) *Tourism in Developing Countries*. London: International Thomson Business.

Payne, A. and Phillips, N. (2010) *Development*. Cambridge: Polity Press.

Rao, M. (2002) 'Challenges and Issues for Tourism in the South Pacific Island States: The Case of the Fiji Islands.' *Tourism Economics* 8(4): 410–29.

Ravonoloa, K. (2009) *Personal Communication*.

Ravuvu, A.D. (1987) *The Fijian Ethos*. Suva, Fiji: Institute for Pacific Studies, University of the South Pacific.

——(1988) *Development or Dependency: The Pattern of Change in a Fijian Village*. Suva: University of the South Pacific.

Richardson, J. and Fluker, N. (2004) *Understanding and Managing Tourism*. New Jersey: Pearson Education.

Samy, J. (1980) 'Crumbs from the Table? The Workers Share in Tourism.' *Pacific Tourism: As Islanders See It*. Suva: Institute of Pacific Studies, 67–82.

Scott, R.J. (1970) 'The Development of Tourism in Fiji since 1923.' *Transactions and Proceedings of the Fiji Society* 12.

Sharpley, R. (2000) 'Tourism and Sustainable Development: Exploring the Theoretical Divide.' *Journal of Sustainable Development* 8(1): 1–19.

——(2009) *Tourism Development and the Environment: Beyond Sustainability.* London: Earthscan.

Sharpley, R. and Telfer, D. (2002) *Tourism and Development: Concepts and Issues.* Clevedon: Channel View Publications.

Smith, V. (ed.) (1978) *Hosts and Guests: The Anthropology of Tourism.* Oxford: Blackwell.

Sofer, M. (1990) 'The Impact of Tourism on a Village Community. A Case Study of Votua Village, Nadroga/Navosa, Fiji.' *Journal of Pacific Studies* 15: 107–30.

Stake, R.E. (2000) 'Case Studies.' In N.K. Denzin and Y.S. Lincoln (eds) *Handbook of Qualitative Research.* Second edition. London: Sage, 435–54.

Torres, R.B. and Momsen, J.H. (eds) (2011) *Tourism and Agriculture: New Geographies of Consumption, Production and Restructuring.* London: Routledge.

UNWTO (United Nations World Tourism Organization) (2008) *Measuring Tourism: The UN TSA Approach vs. the WTTC Approach: Brunei as a Case Study.* Madrid: UNWTO.

——(2010) *Compendium of Tourism Statistics: 2009 Edition.* Madrid: UNWTO.

Veal, A.J. (2006) *Research Methods for Leisure and Tourism: A Practical Guide.* Third edn. Harlow: Prentice Hall.

Waddington, D. (1994) 'Participant Observation.' In C. Cassell and G. Symon (eds) *Qualitative Methods in Organizational Research: A Practical Guide.* London: Sage Publications, 107–22.

Walsh, J.P. (1996) *Research Methods in Social Sciences.* Fifth edn. London: Edward Arnold.

Weaver, D. (1998) *Eco-tourism in the Less Developed World.* Oxford: CABI International.

Weaver, D. and Oppermann, C. (2000) *Tourism Management.* Second edn. Brisbane: John Wiley & Sons.

World Travel and Tourism Council (WTTC) (2013) *Travel and Tourism Economic Impacts.* Fiji.

Young, J. and Vinning, G. (2007) *Fiji: Commodity Chain Study.* Rome: Food and Agricultural Organization of the United Nations (FAO).

7 Community-based tourism in Fiji

A case study of Wayalailai Ecohaven Resort, Yasawa Island Group

Dawn Gibson

Introduction

The growth of tourism in developing countries has led to increased interest in tourism as a development tool for alleviating poverty (Chok, Macbeth and Warren, 2007; Sofield *et al.*, 2004; UNESCAP, 2003). At the same time, a need has emerged for more sustainable tourism planning, policies and programmes that consider tourist expectations of resource management as well as the needs of local communities, who in developing countries are often marginalised rural communities (UNEP, 2012). As a consequence, there has been an increased focus on indigenous tourism and pro-poor tourism, and many ecotourism and community-based ecotourism (CBE) schemes claim benefits to local communities, though as yet there is little evidence to date to substantiate such claims (Goodwin, 2007). Furthermore, when considering tourism's contributions to poverty reduction, one must consider 'how, and to what extent tourism can address the wider poverty agenda by contributing to health, education, welfare and community capacity building' (Goodwin, 2007: 86). Arguably, indigenous CBE, which has grown in developing countries with rare and exotic biodiversity and indigenous cultures, can indeed revive or sustain local cultural practices and educate and entertain tourists, but indigenous peoples rarely have control over tourism development (Goodwin, 2007: 85; Liu and Wall, 2006). More often, they are objects of the 'tourist gaze' (Urry, 2002).

Community-based tourism

Community-based tourism (CBT) development is promoted in many developing countries as a tool that enables the equitable distribution of economic benefits from tourism, encourages local involvement in the decision-making process, and better meets the needs of local communities and indigenous peoples (Britton, 1982; Brohman, 1996; de Kadt, 1979; Tosun, 2000). In the South Pacific, CBT or CBE is promoted as a development tool for rural and marginalised areas, including remote outlying islands (Ateljevic and Doorne, 2004: 5). However, some suggest that community development in tourism is merely rhetoric, and question the extent to which local residents truly share in the economic benefits of tourism (Joppe, 1996; Mitchell, 2003). What involvement will communities have? How will this be done? Will it just be a limited number of low-paying seasonal jobs or something more significant? Should communities be involved at all? However, despite such criticisms, for the long-term sustainability of tourism development, community involvement and support is often considered vital (Armstrong, 2012; Tosun, 2002).

Scheyvens defined community-based tourism enterprises as 'those in which the local communities have a high degree of control over the activities taking place, and a significant proportion of the economic benefits accrue to them. They may also be characterised by local ownership and a low level of leakage' (Scheyvens, 2002: 10). Even where local indigenous communities have a high degree of control, levels of power and economic benefits are not necessarily equitable. In Fiji, for example, community participation does occur but power and control generally remain in the hands of chiefs, elders and wealthy elites, who are predominantly male (Gibson, 2013).

Definitions of community participation in the development process vary, but most agree that the process should be voluntary, educational, empowering and include more participatory decision making (Ashley, Roe and Goodwin, 2001; Simpson, 2007, 2008). Participation exists, for example, where grassroots people can form partnerships with authorities who help them identify problems and needs, and empower them to take responsibility for planning, managing and controlling their futures (Tosun, 2000). Stone claimed active community participation was when development was designed so that 'intended beneficiaries are encouraged to take matters into their own hands, to participate in their own development through mobilising their own resources, defining their own needs, and making their own decisions about how to meet them' (Stone, 1989: 207).

Pro-poor tourism

Since the late 1990s, the concept of pro-poor tourism (PPT), with its alleged potential to contribute to poverty alleviation, has received extensive support from donors, development agencies, tourism organisations and governments (Scheyvens, 2009). In contrast to sustainable tourism, which focuses on protection and conservation, PPT aims to increase net benefits to the poor whilst considering environmental concerns. Researchers, consultants and aid agencies have promoted PPT approaches since the late 1990s (Harrison, 2008).

Furthermore, PPT is not a model or theory, but 'an orientation or approach to any form of tourism which focuses on the net benefits accruing to poor people in tourist destination areas' (Harrison, 2008: 855–56). It goes beyond a community focus by promoting strategies that specifically focus on the poor, although others may also benefit. PPT strategies can generate different benefits to local communities, which can be divided into three types: economic benefits, livelihood benefits and intangible benefits, which enhance participation and partnerships amongst different stakeholders (Scheyvens, 2012: 223). To increase the benefits from PPT, the development of community tourism is important. Although impacts of PPT initiatives may be limited, they can provide such invaluable financial and livelihood benefits as better access to information and infrastructure and pride in local cultures and traditions (Ashley *et al.*, 2001; Simpson, 2007). However, obstacles to implementing PPT benefits exist, including poor understanding of tourism, a lack of skills, poor-quality products and limited access to markets. These can be countered by increased consultation with the poor, especially when developing infrastructure and services for tourists (Ashley *et al.*, 2001).

Initially, PPT initiatives focused on such niche tourism markets as ecotourism and CBT, but it is now suggested that even mass tourism could increase participation of the poor (Bleitrach and Foch, 2010), by considering alternative livelihood initiatives such as handicrafts, traditional performances, tour guiding and the supply of agricultural produce (Gibson, 2013: 85; Kieti, Jones and Wishitemi, 2009). The tourism industry is thought to be suitable for pro-poor initiatives, because it is 'labour-intensive, inclusive of women and the informal sector; based on natural and cultural assets of the poor; and suitable for poor rural areas with few other growth options' (Ashley and Roe, 2002: 61).

Research by Scheyvens and Russell (2010) into tourism and poverty alleviation in Fiji established that although not all (or only) the poor may benefit directly from tourism, benefits could be spread more evenly if policies for communal benefits were developed by businesses and government. Therefore, although local chiefs and indigenous owners of CBT resorts are likely to receive the largest proportion of economic benefits from tourism, the community at large will benefit from contributions to education and churches, and from improvements in housing and village infrastructure (water, power, sewerage). As shown in the Wayalailai case study, detailed below, such benefits may possibly be more appropriate indicators of success and fulfil community motivations for CBT in indigenous, close-knit, communal, societies (Gibson, 2013).

Social capital

Social capital is claimed to be a significant influence on community participation in community development, and highly influential in the success of community-based small and medium-sized tourism enterprises (SMTEs) (Pretty and Ward, 2001; Macbeth, Carson and Northcote, 2004; Jones, 2005; Zhao, Brent Ritchie and Echtner, 2011). It is seen to be especially important in enabling rural or peripheral communities to transform themselves from traditional resource-based subsistence economies to those with an emphasis on entrepreneurship in tourism (Johannesson, Skaptadottir and Benediktsson, 2003).

Within indigenous Fijian societies, social relationships cross several hierarchies (for example, village, clan, tribe, province and nation), and are both strong and complicated. Such communities as those in the case study have the potential to use social capital to support their community-based tourism developments, where an important determinant of economic success is the level of social capital and the relationships among project participants (Ostram, 2000). In indigenous communities, physical capital alone is insufficient for economic growth and, when combined with other forms of capital, social capital is an essential component of development.

Ecotourism and CBT in Fiji

Community-based ecotourism has the potential to make a valuable contribution to rural economic development in Fiji. In the 1970s and early 1980s, the government formulated nature-based tourism strategies as a form of alternative development to conventional resort mass tourism (Harrison, 1998). Since then, Fiji's tourism industry has diversified, and a variety of new products have emerged. These range from conventional mass tourism in hotels and resorts, to such niche markets as ecotourism and community-based tourism, and budget products catering to the backpacker or youth tourism markets (Eccles and Costa, 1996).

In 1992, the Fiji government adopted the National Environment Strategy, which supported the concept of sustainable tourism through the increased development of ecotourism. This recognised the benefits of foreign exchange, employment and income generation for landowners, the complexities of the land tenure system, and the need to conserve the environment and cultural heritage. The Fiji government also identified ecotourism as way of increasing the participation of *i-Taukei* (indigenous Fijians) in business, considering ecotourism a 'social and economic development tool, to educate and promote sustainable development, for resource owners and backpacker resort owners' (Verebalavu-Faletoese and Kuridrani, 2006: 8). A further benefit of ecotourism was its small scale and low start-up capital and operating costs, when compared to resort mass tourism (Farrelly, 2009: 3).

Although successive national tourism development plans have recommended a focus on poverty reduction, community participation and sustainable development, the main policy focus is on increasing tourist numbers and foreign investment (Scheyvens and Russell, 2010: 10). In the 2007–16 Tourism Development Plan the Fiji government emphasised the need to achieve a balance between social, cultural, environmental and economic development (Ministry of Tourism, 2007: 4) – one way being, to 'encourage sustainable tourism development with the setting up of ecotourism projects and the protection of the environment in the long run' (Ministry of Tourism, 2007: 4).

Definitions of ecotourism vary, and what is referred to as ecotourism in Fiji could be broadly considered backpacking, budget, indigenous, village-based or CBT in other countries. The range of such activities is neatly summarised in a 2003 strategic environmental assessment of Fiji's tourism development plan, which recommended that the government concentrate on supporting modes of tourism that have lower leakage, few environmental impacts, and attract tourists whose motivations were aligned to ecotourism or CBT (Levett and McNally, 2003: xviii). The benefits of ecotourism ventures for indigenous Fijians were that given the small-scale nature of these businesses, they could be started with little capital investment, would cater for ecotourists interested in an educational cultural experience, be owned and operated by local people, be village or nature based, and have fewer leakages than large-scale tourism. Other envisaged benefits were economic, in the form of contributions to foreign exchange and employment, greater retention of income because of local ownership, and the use of locally produced resources. Social benefits included the preservation of natural and cultural heritage and, in some cases, the revival of cultural practices. Environmentally, ecotourism development could encourage the protection of endangered species, preserve natural and cultural sites, and develop an awareness of unsustainable practices such as logging or slash-and-burn agriculture.

As Harrison and Brandt (2003: 156) have noted, although village-based ecotourism in Fiji is unlikely to replace large-scale resort-based tourism, more could be done to ensure that tourism development is based on environmentally sustainable practice and make a valuable contribution to poverty alleviation, employment creation and the socio-economic development of marginalised rural communities and villagers. It is here that indigenous-owned, community-based tourism can play a useful and important role, as demonstrated in the following case study.

Case study: Wayalailai Ecohaven Resort

Study area

The ethnographic case study of Wayalailai Ecohaven Resort, in the Yasawas, provides an example of a participatory approach to indigenous tourism. Wayalailai Resort, belonging to the province of Vuda, is located on the island of Wayalailai in the Yasawa Island Group in north-western Fiji. Like most resorts in the Yasawas, it provides a stereotypical tropical island 'sun, sea and sand' and adventure holiday, which especially appeals to the more limited-budget backpacker market. Wayalailai Ecohaven Resort has operated since 1996 and received government assistance, in the form of loans and training, from the Ministry of Tourism.

Research methods

Following a detailed literature review, data (which were mostly qualitative) were gathered over a period of three years during visits that varied from a few days to six months. They involved techniques of participant observation at the village and in the resort, and in-depth and focus group interviews of community groups (youth, women, men, elders and staff) to reveal their primary motivations for developing CBT and to identify the impact on poverty

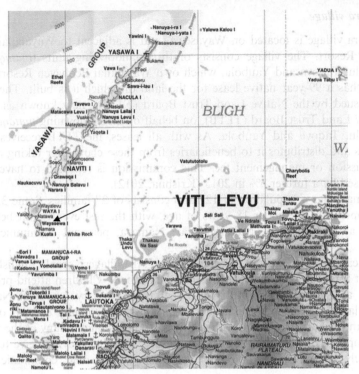

Figure 7.1 Wayasewa (Wayalailai) Island
Source: www.mappery.com

alleviation made by the resort on Wayalailai, as well as the potential cultural challenges accompanying its operation.

In Fiji strict protocols exist regarding the interaction between men and women of different ages, and elders, women and youth were interviewed together and separately. For example, it is unlikely that *i-Taukei* women and youth will speak out in front of male elders and chiefs; even in a group setting, gender roles are very specific and there is little interaction between males and females (Gibson, Pratt and Movono, 2012). Furthermore, conducting a formal 'interview' or a 'focus group' among *i-Taukei*, or seeking responses to a semi-structured questionnaire, can sometimes be inappropriate in such a context. In an effort to please the researcher, indigenous Fijians are likely to provide the answer they think the researcher wants to hear rather than giving their own views (Evening, 2000; Gibson, 2003). A more culturally appropriate form of eliciting responses are *talanoa* sessions, where people meet and talk informally while drinking *yaqona* (kava) around the *tanoa* (communal kava bowl). In this situation, *i-Taukei* are more open and spontaneous in their responses (Gibson *et al.*, 2012).

Namara village

Namara village is located on Wayasewa, and is adjacent to Wayalailai Eco-haven Resort. The village consists of three landowning units (*mataqalis*[1]): Boutolu, Taqova and Yaubola, which own Wayalailai Ecohaven Resort. The resort has a 99-year native lease for the land on which it is built. The lease was issued by the Native Land Trust Board (NLTB), now known as the *i-Taukei* Land Trust Board (TLTB), on behalf of the landowning *mataqalis* of Boutolu, Taqova and Yaubola. As with all leases, the TLTB receives lease monies and distributes it to beneficiaries from these clans after taking a 15% commission or management fee. This commission is reported to have been decreased by a further 5% in 2013 (Krishna, 2012).

Namara has a population of 127 and consists of 27 families. Some 35% of the population are under 18 years of age, with the rest evenly split between males and females (W. Nakalougaga,[2] Namara, personal communication, 2011).

Education levels within the village vary. All villagers speak English and have at least two or three years of secondary school. Children attend primary school at Naboro village and then either the secondary school at Nasawa Secondary School on Waya Island or one of the secondary schools on the mainland, where they board with relatives. Today, though, many of the youth are dropping out of school to work in resorts for what they perceive to be a relatively easy cash income (W. Nakalougaga, personal communication, 2011).

Historical background

The nearest island in the Yasawa Island Group to Viti Levu, Wayalailai is a two-hour trip from Port Denarau via the ferries operated by Awesome Adventures and South Seas Cruises (SSC) (see Figure 7.1). Wayalailai Ecohaven Resort, which is 100% indigenous Fijian community-owned and operated, was the second resort built in the Yasawa Island Group after Coral View on Tavewa Island, and opened in 1996, financed entirely from local sources.

The resort management is accountable to a board of directors, consisting of elders from the villages of Namara, Naboro and Yamata. This reflects the background of its construction, the result of an initiative by the three villages, which collectively decided to finance the resort entirely from donations from every family, and to provide volunteers to build and work at the resort. The old primary school, empty since a landslide in 1985, was converted into dormitories and a dining room, while the *bures* (thatched houses) were built from local reeds and timber using 'free' village labour as social capital. Six were built in a month, after which the resort opened for business. For the first two months, all food and beverages for guests and staff were provided from donations using local resources. Two months later, they were able to use the earnings from guests to purchase goods from the mainland.

Built on two levels overlooking the sea and Kuata Island, Wayalailai is one of the largest backpacker resorts in the Yasawas, and sleeps up to 80 or 90 guests at a time. Most resort employees come from the three villages, especially Namara, though a few specialist staff, for example, engineers, electricians and chefs, are from elsewhere in Fiji.

Social capital: benefits and costs

Wayalailai has a large pool of social capital to draw from, as it is owned by three clans or *mataqali*. To obtain labour, the resort must rely on the good will of the clan, and although the labourers are 'free', they are not guaranteed. In fact, the main contributors of social capital, from the clans, are women and young male clan members. Male elders rarely contribute directly, except when ceremonial exchanges are performed, but they are responsible for selecting the people to represent their family. Social capital has undoubtedly benefited the resort. Without the 'free' labour provided by the community, its construction would have been extremely costly and it would have taken much longer to complete. However, in providing such capital, a strong sense of ownership has developed among the clans. As members have built the resort for 'free' and donated their time, labour and food, they feel that not only are they 'owners', but also that they are entitled to use the resort and reap the benefits. This has led to abuse by villagers and Wayalailai management has implemented strict regulations regarding clan access and behaviour at the resort.

Impacts of community-based tourism initiatives

The clans of Wayalailai hoped that ownership of the resort and tourism would provide an alternative livelihood for their people. The benefits they have received include employment and much-needed cash incomes to help fulfil traditional obligations, pay church tithes and school fees. Over the years, the community has discovered that tourism has brought benefits and some negative impacts but the overall feeling is that tourism has been beneficial, in that it has enabled them to fulfil their dreams, participate in ceremonial obligations and compete with other CBT resorts in the Yasawas Group (V. Ratugolea,[3] personal communication, 18 April 2010). Interestingly, villagers consider fishing and farming as forms of self-employment, but 'real work' is only when you are employed by the resort. They feel that their ownership of Wayalailai has given them the opportunity to participate as equals in traditional *i-Taukei* society, and has substantially increased community pride (Gibson, 2013).

Socio-economic impacts of CBT

Economic benefits to the clans provided by Wayalailai include (mainly part-time) employment. The resort employs about 30 staff at any one time, of whom ten are full time (five women and five men), and 20 are part time. The staff rosters at the resort ensure that every week households have at least one person earning a cash income. As with most tourism resorts, employment is seasonal and the number of employees varies, depending on occupancy, new developments or maintenance requirements. Nevertheless, as identified by the United Nations World Tourism Organization (UNWTO, 2004, in Goodwin, 2007: 92), the researcher discovered that these cash contributions, although only between F$50–$150 a week, make a significant contribution to household income and supplement cash obtained from subsistence farming. Findings from employee interviews indicate that villagers are satisfied with supplemented income, which is used to purchase food and such luxuries as *yaqona*, cigarettes, mobile phone recharge cards and the occasional trip to the mainland.

There are also collective benefits in the areas of housing and sanitation, religion and education. By the end of 1996, a housing scheme, funded by the resort, built ten new houses, two for every *mataqali*. House construction continues, with families making submissions to elders for building funds. Namara villagers receive free electricity between 6.00 am and 10.30 pm, and all households have access to fresh, indoor plumbing and flush toilets. As Scheyvens and Russell (2010) discovered in their study of villages in Fiji associated with backpacker resorts, benefits from tourism through improved housing, schooling and village beautification, together with increased interaction with tourists, had also enhanced village pride. As well as the benefits already outlined, clans on Wayalailai have the discretionary income to spend on consumer goods such as clothing, and household goods such as furniture, televisions, DVD players, refrigerators, gas ovens, mobile phones and laptops.

Religion is extremely important to the clans of Wayalailai (and *i-Taukei* communities in general). Wayalailai villagers are Methodist, and since the opening of the resort two churches have been built in Namara and Yamata, with a third under construction in Naboro at the time of writing. In addition, incomes from the resort assist families in paying the Methodist church tithe of FJ$65 a year per household, amounting to approximately FJ$19,500 per year for Wayalailai.

There are also educational benefits. A boarding school for kindergarten and primary school students at Naboro catering to villagers from Wayalailai operates from Monday to Friday, with parents taking turns to cook and provide meals. This also enables parents with young children to work during the week, and have children at home over the weekend. Secondary school students attend school on the mainland or at the neighbouring island of Waya and work part time at the resort to obtain money for school fees, uniforms and textbooks. Other monies have been reinvested in the resort. The original *bures* have been rebuilt, and a new coffee house, café and dormitory have been constructed.

Perceived negative socio-cultural impacts of CBT/CBE

Studies show that tourism can have negative as well as positive impacts on resident communities (Friday, 2003; George, 2004; Martin, 1998), and while villagers in Wayalailai generally feel that tourism has been beneficial, village elders and older staff members expressed concern at the changing behaviour of young men and women in the village. Clans on Wayalailai live a simple, frugal, predominantly subsistence lifestyle, governed by strict codes of conduct and dress. Alcohol consumption is banned in the village, women must wear tops with sleeves (no tee-shirts) covering their elbows, and *sulus* (sarongs), skirts or dresses must reach at least mid-calf. In the evenings men, too, must wear *sulusi*. Shorts or long trousers are not allowed.

With earnings from tourism, some of these expectations are being challenged. New forms of consumption have emerged and traditional authorities are being questioned. Among young workers, for example, alcohol consumption and cigarette smoking have increased, and *yaqona* consumption by many is excessive, to the extent that the resort has implemented policies to regulate consumption due to high levels of absenteeism.

Women are beginning to dye their hair, wear make-up and, when off the island, wear jeans, shorts, tee-shirts, baseball caps and sunglasses, all of which are banned in the village. Although elders and traditional leaders on Wayalailai attribute many of these changes to tourism and backpackers, the extent to which these changes are 'demonstration effects' from tourism, or results of modernisation and increased access to Western consumer goods, or gifts from family who have migrated overseas, is arguable (Scheyvens and Russell, 2010: 20). Village women purchase many of their items of clothing from secondhand stores in towns – e.g. Lautoka or Nadi on the main island of Viti Levu, which import clothes from Australia and New Zealand – so this potentially has more influence on their clothing choices than young backpacker tourists. It may indeed be the case that, as in the Caribbean, 'nontourist influences are more important predictors of ... consumption behaviour' (McElroy and de Albuquerque, 1986: 33). Others have also noted that tourism cannot be the only determinant of cultural change (Berno 1995; Crick 1989; MacNaught, 1982), and that local people are also influenced by examples of Western lifestyles in advertisements, films, television, magazines and such social networking sites as Facebook (Fisher, 2004: 230).

People are now missing church services, some because they have to work at the resorts on Sundays, while others may have consumed too much *yaqona* or alcohol the night before. Such behaviour is considered by elders to be disrespectful, and many fear their culture is slowly being changed by tourism. Furthermore, with better access to education and employment, young men and women are starting to question decisions of their elders at village meetings. Elders consider this to be disrespectful, for young people do not traditionally have the right to speak out or disregard the wishes of their elders.

Indeed, elders also feel that one result of the new source of income from tourism has been the breakdown of the family unit. Today, with both parents working either at the resorts or on the mainland, close family members bring up their children. Children attend secondary school at Waya, or on the mainland, where they board or stay with relatives.

Environmental impacts of CBT

For indigenous Fijians, their relationship with the *vanua* (land) is more than an economic relationship; it is a spiritual association that is a key feature of their individual and collective identity and central to a holistic world view, in which humans are part of, rather than separate from, the land (Ravuvu, 1983: 70). Given their dependency on, and interconnectedness with, the environment, they grow up caring and protecting their *vanua*, abide by the ways of the land (*vakavanua*), and see their community as a key component of their identity (Brison, 2001; Nainoca, 2011). Villagers feel a sense of responsibility and stewardship for their environment, which they value and consider important for their survival. This practice is called *mamaroi* or *maroroya*. As children, growing up in the village, Fijians are taught to take care of their *vanua*, family and resources for the future.

Arguably, tourism development might be having an effect on this relationship. In particular, as the resort expands and community development occurs, evidence from surveys of Wayalailai staff and villages show that environmental impacts are emerging which need to be addressed. Increased numbers of visitors and developments associated with them, e.g. flush toilets and increased waste, have begun to have negative impacts on the environment.

> The increase of tins on the island (from tinned food and beverages), the use of bottled drinks in the bar and careless disposal is causing pollution. We are facing problems like lots of seaweeds and the reef being spoilt by boat anchors and cutting down of trees on Kuata and Wayalailai increase possibility of erosion. It is also hard to cater for water for many people during dry season.
>
> (I. Galo,[4] personal communication, Wayalailai, 2009)

> We have several toilets with septic tanks which are affecting our ocean. Rainy days allow dirty water to flow down to our beautiful sea and this causes bad seaweed to grow.
>
> (R. Vata,[5] personal communication, Wayalailai, 2009)

Deforestation to build the resort and village houses has led to landslides and siltation which has affected the reefs. Sand, coral and volcanic rocks have been removed for construction. Runoff from the overflow of septic tanks has led to increased nutrients in the sea and seaweed growth on rocks surrounding the resorts and villages.

> Damaging of our beautiful corals, affected by the anchors of our boats that take tourists to the reefs.
>
> (J. Nawaqa,[6] personal communication, Wayalailai, 2009)

> Our reef is not as healthy as before (13 years back), could be because of the sunscreen or other kinds of stuff tourists use while swimming.
>
> (M. Nailiva,[7] personal communication, Wayalailai, 2009)

> Washing of clothes, bedsheets, towels everyday, and detergents are washed away in the soil and this will be a problem in the next ten years.
>
> (S. Waqa,[8] personal communication, Wayalailai, 2009)

Although negative impacts have become evident over the last few years and must be addressed, in general, the clans feel that the development of Wayalailai Ecohaven Resort has been successful and has increased pride, self-esteem and status within the larger community of Vuda and other *i-Taukei* provinces in Fiji.

Conclusion

This chapter reviewed research and literature on community-based tourism and the role of tourism in poverty alleviation. Using a case study of Wayalailai Ecotourism Resort in the Yasawa Island Group, it discussed how community-based tourism can provide social and economic benefits to an indigenous community, promote ecotourism and long-term sustainability of the product.

Community-based tourism is supported by the Fiji government for the socio-economic benefits it can bring (Jarvis and Hobman, 2006). However, for tourism to contribute to sustainable development, it must be economically viable, ecologically sensitive and culturally appropriate (Wall, 1997). Hall and Lew (2009: 230) noted that ultimately, the planning and management of tourism impacts is a matter for public policy, although, with increased tourism development and concerns about tourism impacts, tourism businesses must consider the wider social and natural environments within which they operate.

This study indicates that rather than evaluating success solely in financial or economic terms, assessment should also include such cultural dimensions as the ability of indigenous entrepreneurs to balance traditional and business obligations and maintain their status within indigenous and local society. It is, after all, their business. Overall, clan members believe the resort is a success, but place a high level of importance on village development, for example, housing, running water, toilets, payment of church tithes and school fees, increased living standards, and the ability to contribute to traditional obligations and ceremonies. By contrast, profit maximisation, saving and reinvestment in the resort are considered to be of secondary importance. CBT at Wayalailai has provided extensive economic and social benefits for a once marginalised, remote island community, and is an example, of how, with planning and consideration of cultural aspirations, tourism potential for alleviating poverty can have substantial impacts for marginalised communities.

Notes

1 Landowning descent group structure. Several *tokatoka* form a *mataqali*, or clan.
2 *Turaga ni koro* or village headman, Namara village. The *Turaga ni koro* is the keeper of village records and demographic statistics.
3 Resort manager, Waylailai Ecohaven Resort.
4 Wayalailai staff member and Namara villager.
5 Wayalailai staff member and Namara villager.
6 Wayalailai staff member and Namara villager.
7 Wayalailai staff member and Namara villager.
8 Wayalailai staff member and Namara villager.

References

Armstrong, R. (2012) 'An Analysis of the Conditions for Success of Community Based Tourism Enterprises.' *International Centre for Responsible Tourism.* Occasional Paper OP 21(2012): 1–52.

Ashley, C. and Roe, D. (2002) 'Making Tourism Work for the Poor: Strategies and Challenges in Southern Africa.' *Development Southern Africa* 19/1: 61–82.

Ashley, C., Roe, D. and Goodwin, H. (2001) *Pro-poor Tourism Strategies: Making Tourism Work for the Poor. A Review of Experience.* Pro-poor tourism report No. 1. ODI, IIED, CRT.

Ateljevic, I. and Doorne, S. (2004) 'Diseconomies of Scale: A Study of Development Constraints in Small Tourism Firms in Central New Zealand.' *Tourism and Hospitality Research* 5/1: 5–24.

Berno, T. (1995) 'The Socio-cultural and Psychological Effects of Tourism on Indigenous Cultures.' Unpublished PhD thesis, University of Canterbury, Christchurch, New Zealand.

Bleitrach, V. and Foch, A. (2010) 'Lessons Learned from this Issue. Should Tourism be Promoted in Developing Countries?' *Private Sector and Development, Proparco's Magazine* 7, September 2010.

Brison, K.J. (2001) 'Constructing Identity through Ceremonial Language in Rural Fiji.' *Ethnology* 40/4: 309–27.

Britton, S.G. (1982) 'The Political Economy of Tourism in the Third World.' *Annals of Tourism Research* 9: 331–58.

Brohman, J. (1996) 'New Directions in Tourism for Third World Development.' *Annals of Tourism Research* 25/1: 48–70.

Chok, S., Macbeth, J. and Warren, C. (2007) 'Tourism as a Tool for Poverty Alleviation: A Critical Analysis of "Pro-poor Tourism" and Implications for Sustainability.' *Current Issues in Tourism* 10/2–3: 144–65.

Crick, M. (1989) 'Representations of International Tourism in the Social Sciences: Sun, Sex, Sights, Savings and Servility.' *Annual Review of Anthropology* 18: 307–44.

de Kadt, E. (1979) 'Social Planning for Tourism in the Developing Countries.' *Annals of Tourism Research*, January/March: 36–48.

Eccles, G. and Costa, J. (1996) 'Perspectives on Tourism Development.' *International Journal of Contemporary Hospitality Management* 8/7}: 44–51.

Evening, E.S.H. (2000) 'A Case Study of Investigation of the Factors Responsible for Limiting the Marketing Exposure of Small-scale Village-based Tourism Schemes in Fiji.' Unpublished Master's thesis. Lincoln University, Canterbury, New Zealand.

Farrelly, T.A. (2009) *Business va'avanua: Cultural Hybridisation and Indigenous Entrepreneurship in the Bouma National Heritage Park, Fiji.* Unpublished PhD thesis. Massey University, Palmerston North, New Zealand. mro.massey.ac.nz/bit stream/handle/10179/1166/02_whole.pdf?sequence=4 (accessed 4 June 2013).

Fisher, D. (2004) 'The Demonstration Effect Revisited.' *Annals of Tourism Research* 31/2: 428–46.

Foley, D. (2006) 'Does Business Success Make You Any Less Indigenous?' *Indigenous Entrepreneurship*, 241–57. www.swinburne.edu.au/lib/ir/onlineconferences/agse2006/ foley_p241.pdf (accessed 10 January 2013).

Friday, J. (2003) 'Performing Authenticity: The Game of Contemporary Backpacker Tourism (Australia).' Unpublished PhD thesis. Lakehead University, Canada.

Furneaux, C. and Brown, K. (2007) *Indigenous Entrepreneurship: An Analysis of Capital Constraints.* AGSE, 669–82. www.aphref.aph.gov.au_house_committee _atsia_indigenousenterprises_subs_attachmenta33.pdf (accessed 3 January 2013).

George, E.W. (2004) 'Commodifying Local Culture for Tourism Development: The Case of One Rural Community in Atlantic Canada.' Unpublished PhD thesis. University of Guelph.

Gibson, D. (2003) 'More than Smiles: Employee Empowerment Facilitating the Delivery of High Quality Consistent Services in Tourism and Hospitality.' Unpublished Master's thesis. University of the South Pacific, Suva, Fiji.

——(2013a) 'The Cultural Challenges Faced by Indigenous-owned Small Medium Tourism Enterprises (SMTEs) in Fiji. Case Studies from the Yasawa Islands.' *The Journal of Pacific Studies* 32: 106–31.

——(2013b) 'Living in the Moment: Cultural Challenges Faced by Indigenous Owned Budget Resorts in Fiji – Case Studies from Wayalailai, Yasawa Island Group.' Unpublished PhD thesis. Suva: University of the South Pacific.

Gibson, D., Pratt, S. and Movono, A. (2012) 'Tribe Tourism: A Case Study of the Tribewanted Project on Vorovoro, Fiji.' In S. Fullagar, K. Markwell and E. Wilson (eds) *Slow Tourism: Experiences and Mobilities.* Bristol: Channel View, 322–47.

Goodwin, H. (2007) 'Indigenous Tourism and Poverty Reduction.' In R. Butler and T. Hinch (eds) *Tourism and Indigenous Peoples.* Oxford: Butterworth Heinemann, 84–94.

Hailey, J.M. (1985) *Indigenous Business in Fiji.* Honolulu: Pacific Islands Development Programme East-West Centre.

Hall, C.M. and Lew, A.A. (2009) *Understanding and Managing Tourism Impacts: An Integrated Approach.* London: Routledge.

Harrison, D. (ed.) (1998) *Ecotourism and Village-based Tourism: A Policy and Strategy for Fiji.* Suva, Fiji: Government Printer.

——(2008) 'Pro-poor Tourism: A Critique.' *Third World Quarterly* 29/5: 851–68.

Harrison, D. and Brandt, J. (2003) 'Ecotourism in Fiji.' In D. Harrison (ed.) *Pacific Island Tourism*. New York: Cognizant Publications, 139–51.

Jarvis, J. and Hobman, E. (2006) *Flashpackers – Backpackers and Independent Travellers in Fiji 2006*. Melbourne: Tourism Research Unit & National Centre for Australian Studies, Monash University.

Johannesson, G., Skaptadottir, U. and Benediktsson, K. (2003) 'Coping with Social Capital? The Cultural Economy of Tourism in the North.' *Sociologia Ruralis* 43/1: 3–16.

Jones, S. (2005) 'Community-based Ecotourism: The Significance of Social Capital.' *Annals of Tourism Research* 32/2: 303–4.

Joppe, M. (1996) 'Sustainable Community Tourism Development Revisited.' *Tourism Management* 17/7: 475–79.

Kieti, D.M., Jones, E. and Wishitemi, B. (2009) 'Alternative Models of Community Tourism: Balancing Economic Development and the Aspirations of the Poor.' *Tourism Review International* 12: 275–90.

Krishna, I. (2012) 'TLTB Announces Fees Reduction in 2013.' *FijiLive*, 22 October. www.fijilive.com/fijiliive-printstory.Fijilive?48400.Fijilive (accessed 4 December 2012).

Levett, R. and McNally, R. (2003) *A Strategic Environmental Assessment of Fiji's Tourism Development Plan*. www.worldwildlife.org/what/wherewework/coraltriangle/ WWFBinaryitem7758.pdf (accessed 10 June 2013).

Lindsay, N.J. (2005) 'Toward a Cultural Model of Indigenous Entrepreneurial Attitude.' *Academy of Marketing Science Review* 5. www.amsreview.org/articles/lind say05-2005.pdf (accessed 13 January 2013).

Liu, A. and Wall, G. (2006) 'Planning Tourism Employment: A Developing Country Perspective.' *Tourism Management* 27: 159–70.

Macbeth, J., Carson, D. and Northcote, J.K. (2004) 'Social Capital, Tourism and Regional Development: SPCC as a Basis for Innovation and Sustainability.' *Current Issues in Tourism* 7/6: 502–22.

MacNaught, T. (1982) 'Mass Tourism and the Dilemmas of Modernisation in Pacific Island Communities.' *Annals of Tourism Research* 9/3: 359–81.

Martin, B.M. (1998) 'Tourism as a Means of Economic and Sociocultural Adaptation in a Fijian Village.' Unpublished PhD thesis. University of Colorado.

McElroy, J. and de Albuquerque, K. (1986) 'The Tourism Demonstration Effect in the Caribbean.' *Journal of Travel Research* 25/31: 31–34.

Milne, S. (2005) *The Training Needs of South Pacific Tourism SME Owners and Managers 2005*. csrs2.aut.ac.nz/NZTRI/nztrinew/documents/SPTO_Training_Needs _Final_Report.pdf (accessed 10 July 2013).

Ministry of Tourism (2007) *Fiji's Tourism Development Plan 2007–2016*. Department of Tourism, Ministry of Tourism and Environment, Suva.

Mitchell, R.E. (2003) 'Community-based Tourism: Moving from Rhetoric to Practice.' *E-Review of Tourism Research* 1/1: 1–4.

Nainoca, W.U. (2011) 'The Influence of the Fijian Way of Life (bula vakavanua) on Community-based Marine Conservation in Fiji, with a Focus on Social Capital and Traditional Ecological Knowledge.' Unpublished PhD thesis. Massey University, Palmerston North, New Zealand.

Ostram, E. (2000) *Social Capital: A Fad or Fundamental Concept?* Bloomington: Centre for the Study of Institutions, Population and Environmental Change, Indiana University, 172–214. www.exclusion.net/images/pdf/778_latuk_ostrom.pdf (accessed 21 August 2012).

Pretty, J. and Ward, H. (2001) 'Social Capital and the Environment.' *World Development* 29/2: 209–27.

Ravuvu, A.D. (1983) *Vaka i-Taukei: The Fijian Way of Life.* Suva: Institute of Pacific Studies, University of the South Pacific (reprinted 2012).

Roe, D., Goodwin, H. and Ashley, C. (2002) *The Tourism Industry and Poverty Reduction: A Business Primer.* London: Pro-Poor Tourism Briefing No. 2/2002.

Saffu, K. (2003) 'The Role and Impact of Culture on South Pacific Island Entrepreneurs.' *International Journal of Entrepreneurial Behaviour and Research* 9(2): 55–73.

Scheyvens, R. (2002) *Tourism for Development Empowering Communities.* Harlow: Prentice Hall.

——(2009) 'Pro-poor Tourism: Is there Value beyond the Rhetoric?' *Tourism Recreation Research* 34/2: 191–96.

——(2012) *Tourism and Poverty.* Abingdon: Routledge.

Scheyvens, R. and Russell, M. (2010) *Sharing the Riches of Tourism.* Palmerston North: School of People, Environment and Planning, Massey University. www.aid. govt.nz/webfm_send/314 (accessed 31 May 2014).

Simpson, M.C. (2007) 'An Integrated Approach to Assess the Impacts of Tourism on Community Development and Sustainable Livelihoods.' *Community Development Journal* (advance access published 17 October 2007): 1–23.

——(2008) 'Community Benefit Tourism Initiatives – A Conceptual Oxymoron?' *Tourism Management* 29: 1–18.

Sofield, T., Bauer, J., Delacy, T., Lipman, G. and Daugherty, S. (2004) *Sustainable Tourism-Elimination Poverty (ST-EP): An Overview.* Queensland, Australia: CRC for Sustainable Tourism.

Stone, L. (1989) 'Cultural Cross-roads of Community Participation in Development: A Case from Nepal.' *Human Organisation* 48/3: 206–13.

Tosun, C. (2000) 'Limits to Community Participation in the Tourism Development Process in Developing Countries.' *Tourism Management* 21/6: 613–33.

——(2002) 'Host Perceptions of Impacts. A Comparative Tourism Study.' *Annals of Tourism Research* 29/1: 231–53.

UNEP (United Nations Environment Programme) and World Tourism Organization (2012) 'Tourism in the Green Economy – Background Report.' Madrid: UNWTO. www.unep.org/greeneconomy/Portals/88/documents/ger/ger_final_dec_2011/Tourism %20in%20the%20green_economy%20unwto_unep.pdf (accessed 20 September 2012).

UNESCAP (2003) *Poverty Alleviation through Sustainable Tourism Development.* New York: UN. unescap.org/ttdw/Publications/TPTS_pubs/Pub_2265_fulltext.pdf (accessed 23 September 2012).

Urry, J. (2002) *The Tourist Gaze.* Second edn. London: Sage.

Verebalavu-Faletoese, J. and Kuridrani, L. (2006) *Evaluation Report of Ecotourism Projects in Fiji.* Suva, Fiji: Ministry of Tourism.

Wall, G. (1997) 'Is Eco-tourism Sustainable?' *Environmental Management* 24/1: 483–91.

Zhao, W., Brent Ritchie, J.R. and Echtner, C.M. (2011) 'Social Capital and Tourism Entrepreneurship.' *Annals of Tourism Research* 38/4: 1570–93.

8 Tourism and CSR in the Pacific

Regina Scheyvens and Emma Hughes

Introduction

For several decades, academics have criticised the negative impacts of tourism on small island states, and large-scale developments have often been signalled as especially problematic. However, governments of Pacific island countries (PICs), as well as donors and multilateral agencies, also continually promote tourism and encourage investment in the sector, believing that more tourists and foreign exchange will result in direct benefits for their economies and peoples. Indeed, when the global financial crisis emerged, some governments relied on tourism to help them through this difficult time, which is why the Fijian government almost doubled its tourism budget from FJ$12 million in 2008 to FJ$23.5 million for 2009 (*Sydney Morning Herald*, 2009).

Meanwhile, there are increasing calls for tourism businesses to be more socially responsible (Mowforth and Munt, 2009: 198–99). Following pressure from shareholders, tourism watchdog groups, consumers, environmental organisations and host country governments, segments of the industry are changing their practices. Ideally, this could lead to more benefits for the people and environments in which tourism businesses operate. There are concerns, however, that corporate social responsibility (CSR) in tourism is merely a way of businesses avoiding external regulation of their activities, and that the CSR initiatives are no more than window dressing. Hotels, for example, may support a turtle nesting site but deny labour rights to hundreds of employees.

To date, little attention has been paid to CSR in tourism in PICs – a gap this chapter seeks to address. After a general discussion of how CSR fits in with other new approaches to tourism, the motivations of tourism companies engaging in CSR are examined, and the potential benefits and limitations of CSR are discussed. Pacific island examples, particularly from Vanuatu and Fiji, will be utilised. Tourism is important to Pacific island economies, so while acknowledging past criticisms of tourism in the region – several of which have been raised in other chapters of this book – we believe it is vital to find ways to practise tourism in a more sustainable, equitable fashion. In particular, hotel and resort owners, cruise ship operators and tour operators in the Pacific currently cater for most tourists visiting the region, and are in a prime position to further local development by adopting new approaches to tourism.

New approaches to tourism

In the past, a strong alternative tourism movement posited that small-scale, locally owned, community-based and eco-friendly tourism was the way to minimise negative impacts of tourism and enhance benefits for local residents (see e.g. Murphy, 2013; Scheyvens, 2002). Now, however, there are claims that even large-scale, conventional tourism can be planned in a way that is sustainable and contributes significantly to local development. Some such thinking is informed by Weaver's work on 'sustainable mass tourism', which argues that large tourism businesses might be best placed to contribute to more sustainable tourism:

> the same corporations that control the mega-resorts are probably in the best position to effect the transition towards sustainability, relative to their smaller counterparts. This is owing to the critical mass that allows them to allocate significant resources specifically for environmental and social purposes.
>
> (Weaver, 2001: 167)

Others considering how tourism could be practised in a more ethical and sustainable manner have focused on such concepts as 'altruistic' and 'responsible' tourism (Singh, 2002; Goodwin, 2011). Since the 1990s, the literature on pro-poor tourism (PPT) has been especially influential. Proponents of PPT suggest that the poor will benefit more from tourism if we work at a range of scales, including large-scale enterprises, and include the private sector (Mitchell and Ashley, 2010). This purportedly would lead to improvements in local development, better labour practices in hotels and resorts, and stronger linkages between such related sectors as agriculture and fisheries. Work in this area includes examination of tourism value chains, mapping the sale of products and services to tourists back to their origins, and identifying beneficiaries at every stage of the value chain (Mitchell and Phuc, 2007). It is important to note, however, that PPT has been especially criticised for not directly addressing the inequalities so often associated with a neoliberal approach to development (Harrison, 2008; Schilcher, 2007).

PPT is part of the wider debate about CSR, corporate citizenship and the role of the private sector in meeting the Millennium Development Goals (MDGs). In these debates, which cut across sectors, tourism plays a minor role. However, the focus of PPT on changing business behaviour has parallels in CSR and MDG debates, where the emphasis has shifted from short-term 'doing good' to finding win-win situations in which companies can profit by 'doing good' (Ashley and Haysom, 2006: 267).

CSR in tourism: the state of the play

CSR refers to a company's responsiveness to the 'triple bottom line' of financial, social and environmental outcomes, and CSR can clearly be good for business. In the hotel sector this includes: increasing competitive advantage (Inoue and Lee, 2011); establishing legitimacy (Williams, Gill and Ponsford, 2007); building reputation; avoiding the imposition of external regulation (Kalisch, 2002); attracting and retaining employees and customers (Ashley and Haysom, 2006); mitigating risk to the business, and accessing branding, marketing and finance options (Ashley *et al.*, 2007). Although studies on the impact of CSR on company performance show mixed results (Coles *et al.*, 2013), literature on the benefits of CSR in the tourism sector still focus on the advantages to business. By contrast, there is comparatively little consideration of the social and economic impact of CSR on host destinations.

While the tourism sector reportedly lags behind other industries in adopting CSR (Coles *et al.*, 2013), owners of hotels and tour operators are under increasing pressure to embed CSR in their business practices. Tourists are said to want ethical practice in tourism (de Grosbois, 2012; Dodds and Joppe, 2005), and there is an imperative to protect the local environment and culture as part of the tourism 'product' (Kalisch, 2002). Numerous awards, accreditation systems and reporting frameworks are also now available (Dodds and Joppe, 2005), and industry conferences now commonly have such themes as ethical tourism, sustainable tourism and responsible tourism: 'The word "responsible" has taken over this year's World Travel Market. Wherever you turn, "responsible" seems to be the buzzword' (Alcantara, 2008).

Overall, CSR has focused on environmental initiatives in tourism rather than social or economic issues (Ashley and Roe, 2002; Dodds and Joppe, 2009). This is consistent with global concerns over climate change and is reflected in reporting and measurement indices, as environmental initiatives lend themselves more readily to statistical data analysis (Font *et al.*, 2012). In addition to creating a good impression on potential customers, such environmental measures as energy efficiency are popular among businesses because they can save money. Tearfund's research into the business practices of 65 UK-based tourism operators found that while they have made strides in addressing environmental issues, they were less determined than other industries to address social and economic issues (Mowforth and Munt, 2009: 199). The focus on environmental measures might also be influenced by such hotel accreditation schemes as Green Globe, which have environmental actions as their foundation.

While the initial impetus for CSR in tourism emerged from concern for the environment, attention is increasingly on social and economic dimensions (Holcomb *et al.*, 2007) and there are examples of social and cultural audits of CSR practices (Harrison and Campus, 2004). Social and economic support for host communities is highly significant in low-income countries, more so for countries heavily reliant on tourism, especially in small island developing states (SIDS). Indeed, it has been suggested that CSR practices in developing countries commonly have social programmes, which often include health, education and youth development (Levy and Hawkins, 2008). While such social initiatives are hard to quantify and to report, the importance of community engagement is recognised by such tourism organisations as Green Hotelier, and hotel CSR reports are starting to document a range of initiatives from philanthropic donations and disaster relief, to volunteering, training and partnership with community organisations.

Debating the value of CSR in tourism

Clearly, CSR can generate benefits for hotels and tour operators, but the benefits to communities are less obvious. Indeed, some critics suggest that CSR diverts attention away from problems experienced in local communities and environments when big business is in charge:

> The fact that Corporate Responsibility is so popular today is an indication that big business is feeling the heat. But the solutions they advocate and pursue – voluntary unenforced codes of conduct, piecemeal eco-improvements, token philanthropic donations, endless rounds of meaningless 'engagement' with 'stakeholders' who might otherwise be publicly criticising them, dubious but lucrative techno-fixes – are actually dangerous diversions.
> (Worth, 2007: 7, cited in Mowforth and Munt, 2009: 199)

More specifically, the potential for CSR to contribute meaningfully to community development and well-being can be constrained by numerous factors.

- *The limits of self-regulation.* For any tourist corporation, business will always be the primary objective. Corporations are unlikely to prioritise community needs unless it is in their self-interest or they are being subjected to external regulation or pressure. Business and community interests may coincide, as when the community seeks ongoing contributions from the company and the company wishes to minimise conflict. However, except for lease agreements for customary land, agreements and accords are generally voluntary and non-enforceable. This limits what can be achieved in practice. Arguably, 'greenwashing' is common, self-regulation is 'at best questionable and at worst meaningless' (Mowforth and Munt, 2009: 208), and companies sign up to accords as a way of avoiding external regulation. The same authors question whether in fact CSR 'promote[s] genuine change in practices or cosmetic change which serves as good publicity but makes little effective difference' (Mowforth and Munt, 2009: 223).
- *The gap between reporting and practice.* A study examining the operational practices of ten international hotel groups not only found discrepancies

between reporting and practice, but also identified many policies that were simply complying with requirements to meet the legal and economic concerns of stakeholders (Font *et al.*, 2012). In practice, where CSR initiatives are implemented there may be contradictions – as when a company donates to a local school and yet has a poor record in empowerment and human rights, pays low wages, does not remunerate overtime or offer secure contracts, and gives few opportunities for promotion (Beddoe, 2004). It might also fail to detail the impacts or quality of its CSR policies (de Grosbois, 2012; Holcomb *et al.*, 2007; Esrock and Leichty, 1998).

- *Lack of ability to reach the very poor.* CSR strategies, though focusing on 'stakeholders', may exclude the poorest. As Jenkins (2005: 540) points out, '[a]lmost by definition, the poor are those who do not have a stake'. Similarly, Boyle and Boguslaw note that short-term, uncoordinated initiatives are unlikely to benefit the poorest segments of society, as they 'do not change the structures that keep poor people poor' (Boyle and Boguslaw, 2007: 114). Studies attempting to quantify the impact of tourism on poverty reinforce this view, demonstrating that although the poor benefit from tourism, lowest-income households are not the primary beneficiaries (e.g. Blake *et al.*, 2008: 124). Consequently, some authors propose long-term strategies within the private sector, coordinated with government and non-governmental organisations (NGOs), to provide a strong regulatory framework that attracts international support (e.g. Boyle and Boguslaw, 2007; Kasim, 2006; Meyer, 2006; Ashley *et al.*, 2007; Schilcher, 2007).
- *Limits to scale and scope.* Many CSR initiatives are tokenistic. Research from Southern Africa suggests that while tourism corporations are often philanthropic, for example, in seeking guest donations for a community development fund, few are committed to more enduring changes to their business strategies and practices (Ashley and Haysom, 2006). Similarly, as noted above, many companies limit their CSR efforts to environmental initiatives. Overall then, the scope of most CSR initiatives in tourism is limited and makes a relatively small contribution to local well-being. In fact, CSR budgets usually represent a tiny fraction of annual turnover and there may be other ways of achieving greater impact. The South African hotel Spier Leisure, for example, noted that a shift in as little as 10% of procurement to local suppliers would surpass its CSR budget (Ashley and Haysom, 2006: 273).

Ashley and Haysom use Locke's (2002) typology to categorise the different approaches of tourism organisations to CSR along a continuum of minimalist support to stakeholders through to a social activist approach with the intention of catalysing change (Table 8.1). As suggested above, the philanthropic approach of most companies remains minimalist. Rather than arising from a commitment to equity, sustainability and partnership with local communities, their interest in local community development is primarily pragmatic.

CSR in practice: examples from the Pacific

Despite the concerns raised above, CSR in the tourism industry can play a significant role in improving community well-being in PICs. Bradly's (forthcoming) qualitative study of the community investment practices of 42 tourism companies in Fiji, for example, showed that they regularly provided philanthropic donations, volunteers, a range of services and direct funding. Harrison and Prasad (2013) document a range of 'substantial, if largely ad hoc' CSR activities in one of Fiji's key tourist regions, and cite a claim that over the last decade, the Fiji Hotel and Tourism Association raised FJ$5 million for the Coral Coast community (Harrison and Prasad, 2013: 752). Scheyvens's recent fieldwork in Fiji and Vanuatu also provides multiple examples of community benefit.

Meyer's (2006) typology of core and non-core practices with respect to building linkages can usefully be applied to CSR activities: core business practices include employment and training responsibilities, and procurement of food and building supplies, for example, while non-core business practices encompass outsourcing, mentoring, donations and capacity-building activities (Meyer, 2006: 12). Such non-core CSR activities tend to be favoured in promotional material associating hotels with charitable donations (Holcomb *et al.*, 2007), a practice referred to by Esrock and Leichty (1998) as 'good deeds' reporting, but responsibility in core practices often has the potential to establish longer-term benefits and should not be overlooked.

Non-core practices

Community engagement. Resorts can bring significant social and economic benefits to local communities through engaging their services and skills.

Table 8.1 Different approaches to CSR in tourism

Approach to CSR	Examples in the tourism sector
Minimalist	Tokenistic support to stakeholders, e.g. donations of used equipment to neighbouring communities
Philanthropic	Support for conservation and development projects (e.g. donations to local environmental groups, schools and health clinics). Guests are encouraged to donate to specific environmental and/or social development initiatives
Encompassing	Company management style and values reflects a desire to run a more socially responsible business. Partnerships with local communities over the long term ensure the business is not undermining social or environmental well-being and provide ongoing support for local development initiatives and for local businesses (rather than ad hoc donations)
Social activist	Strong philosophical approach that is not based on profit maximisation. Motivation is to catalyse change

Source: Structure based on Locke, 2002, cited in Ashley and Haysom, 2006

Research conducted by Scheyvens in Fiji in 2009–10 and Vanuatu in 2011, shows that CSR can bring a number of economic, social and cultural benefits:

- local craftspeople and musicians are contracted by hotels and resorts to entertain guests, leading to a welcome cash inflow to some households;
- hotels and resorts run village tours or school tours and pay a set fee per head (usually around FJ$5) to the school or to the Village Development Committee, which plans projects for communal benefit, such as village hall construction;
- money donated to schools (which amounted to FJ$4,000 per annum at one Yasawa Islands primary school) is usually used for school equipment, transportation for students, or food for students boarding at the school;
- hotels and resorts sometimes engage in such projects as building and equipping schools or providing rainwater tanks;
- resorts and hotels respond to direct requests from the community, for example, for scholarships, sports equipment and donations to schools or churches. One such example is Octopus Resort in the Yasawa Islands of Fiji, which offered scholarships to students from a neighbouring village to attend secondary school on the mainland;
- resorts and hotels provide assistance to communities during and after natural disasters. In January 2009, for example, after severe floods in Fiji, chefs from a resort cooked food at the evacuation centres for almost three weeks, and the resort's parent company contributed FJ$1 million to help repair the district school.

While much of the assistance indicated above is of a rather piecemeal nature, there are exceptions. At Eratap, a 12-villa boutique resort in Vanuatu, the owners annually give $1 million vatu (about NZ$14,000) to a major community project, decided by villagers at nearby Eratap at a community meeting. Funds are used for major projects that benefit the entire village, for example, improving water supply or upgrading roads. As the resort owner notes:

> You're a little like an economic zone in the middle of nowhere. You're a bit like, you know, how mines all of a sudden open up in a place so remote it's unbelievable, and they create this minor city in the middle of nowhere. Now mining has a negative impact, ultimately on the environment, whereas a resort, if developed correctly, can actually really benefit a place.
>
> (Tony Pittar, owner, 2011)

Joint ventures. Joint ventures involving communities and established hotels or resorts are good examples of CSR. Community-based tourism ventures in which communities have a high degree of control may seem ideal, but in practice many communities lack the skills, resources, experience or networks to engage successfully in tourism and may prefer to work with other stakeholders. Joint ventures are one example of such partnerships, where community resources are used for tourism in exchange for profit sharing, jobs, a share of ownership, and other material benefits from a private-sector partner. They enable communities to gain skills and confidence in dealing with tourists without bearing ultimate responsibility for the effective running of the business. Examples of such voluntary practices are found in Fiji and Vanuatu, while Cook Islands legally requires foreign investors to form a joint venture with a local partner, though this provision is sometimes manipulated in practice.

Business mentoring. Established tourism businesses can also mentor fledgling community enterprises, helping them become established or develop strategies to overcome constraints to business success. Even in Vanuatu, where government has created 'reserved investments' (meaning that only ni-Vanuatu can own small tour operator businesses), it can be incredibly difficult for local owners to partner larger businesses which could provide them with customers (Scheyvens, field research 2011).

In Fiji, examples of mentoring are found at two resorts which helped to establish a community-operated trekking business and a taxi service. In the former, the owner of Uprising Resort and his management team helped nearby villagers establish an adventure tourism business which involved guiding visitors on a rainforest walk to a waterfall, and then boating down a river. The resort provided the necessary health, safety and hospitality training to six guides, young men who were previously unemployed, and also purchased the correct equipment (e.g. boots and life jackets). A village elder noted how these young men had benefited through this venture: 'We are very surprised with the level of skills they have come out with ... It strengthened their communication skills' (Scheyvens, field research, 2009). Uprising also provided expertise in marketing and sales, tapping into their own pool of customers, and planned for the community eventually to take over full management of the enterprise.

In the second case, Sonaisali Resort, owned by an Australian family, helped landowners establish a taxi business, assisting them with their business planning and in negotiating a good price for five new cars. Naisali Taxis was born. It is a rare case of a business owned by *i-Taukei* (indigenous Fijians) and landowners are immensely proud of their achievement. As one *mataqali* (clan) member notes, their success had shown 'that Fijians can excel in business, like our Indian counterparts' (Scheyvens, field research, 2010).

Environmental initiatives. As elsewhere, hotels and resorts in PICs are happy to support a range of environmental initiatives, especially when this saves money. Consequently, energy-efficient lighting, re-use of towels, and recycled grey water are adopted by a wide range of mainstream tourism businesses. In addition, many resorts and hotels contribute to environmental causes, perhaps through supporting a marine protected area or conservation organisation, or contributing to mangrove rehabilitation. Such initiatives benefit everyone in the region who relies on coastal resources. A less common initiative is illustrated by the marine conservation centre of the Shangri-La Fijian Resort, which offers environmental education to guests and local residents, including school children.[1]

Core practices

Procurement. An effective mechanism for widely distributing tourism revenues is through greater procurement of local goods and services by food and accommodation providers. This offers important economic opportunities for poorer members of communities, in particular, who lack capital to establish their own tourist enterprises or skills to find formal sector employment (Ashley and Roe, 1998). In Fiji, when Uprising Resort was being constructed, FJ$20,000 was spent on thatch, which directly benefited three local villages, and locally made furniture, table mats, sun loungers and timber were also purchased (Scheyvens, field research, 2009). More widely, communities also benefit by selling fresh or processed food to hotels and restaurants.

However, there are constraints to such practices. Berno (2006) estimated that approximately FJ$30 million was spent annually on importing food products for hotels that could be grown or produced in Fiji, and she later asserted that mass tourism is the most difficult sector in which to promote 'farm-to-fork' linkages (Berno, 2011: 99). Others suggest that concerns about consistency, quantity, quality and food safety prompt major hotel brands to import up to 80% of their food. By contrast, small- to medium-scale resorts and hotels are more able to use local markets and local suppliers, and some purchase 70% of their food from within Fiji (Scheyvens and Russell, 2010).

In Vanuatu, the situation is similar to Fiji, and it is reported that nearly 28 tonnes of fresh produce was being imported into Vanuatu every week (Mael, 2011). Furthermore, as cruise tourism grows, further opportunities for local producers will be lost. Asked why Carnival Cruises purchased so little local produce in Vanuatu, a manager explained: 'We can't risk non-delivery when there's 2,000 people to feed. And there's a very small window of opportunity for providing supplies, as we're only in port for a short time' (Michael Mihajlov, destinations manager, Carnival Australia, June 2012).

The potential impact of ethical procurement policies is significant enough for Ashley *et al.* (2007: 17) to suggest that 'in some instances, incorporating local enterprises into hotel supply chains supports more households than direct employment'. Ethical issues aside, if there is to be increased procurement of local foods, greater consistency in quantity and quality – and stronger linkages between producers and hotels – are required. Unfortunately, as Milne (2005) notes, tourism's connections with local Pacific economies have weakened over time.

Employment conditions and training. Another core practice in which CSR can lead to significant improvements is employment. This refers not only to access to a job and wages, but also to employment conditions and opportunities for training and progression. The most progressive hotels and resorts implement broad policies that support labour rights and employee well-being (including training, health and retirement schemes), going beyond what is required by law. One major hotel in Fiji, for example, operated a health insurance scheme into which the employer paid FJ$7.50 a week if the employee paid FJ$2.50. Meanwhile, Poppy's on the Lagoon Resort in Vanuatu has an optional education fund for employees, matching employee contributions towards their own education or in support of a selected relative (Scheyvens, field research, 2012).

Hotels wishing to be seen as responsible are responsive to the needs of employees. One such case is the Iririki Resort in Vanuatu, where staff rosters were reduced from six to five days. Employees continued to work a 44-hour week, and their overall pay was unchanged, but there was an immediate boost in staff morale. As Fahad Hayat, a manager, notes: 'working six days a week is hard. They don't see their families much at all. And in Vanuatu they are very family oriented people' (Scheyvens, field research, 2011). It is hoped the change will result in less sick leave being taken and higher productivity. Another distinctive feature of this resort is that 70% of its employees are on permanent contracts (i.e. on one-year or longer contracts). This contrasts with a similar-sized resort in Fiji where less than 30% of staff members (83 of 248 employees) were on permanent contracts. There, most (133 of 248) were on temporary (monthly) contracts, with a few on casual (one-off) contracts. As a receptionist remarked, 'You just look at the monthly roster. If your name doesn't appear you know you just stay home' (Scheyvens, field research, 2009).

Discussion and conclusions: CSR in tourism as a development tool

CSR initiatives can be categorised according to the four approaches shown in Table 8.1: minimalist, philanthropic, encompassing, and social activist. Despite some progress, many tourism companies in PICs engage only at the minimalist or philanthropic level. As noted by several academics (Campling and Rosalie, 2006; Scheyvens and Momsen, 2008), such large corporations have long been criticised for their negative social and environmental impacts and their failure to contribute to sustainable development.

Nevertheless, CSR has the potential to contribute more broadly, particularly when core practices are taken into consideration. Indeed, Telfer and Sharpley take a positive view, arguing that 'these corporations also bring investment funds, know-how, expertise, managerial competence, market penetration and control, and opportunities for local entrepreneurs' (Telfer and Sharpley, 2008: 88). We, too, suggest that tourism corporations can make more than a minimalist contribution to CSR by capitalising on their core strengths, for example, by facilitating economic opportunities via training, good employment practices and fair procurement strategies (Ashley *et al.*, 2007; Porter and Kramer, 2011; Scheyvens, 2011).

Lessons as to how CSR can benefit communities in small island nations can be learned from the Caribbean, where many SIDS are similarly dependent on tourist revenues. There, backward linkages have been established in the supply chain (Dodds and Joppe, 2009), and partnerships created with the community (Meyer, 2006), local producers and farmers (Ashley *et al.*, 2006). The focus here is on both core and non-core business opportunities, and such encompassing initiatives move well beyond a minimalist or philanthropic approach.

In PICs, responsible practices by tourism providers are making significant contributions to community livelihoods and well-being. Resorts such as Octopus provide secondary school scholarships, and Eratap make substantial contributions to a community development fund. Other hotels have training schemes, career structures and insurance policies for their employees. Resorts like Uprising follow a social activist approach in supporting communities through maximising local procurement and encouraging local business development. While clearly positive, however, such developments are not necessarily typical in a highly competitive industry, where long-term strategies to improve ethical business practice can easily be undermined by a short-term need for profit.

More can be done to encourage tourism businesses to adopt encompassing approaches to CSR, which would result in genuine partnerships with local communities. As a consequence, core business activities would be characterised by closer links with local suppliers, improved working conditions and labour rights, more job security and better training, and assistance to local enterprises. Industry associations could encourage best practice by disseminating information, contracting international chefs to run workshops on incorporating local produce into menus, and promoting responsible tourism awards.

For PICs to remain attractive destinations, the impacts of tourism need to be managed. Effective CSR practices can contribute significantly to this process, but at present they are relatively little developed in PICs. Utting (2007) suggests that in an ideal world, CSR would promote social protection, employee rights and empowerment, and wider distribution of benefits. Such a position is at the social activist end of the spectrum and, clearly, substantial improvement in these areas is possible in Fiji and Vanuatu, as well as other PICs. However, businesses are not public-sector institutions or voluntary agencies. As Standing (2007: 2) notes, 'Companies should not be expected to take over governments' responsibility for social policy – the state should set the rules and regulate in the interests of all groups equitably and efficiently'. The state can create an appropriate regulatory environment where tourism companies are encouraged to bring more social benefits to the communities in which they operate (Harrison, 2008; Sofield, 1993). In this way, CSR has a greater potential to reach the poor and support socio-economic development over the long term.

Notes

1 See www.shangrila.com/yanucaisland/fijianresort/about/corporate-social-responsibil ity/ (accessed 8 November 2013).

References

Alcantara, N. (2008) 'New Era Begins in Maldives Amid Challenges, but Tourism is Optimistic.' *World Tourism Directory News*. www.worldtourismdirectory.com/news/ 442/new+era+begins+in+maldives+amid+challenges,+but+tourism+is+optimistic (accessed 11 November 2008).

Ashley, C., de Brine, P., Lehr, A. and Wilde, H. (2007) *The Role of the Tourism Sector in Expanding Economic Opportunity*. John F. Kennedy School of Government, Harvard University.

Ashley, C., Goodwin, H., McNab, D., Scott, M. and Chaves, L. (2006) 'Making Tourism Count for the Local Economy in the Caribbean: Guidelines for Good Practice.' Pro-Poor Tourism Partnership.

Ashley, C. and Haysom, G. (2006) 'From Philanthropy to a Different Way of Doing Business: Strategies and Challenges in Integrating Pro-Poor Approaches into Tourism Business.' *Development Southern Africa* 23(2): 265–80.

Ashley, C. and Roe, D. (1998) *Enhancing Community Involvement in Wildlife Tourism: Issues and Challenges*. IIED Wildlife and Development Series No.11. International Institute for Environment and Development, London.

——(2002) 'Working with the Private Sector on Pro-Poor Tourism.' Opinions and Experience from Two Development Practitioners. ODI.

Beddoe, C. (2004) 'Labour Standards, Social Responsibility and Tourism.' Tourism Concern, UK.

Berno, T. (2006) 'Bridging Sustainable Agriculture and Sustainable Tourism to Enhance Sustainability.' In G. Mudacumura, D. Mebratu and M. Haque (eds) *Sustainable Development Policy and Administration*. New York: Taylor & Francis.

——(2011) 'Sustainability on a Plate: Linking Agriculture and Food in the Fiji Islands Tourism Industry.' In R.M. Torres and J.H. Momsen (eds) *Tourism and Agriculture: New Geographies of Consumption, Production and Rural Restructuring*. London and New York: Routledge.

Blake, A., Arbache, J.S., Sinclair, M.T. and Teles, V. (2008) 'Tourism and Poverty Relief.' *Annals of Tourism Research* 35(1): 107–26.

Boyle, M.E. and Boguslaw, J. (2007) 'Business, Poverty and Corporate Citizenship.' *Journal of Corporate Citizenship* (26): 101–20.

Bradly, A. (2014) 'The business-Case for Community Investment: Evidence from Fiji's Tourism Industry.' *Social Responsibility Journal*, forthcoming: 1–28.

Campling, L. and Rosalie, M. (2006) 'Sustaining Social Development in a Small Island Developing State? The Case of Seychelles.' *Sustainable Development* 14: 115–25.

Coles, T., Fenclova, E. and Dinan, C. (2013) 'Tourism and Corporate Social Responsibility: A Critical Review and Research Agenda.' *Tourism Management Perspectives* 6: 122–41.

de Grosbois, D. (2012) 'Corporate Social Responsibility Reporting by the Global Hotel Industry: Commitment, Initiatives and Performance.' *International Journal of Hospitality Management* 31(3): 896–905.

Dodds, R. and Joppe, M. (2005) *CSR in the Tourism Industry? The Status of and Potential for Certification, Codes of Conduct and Guidelines.* Washington: IFC/World Bank.

——(2009) 'The Demand for, and Participation in Corporate Social Responsibility and Sustainable Tourism – Implications for the Caribbean.' *ARA Journal of Travel Research* 2(1): 1–24.

Esrock, S.L. and Leichty, G.B. (1998) 'Social Responsibility and Corporate Web Pages: Self-Presentation or Agenda-Setting?' *Public Relations Review* 24(3): 305–19.

Font, X., Walmsley, A., Cogotti, S., McCombes, L. and Häusler, N. (2012) 'Corporate Social Responsibility: The Disclosure-Performance Gap.' *Tourism Management* 33: 1544–53.

Goodwin, H. (2011) *Responsible Tourism.* London and New York: Routledge.

Harrison, D. (2008) 'Pro-Poor Tourism: A Critique.' *Third World Quarterly* 29(5): 851–68.

Harrison, D. and Campus, N. (2004) 'Working with the Tourism Industry: A Case Study from Fiji.' *Social Responsibility* 1 (1–2).

Harrison, D. and Prasad, B. (2013) 'The Contribution of Tourism to the Development of Fiji and other Pacific Island Countries.' In C.A. Tisdell (ed.) *Handbook of Tourism Economics: Analysis, New Applications and Case Studies.* Singapore: World Scientific.

Holcomb, J.L., Upchurch, R.S. and Okumus, F. (2007) 'Corporate Social Responsibility: What are Top Hotel Companies Reporting?' *International Journal of Contemporary Hospitality Management* 19(6): 461–75.

Hoti, S., McAleer, M. and Shareef, R. (2005) 'Modelling Country Risk and Uncertainty in Small Island Tourism Economies.' *Tourism Economics* 11(2): 159–83.

Inoue, Y. and Lee, S. (2011) 'Effects of Different Dimensions of Corporate Social Responsibility on Corporate Financial Performance in Tourism-Related Industries.' *Tourism Management* 32(4): 790–804.

Jenkins, R. (2005) 'Globalization, Corporate Social Responsibility and Poverty.' *International Affairs* 81(3): 525–40.

Kalisch, A. (2002) *Corporate Futures: Social Responsibility in the Tourism Industry.* London: Tourism Concern.

Kasim, A. (2006) 'The Need for Business Environmental and Social Responsibility in the Tourism Industry.' *International Journal of Hospitality & Tourism Administration* 7 (1): 1–22.

Levy, S.E. and Hawkins, D.E. (2008) 'Peace through Tourism: Commerce based Principles and Practices.' Paper presented at the Peace through Commerce e-Conference, theme 8: A Perspective from the Tourism Industry. api.ning.com/files/kqj8PjwXzUC0*fJJE6tpasBjQSIwiGMyReuje0glgwbc62zfLfcRGjVW3cPH-h WNkQpR*-iz8YuNrIiGrXPquCDskvCYmEj-/LevyandHawkinsJBESubmission.pdf (accessed 30 October 2009).

Locke, R.M. (2002) 'Note on Corporate Citizenship in a Global Economy.' *Massachusetts Institute of Technology Industrial Performance Center Working Paper.* Cambridge: MIT.

Mael, J.T. (2011) *Vanuatu Domestic Market Study: The Potential Impact of Increased Tourist Numbers on the Domestic Market for Selected Fresh Vegetable Produce.* Rome: Food and Agriculture Organization of the United Nations.

Meyer, D. (2006) *Caribbean Tourism, Local Sourcing and Enterprise Development: Review of the Literature.* London: Pro-Poor Tourism Partnership.

Milne, S. (2005) *The Economic Impact of Tourism in SPTO Member Countries.* Suva: South Pacific Tourism Organisation.

Mitchell, J. and Ashley, C. (2010) *Tourism and Poverty Reduction: Pathways to Prosperity.* London: Earthscan.

Mitchell, J. and Phuc, L.C. (2007) *Final Report on Participatory Tourism Value Chain Analysis in Da Nang, Central Vietnam.* London: Overseas Development Institute.

Mowforth, M. and Munt, I. (2009) *Tourism and Sustainability: Development, Globalisation and New Tourism in the Third World.* London and New York: Routledge.

Murphy, P.E. (2013) *Tourism: A Community Approach.* Vol. 4. London and New York: Routledge.

Porter, M.E. and Kramer, M.R. (2011) 'The Big Idea: Creating Shared Value. How to Reinvent Capitalism – And Unleash a Wave of Innovation and Growth.' *Harvard Business Review* 89(1–2).

Scheyvens, R. (2002) *Tourism for Development: Empowering Communities.* Harlow: Prentice Hall.

——(2011) *Tourism and Poverty.* New York: Routledge.

Scheyvens, R. and Momsen, J. (2008) 'Tourism and Poverty Reduction: Issues for Small Island States.' *Tourism Geographies* 10(1): 22–41.

Scheyvens, R. and Russell, M. (2010) *Sharing the Riches of Tourism: Summary Report – Fiji.* Palmerston North: Massey University.

Schilcher, D. (2007) 'Growth Versus Equity: The Continuum of Pro-poor Tourism and Neoliberal Governance.' *Current Issues in Tourism* 10(2–3): 166–93.

Singh, T.V. (2002) 'Altruistic Tourism: Another Shade of Sustainable Tourism. The Case of Kanda Community.' *Tourism* 50(4): 361–70.

Sofield, T. (1993) 'Indigenous Tourism Development.' *Annals of Tourism Research* 20: 729–50.

Standing, G. (2007) *Decent Workplaces, Self-Regulation and CSR: From Puff to Stuff?* Working Paper 62. New York: United Nations Department of Economic and Social Affairs. www.un.org/esa/desa/papers/2007/wp62_2007.pdf (accessed 10 May 2010).

Sydney Morning Herald (2009) 'Expect Bargain Holiday Deals as Fiji Tourism Slumps.' 12 February. www.smh.com.au/travel/activity/surfing-and-diving/expect-bargain-holiday-deals-as-fiji-tourism-slumps-20090212-85o2.html (accessed 18 October 2013).

Telfer, D.J. and Sharpley, R. (2008) *Tourism and Development in the Developing World.* London: Routledge.

Utting, P. (2007) 'CSR and Equality.' *Third World Quarterly* 28(4): 697–712.

Weaver, D. (2001) 'Mass Tourism and Alternative Tourism in the Caribbean.' In D. Harrison (ed.) *Tourism and the Less Developed World: Issues and Case Studies.* Wallingford: CABI.

Williams, P., Gill, A. and Ponsford, I. (2007) 'Corporate Social Responsibility at Tourism Destinations: Toward a Social License to Operate.' *Tourism Review International* 11: 133–44.

9 The relationship between tourism, the pearl and mother of pearl shell jewellery industries in Fiji

Anand Chand, Suwastika Naidu,
Paul C. Southgate and Theo Simos

Introduction

This chapter examines the relationship between tourism and the round pearl and mother-of-pearl (MOP)[1] shell jewellery industries in Fiji. Since the early 1900s cultured pearls have attracted both women and men the world over. There is particular demand for cultured 'black' pearls, which have become an icon of the Pacific islands. Black pearls are cultured primarily in French Polynesia and the success of this industry, valued at around US$180 million per annum and second only to tourism as an export earner, has encouraged other Pacific nations to begin pearl culture. One of these is Fiji. Since 2000 Fiji has developed a cultured round pearl industry that has rapidly gained a global reputation for producing high-quality cultured pearls with unique colours (Southgate *et al.*, 2008; Anon., 2008). More recently, this industry has diversified and half-pearls (known as *mabé*[2]) are now an additional export product. These pearl products are much in demand in the USA, Japan, Hong Kong, China and the European Union countries. There is also considerable domestic demand for pearls and such related products as MOP shell jewellery in Fiji. This chapter examines the relationship between tourism and the pearl and MOP shell jewellery industries in Fiji.

Souvenirs are an important component of the tourist experience and most tourists take home souvenirs and gifts, including jewellery, as mementos of their visit (Zalatan, 1998; Zauberman *et al.*, 2009; Wilkins, 2011). As Wilkins (2011: 239) mentioned, 'the souvenir is an important component of the tourist experience with most tourists bringing back souvenirs, gifts, jewellery as evidence ... people like to be reminded of special moments in their lives and souvenirs remind them of those special moments'.

At the global level, there is a considerable literature on tourist purchases of souvenirs and handicrafts (see Littrell *et al.*, 1993; Anderson and Littrell, 1996; Kim and Littrell, 2001; Wilkins, 2011). There is also a considerable scientific and 'grey' literature on aspects of pearl cultivation. However, little has been written on the marketing aspect of pearls and MOP shell jewellery. Most of the scientific literature has focused on the biological aspect of pearls and MOP production (e.g. Southgate and Lucas, 2008), and not on the social science or socio-economic aspects of the pearl industry. Literature on the purchase of pearls and MOP shell jewellery by tourists is extremely limited and there are hardly any scholarly journal articles on tourists' purchase of pearls and MOP shell jewellery.

Literature on such topics within the South Pacific is even scarcer. In *The Marketing of Marine Products from the South Pacific*, Philipson (1989) devoted a chapter to the export of raw MOP shells to Japan, South Korea and Taiwan for manufacture of button blanks and jewellery. He also mentioned a Chinese firm in Vanuatu and Fiji that made button blanks from MOP and trochus shells, and suggested there was some opportunity for this activity for South Pacific countries. In addition, he reported high demand for MOP and trochus shells in Asia, and suggested that in the 1900s prices for these commodities had steadily increased, arguing that although MOP from black-lip pearl oysters and trochus shells was used to make buttons, it was more valuable when infused as 'inlay' in wooden handicraft items and furniture. Furthermore, Tisdell (2011) discussed aspects of the making and marketing of MOP shells ornaments in the Oceania region. The *Pearl Oyster Bulletin*[3] published by the Secretariat of the Pacific Community (SPC) in Nouméa, New Caledonia, also periodically presents information on pearls and MOP shells ornaments. However, there is a clear research gap and this chapter adds to our knowledge of pearls and MOP shell jewellery within the context of tourism.

Research methods

This chapter is based on primary base-line empirical research conducted in Fiji between 2010 and 2013 as part of the Pacific Agriculture Research Development Initiative (PARDI), a collaborative project, funded by the Australian government, involving four Australian universities, the SPC and the University of the South Pacific (USP).

Several research methods were used to gather data: document review, structured and semi-structured interviews, and covert participatory research. First, we reviewed the existing literature (journal articles and book chapters) and grey literature, including unpublished reports, documents and bulletin articles. Second, we carried out a preliminary scoping study by interviews to have a better understanding of the pearl and MOP shell jewellery industries. This was conducted primarily through informal interviews with a variety of stakeholders, including eight pearl farmers, officers of the Fiji Fisheries Department, MOP shell jewellery artisans, handicraft makers, wholesalers, retailers and salespersons of round pearls and MOP products. During the preliminary scoping study, the authors also used a covert participatory research method to obtain an idea of the sales techniques used by retailers at the lower end of the market (especially small handicraft sellers) when selling products not made in Fiji. For this purpose, researchers acted as buyers, purchased some items, and talked to salespeople at handicraft stalls and hotel stores to obtain information. The research findings reveal that salespersons, especially at handicraft stalls and flea markets, deliberately lied to buyers and potential buyers; only at such up-market stores as Prouds and Tappoos did salespeople tell the truth about the origin of the pearls they sold.

Once the scoping study was complete, questionnaires were designed and, in the third phase of the study, pearl stakeholders were interviewed to obtain in-depth information about both the pearl and the MOP shell jewellery industries in Fiji.

In the fourth phase of research, 80 tourists were interviewed, through the use of a semi-structured questionnaire, to gather their views on pearls and MOP shell jewellery. Interviews were conducted over a two-year period between January 2011 and December 2013. We used 'convenience' and 'purposive' sampling techniques and selectively interviewed tourists who were

Table 9.1 Locations of interviews, sample size and type of tourists interviewed, January 2011–December 2013

Location of interviews of tourists in Fiji	Distribution of sample/category of tourists	Total number of tourists interviewed
Suva (interviews conducted at handicraft stores, flea markets, at Rock Market, the 'Hibiscus Festival', Fiji Arts Council-organised events and upmarket stores)	Up-market level (luxury) tourists = 5 Middle-level tourists = 5 Lower-bracket tourist =10	20
Pacific Harbour (interviews conducted at handicraft stores and at the Pearl Hotel)	Middle-level tourists = 5	5
Coral Coast (interviews conducted at three hotel stores; Warwick, Novatel Fijian, Fijian Resort)	Up-market level tourists = 5 Middle-level tourists = 5 Lower-bracket tourist = 5	15
Nadi (interviews conducted at handicraft stores, flea market and upmarket store at Sheraton, Sofitel and Port Marina)	Up-market level tourists (luxury and honeymoon) =10 Middle-level tourists = 5 Lower-bracket tourist = 10	25
Savusavu Town (interviews conducted at handicraft stalls and Savusavu airport)	Middle-level tourists = 5 Lower-bracket tourist = 5	10
Lautoka (interviews conducted at handicraft stalls in Lautoka Municipal Market)	Lower-bracket tourist = 5	5
Total	Up-market level tourists = 20 Middle-level tourists = 25 Lower-bracket tourist = 30	80

browsing through and purchasing pearls and MOP shell jewellery at various retail outlets in Fiji. So that there was a wide representation of tourists' views, from backpackers to up-market visitors, interviews were conducted at handicraft stalls and souvenir shops in Suva, Nadi, Lautoka and Savusavu; at souvenir shops in hotels in Pacific Harbour, Baravi, Coral Coast and Nadi; and at such up-market stores as Prouds, Tappoos, Jacks and Jewels. The sample size and location of interviews of tourists are indicated in Table 9.1.

Interviews lasted 10–15 minutes and respondents were asked seven questions:

1 Did they purchase pearls and MOP shell jewellery in Fiji?
2 If they answered yes to question 1, what did they buy?
3 Did they know the country of origin of pearl and MOP items?
4 Would they prefer to buy genuine Fiji-made souvenirs?
5 What kinds of designs in the MOP shell would they prefer that are not currently available in Fiji?
6 Did they feel 'morally' good and 'happy' if they are helping local Fijian people by buying 'Fiji-made' pearls and MOP products?
7 Did they want to purchase souvenirs produced in an 'environmentally friendly' manner?

Table 9.2 Country of origin and gender of tourists interviewed

Country of origin	Gender of tourists interviewed		Total number of tourists interviewed	Total %
	Male	*Female*		
Australia	15	14	29	36.3
New Zealand	9	12	21	26.2
USA	6	5	11	13.7
Japan	7	1	8	10.0
China	3	3	6	7.5
Europe	3	2	5	6.3
Total	43	37	80	100
	(54% of total sample)	(46% of total sample)		

Table 9.3 Age distribution of tourists interviewed

N	Age category (years)	Number of tourists	Percentage (%)
1	18–24	19	23.8
2	25–31	16	20.0
3	32–38	15	18.8
4	39–45	10	12.4
5	46–52	12	15.0
6	53 and above	8	10.0
Total		80	100

Slightly more than one third (36%) of the tourists interviewed were from Australia, a quarter (26%) from New Zealand, 14% from the USA, and 6–10% were from Japan, China and Europe. About 54% of total sample were male tourists and 46% were females. Table 9.2 shows the country of origin and gender distribution of tourists interviewed.

The pearl and MOP shell jewellery industries in the South Pacific and Fiji

Pearls are the South Pacific region's most valuable aquaculture commodity. Production is valued at US$200 million per annum (Southgate *et al.*, 2008) and the region is well known for producing high-quality and high-valued 'black' and rainbow-coloured round pearls and half pearls (*mabé*) (Ponia, 2010). These pearls are cultured in black-lip pearl oysters (*Pinctada margaritifera*[4]), and after the pearl harvest, the oysters are killed and the shells used to make MOP jewellery. However, only a few countries in the South Pacific produce commercial quantities of cultured pearls: French Polynesia, the Cook Islands and Fiji primarily produce round pearls, while Tonga produces only *mabé*.

Historically, MOP shells have been used by artisans globally to make jewellery for sale to locals and tourists. The MOP shells are also used as inlay in wooden handicrafts and furniture, while black-lip MOP shells are much in demand in Asia for making jewellery, buttons, and as inlay in wooden furniture. Indeed, it has been estimated that in the 1990s, around 6,000 tonnes of MOP shells were harvested annually worldwide, of which 1,500 tonnes (25%) originated in South Pacific islands (Southgate *et al.*, 2008), and in 1990 it was suggested that demand for MOP shells generally outstripped supply, thus raising the price of MOP shells as a commodity (Philipson, 1989).

The origins of the pearl farming in Fiji can be traced back to the 1960s, when a Japanese pioneer named Tokito began experiments in pearl cultivation at Gau Island and, later, in Savusavu and in Rakiraki. He married an indigenous Fijian, and at the time of writing (May 2014), he and his two sons were operating a small pearl farm near Rakiraki, a town on the north coast of Viti Levu. In the 1990s, the Fiji government took an initiative to develop a pearl industry in Fiji and this provided a basis for the emergence of other pearl farms. At the time of writing there were eight pearl farms in Fiji: J. Hunter Pearls (Savusavu, Kioa Island), Valili Pearl Company (Wailevu, Savusavu), Paradise Pearl Company (Malake Island, Rakiraki), Tokito Pearl Company, Civa Pearl Company (Taveuni), Peckham Pearl Company (Taveuni), Navatadua Pearl Farm (Raviravi), and Desci Malolo Pearl Company (Namarai, Rakiraki). J. Hunter Pearls is by far the largest pearl farm in Fiji (see Table 9.4). Figure 9.1 shows the geographical location of the eight pearl farms in Fiji.

Table 9.4 provides details of the eight pearl farms in Fiji, including their location, ownership, ethnicity, size and production capacity. J. Hunter Pearls,

Table 9.4 Pearl farms in Fiji: location, ownership, ethnicity and production capacity, 2010–14

Pearl farmers (in order of size)	Location	Ownership/ethnicity	Issues
1 J. Hunter Pearls (largest farm)	Two farms: 1 Savusavu 2 Kioa Island (Buca Bay, Vanua Levu)	Mr Justin Hunter. Part-European and ethnic Fijian-Fiji citizen. Partnership with Taylor Shellfish Company from the USA	– Largest farm in Fiji (started 13 years ago) – Produces 80% of all pearls produced in Fiji – Owns a spat hatchery
2 Valili Pearls (medium-size farm)	Vatulele, Wailevu Bay, Vanua Levu	Ratu Jone Maivalili (ethnic Fijian-Fiji citizen)	– Medium-size farm (started seven years ago) – Produces ~10% of Fiji pearls – Supported by J. Hunter Pearls, e.g. sharing of technicians and auction sale overseas
3 Pearls of Paradise (small farm)	Malake Island, Rakiraki, Viti Levu	Joint venture between Mr Raghu Chowdhary (Indian) and Mr Tim Okatai (Cook Island pearl farmer)	– Small to medium-size farm (started four years ago) – Produces ~5% of Fiji's pearl production – Supported by Cook Island partner
4 Civa Pearls (small farm)	Bouma, Tavenui	Mr Claude-Michel Prevost (Frenchman born in Canada who has lived in Tahiti and has experience of pearl farming in Tahiti)	– Small to medium-size farm (started three years ago and in infant stage) – Produces ~3% of Fiji pearls
5 Tokito Pearls Ltd (small farm)	Nanuyakoto Island, Rakiraki, Viti Levu	Mr Tokito (Japanese, now Fiji citizen) and sons Kenji and Joji (part-Fijian)	– Small farm (pioneer: first farmer in Fiji) – Produces ~1% of round pearl production – Specialises in producing good-quality *mabé* (half-pearl)
6 Peckham Pearls (small farm)	Matei Point, Taveuni	Mr and Mrs Peckham	– Small farm – Produces ~1% of Fiji pearls – Production declining
7 Desci Malolo Pearl Farm (small farm)	Namarai, Rakiraki, Viti Levu	Mr Atilla (from Brisbane, Australia)	– Infant farm, started two years ago – Had problems obtaining oysters – Production slowly growing
8 Navatadua Pearl Farm (very small farm)	Raviravi, Vanua Levu	Co-operative consisting of ethnic Fijian women	– Small farm run by inexperienced women – Produces poor-quality pearls – Production static

Source: Tabulated from primary research data by Chand, Naidu, Southgate and Simos, 2010–14

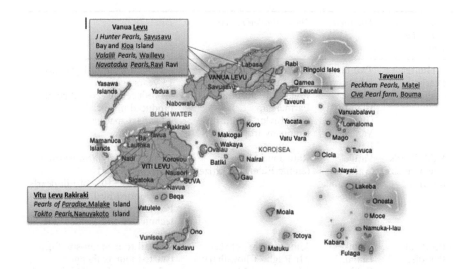

Figure 9.1 Geographical location of eight pearl farms in Fiji
Source: Locations based on primary research by Chand, Naidu, Southgate and Simos, 2010–14

located in Savusavu, is the largest pearl farm and accounts for 80% of cultured round pearls produced in Fiji. Established in 2000, this company is in partnership with the Taylor Shellfish Company of the USA and has an international reputation for high-quality pearls. In 2005, the brand name 'Fiji Pearls' was created by J. Hunter Pearls. The Valili Pearl farm, located in Savusavu is the second largest farm and is owned by Jone Maivalili, an ethnic Fijian chief, a short distance from J. Hunter Pearl farm. Paradise Pearl farm at Malake Island (Rakiraki), is the third largest and is a joint venture between Raghu Chowdhary (an Indian citizen) and Tim Okatai, a Cook Island pearl farmer. Tokito Pearl farm is located in Nanuyakoto Island (Rakiraki) and is owned by Tokito, the Japanese pearl pioneer, who is now a Fiji citizen. The farm is managed by him and his two sons, Kenji and Joji (part-ethnic Fijians). Civa Pearl farm is located in Taveuni Island and is owned by Claude-Michel Prevost, a French Canadian, who has lived in Tahiti, where he experienced pearl farming. Peckham Pearl, in Taveuni, is owned by Tom Peckham, while Desci Malolo Pearl farm, located in Namarai (Rakiraki), is owned by a pharmacist from Brisbane, Australia. Finally, the Navatadua Pearl farm is located in Raviravi (near Labasa) and operates as a cooperative, employing about ten ethnic Fijian women.

Table 9.5 Types of round pearl and MOP shell jewellery available in Fiji and country of origin

Types of round pearl and MOP shell jewellery available in Fiji	Country of origin
1 High-quality, expensive *Fiji-made* round *black* pearls and *mabé*	Fiji
2 High-quality, expensive *Pacific* cultivated round *black* pearls	Tahiti, Cook Islands
3 High-quality, expensive *imported* round *white* pearls	China, Indonesia, Philippines, Japan and Taiwan
4 Low-quality, cheap *imported* round *white* pearls	China, Indonesia, Philippines
5 Low-quality, cheap *imported* round *dyed white* pearls	China, Indonesia, Philippines
6 Low-quality, cheap *imported white* MOP shell jewellery	China, Indonesia, Philippines
7 Low-quality, cheap *imported black* MOP shell jewellery	Indonesia, Philippines
8 *Fiji-made*, cheap MOP *black* shell jewellery	Fiji

Table 9.6 Cultured *Fiji-made* pearls and their value in Fiji

Fiji-made round pearl products	Price range in FJ$ (depending on quality/grade/gold/silver chain/with diamond setting of pearls)
1 Pearl necklace strands (40–50 pearls in each strand)	$10,000–$80,000 (depending on quality and grade of pearls)
2 *Keshi*[1] necklaces (40–50 pearls)	$5,000–$10,000 (depending on quality and grade of pearls)
3 *Mabé* (half-pearl to one *mabé* pearl in gold or silver ring/chain, some with diamond setting)	$300–$1,000 (depending on quality and grade of pearls)
4 Pearl chains (one pearl in gold or silver chain, some with diamond setting)	$200–$2,000 (depending on quality and grade of pearls)
5 Pearl bracelets (10–15 pearls in each strand)	$200–$1,000 (depending on quality and grade of pearls)
6 Pearl earrings (one set of two pieces)	$100–$500 (depending on quality and grade of pearls)

Source: Tabulated from data of primary research by Chand and Naidu, 2010–14
Note: [1] *Keshi* pearls are non-nucleated pearls that are generally smaller than cultured round pearls.

Round pearl and MOP shell jewellery available in Fiji

Table 9.5 shows the types of pearl and MOP shell jewellery available in Fiji and the items' country of origin. The various pearl and MOP products and their price ranges in Fiji are shown in Tables 9.6 and 9.7, respectively.

Methods of selling pearls and MOP shell jewellery: research findings from salespersons

Sale via auctions

Pearl companies in Fiji use several methods to sell 'Fiji-made' pearls. The first method is selling at pearl auctions in Japan and Hong Kong. Three companies – J. Hunter Pearls (Savusavu), Valili Pearls (Savusavu), and Pearls of Paradise (Rakiraki) – sell their best high-quality pearls (gem and 'A'-grade pearls) at annual pearl auctions in Japan and Hong Kong. Since 2013, J. Hunter Pearls has also sold good-quality pearls to a company in Germany, while Pearls of Paradise also sells some 'A'-grade pearls at auctions in Japan, Hong Kong and mainland China, but in relatively small quantities.

Sale at up-market stores in luxury hotels and resorts

The second method of selling 'A'- and 'B'-grade pearls is through up-market retail stores (such as Prouds, Tappoos, Jacks and Jewels) in luxury hotels and resorts. Two pearl farmers have exclusive contracts with two up-market stores: J. Hunter Pearls has an exclusive contract with Prouds, and Pearls of Paradise has a contract with Tappoos Ltd, Jacks Ltd and Jewels Fiji Ltd. These four up-market retail stores also import black pearls from Tahiti and the Cook Islands and good-quality, round *freshwater white* pearls (which are not produced in Fiji) from Asia (China, Japan, the Philippines and Indonesia) to supplement their range of pearl products to sell to tourists.

Table 9.7 MOP shell jewellery and its value in Fiji

	MOP products/items	Average retail price (FJ$)
1	MOP *white and black* shell chains (one small shell piece and string)	$5–$10
2	MOP *black* shell chains (big shell piece and string, Fiji-made)	$20–$50
3	MOP *white and black* shell necklaces (3–5 small shell pieces)	$10–$15
4	MOP *white and black* bracelets (5–10 small shell pieces)	$5–$10
5	MOP *white and black* shell earrings (2 small shells pieces)	$5–$10
6	MOP *black* shell *Magimagi* (Fijian ladies' belt, Fiji-made)	$20–$50

Source: Tabulated from data of primary research by Chand and Naidu, 2010–14

Sale at up-market stores in cities and towns

The third method of selling 'A'-, 'B'- and 'C'-grade pearls is through such up-market retail stores as Prouds, Tappoos, Jacks and Jewels in cities and towns. Pearl farmers also sell pearls to tourists direct from the farm, especially to yacht tourists and those on farm tours in Savusavu.

Sale at low-market end (e.g. handicraft stalls, flea markets)

Low-quality imported pearls and MOP shell jewellery are sold by handicraft stalls, flea markets, and by Fijian women entrepreneurs at hotels and resorts. These retailers sell cheap, low-quality, round white, as well as dyed black pearls and MOP shell jewellery to tourists and locals. The retailers purchase such items from five wholesalers who import them from China, Indonesia and the Philippines, buying them for between FJ$0.50 to $5.00 and selling them from FJ$2.00 to FJ$20.00.

Buyers of pearl and MOP shell jewellery: research findings from salespersons

Interviews with salespersons at handicraft stores and retail stores over the period July 2010–March 2014 revealed that tourists are the major buyers of round pearls and MOP shell jewellery in Fiji. Locals usually buy inexpensive 'B'-grade and low-quality pearls and MOP shell jewellery. Table 9.8 shows the segmentation of the tourist buyers.

Tourists in Fiji have the opportunity to buy across four ranges of pearl and MOP shell jewellery, as described in Table 9.8. The table shows that wealthy 'up-market tourists or business people' buy expensive, good-quality *black* and *white* round pearls, while 'middle-income tourists' buy semi-expensive pearls, and 'budget-range tourists' and 'lower-end tourists' were more inclined to buy cheap, non-genuine pearls and MOP shell jewellery, rather than expensive items.

Chinese and Japanese buyers

Interviews with salespersons in various up-market stores and luxury hotels revealed that the major buyers of high-quality, expensive round *black* pearls are Asians and Europeans. Within the Asian category, the Chinese and Japanese are the main buyers, and most are business people rather than holi-daymakers. They usually purchase high-quality, expensive round black pearl strands (worth FJ$10,000–$80,000), and jewellery such as rings and chains with gold, diamond and silver settings (price range FJ$2,000–$10,000). It is noteworthy that the Chinese and Japanese do not buy high-quality, expensive round white pearls because they are easily available in China and Japan. According to a sales assistant at Prouds in Port Denarau:

Table 9.8 Market segmentation of tourists who buy pearl and MOP shell jewellery

No.	Class of tourists	Where tourists buy from	Price range
1	Up-market tourists/ business people (5–6-star hotels/ resorts), e.g. Sheraton, Denarau, etc.	– Buy from up-market department stores in 5–6-star hotels/resorts and major cities (e.g. from Prouds, Tappoos, Jacks, Jewels stores) – Buy from Prouds, Tappoos, Jewels stores. Yacht tourists buy directly from pearl farmers in Savusavu and Tavueni	Price range FJ\$5,000–\$80,000 (for strand of 40–50 pearls)
2	Middle-range tourists/cruise ships (3–4-star hotels/ resorts/cruise ships)	Buy from department stores in the hotels and cities	Price range FJ\$500–\$5,000
3	Budget-range tourists (1–2-star hotels, motels)	Buy from handicraft stores/stalls of Fijian ladies in hotels, stores in cities/towns, handicraft stalls/market, etc.	Price range FJ\$10–\$200. They buy low-priced pearls and MOP shell jewellery
4	Lower-end/ backpacker tourists	Buy from handicraft stores in cities/towns and handicraft stalls/flea market. Buy cheap, low-grade imported pearl items	Price range FJ\$5–\$20. They buy low-priced, non-genuine pearls and MOP shell jewellery

Source: Created by authors from primary empirical research data, collected 2010–14

> I work in the pearl jewellery section of the shop and the Chinese and Japanese are the biggest buyers of good quality expensive *black* pearls. They usually buy the whole strand of necklace and not single pieces of *black* pearls. They hardly buy *white* pearls.
> (Interview with Sarita Devi, Prouds Store in Port Denarau, December 2013)

While we were carrying out research in Suva, the few Chinese buyers we met were unwilling to explain why they purchased black pearls. However, we were able to interview three Chinese academics at the University of the South Pacific and their responses were instructive. One noted:

> Most of the Chinese buyers who buy pearls in Fiji are jewellers and it is hard to find 'A' quality expensive *black* pearls in China and there is a big demand for the black pearls. So the Chinese jewellers visit Fiji to buy a whole strand with 50 pearls for say US\$10,000 and take them to China and dismantle the strand and make 50 individual necklaces, chains and sell each item for US\$2,000 and hence making a good profit.
> (Interview at the University of the South Pacific, March 2014)

She also suggested that in Chinese culture, black pearls are supposed to bring 'good luck' to people, and so most Chinese people keep black pearls at home, while others wear them as jewellery.

European buyers

Rich and middle-income Europeans are also major buyers of high-quality, expensive round black pearls. They also purchase high-quality white round pearls imported from Indonesia, the Philippines, Japan, and Taiwan and China, while their less wealthy compatriots, the 'budget-range tourists' and 'lower-end tourists', were more inclined to buy cheap, non-genuine pearls and MOP shell jewellery rather than expensive items. By contrast, the honeymoon couple getting married in Fiji would also buy expensive black or white pearl jewellery during their stay.

Table 9.9 Responses from interviews of 80 tourists in Fiji, January 2011– December 2013

	Yes		No	
	Number	*%*	*Number*	*%*
Q1 Did they purchase any pearls and MOP shell jewellery in Fiji?	71	88.8	9	11.2
Q2 If yes to question 1, what did they buy?	23 = Pearls	28.6	n/a	n/a
	48 = MOP items	71.4	n/a	n/a
Q3 Did they know the 'country of origin' of pearl and MOP items?	13	16.3	67	83.7
Q4 Would they prefer to buy genuine 'Fiji- made' souvenirs?	74	92.5	6	7.5
Q5 What kinds of designs in the MOP shell would they prefer which are currently not available in Fiji?	72 = Genuine traditional Fijian designs	90.0	8 = Any designs	10.0
Q6 Did they feel 'morally' good and 'happy' if they were helping local Fijian people by buying 'Fiji-made' pearls and MOP products?	63	78.8	17	21.2
Q7 Did they want to purchase souvenirs that had been produced in an 'environmentally friendly' manner?	67	83.8	13	16.2

Source: Interviews of 80 tourists in Fiji, January 2011–December 2013

Research findings from 80 tourists

The following section details the responses of 80 tourists to questions they were asked over the period January 2011–December 2013 (see Table 9.9).

Of the respondents, 71 (88.8%) had purchased pearls and MOP shell jewellery in Fiji and only 9 (11.2%) had not purchased any such items. More specifically, 23 (28.6%) had purchased pearls and 48 (71.4%) had purchased MOP shell jewellery. However, 67 (83.7%) did not know the country of origin of the pearl and MOP shell jewellery, even though 74 (92.5%) said they preferred to purchase 'Fiji-made' souvenirs and 90% expressed a preference for items with genuine 'traditional Fijian' designs. Interviews also revealed that tourists preferred gifts and souvenirs that captured unique designs of traditional and modern Fijian culture and environment, and wealthier tourists in luxury hotels and resorts expressed themselves willing to pay higher prices for authentic Fiji-made pearls, MOP shell jewellery and souvenirs.

One tourist from the USA commented:

> I travel a lot in the Pacific and I like genuine traditional Pacific island designs. When I am in Fiji, I want to buy gifts which have unique and traditional features of Fiji.
>
> (Interview, June 2013)

Some 63 (78.8%) professed to feel good about helping local people by buying souvenirs and expressed a willingness to spend FJ$10–$40 on locally made jewellery and souvenirs. As an Australian tourist commented:

> I want to buy Fijian souvenirs and gifts and not those that are imported from Asia. I want to spend my money to help Fijian people and prefer to buy souvenirs that are *made by local people*. I feel *morally satisfied* by doing this.
>
> (Interview, January 2013, emphasis added)

Finally, 63 (83.8%) of respondent tourists stated they preferred to purchase souvenirs that had been produced in an 'environmentally friendly' manner. An Australian cruise ship visitor commented:

> My wife and I come to Fiji on the cruise boat at least once a year and we love to see nice clean sea. We want to buy pearls that are cultivated in a nice clean environment. Fiji has a cleaner environment compared to Asia and this needs to be maintained.
>
> (Interview, July 2013)

This clean 'Fiji image' helps in the sale of Fiji pearls and MOP shell jewellery. Tours of pearl farms are offered by several companies, including J. Hunter Pearls in Savusavu (Vanua Levu) and Pearls of Paradise in Malake Island off

Rakiraki (Viti Levu). During these tours, tourists see for themselves how pearls are cultivated and learn about the production and cultivation process, and when the tour is over they can purchase round pearls and MOP shell jewellery at discounted prices from the farm's showroom. According to Southgate and Lucas (2008), pearl production in Fiji has had very little impact on the environment. As he notes, 'all eight pearl farms in Fiji are located in a pristine clean environment and they have no deleterious impact on the Fijian eco-system', adding that, 'the impact of pearl farms on the environment is almost negligible when properly managed' (Southgate and Lucas, 2008: 2).

Tourism and economic impact of pearl production and MOP shell jewellery industries

Tourism impacts positively on the pearl and MOP jewellery industries in several ways. First, by purchasing such items, tourists contribute financially to Fiji's gross domestic product (GDP) and its foreign exchange. There are no data from the Bureau of Statistics but, on the basis of their research, the authors estimate that the pearl and MOP shell jewellery industries contribute around FJ$12.0 million to the Fijian economy.[5] Of this total, round pearls contribute approximately FJ$7.0 million and MOP shell jewellery contributes around FJ$5.0 million.

Second, the pearl and MOP jewellery industries help create employment. Official government data on employment in the pearl and MOP jewellery industries are similarly scarce, but from our interviews with pearl stakeholders we estimate that around 1,130 Fijians are employed in the two industries (Table 9.10).

Employment is both formal and informal. Most of it is permanent, except for 16 farm employees recruited during pearl-harvesting season (once a year) and men and women who fish on a part-time, informal basis, only collecting MOP shells from the sea if they come across them. In addition, handicraft workers and employees sell all types of handicrafts and do not focus exclusively on pearls and MOP shell jewellery.

Table 9.10 Employment in the pearl and MOP shell jewellery industry in Fiji

Types of jobs	Number
1 Handicraft artisans and their employees	371
2 Pearl farm employees (eight farms x average of ten employees)	80
3 Fijian women retailers in flea market and hotels	200
4 Importers and wholesalers of MOP shell jewellery and their employees	30
5 Retailers and salesperson in small souvenir stores	100
6 Salespersons in up-market stores in cities/towns/hotels/resorts	299
7 Fishermen and women who collect MOP shells	50
Total	1,130

Source: Primary empirical research data collected, 2010–14

A statement by a Nadi handicraft manufacturer and retailer captures this point:

> I have a handicraft stall at the Nadi Handicraft Centre in Nadi town and I employ five people full time in my company. Four people are employed for making handicraft (including MOP shells) and one person helps with the selling of the handicraft at my stall. I also employ one more sales boy to help me during the busy times when most tourists come to Fiji.
>
> (Interview with Mr Mohammed Niaz, October 2013)

Third, the pearl and MOP shell jewellery industries have provided earning opportunities for poor Fijian woman in villages near hotels and resorts, where they can sell MOP shell jewellery and other handicrafts, thus supplementing their income from farming and cash crops.

In particular, tourist purchases of pearls and MOP shell jewellery provide income to (largely indigenous Fijian) shell collectors, artisans, handicraft wholesalers and retailers. As a Fijian woman from Savusavu said:

> I have been selling shell jewellery to tourists for the last ten years at Savusavu airport and I am able to make $120 per week. This income is important for my family. My husband died few years ago and this money helps me to survive and send my three daughters to school.
>
> (Interview with Mere, December 2013)

Those residing near the eight pearl farms in rural areas have an opportunity to earn some cash. For example, if we assume that two people work at the same farm, then they earn combined wages of approximately FJ$200 per week, which is enough to feed a family (interview with a farm worker in Savusavu, December 2013). Furthermore, workers' wages are fed back into the economy as they are also consumers.

Conclusions and scope for future research

This chapter has examined the relationship between tourism and the round pearl and MOP shell jewellery industries in Fiji, and highlighted the considerable benefits tourism brings to these industries. It has established that the main buyers of expensive round black pearls are Asians (Japanese and Chinese) and rich tourists from the USA, Europe, Australia and New Zealand. Tourists at the lower end of the market (such as backpackers and others) are more inclined to buy cheap, non-genuine pearls and MOP shell jewellery.

It has been argued that the pearl industry contributes to the Fijian economy through increasing the GDP and foreign exchange earnings, and by providing employment and income. Furthermore, tourists prefer genuine 'Fiji-made' pearls and MOP shell jewellery to those imported from Asia. Since 2013, the Fiji government (through the Ministry of Trade and Commerce) has embarked on a policy to promote 'Fiji-made' products (including jewellery) so that the country imports less from overseas. However, a major problem is that local production of MOP shell jewellery is insufficient to meet market demand. Fiji will thus need to continue to import cheap handicrafts, including pearls and MOP shell jewellery, to meet the demand from less high-spending tourists, and its cultivated upper-grade round black pearls will continue to face competition from imported *black* pearls from Tahiti, the Cook Islands, Indonesia, the Philippines and China.

Although there has been a considerable volume of research undertaken on the topic of souvenirs and the types of souvenirs purchased, further research is needed on souvenir purchases related to pearls and MOP shell jewellery. As indicated at the beginning of this chapter, there is a dearth of scholarly journal articles on this topic. We need a better understanding of the relationship between tourism and the cultured pearl and the MOP shell jewellery industries, to assess more accurately tourist preferences for pearl-related items, to target production more efficiently, and thus to increase the benefits these bring to the economy of Fiji.

Notes

1 We are examining two different products. The first is cultured round pearls and the second is MOP shell jewellery. Pearls are cultured in black-lip pearl oysters, the shells of which are lined with MOP. After the final harvest of pearls, oysters are killed and the shells (bi-product) are used to make jewellery. MOP shells collected from the ocean are also used by Fijian women and men to make jewellery for the tourist market.
2 *Mabé* is a Japanese word for a half-pearl.
3 See www.spc.int/coastfish/en/publications/bulletins/pearl-oyster.html.
4 *Pinctada margaritifera* is the scientific name for black-lip pearl oysters.
5 These are crude estimates, based on information provided by stakeholders in the pearl industry and MOP jewellery industries.

References

Anderson, L. and Littrell, M.A. (1996) 'Group Profiles of Women as Tourists and Purchasers of Souvenirs.' *Family and Consumer Sciences Research Journal* 25(1): 28–55.

Anon. (2008) 'Justin Hunter and Pearls Fiji.' *Pearl World: The International Pearling Journal* 16(4): 10–15.

Chand, A. and Naidu, S. (2010–14) *Data from Primary Research on Fiji Pearl and MOP Shell Jewellery Industries.*

Chand, A., Naidu, S., Southgate, P. and Simos, T. (2010–14) *Data from Primary Research on Fiji Pearl and MOP Shell Jewellery Industries.*

Hambrey Consulting (2011) *Opportunities for the Development of the Pacific Islands Mariculture Sector.* Report prepared for the Secretariat of Pacific Community (SPC), Suva, Fiji. November.

Hammersley, M. and Atkinson, P. (1983) *Ethnography: Principles in Practice.* London: Tavistock.

Kim, S. and Littrell, M.A. (2001) 'Souvenir Buying Intentions for Self-versus Others.' *Annals of Tourism Research* 28(3): 638–57.

Littrell, M.A., Anderson, L.F. and Brown, P.J. (1993) 'What Makes a Craft Souvenir Authentic?' *Annals of Tourism Research* 20: 197–215.

www.motibhai.com/prouds.html (accessed 6 May 2014).

Philipson, P.W. (ed.) (1989) *The Marketing of Marine Products from the South Pacific.* Suva: The Institute of Pacific Studies, USP.

Ponia, B. (2010) *A Review of Aquaculture in the Pacific Islands 1998–2007: Tracking a Decade of Progress through of Fiscal and Provisional Statistics.* New Caledonia: Secretariat of Pacific Community. www.spc.int/DigitalLibrary/Doc/FAME/Reports/ Ponia_10_AquacultureReview (accessed 27 September 2013).

The South Pacific Commission (2000) *Pearl Oyster Bulletin, Various Years: 1990–2014.* Suva, Fiji.

Southgate, P.C. and Lucas, J.S. (eds) (2008) *The Pearl Oyster.* Oxford: Elsevier, 303–55.

Southgate, P.C., Strack, E., Hart, A., Wada, K.T., Monteforte, M., Carino, M., Langy, S., Lo, C., Acosta-Salmon, H. and Wang, A. (2008) 'Exploitation and Culture of Major Commercial Species.' In P.C. Southgate and J.S. Lucas (eds) *The Pearl Oyster.* Oxford: Elsevier, 303–55.

www.tappoo-group.com/tappoo.html (accessed 6 May 2014).

Tisdell, C. and Poirine, B. (2008) 'Economics of Pearl Farming.' In P.C. Southgate and J.S. Lucas (eds) *The Pearl Oyster.* Oxford: Elsevier, 473–96.

——(2011) 'Environmental Governance, Globalisation and Economic Performance.' In J. Aurifeille, C. Medlin, C. Tisdell, J. Lafuente and J. Aluja (eds) *Globalisation, Governance and Ethics. New Managerial and Economic Insights.* USA: Nova Science Publishers.

Wilkins, H.C. (2011) 'Souvenirs: What and Why we Buy.' *Journal of Travel Research* 50(3): 239–47.

Zalatan, A. (1998) 'Wives' Involvement in Tourism Decision Processes.' *Annals of Tourism Research* 25(4): 890–903.

Zauberman, G., Ratner, R.K. and Kim, B.K. (2009) 'Memories as Assets: Strategic Memory Protection in Choice over Time.' *Journal of Consumer Research* 35(5): 715–28.

10 Linkages between tourism and agriculture

Stakeholder perspectives and online marketing and promotion on the Island of Niue in the South Pacific

Evangeline Singh, Simon Milne and John Hull

Introduction

The economy of Niue, like most economies of South Pacific small island developing states (SIDS), mainly consists of the traditional agriculture sector and tourism industry (Prasad, 2003; SIDSNET, 2007). The agriculture sector, which supports 85% of the population in Niue and other SIDS in the region for subsistence, employment or income, has steadily declined in its ability to generate revenue, provide subsistence income and sustain economic growth (Prasad, 2003; Barker, 2000; SIDSNET, 2007).

The development of closer links between agriculture and tourism is critical to ensure that they develop sustainably, especially when the former has been struggling to sustain economic growth in many island nations (Harrison, 2004; Mason and Milne, 2006). SIDS governments and aid donors in the Pacific are committed to promoting sustainable tourism in the region. The push for sustainable forms of tourism by these stakeholders reflects their intentions to create niche products rather than the usual 'sun, sand and sea' types of mass tourism which are being offered by many Pacific SIDS (Black and King, 2002; Harrison, 2004). The development of linkages between the tourism industry and agriculture sectors has the potential to sustain future development and increase income for local communities.

The strength of linkages between tourism and agriculture is influenced by factors related to demand, supply, production and marketing (Belisle, 1983; Torres, 2003). The already existing market for local food and culture provides Pacific SIDS with the opportunity to expand both their agricultural and tourism industries in order to achieve sustainable development. According to the Niue Visitor Departure Survey, in particular, for returning Niueans there is a desire to connect to their cultural roots – something that they look for when they visit Niue with their spouses and children (Milne and Singh, 2008). Returning Niueans are especially eager to experience village-, food- and agriculture-related experiences during their time spent on the island – something that is especially important for the young returning Niueans who are enthusiastic to eat local food and participate in activities that help them experience a village lifestyle. Although linkages between agriculture and tourism have the ability to sustain resources for future social, economic and ecological benefits (Busby and Rendle, 2000; International Agricultural Research Centre, 2005; Flyman, 2003), the linkage concept has not been exploited much in Pacific SIDS.

Linkages between tourism and agriculture largely fail to emerge for a number of reasons: imported food is cheaper than local produce, hotels accept an opportunity cost to ensure superior quality and regularity of supply, and tourism operators are not fully aware of the type and quantity of locally grown produce (Brohman, 1996; Sims, 2009; Telfer and Wall, 1996). Also, tourists' preferences or at least their perceived preferences for 'international' food may further limit the linkages between tourism and agriculture (Pratt, 2013). Sometimes local farmers do not want to change their traditional crop production because they lack information on the types and quantities of food needed by the tourism industry, are unable to maintain regular supplies, and/or they feel inhibited from dealing with small and medium-sized tourism enterprises (SMTEs) (Belisle, 1983; Berno and Oliver, 2010; Brohman, 1996; Telfer and Wall, 1996). Also, linkages might be severed through loss of networks due to a change in such key personnel as a resort manager or executive chef, who may have been employed by the resort only on a short-term contract (Pratt, 2013).

Tourism has the potential to stimulate demand in other economic sectors, such as agriculture, so it is important that linkages are created between them. If the benefits of tourism are to be distributed through the local communities, strong linkages between the industry and the agriculture sector need to be developed; these linkages would also assist in reducing the economic dependence of Pacific SIDS on imports (Torres, 2002). Enhancing the linkages between tourism and agriculture represents an important potential mechanism to stimulate and strengthen the traditional local agricultural sector and to improve the distribution of the benefits of tourism to rural people (Burnett, 2007; Mason and Milne, 2006).

Closer linkages with the tourism industry provide opportunities for niche markets, which have always remained a key challenge for sustainable agriculture (Mason and Milne, 2006; Torres, 2003). According to the Niue Visitor Departure Survey, the average Niuean visitor is highly educated, relatively wealthy and has a thirst for 'unique and local' experiences that revolve around local agriculture, food- and village-related activities, in order to get a 'sense of place' (Milne and Singh, 2008). The interaction of visitors and host communities provides mutual experiential benefits. By developing an appreciation of local communities and their customs and traditions, a process of mutual respect and understanding between societies can be greatly enhanced, and the achievement of successful interaction between hosts and guests will benefit and sustain the well-being of local communities (Wearing and Neil, 2009). Visitor experience, through the process of direct interaction and information sharing between farmers and consumers, will in time forge stronger bonds between them and cement the foundations of locally and regionally self-sufficient food systems (Earles, 2005; Feenstra, 1997).

The internet is an important tool for promoting linkages between tourism and agriculture because of its prominent role in providing information to potential tourists. Travellers require information before they travel to a destination and once they arrive (Huang and Lee, 2009). The ease with which information about a destination's facilities and events can be accessed is a critical component of the area's success and of visitor satisfaction (Sheldon, 1993; Small Farm Center, 2006). The provision of destination information to tourists not only affects their destination choice but also their satisfaction at the destination and their potential repeat visit (Huang and Lee, 2009).

The internet can enhance the linkages between tourism and the local economy in SIDS through the use of websites that offer comprehensive information on surrounding activities (Levinson and Milne, 2004; Milne, 2009; Poon, 1993; Soteriades *et al.*, 2004). For example, a hotel's website could act as a portal to nearby suppliers and surrounding community interests; it could include a menu that is linked to local farmers who supply food, and provide information on local handicrafts or community events. Information sharing through the internet can increase tourists' spending opportunities and build good will between a core tourism operation and its surrounding community (Levinson and Milne, 2004; Mason and Milne, 2006).

In this chapter, the perspectives of stakeholders in Niue on the strength of the linkages between agriculture and tourism are explored, and the current marketing and promotion of tourism products, especially local experiences available on the island, are reviewed. The objectives are to discuss the following: first, linkages between local agriculture and the tourism industry; and second, marketing and promotion of food- and agriculture-related experiences to tourists through an audit of popular websites that provide information to potential visitors.

This chapter discusses the data-collection techniques used to gather information on the existing linkages between tourism and agriculture in Niue. It then highlights the perspectives of key stakeholders, for example, growers, SMTEs and government officials, on the strength of current linkages between the two sectors. A review is provided of the marketing of tourism products and experiences, with a major focus on agriculture-related activities for tourists. Popular websites that provide tourism information are audited to examine what information they provide, especially on culture, agriculture, food- and village-based experiences for tourists prior to their travel to Niue. The chapter concludes by emphasising the levels of agreement of stakeholders on the existing linkages between tourism and agriculture and the effectiveness of the tourist information currently provided by major websites in Niue.

Tourism in Niue

Niue has a population of fewer than 1,500 people and its tourism industry contributes 13% towards the country's gross domestic product (GDP), while the agriculture sector remains the highest contributor (34%) (FAO, 2005; South Pacific Travel, 2003). Niue's tourism industry is small. There is only one hotel in Niue, the government-owned, donor-assisted Matavai Resort, and 18 other accommodation units that are operated as private businesses. These consist of six guest houses, six motels, four rental homes, a homestay and a backpacker unit, and together they offer 74 rooms that can accommodate, in total, 174 tourists (Singh, 2012: 97). In recent years, visitors have numbered about 5,000–6,000 tourists annually (UNWTO, 2012). Prior to 2010, Niue received an annual total of fewer than 5,000 (Niue Tourism, 2012). New Zealanders make up 72% of the tourist arrivals, followed by Australians (13%) and other Pacific Islanders (7%) (Singh, 2012). As Niue does not have the vast stretches of beach offered by other Pacific SIDS, its tourism industry differs from theirs, attracting visitors who are not the typical 'sun, sand, sea tourists' (Statistics Niue, 2010). According to Singh (2012), tourists who visit Niue are mainly middle-aged, university-educated professionals who are holidaymakers. Most are on their first visit to Niue and are accompanied by their partner or spouse. Prior to their arrival, the major websites they use to obtain information about Niue are those of the Niue Tourism Office (www.niueisland.com), the Niue government site (www.gov.nu), and the South Pacific Travel Organisation (SPTO, www.spto.org) (Singh, 2012).

The peak tourism season is mainly from June to September. This coincides with New Zealand's winter season, and more than 70% of the tourists to Niue are New Zealanders who are eager to escape the cold weather for a warmer, affordable holiday that is close to home. A second peak season is from December to January, which coincides with the end-of the-year holiday season, especially for Niueans living overseas, who prefer to return to Niue to spend Christmas and New Year with friends and family (Singh, 2012; Statistics Niue, 2010).

Statistics are in short supply in Niue but, with assistance from government officials, 34 SMTE operators were identified, of whom 26 are of Niuean origin. These 34 operators run about 95% (62) of SMTE operations in Niue, which can be broken down as follows: tourist accommodation (19), tours and activities (14), shops (10), restaurants and cafés (8), vehicle rental (4), travel agencies (2) and other operations, for example, sellers of hydroponic vegetables, organic vanilla and ebony carvings (5). These enterprises include all existing tourist accommodation, tours and activities, restaurants and cafés, vehicle rentals, travel agencies and most (80%) of the shops in Niue in 2008/09, when fieldwork was conducted on the island.

In 2005, it was estimated that the number of locals employed in Niue's tourism sector ranged from 40 to 80, of a total labour force of approximately 750 (Milne, 2005). In this study, the focus was on the full-time and part-time employees of SMTEs. Nearly half of the SMTE operators (16 out of 34) indicated that they were small family businesses and employed no other workers, while 11 (out of 34) SMTE operators said they employed one to three full-time workers, primarily as managers, cooks, kitchen hands, groundsmen, cleaners, waitresses, shop assistants, mechanics, garage keepers, office workers and fishermen. Finally, 13 (of 34) SMTE operators indicated that they employed one to three part-time workers during the peak tourism season, primarily as gardeners, cleaners, waitresses, night porters and handymen.

Methods

To explore the strength of linkages between agriculture and tourism in Niue, data were collected from key stakeholders, including growers, SMTEs and government officials. As a consequence, semi-structured interviews, on a one-to-one basis, lasting between 30 and 60 minutes, were conducted with 29 growers, 34 SMTEs and 12 government officials in Niue. In addition, web audits were conducted for popular websites that provide tourist information to potential visitors to Niue. These included the abovementioned websites of the Niue Tourism Office, Niue government and SPTO. These three websites were examined for the information they provided to tourists on products and services available on the island relating to local food, culture, villages, agriculture and nature.

Stakeholders' perspectives on current tourism and agriculture links

It should be noted that agriculture in Niue is focused primarily on subsistence, and that consequently the availability of surplus produce for sale fluctuates throughout the year. Interviewee responses, which are discussed in this section, reflect this situation.

A significant proportion of SMTEs (44.1%), and most growers (55.6%) and government officials (66.7%) said that linkages between tourism and agriculture are very weak. Another 20.6% of SMTEs and 29.6% of growers suggested there were no linkages between the tourism and agriculture sectors. Restaurant and shop operators stated that imported food accounted for 80%–90% of their total food costs, especially during the peak tourism season (June to September and December to January). By contrast, during the off-peak tourism season, imported food accounted for only 40%–50% of their costs. Government officials noted that as the tourism sector expanded, locals would have an incentive to grow more to meet at least some of the demand for fruit and vegetables in season.

The reasons linkages between tourism and agriculture are minimal is because of inconsistent supply of local produce, lack of opportunities for tourists to interact with locals, and shortage of tourist information on what food and activities are available. The lack of linkages is also due to the absence of communication between them, and the failure of officials at the Tourism Office to appreciate the importance of agriculture and related activities. It was also felt that SMTEs and local communities were neglected by organisers of tourism-related functions, who selected their favourite caterers to provide food. As an example of a failure to communicate, a grower complained that the Tourism Office did not publicise when around-the-island tours and other tourist activities were to take place, so growers were unable to ensure local food was made available at village stops.

Another explanation for the minimal linkages between the two economic sectors is the lack of creativity among locals to develop recipes that include local produce, which is rarely on the menus at cafés and restaurants. Examples of locally grown fruits, vegetables and meats that *could have been* used in local meal preparation but were *not*, include: tomatoes and lettuces in burgers and panini wraps, banana and pineapple in local fruit salads, taro, *bele* (a local green leafy vegetable), fish, coconuts and pig in *umu* (food cooked underground, i.e. an earth oven), and yams and pawpaw in *takihi* (sliced pawpaw and taro in coconut cream). One explanation provided by interviewees for the absence of such produce from the table was that local communities enjoyed too comfortable a lifestyle and had no incentive to supplement their income.

There is a general feeling, at least among some SMTE operators, that government policy is inadequate. Indeed, about 44% of SMTE operators considered that such linkages that did exist between tourism and agriculture were accidental rather than deliberate, and that tourism officials emphasised only government's plans for increasing accommodation, and neglected tourism's links to agriculture. At the same time, though, they considered that while stakeholders in both sectors were unsure of how linkages could be made, the tourism industry would require the support of the agricultural sector if it were to develop sustainably, and the Tourism Office needed to initiate communication with the agriculture department and growers to create linkages and develop local agricultural products for the tourism sector.

Government officials pointed out that with 85%–90% of the population in Niue engaged in subsistence agriculture, barely 10% participates in commercial agriculture on a regular basis, and subsistence farmers take crops to market only on an *ad hoc* basis, if and when they have any surplus produce. Furthermore, the links with tourism are few. Tourist business operators, for example, rarely visit the market, so growers rely on friends and relatives to buy their produce and craft items. Indeed, they may sometimes distribute their produce to friends and relatives because they are unable to sell items on market days. For their part, if they go to the market at all, tourists will usually arrive at about 10.00 am, by which time most of local food has been sold. As a consequence, growers felt that, to date, tourism had not grown sufficiently to motivate them to increase their productive capacity to meet tourist demand.

Some interviewees felt that recently there has been some progress. More fruit and vegetables have been planted because the government is promoting the consumption of a balanced diet for healthy living. If successful, this extra capacity could also help create linkages to the tourism sector by meeting the demand for locally grown produce and minimising imports. However, this might not be enough, and the government needs to promote and educate tourists to experience local food and products other than fruit and vegetables. Only then are growers likely to show an interest in satisfying demand. As a government official noted, however, by meeting the demands of the tourism industry, the agriculture sector would not have to face the constraints of high freight costs and the difficulties of searching for export markets.

Structurally, the agricultural sector is not geared towards meeting the needs of the tourism sector, and there is no liaison across the two sectors. Informants noted that, in the past, projects bringing together tourism and agriculture, usually assisted by donor funding, had not been properly managed and had ended when funds ran out. What happens, instead, is that what a grower chooses to plant, produce and sell at the local market depends on their personal interest and preference. The small commercial agriculture sector, which in other circumstances might meet tourist and local demand, is focused primarily on export crops, such as noni, vanilla and taro. Even local produce, for example fresh fish and fruit, is in short supply, especially when tourist demand is at its height, and the result is to reinforce the demand for imported food.

In these circumstances, there is a general lack of motivation all round. Growers need to be motivated to grow more produce for sale, especially fruit and vegetables, because these are not traditional food sources, while consumers prefer imported fruits and vegetables, probably because they are easier to buy than to grow and are consistent in quantity and quality throughout the year.

It was felt that there is no easy answer to these problems and perceptions varied among stakeholders. One requirement perhaps is planning, which is necessary if the agricultural sector is to provide a diversity of local produce, handicrafts and activities to the tourism industry. In this respect, government officials feel that growers should be divided into small groups, with every group focusing on a specific product, rather than all growing the same produce, presenting them at the market at the same time, and thus creating a glut. Others felt that some of the problems rested with the government itself. With more than 400 employees (New Zealand Ministry of Foreign Affairs and Trade, 2010), it is the main employer on the island. It was argued, though, that government workers have limited time to set up agriculture-related experiences for tourists. More generally, population decline and a lack of interest shown by youths for agriculture is alarming for both the tourism and agriculture sectors, as fewer locals are left to work the land and set up businesses.

Another requirement is for the tourism sector to make an effort to promote the consumption of local food and inform tourists of the types of produce and traditional meals that are available. A third need is for locals to understand the experiences and products tourists would like while in Niue.

A different but related problem concerns the separation of tourists from locals when they are visiting Niue. There is a scarcity of accommodation for visitors in the villages, and the accommodation sector is dominated by donor-assisted government investment in the island's only resort. A few small-scale operations are run by locals, but because tourists normally stay either at the hotel or in motels, they miss out on village life and interaction with Niueans. This is a loss for both sides, as local people are unable to share their knowledge, history and traditional stories with tourists, and little attention is given to exploiting Niue's lifestyle, environmental sustainability, or such individual life skills as fishing, planting and hunting, for tourism development, even for returning Niueans. Here again, it was argued that the government could do more to encourage villagers and the younger generation to engage in entrepreneurial activities, which could provide additional opportunities for tourists to interact with locals and experience Niuean culture.

Marketing of agriculture and tourism links

The internet is a key tool for enhancing the linkages between tourism and agriculture because of its role in providing tourist information to potential visitors before they travel. In a recent Niue departure survey, nearly 80% of visitors stated that the internet had been an important source of information when they planned their trip (Milne and Singh, 2008)

Audit of the popular websites that provide online tourism information

The three major websites (www.niueisland.com, www.gov.nu and www.spto. org) containing information on Niue for potential tourists were reviewed at the time of the research (2008/09) and again in 2012, after the field work, to see if they provided sufficient information to tourists about the products and services relating to agriculture- and village-based experiences.

The Niue Tourism Office website mentions a few unique cultural experiences, including local pageants, show days, such traditional commemorations as ear-piercing and hair-cutting ceremonies, and Christian churches (website revived during 2008/09). The small number of cultural experiences mentioned are very briefly described, with few pictures and minimal information, and have no reviews or recommendations from locals and tourists. The web page failed to give confirmed dates for these cultural events in: '… for the latest confirmed dates, check the Events Calendar or contact the Niue Tourism Office …' (www.niueisland.com, 2009).

Tourists cannot experience any of the cultural events mentioned by the website because no information is provided about them, such as when they take place, contacts for bookings or descriptions of the events. The website needs to be at the forefront of marketing and promoting culture-related events on the island by listing more cultural events available and providing thorough information on what every activity offers. Reviews from tourists and locals who have experienced the cultural events and more pictures showing the significance of the activities are also necessary. The website should also inform potential tourists how they could participate in the cultural events, for example, enabling them to book ahead, giving information about costs, and detailing anything they need to know before engaging in the activity.

The website mentions a few traditional local foods – for example, taro, cassava and breadfruit – which can be bought at the market, but fails to inform tourists of the best time (i.e. early in the morning) to visit the market to purchase fresh local produce. Limited information and pictures are available on the range of local produce available at the market and local shops, and while the Tourism Office web page on local dining provides brief information on the local produce and prepared food that tourists can experience on show days, it does not give the time of the events:

> ... the very best range of traditional local food is found at the annual village show days – each of Niue's fourteen villages hosts a show day every year to showcase local cooking, craft, sporting and cultural skills. A large earth oven, or 'umu' is prepared and visitors can sample some rarely found and delicious treats. Try to co-ordinate your visit with one of these show days, for it will expose you to the full fabric of Niuean life.
>
> (www.niueisland.com, 2009)

Unfortunately, the lack of information on the major websites that promote Niue results in tourists missing the opportunity to experience local food on show days. They should indicate the wide selection of local food available on show days, add photographs, and inform tourists of when the food can be obtained on show days, at markets and other times that are possible.

The Tourism Office website lists some places for dining out but does not detail the types of dishes and traditional meals offered, or their cost, and has no pictures of dishes available at the island's restaurants and cafés, provides no information on their opening times or how bookings can be made. The site could offer sample recipes and show the problems involved in buying and cooking local foodstuffs; instead, visitors to the site are told: 'for the most up-to-date list of opening hours, check with the Niue Tourism Office ... Matavai resort ... bookings essential ... ' (www.niueisland.com, 2009).

The situation is similar in relation to local entertainment. The Niue Tourism Office website indicates a few available activities for local entertainment but, again, the information is limited. The entertainment is not really described and no information is given as to when it will take place:

> ... traditional festive nights – these large events are less common but normally coincide with a political event or sponsorship drive. Highly recommended but won't take place without a lot of advance notice. Check with the Niue Tourism Office ...
>
> (www.niueisland.com, 2009)

The web page does not say what tourists can expect in the way of local entertainment and sport, how much it will cost, how they can book, and whether or not there are specific cultural norms to be followed by those who attend. It would be much better if such information were provided, along with pictures and reviews to give potential visitors a 'feel' for what is on offer, and contact information of the organisers.

In revisiting the coverage of links between tourism and agriculture by the Niue Tourism Office website, it was found that the site had been upgraded in 2012. Pictures of and information about local foods had been added; there was information on the island's culture, and tourists were encouraged to post reviews of their experiences on the island. It was also evident that the Tourism Office was making an effort to post news articles and media releases written by local villages and journalists. While yet more information could have been given on food and cultural activities, the value of the website in providing information was clear, and it was now reinforcing the tourist experience and the local community's experience of tourism.

The second website examined during fieldwork was that of the Government of Niue (www.gov.nu) and this barely mentioned local food and agriculture, with only one picture of local produce and no information at all about the growers or their communities. As indicated earlier, information and pictures of island life, culture, agriculture, food and villages would have been an improvement, as would a link to the website of the Tourism Office. On examining this site again in 2012, it was found to contain government press releases, and included an online newsletter (*Tau Tala Niue*), which detailed stories and pictures of current happenings in Niue, major local events, show days and competitions, welcoming performances for visitors at the airport, and a story on the coming into service of the new A320 Air New Zealand flight. Although published only irregularly, the newsletter helps provide the visitor with a 'sense of place', and demonstrates that government officials do see an opportunity to create linkages between the tourism and agriculture sectors through an effective dissemination of tourist information to potential visitors.

The third website audited from 2008 to 2009 was that of the SPTO (www. spto.org/spto/cms/destinations/niue/). When first audited, it contained little information on how tourists could experience local produce, highlighting only one café (Jenna's) as a place to find local food. No information was provided on food sold in other local restaurants and cafés, or on tours and other activities available for tourists, and there were no contributions from residents or tourists. Furthermore, there were no links with the government of Niue or the Tourism Office websites. Reviewed again in 2012, the only change seemed to have been an increase in the number of accommodation providers from 12 in 2009 to 16 in 2012. Much remains to be done on this website if it is to be effective.

Individual SMTE websites

Slightly more than one quarter (26.5%, or nine out of 34) of the SMTE operators had their own website during the initial fieldwork period. They mainly rely on the Niue Tourism Office to promote their services, take online bookings, list facilities for renting vehicles, and give details of shops, cafés, restaurants and tours. Word of mouth is also commonly used to promote the products and services offered by SMTE operators on the island. In addition, some of them promoted their products and services in a weekly newsletter distributed at the airport. They also sporadically use wholesalers and travel agents in New Zealand and Australia, the South Pacific Travel website, radio, pamphlets and business cards, magazine articles and local notice boards to promote their products and services and communicate with tourists, though none of these is used regularly. Overseas suppliers are contacted mainly through email, while local suppliers of food and services are contacted directly in person or by phone.

The websites of three accommodation enterprises were audited: Kololi (www.niueaccommodation.nu), Coral Gardens (www.coralgardens.nu) and Namukulu (www.namukulu-motel.nu). All focus primarily on providing information such as their size and rates. Examples are as follows:

> Kololi's offers the following rooms: 3 self contained units (chalet type), two 2-bedroom units, one 1-bedroom unit, all units have separate bedrooms, a lounge, adjoining kitchen and separate bathroom ...
>
> (Kololi, www.niueaccommodation.nu, 2009)

> Coral Gardens Motel is situated on the main road at Makapu Point six kms north of the main village and port of Alofi. Five studio-type comfortable fales have cliff top ocean views and have been designed for holidaymakers and professionals visiting Niue ...
>
> (Coral Gardens, www.coralgardens.nu, 2009)

> Namukulu Cottages & Spa is situated just 10 minutes drive from Alofi in totally tranquil tropical surroundings and has 3 fabulous Cottages of superior quality, each with magnificent panoramic sea views.
>
> (Namukulu, www.namukulu-motel.nu, 2009)

These websites had few web links to other SMTEs and the main tourism information sites in Niue. Coral Gardens' website is linked to one other website (the rental operator Alofi Rentals); Namukulu's website is linked to the main tourism office and Air New Zealand; Kololi's website has no link to any other websites.

No information or pictures of local food, agriculture, culture or people are featured on the three accommodation websites. However, the Kololi website did provide brief information on the type of activities and experiences available for tourists in Niue, for example, caving, rainforest and reef walks, and whale and dolphin watching. In addition, Coral Gardens' website provided very general information on Niue:

Food supplies are available from several stores in Alofi. Most goods are imported from New Zealand. Market Day on Niue is Friday – be early for fresh fruit, coconuts, uga crab and traditional Niuean cooked foods.

(Coral Gardens, www.coralgardens.nu, 2009)

Namukulu's website provides brief information on restaurants:

There are 11 eating places on the Island, mostly situated in Alofi. Jenna's Café is a favourite place for a buffet on Tuesday nights. Washaway Café at Avatele is the place to go on Sunday afternoon and evening. Other popular places are Crazy Uga Bar & Café, FalalaFa Bar & Café and Gills Indian Restaurant.

(Namukulu, www.namukulu-motel.nu, 2009)

The websites of tour operators Kayak Niue (kayakniue.nu) and Niue Dive (www.dive.nu) mainly provide information only on the activities they offer. Neither of them says anything about local food, agriculture, cultural activities or any other attractions.

In 2008/09, potential was not being realised on these websites. It would be much better if they could advertise local opportunities for tourists to spend their money, and thus foster good will between the tourism sector and the local community. Such information would also assist tourists when planning their trip to Niue, and possibly lead to them extending their stay and having a more satisfying visit.

When the websites of the tour operators were revisited in 2012, only two noticeable upgrades had been made in 2012. That of Coral Gardens had become linked to the Niue Travel Guide (niue.southpacific.org) and the Niue Tourism Office (www.niueisland.com), while Namukulu's had become linked to several sites, including Qantas and local car rental companies. It had also developed links with Trip Advisor and *Lonely Planet*, enabling visitors to report on their experience of Niue. In short, the tour operators were beginning to realise the value of a more extensive range of tourist information on their websites.

In 2012, the role of local communities in nurturing links between tourism and agriculture, and their online activities were reviewed. Noticeably, they were providing some information that was absent from the websites of the public and private sector. In 2012, for instance, the village of Mutalau was presenting an island night every Saturday, enabling tourists to experience local cuisine, traditional activities and cultural entertainment (www.niueisland.com/content/restaurants). It had also set up a Facebook page, to communicate and share information with Niueans living overseas, hoping they would return to Niue to visit their friends and relatives, and an online user group (groups.yahoo.com/group/cyber_muta), used *inter alia* to raise funds for village activities.

Conclusion

Tourism and agriculture stakeholders on Niue feel that the existing linkages between the two sectors are minimal and are restricted to the occasional supply of fruit and vegetables. They suggest this situation has arisen because supplies of local produce are irregular, opportunities for visitors to interact with locals and experience Niuean culture are limited, and there is little information available to tourists before they travel to Niue about what they can eat and do when they arrive. Other reasons given include insufficient numbers of tourists and a corresponding lack of incentive to provide for their needs in the agricultural sector, and the failure of participants in tourism and agriculture to communicate with each other or to appreciate the mutual benefits that collaboration would bring (Dahles and Meijl, 1999; Meyer, 2007; Milne and Nowosielski, 1997).

If these problems are not addressed, and the information for tourists on the website remains inadequate, Niue will miss out on the economic benefits and local multiplier effect generated by the tourism industry. Closer links would contribute to the sustainability of both sectors.

References

Barker, J.C. (2000) 'Hurricanes and Socio-economic Development on Niue Island.' *Asia Pacific Viewpoint* 41(2): 191–205.

Belisle, F.J. (1983) 'Tourism and Food Production in the Caribbean.' *Annals of Tourism Research* 10(4): 497–513.

Berno, T. and Oliver, R. (2010) *Me'a Kai: The Food and Flavours of the South Pacific*. Auckland: Random House.

Black, R. and King, B. (2002) 'Human Resource Development in Remote Island Communities: An Evaluation of Tour-guide Training in Vanuatu.' *International Journal of Tourism Research* 4(1): 103–17.

Brohman, J. (1996) 'New Directions in Tourism for Third World Development.' *Annals of Tourism Research* 23(1): 48–70.

Burnett, D. (2007) *Diagnostic Trade Integration Study: Agriculture, Livestock and Forestry*. Port Vila, Vanuatu: United Nations Development Programme.

Busby, G. and Rendle, S. (2000) 'The Transition from Tourism on Farms to Farm Tourism.' *Tourism Management* 21(1): 635–42.

Dahles, H. and Meijl, T. (1999) 'Local Perspectives on Global Tourism in the Asia-Pacific Region.' International Institute for Asian Studies (IIAS), *Newsletter* 19, The Netherlands: IIAS.

Earles, R. (2005) *Sustainable Agriculture: An Introduction*. California: National Sustainable Agriculture Information Service, Appropriate Technology Transfer for Rural Areas (ATTRA).

Feenstra, G. (1997) *What is Sustainable Agritourism?* California: Sustainable Agriculture Research and Education Program, University of California.

Flyman, M.V. (2003) *Bridging the Gap between Livestock Keeping and Tourism in Ngamiland District, Botswana*. Gumare, Botswana: Agency for Cooperation and Research in Development (ACORD).

FAO (Food and Agriculture Organization) (2005) *Pacific Islands: Support to the Regional Programme for Food Security.* Project: GTFS/RAS/198/ITA. Rome: FAO.

Harrison, D. (2004) 'Tourism in Pacific Islands.' *The Journal of Pacific Studies* 26(1): 1–28.

Huang, W.J. and Lee, B.C. (2009) 'Capital City Tourism: Online Destination Image of Washington, DC.' In: W. Hopken, U. Gretzel and R. Law (eds) *Information and Communication Technologies in Tourism.* New York: Springer Wien, 355–68.

International Agricultural Research Centre (2005) *Community Participation.* Washington, DC: Consultative Group on International Agricultural Research Secretariat, The World Bank.

Levinson, J. and Milne, S. (2004) 'From Brochures to the Internet: Tourism, Marketing and Development in the Cook Islands.' *The Journal of Pacific Studies* 26(1&2): 175–98.

Mason, D. and Milne, S. (2006) 'Generating Agritourism Options in the Caribbean: A Cost Effective Model.' In C. Jayawardena (ed.) *Caribbean Tourism: More than Sun, Sand and Sea.* Jamaica, WI: Ian Randle Publishers, 61–75.

Meyer, D. (2007) 'Pro-poor Tourism: From Leakages to Linkages – A Conceptual Framework for Creating Linkages between the Accommodation Sector and "Poor" Neighbouring Countries.' *Current Issues in Tourism* 10(6): 558–83.

Milne, S. (2005) *The Economic Impact of Tourism in SPTO Member Countries.* Report for SPTO/EU, Suva.

——(2009) *Tonga Tourism Support Programme: Economic Linkage Study.* NZAID Report. www.nztri.org.nz (accessed 7 July 2013).

Milne, S. and Nowosielski, L. (1997) 'Travel Distribution Technologies and Sustainable Tourism Development: The Case of South Pacific Microstates.' *Journal of Sustainable Tourism* 5(2): 131–49.

Milne, S. and Singh, E. (2008) *Visitor Departure Survey (June to October 2008).* Niue Tourism Research Reports: Report 1. New Zealand Tourism Research Institute (NZTRI), Auckland University of Technology, 1–110. www.nztri.org/node/319 (accessed 21 July 2010).

New Zealand Ministry of Foreign Affairs and Trade (2010) *Niue: Country Information.* www.mfat.govt.nz/Countries/Pacific/Niue.php.

Poon, A. (1993) *Tourism, Technology and Competitive Strategies.* Oxford: CABI Publishing.

Prasad, N. (2003) 'Small Islands' Quest for Economic Development.' *Journal of Asia-Pacific Development* 10(1): 47–67.

Pratt, S. (2013) 'Minimising Food Miles: Issues and Outcomes in an Ecotourism Venture in Fiji.' *Journal of Sustainable Tourism* 21(8): 1148–65.

Sheldon, P.J. (1993) *Issues in the Development of Destination Information Systems.* San Francisco: Pacific Asia Travel Association.

SIDSNET (Small Island Developing States Network) (2007) *The South Pacific.* Division for Sustainable Development of the United Nations. New York: SIDSNET.

Sims, R. (2009) 'Food, Place and Authenticity: Local Food and the Sustainable Tourism Experience.' *Journal of Sustainable Tourism* 17(3): 321–36.

Singh, E. (2012) *Linkages between Tourism and Agriculture in South Pacific SIDS: The Case of Niue.* Unpublished doctoral thesis. Auckland, New Zealand: Auckland University of Technology.

Small Farm Center (2006) *Fact Sheets for Managing Agri- and Nature-tourism Operations.* Davis, CA: University of California. www.sfc.ucdavis.edu/agritourism/factsheets/.html.

Soteriades, M., Aivalis, C. and Varvaressos, S. (2004) *E-marketing and e-commerce in the Tourism Industry: A Framework to Develop and Implement Business Initiatives.* Athens, Greece: Association of Greek Tourist Enterprises (SETE).

South Pacific Travel (2003) *Regional Tourism Strategy for the South and Central Pacific: Strategy for Growth.* Suva, Fiji: South Pacific Tourism Organisation.

Statistics Niue (2010) *Visitor Statistics: Economic Planning and Statistics.* Alofi, Niue: Government of Niue. www.spc.int/prism/Country/NU/stats/index.htm (accessed 16 February 2014).

Telfer, D.J. and Wall, G. (1996) 'Linkages between Tourism and Food Production.' *Annals of Tourism Research* 23(3): 635–53.

Torres, R. (2002) 'Toward a Better Understanding of Tourism and Agriculture Linkages in the Yucatan: Tourist Food Consumption and Preferences.' *Tourism Geographies* 4(3): 282–306.

——(2003) 'Linkages between Tourism and Agriculture in Mexico.' *Annals of Tourism Research* 30(3): 546–66.

UNWTO (United Nations World Tourism Organization) (2012) *UNWTO Tourism Highlights, 2012 Edition.* Madrid: UNWTO. mkt.unwto.org/sites/all/files/docpdf/unwtohighlights12enhr.pdf (accessed 16 July 2013).

Wearing, S. and Neil, J. (2009) *Ecotourism: Impacts, Potentials and Possibilities.* Second edn. Oxford: Elsevier.

Websites

Coral Gardens, www.coralgardens.nu (last accessed 5 May 2014)
Government of Niue, www.gov.nu/wb/ (last accessed 7 July 2013)
Kayak Niue, kayakniue.nu (last accessed 5 May 2014)
Kololi, www.niueaccommodation.nu (last accessed 5 May 2014)
Namukulu, www.namukulu-motel.nu (last accessed 5 May 2014)
Niue Dive, www.dive.nu (last accessed 5 May 2014)
Niue Tourism Office, www.niueisland.com (last accessed 7 July 2013)
SPTO, www.spto.org/spto/cms/destinations/niue/ (last accessed 7 July 2013)

Part IV

Pacific island countries and the outside world

11 Air transportation and tourism linkages in the South Pacific islands

Semisi Taumoepeau

Introduction: the changing organisation of international air travel

Small is not necessarily beautiful. Possibilities for economic growth in most Pacific island countries (PICs) are limited because they are small in size and population, geographically isolated, lack natural resources, and their domestic markets alone do not justify frequent air traffic. As a consequence, airlines cannot make economies of scale and operate with low load factors, making airline operations even more economically unsustainable. Problems are compounded because in developed countries, the source of most PIC tourists, airport charges are high, as are costs of fuel, spare parts and replacement aircraft, whether leased or purchased. In view of such constraints, their options are limited. Partnerships with regional airlines are one possibility, while another is to operate their own national airline, either alone or bilaterally with other partners, which may have nationalistic appeal but inevitably raises financial problems. At the management level, governments are often unable to define airline objectives or exert adequate financial control and yet will be committed to heavy financial outlay for aircraft and ongoing government operational subsidies. Another option for government is to deregulate, increase the competition (which will then affect the viability of their own airline) and encourage low-cost carriers (LCCs) to enter the market, a policy which, it is suggested in this chapter, has led to substantially increased tourist numbers in some PICs.

The emergence of the low-cost carriers

Since the end of the Second World War, international air services were operated between countries under strict bilateral air services agreements (ASAs)[1] negotiated between the two countries. Typically, these ASAs specified which airlines could fly between two countries, the routes, the airports, whether or not airlines could fly beyond third and fourth services (fifth freedom rights), the frequency and the operating capacity. In addition to the ASAs, the countries could restrict ownership and control, limit foreign ownership, and control some defence, safety and strategic issues. However, during the past three decades there has been a global trend to liberalise some of these aviation requirements as countries recognised the benefits of allowing market forces to take over flights, trade, tourism and international investment. Liberalisation of air services started from the USA with the Airline Deregulation Act of 1978, which pursued an active policy of liberalisation through the so called 'open skies' agreement at an international level. This was followed by the European Union in the 1990s and at the time of writing was being introduced into the Asia-Pacific region (Graham *et al.*, 2010).

Southwest Airlines adopted a low-cost business model shortly after deregulation was passed. In the USA and, later, in Europe, airline liberation facilitated the emergence of value-based or low-cost carriers (LCCs) (Freiberg *et al.*, 1998). These are relatively small airlines, which offer services with a single cabin class and reduced provision in flight services. The LCC model tends to overhaul and simplify processes, often involving a one-type aircraft fleet structure, higher aircraft utilisation and lower distribution costs to improve efficiency.

The start of the deregulation era triggered global deregulation towards a fully fledged commercialisation of airlines; then followed privatisation, mergers and alliances. Nationalistic and ownership constraints were gradually removed in response to increasing trade, tourism and air transport liberalisation (Doganis, 2006). Wherever possible, code-sharing arrangements between carriers enhanced services and created marketing advantage in online connecting services and helped escape the regulatory framework. Liberalisation, privatisation, foreign ownership and transnational mergers are thus transforming the structure of the international airline industry. As a consequence, there will be great pressure to reform the international regulatory system, especially in such traditionally regulated regions as Asia and the Pacific countries.

Increasingly in several countries of the Asia-Pacific region, several variations of LCC models have emerged. The first LCC established in the Asian region was Malaysia's Air Asia in 2001, an LCC universal model in a fully fledged liberalised aviation regime. It was quickly followed by other new carriers, emerging either through a subsidiary formation of an existing national airline, for example, Tiger Airways from Singapore Airlines (Wijaya, 2010), or as a newly formed LCC in a highly regulated aviation regime, for example, Spring Airline in China in 2005. In India, Air Deccan adopted an LCC universal model in a partly regulated aviation regime at the same time (O'Connell and Williams, 2006; CAPA, 2012). Examples of LCC models in the Pacific, operating from metropolitan centres, are Jetstar and Pacific Blue[2] in Australia and New Zealand (CAPA, 2012).

Table 11.1 Regional South Pacific-based airlines as of 1 July 2013

Airlines based in the South acific Islands	Operational structure	Code share partners in the South Pacific region	South Pacific destinations	Types of aircraft/fleet
Regional international routes				
Aircalin (SB)	TSA	NZ	Nouméa to Auckland, Brisbane, Nadi	1 A320, 2 A330
Air Kiribati (VK)	TSA	ON	Code shares with all Our Airline services	1 B737, 1 Casa, 1 Harbin Y-12
Air Niugini (PX)	TSA	QF	Port Moresby to Brisbane, Cairns, Honiara, Nadi, Singapore, Tokyo	2 B737, 1 B757, 3 B767, 1 B787, 13 Dash 8, 6 Fokker 100, 1 ATR72, 1 ATR42
Air Pacific (Fiji Airways)[1] FJ	TSA	NZ,IE, NF,QF	Nadi to Apia, Auckland, Brisbane, Christchurch, Funafuti, Honiara, Honolulu, Kiritimati, Los Angeles, Melbourne, Port Vila, Sydney, Tarawa, Tonga, Suva, Auckland	3 A330, 4 B737, 2 B747
Air Tahiti Nui (TN)	TSA	NZ,QF	Papeete to Auckland, Los Angeles, New York, Paris, Sydney, Tokyo	5 A340
Air Vanuatu (NF)	TSA	NZ,FJ	Port Vila to Auckland, Brisbane, Honiara, Melbourne, Nadi, Nouméa, Sydney	1B737, 1 ATR 72, 3 Harbin Y-12
Inter Island Airways	TSA	–	From Pagopago to Apia	1 Dornier 328, 1 Britten Noman
Our Airline (Air Nauru) ON	TSA	4A	From Brisbane to Honiara, Majuro, Nadi, Nauru, Tarawa	1 B737
Polynesian Airlines (PH)	TSA	–	From Apia to Pagopago	2 Twin Otter
Solomon Airlines (IE)	TSA	FJ	From Honiara to Brisbane, Nadi	1 A320, 1 DHC8, 3 Twin Otter, 2 Britten Norman Islander
Virgin Samoa (VS) (partnership with Virgin Australia)	LCC	VA	From Sydney and Auckland to Apia	1 B737

Notes: TSA = traditional serviced airline; LCC = low-cost carrier. [1] In May 2012 Air Pacific announced that it would reintroduce the name Fiji Airways to reinforce its role as the proud national airline of Fiji.

Air transportation in the South Pacific

In the South Pacific region, opportunities for economic growth tend to be limited, reflecting a narrow base, small domestic markets and high transport costs to external markets (Scheyvens and Russell, 2009; Taumoepeau, 2010a). Several elements of commonality across many South Pacific countries include the close proximity of the sea, the smallness and fragmented character of the land areas, and the vast distances that have to be spanned to maintain contact within any one island group, let alone between groups or with the rest of the world (Kissling, 2002; SPTO, 2013).

Traditionally in the South Pacific, air services from such metropolitan gateways as Sydney and Auckland have dominated air transportation. Tourism industries in the region could not survive without the visitors generated by these overseas-based carriers. From the early 1980s, air transportation and tourism became integral to the growing economies of these island nations (Kissling, 2002).

Most of these countries started their own national airlines not only for economic reasons, but also for national pride. However, in recent years, heavy financial losses led to most of these national airlines being restructured, entering into commercial partnerships with metropolitan carriers, or going into bankruptcy. The costs of owning and operating a national airline are still extremely high in these sparely populated and remote South Pacific countries (Taumoepeau, 2009).

Most airlines in the region are wholly or partially owned by governments and still operate on the old traditional service structure (i.e. aircraft configured into two or three classes, with a full on-board catering service), enjoying government subsidies, tax concessions and operating under bilateral ASAs. Even by the mid-2000s, the aviation industry of most countries in the region was still highly regulated, dominated by a few long-established national airlines (owned or partly owned by their respective governments), for example, Air Pacific (Fiji Airways), Air Vanuatu, Polynesian Airlines and Air Niugini. However, deregulation and multilateral air services agreements have opened up such destinations as the Cook Islands, Samoa, Tonga and Vanuatu for LCC services, and LCCs have opened more frequency and increased capacity and secondary routes at much lower fares than offered by traditional airlines over the past 15 years (Kissling, 2002, Taumoepeau, 2010a).

Support from host governments is ongoing as national airlines continue to play an increasing public utility service role as well. The level and degree of government involvement in the national airlines and tourism development varies, depending on government national objectives and the stage of the nation's economic development. In general, bilateral agreements are increasingly seen to restrict the development of a multinational industry and the case for a liberal multilateral regime is growing stronger in the South Pacific region.

Table 11.1 shows that most regionally based carriers are still on the traditional two- or three-class cabin configuration, utilising a range of different types of aircrafts, depending on the host government aspirations, geographic locations and routes being served. Such airlines as Fiji Airways have established code share partners with other airlines in the region.

Constraints in air transportation in the South Pacific

The Pacific Islands market is characterised by small economies, limited natural resources for exports, and populations dispersed across many isolated islands (Milne, 2005; Scheyvens and Russell, 2009). The current provision of air services is fragmented, often involving long routes with thin traffic and low freight levels (Taumoepeau, 2010a). As a result, South Pacific airlines face considerable constraints in managing returns through low passenger and cargo levels and achieving sufficiently high levels of aircraft utilisation. The more commercial Pacific air routes, which are closer to Australia and New Zealand, are generally tourism related and are enjoying recent growth in international arrivals from these two countries.

Recent studies by Taumoepeau (2010a) show why regional airlines are not economically sustainable. Contributing factors include:

- Remoteness and length of distances between islands and airfields.
- Limited size of the markets and low volume.
- Specific overrun factors and high airport charges.
- Low load factor and some thin sectors that are not economically sustainable.
- Soft currencies (local regional currencies) earned by regional airlines that must be converted to US dollars to purchase such major operational items as spare parts, fuel and aircraft leases.

Domestic airlines in the South Pacific

Domestic routes operate mainly as a 'public utility' service and support the distribution of tourist traffic domestically. In the South Pacific region, different types of small turbo propeller aircraft are used, depending on the route, airfields used, market demand and availability of finance or donor funding to lease or buy the equipment (Table 11.2). Having different types of aircraft necessitates additional costs, as training, maintenance and spare parts are expensive. In most cases, timetable and airline schedules are changed regularly and tend to limit the accessibility of the mainstream international tourist market to some of these islands. Most domestic airlines provide a public utility service because it is required by the host governments and are thus losing money, even though they are subsidised by their respective governments. Increased tourism traffic, however, helps to improve the economic sustainability of most domestic airlines in the South Pacific and most provide feeder services to the main gateways in the region, thus enabling more international tourists to visit the small islands.

Table 11.2 Main domestic airlines of the South Pacific region as of 1 July 2013

Domestic routes		Types of aircraft
Air Caledonie	New Caledonia domestic routes	1 ATR42, 2 ATR72
Air Kiribati 4A	Kiribati domestic routes	1 CASA C212, 1 Harbin Y12
Airlines PNG	PNG domestic routes	10 De Havilland Dash 8, 10 Twin Otter, 1 ATR72
Air Marshall Islands	Marshall Islands domestic routes	1 Bombardier Dash 8, 2 Dornier 228
Fiji Airways (Pacific Sun)	Fiji domestic routes	2 ATR42, 3 Twin Otter
Air Rarotonga (GZ)	Rarotonga domestic routes	1 Cessna, 4EMB Bandeirante, 1 SAAB 340A
Air Tahiti (VT)	Tahiti domestic routes	3 ATR42, 7 ATR72, 1 Beechcraft King Air, 1 Twin Otter
Air Vanuatu (NF)	Vanuatu domestic routes	1 ATR 72, 3 Harbin Y-12
Inter Island Airways	American Samoa domestic routes	1 Dornier 328, 1 Britten Noman Islander
Northern Air	Fiji domestic routes	2 Britten Norman Islander, 4 Embraer Banderainte
Real Tonga (RT)	Tonga domestic routes	1 MA60, 1 Harbin Y12, 1 Queen Air, 1 Britten Norman Islander
Samoa Air	Samoa domestic routes	2 Britten Norman Islander, 1 Cessna 172
Solomon Airlines (IE)	Solomon domestic routes	1 DHC8, 3 Twin Otter, 2 Britten Norman Islander

Source: Compiled by the author

Low-cost carriers and tourism to PICs

While the level of tourism activity, the size of the industry, the degree of foreign participation and the rate of tourism development all differ markedly from one country to another, it can be generalised that the growth of tourism in PICs has been facilitated by the emergence of LCCs. The first to fly into the Pacific Islands was Kiwi International in 1994, which flew to Tonga and Samoa for a few years. However, it was undercapitalised and in 1996 it failed financially. In 1995, Air New Zealand formed an LCC subsidiary, Freedom Air, and competed with Kiwi International on regional flights, which quickly put Kiwi International out of business. The Freedom Air business then merged with the restructured Air New Zealand in 2008. Elsewhere, Jetstar (a low-cost subsidiary of Qantas) started flying A320s to Fiji from 2010 and has helped to boost tourism to Fiji from the large Australian market (Taumoepeau, 2013).

The re-introduction of LCC services to the Pacific started in September 2004 to Fiji and Vanuatu from Sydney, in March 2005 to the Cook Islands, and in October 2005 from Auckland to Samoa and Tonga, by Pacific Blue (owned by Virgin Australia). These new LCC services from Australia and New Zealand produced dramatic passenger growth and substantial economic benefits. They also resulted in considerably reduced fares, much to the benefit of consumers. Fiji, Samoa, Tonga and Vanuatu were the markets targeted by LCCs, and passenger traffic and visitor arrivals in all four target countries increased substantially (Asian Development Bank, 2009, Taumoepeau, 2010b), as shown in Table 11.3.

The increased visitor numbers to these island nations led not only to a significant and tangible return to the community through increased tourism and economic benefits, but also prompted renewed interest from developers keen to invest in infrastructure to support increased numbers of tourists in the region. In the eight months following the launch of Polynesian Blue in October 2005, visitor arrivals to Samoa increased by more than 18% compared to an average annual growth over the prior ten years of just 3.9% (Taumoepeau, 2010b). During the previous decade, the government of Samoa had contributed over WST200 million to the nation's flagship airline; after the introduction of the LCC, such funds could be re-directed to health, education and other essential community services throughout Samoa.

A recent study (Taumoepeau, 2010b) of international arrivals to PICs shows that improved air services, through increased capacity and frequency and lower airfares, have had a major impact on destinations. PICs with a tourism arrival growth rate above 10% (Table 1.1, in Harrison and Pratt, this book) from the period 2005–12 are mostly destinations that receive LCC flights from Virgin Australia or Jetstar. Such destinations are the Cook Islands, Fiji, Papua New Guinea, Samoa, Solomon Islands, Tonga and Vanuatu. Papua New Guinea air services have also improved greatly over the last decade, opening up new gateways in the Asian market. A recent decision by Air New Zealand to increase its capacity and frequency to Niue to three times a week has boosted tourism arrivals, and improved connections from the Asian gateways and Asian airlines connecting to the Northern Marianas and Palau have increased traffic to these destinations. Finally, in New

Table 11.3 Number of international air travellers to key LCC destinations, 2005–09

Country	LCC start date	2005	2006	2007	2008	2009	% growth 2005–09
Cook Islands	March 2005	88,405	92,328	97,316	94,776	100,592	14
Fiji	September 2004	545,145	548,589	539,881	585,031	542,186	7*
Samoa	October 2005	101,807	115,882	122,352	122,222	128,830	27
Tonga	October 2005	43,380	39,451	46,040	49,400	50,645	18
Vanuatu	September 2004	62,213	67,787	81,345	90,657	100,675	46

Source: Taumoepeau, 2013
Note: * 2008 figure used. Tourism arrivals to Fiji in 2009 decreased due mainly to some political problems that reduced the number of travellers from New Zealand and Australia, but the situation has since normalised.

Caledonia, improved services and product development have helped increase international arrivals.

The emergence of LCCs has similarly affected return visits by (and remittances from) islanders living elsewhere, especially Tongans and Samoans. Indeed, while tourism offices in the region have recorded increased tourist arrivals from New Zealand and Australia, local businesses have also reported increased expenditure by travellers. It would seem that savings in air fares are being spent by tourists in shops at destinations, and by returning residents in further assisting local families (Taumoepeau, 2010b).

Statistics provided in other chapters also demonstrate the economic importance of tourism to Pacific island countries. The South Pacific Tourism Organisation (SPTO), for example, estimated the total international tourism revenue (tourist expenditures) for the region to be $1.5 billion in 2005 and more than $2.5 billion in 2010 (SPTO, 2013), and it is evident that in several Pacific island countries, tourism is a vital contributor to gross domestic product (GDP) (Milne, 2005) and a major provider of employment, as indicated in Table 11.4.

However, as Table 11.4 indicates, tourism's importance varies considerably across PICs. Destinations with a well-established airlines network, close proximity to the main trunk routes, and developed infrastructure and tourism plant tend to attract and accommodate more tourists, whereas smaller

Table 11.4 South Pacific regional economic overview of tourism

Country	Tourism GDP % (estimates 2011)	Tourism % employment (estimates 2011)
Cook Islands	75.0	55.0
Fiji	30.0	18.0
Federated States of Micronesia*	8.0	4.0
Kiribati	14.5	10.0
Marshall Islands*	8.0	3.0
Nauru*	8.0	4.0
Niue	20.0	15.0
Palau	50.0	50.0
Papua New Guinea	7.0	6.0
Samoa	20.0	18.0
Solomon Islands	3.0	4.0
Timor Leste*	n/a	n/a
Tonga	12.0	15.0
Tuvalu	3.0	0.7
Vanuatu	35.0	32.0

Source: ADB Pacific Tourism report on individual countries, www.adb.org; South Pacific Community, www.spc.imt, annual statistics for tourism for member countries; National Bureau of Statistics and through consultation with national tourism office officials

Note: * Estimates given by the national tourism offices.

destinations with undeveloped infrastructure and a smaller tourism industry struggle with unsustainable air services and poorer connections.

Continuous economic improvement is not guaranteed. During the 2000s, for example, there was a marked downturn in monies remitted by residents abroad, and natural disasters and earthquakes in Samoa and Tonga further slowed down the expected economic recovery of these countries, while the global financial crisis from 2008 had a severe (but not universal) affect throughout the region. It remains the case, though, that except for Fiji and Papua New Guinea, the population of most South Pacific countries is under 500,000, and the population base is thus too small to support and sustain a national airline with both domestic and international routes. Quite simply, such countries are unable to exploit the economies of scale available in many aspects of airline operations. To compensate, a greater influx of international tourists is needed to contribute towards the costs of operating the regional airlines.

Issues and challenges for South Pacific-based airlines

Despite their vast distances apart, different political structures, varying population base, and different stages of economic and tourism development, airlines of the region seem to share the same common economic character-istics and all are struggling financially. Some constraints have already been discussed. Others include the inability of national governments to define their national airline objectives clearly; their failure to exercise financial control; mistakes in the choice of aircraft, which have usually been too large, and their failure to control ownership and operating costs (Forsyth and King, 1996). To these constraints can be added undercapitalisation, and high maintenance and fuel costs.

In the South Pacific, the number of realistic alternatives for major jet air-craft maintenance is limited. A major consideration is the avoidance of costly positioning flights, and a frequent schedule service to the location where work is to be carried out is obviously an advantage. Operating only one aircraft presents a formidable problem, as it must at some time be withdrawn from service for a number of weeks, and replacement capacity found. The high cost of imported fuels at island airports is also significant; this increased from about 15% of the total airline operational cost in 2001 to more than 30% in 2008 (Taumoepeau, 2009). Maintenance, spare parts, expatriate engineering and pilots are also heavy contributors to the airlines' costs in the islands, as are high airport charges and station costs. All such constraints occur in a situation where reliability and punctuality are essential to the operation of scheduled services, particularly in the South Pacific, where frequencies tend to be low. Tourists must be able to depend on connections and regional airlines must earn a good reputation in this area with the travel trade.

At the regional level, governments are beginning to review their roles in supporting national carriers in the aftermath of heightened costs of security, insurance and safety. A recent study (Taumoepeau, 2010a) of the financial viability of some of regional airlines reveals that such financial issues as oversupply, low demand, undercapitalisation, government intervention and low investment in accommodation are some of the major concerns for regional airlines. Recent strengthening of the US dollar, the aviation currency also used for fuel purchasing, is affecting the airlines, which earn soft currencies but must meet their main expenses in the strong US dollar. Other downturns in traffic have been due to political problems in the region, for example, military coups in Fiji and political unrest in Solomon Islands and Papua New Guinea. Table 11.5 below summarises selected regional airlines core business and challenges to the airlines' economic viability.

As described elsewhere in the chapter, other challenges for airlines' operation in the South Pacific region are caused by geography and isolation, low demand and consistently low volume, small economies and high airport charges as airfields themselves are struggling to gain maintenance revenues for their ailing airfields and navigational aids and buildings. Some necessary thin sectors are not really sustainable but national carriers are nevertheless expected to carry out their roles as laid down by government. Airports and runways in the region are not uniform in standard and runway length, and some are inadequate for A320 and B737 operations (Taumoepeau, 2009).

Table 11.5 Summary of selected regional airlines' viability challenges

Regional airlines	Main core business	Economic viability challenges
Air Rarotonga GZ	Tourism	Need growth in tourism demand, high operational cost
Air Tahiti VT	Tourism	Undercapitalised and need growth in demand, costly equipment used, high operational cost
Air Kiribati VK	Ethnic market	Undercapitalised, small tourism plant, not enough demand, high operational cost
Fiji Airways (Air Pacific) FJ	Tourism	Recent heavy investment in new jet equipment A330 jets. Not enough hotel rooms, competition from LCC and FSA carriers
Polynesian Airline PH	Tourism and ethnic market	Undercapitalised, small tourism demand, unable to manage cost of operation, government intervention
Air Vanuatu NF	Tourism	Undercapitalised, small tourism demand, can have overcapacity, unable to manage cost of operation, competition from LCC carriers
Solomon Airlines IE	Tourism	Undercapitalised, small tourism demand, can have overcapacity, unable to manage cost of operation, competition from LCC carriers

Source: Compiled by the author

Towards new LCC airline structures for the South Pacific

In view of the nature and problems of air transport in PICs outlined in this chapter, it might be useful to outline an alternative approach, which focuses on airline consolidation, new roles by host governments and a strategy for cost containment.

As airline services are necessary for the economic and social development of small islands of the South Pacific, a viable workable model is needed in order to ensure the survival and profitable operation of national carriers in the region. Throughout the Pacific countries there is a need for airline consolidation through alliance partners and code sharing. Host governments need to relax national ownership and move towards air rights liberalisation while ensuring air transportation security, safety and economic sustainability. A cost containment strategy for regional airlines and a step towards a more suitable LCC model or LCC hybrid version is outlined in Table 11.6.

The low-cost model for the Pacific is somewhat different from its Asian counterpart. The region has smaller economies, fewer inhabitants, and the islands are sparsely located and isolated in the vast Pacific Ocean, all of which pose a different set of challenges, not only for the low-cost model, but also for traditional national network airlines.

However, having analysed the challenges facing air transportation in the South Pacific and studying how some of the Asia-Pacific region carriers enter the LCC market, there is a clear case for recommending regional carriers and host governments of the South Pacific to adopt special LCC-type structures and operational patterns for the region. Such new business model(s) could enable more cost-efficient airlines to operate in the South Pacific region.

The future of tourism in the South Pacific Islands depends almost wholly on the provision of frequent, sustainable and reasonably priced air transportation to and within the area. In turn, the growth of aviation in the region depends almost entirely on the international tourism market, as the small economies and populations of most PICs cannot alone sustain improved air services. Unfortunately, a preoccupation with national sovereignty seems to prevent small island states from embracing the concept of airline cooperation, code sharing, and even adopting the LCC model. This is regrettable, as lower airfares and affordable flights for a growing majority of the region's

Table 11.6 South Pacific airline industry adopting a new structure

Airline consolidation	Through alliance partners and code sharing in services
New government roles	Relax national ownership and move towards air rights liberalisation with more concerns towards air transportation security, safety and economic sustainability
Cost containment	Adoption of low-cost model airlines or a suitable LCC hybrid version appropriate for regional operation

Source: Taumoepeau, 2009

population would greatly assist in developing the economies of these isolated countries.

Notes

1 An ASA is an agreement, under the International Civil Aviation Organization (ICAO) protocol, in which two countries sign to allow international air services between their territories. The first ASA was signed between the government of the UK and the government of the USA in Bermuda (hence named the Bermuda Agreement) on 11 February 1946. This established a precedent for the signing of approximately 4,000 such agreements between countries. In recent decades some of the traditional clauses in such agreements have been modified in accordance with more liberal and deregulated or 'open skies' policies adjusted by countries concerned.
2 Pacific Blue was established as a subsidiary of Australian airline Virgin Blue. It was renamed Virgin Australia Airlines (NZ) Ltd in December 2011. Virgin Samoa, which operates one Boeing 737 and flies from Apia to Sydney, Brisbane and Auckland, is a joint venture between Virgin Australia and the Samoan government, both of which own 49% of the airline. Aggie Grey's Resort and Hotel holds the remaining shareholding.

References

Asian Development Bank (2009) *Pacific Economic Monitor.* August 2009.
——(2012) *Annual Report 2011.* Mandaluyong City, Philippines.
——(2013) *Pacific Economic Monitor.* August 2009. www.adb.org/publications/pacific-economic-monitor-march-2013.
CAPA (Centre for Asia Pacific Aviation) (2011) *Low Cost Share of Capacity 2010.*
——(2012) *Low Cost Carriers (LCCs): LCC Capacity Share (%) of Total Seats: 2001–2012**. www.centreforaviation.com/profiles/hot-issues/low-cost-carriers-lccs#lcc (accessed 6 June 2012).
Doganis, R. (2006) *The Airline Business.* Second edn. New York: Routledge.
Forsyth, P. and King, J. (1996) *Cooperation, Competition, and Financial Performance in South Pacific Aviation.* Edited by G. Hufbauer and C. Findlay. Washington, DC: Flying High, Institute for International Economics.
Freiberg, K., Freiberg, J. and Peters, T. (1998) *Nuts! Southwest Airline's Crazy Recipe for Business and Personal Success.* Bantam Doubleday Dell Pub.
Graham, A., Papatheodorou, A. and Forsyth, P. (2010) *Aviation and Tourism: Aviation and Tourism: Implications for Leisure Travel.* Hampshire: Burlington.
Kissling, C. (2002) *Transport and Communications for Pacific Microstates: Issues in Organisation and Management.* Suva, Fiji: Institute of Pacific Studies of the University of the South Pacific.
Milne, S. (2005) *The Economic Impact of Tourism in the SPTO Countries.* Suva, Fiji: SPTO.
O'Connell, J.F. and Williams, G. (2006) 'Transformation of India's Domestic Airlines: A Case Study of Indian Airlines, Jet Airways, Air Sahara and Air Deccan.' *Journal of Air Transport Management* 12: 358–74.
Scheyvens, R. and Russell, M. (2009) *Tourism and Poverty Reduction in the South Pacific.* New Zealand: Massey University.

SPTO (South Pacific Tourism Organisation) (2013) *Report on Pacific Regional Tourism and Hospitality Human Resource Development Plan.* Suva, Fiji.

Taumoepeau, S. (2007) *A Blueprint for the Economic Sustainability of the Small National Airlines of the South Pacific.* Unpublished doctorate thesis. University of the Sunshine Coast, Queensland, Australia.

——(2009) *South Pacific Aviation.* Saarbrucken, Germany: VDM Verlag.

——(2010a) 'South Pacific.' In A. Graham, A. Papatheodorou and O. Forsyth (eds) *Aviation and Tourism: Implications for Leisure Travel.* Hampshire: Burlington, 323–31.

——(2010b) *Impact of Low Cost Airlines on Pacific Island Economies.* New Zealand Tourism and Hospitality Research Conference (NZTHRC) Biannual Conference, AUT, Auckland, 24–26 November 2010.

——(2013) 'Low Cost Carriers in Asia and the Pacific: Development and the Business Structure.' In S. Cross and M. Luck (eds) *The Low Cost Carrier Worldwide.* Ashgate.

Wijaya, M. (2010) *New Heights for Asia's Budget Carriers.* 17 February. www.atimes.com/atimes/Southeast_Asia/LB17Ae01.html (accessed 30 November 2011).

12 Recent developments and changes in demand for tourism in Fiji

Uwe Kaufmann and Haruo Nakagawa

Introduction

With its 330 islands scattered throughout the South Pacific Ocean, the Fiji Islands are a renowned tourism destination throughout the world. Its supply of high-quality tourism and its unique landscape and beaches make Fiji ideal for tropical holidays. With international visitor arrivals growing to more than half a million, the Fiji Islands are the number one tourism supplier in the South Pacific.

From a macroeconomic point of view, the Fijian tourism industry has become the most important driver of the country's foreign exchange earnings. Revenues generated from tourism have increased rapidly. In 1974, FJ$60 million (US$75 million) was generated in revenues from tourism; this figure grew to more than FJ$816 million (US$417 million) in 2009, which is equivalent to about 30% of Fiji's gross domestic product (GDP).

According to figures from the Reserve Bank of Fiji (2008), the hotel and restaurant industry provides direct employment for about 9,000 workers. Including secondary industries and part-time workers, the figure grows to more than 23,400 formal jobs. Given that there are no figures available for the large informal sector reliant on the industry, total employment is likely to be much higher. The tourism industry is a significant part of Fiji's economy, providing significant employment and investment opportunities. Furthermore, tourism services have the capacity to facilitate sustainable economic growth for that country.

However, demand for Fijian tourism is highly dependent on international developments; the more Fiji's economy depends on tourism, the more it depends on international markets, which means Fiji's economy is more vulnerable to international shocks.

From a tourist's perspective, demand for tourism in a particular destination depends on the tourist's income, the cost of tourism in the country, the distance and time it takes to travel to the destination, and other subjective preferences.

Previous studies[1] have indicated that, following economic theory, the change of a tourist's personal income is strongly correlated with the change in the demand for tourism. Accordingly, demand theory suggests that as per capita GDP declines, a potential tourist is less likely to travel on holidays. Furthermore, the development of per capita GDP is strongly correlated to economic growth of the tourist's home country. If the tourist's country of origin is experiencing economic difficulty (e.g. the global financial crisis or other recessions), income pressure on the potential tourist increases. This could affect the tourist's choice of holiday destination and even lead to the tourist not travelling on a holiday vacation at all.

The cost of tourism includes the travel cost in the form of air fares from the country of origin to the tourism destination and the cost of living (accommodation and other costs such as meals) of the holiday. Air fares may decline due to aviation market developments (e.g. liberalisation of the aviation market), or increase due to a hike in fuel prices (e.g. resource price crisis in 2008), changing the final price of the holidays accordingly. Similarly, economic changes in the tourism destination will affect the price of the holidays. For example, an increase in tariffs on tourism-related items will increase the cost of living. Other than the travel cost and cost of living, the distance and time to reach the destination also play a vital role in the tourist's decision making. According to the Australian Bureau of Statistics (2010), 53% of Australian holiday seekers travel to the Asia-Pacific region. The same study finds that short-term trips are on the rise, making the proximity of the tourism destination an even more important factor, also affecting the air fare.

Fiji's relatively close proximity to Australia and New Zealand (ANZ) make it an important holiday destination for tourists from these two countries. To facilitate tourism demand from this region further, Fiji deregulated its aviation market in 2004. As a result of this liberalisation, additional flights offered between Fiji and ANZ increased competitiveness and this significantly lowered air fares from these two important tourism sources. In 2009, more than 62% of all international visitors arriving in Fiji were from these two nations.

Other demand preferences determining the tourism destination are subjective to the tourist himself/herself. Nevertheless, the reputation and the safety and political stability of the potential tourism destination play a role.

Political stability has been especially important and challenging in Fiji. The country has experienced four coups since 1987, the latest being the December 2006 takeover by the Fijian military. The coups have had an immediate adverse impact on tourist arrivals and damaged Fiji's reputation as a tourism destination significantly, jeopardising the tourism sector's role in facilitating sustainable growth.

The following section gives an overview of the changes experienced in Fiji's tourism sector over the recent past. It includes an analysis of arrival figures by country of origin, purpose of visit and length of stay, and the impacts the political unrest and aviation market deregulation have had on the demand for Fijian tourism. Section three discusses economic and econometric demand-for-tourism models in the context of small island countries such as Fiji. The fourth section outlines the econometric specifications used in this chapter to model Fijian tourism demand and presents its results. The fifth part of this chapter discusses future research topics in modelling tourism demand with a focus on changes in air fares. The conclusions are presented in section six.

Overview of Fiji tourism statistics

Figure 12.1 shows that visitor arrivals to Fiji have increased strongly over the past 20 years from less than 250,000 in 1988/89 to more than 585,000 in 2008. However, the figure also indicates that the increase was not free of shocks. In particular, Fiji's history of political instability hurt the country's reputation as a tourism destination.

In 1987 two military coups sent Fijian tourist arrivals into a nosedive. International visitor arrivals fell by more than 26% and tourism earnings declined by more than 20%, contributing to the decline in economic growth experienced in that year. In 1988, the Fijian government took drastic measures to stabilise the economy and offset the adverse effects of the previous year's coups. In two steps, the Reserve Bank of Fiji devalued the currency by a total of 33%. As this made Fijian tourism internationally more competitive, visitor arrivals began to improve. However, it took another two years until tourist arrivals and the revenues generated from tourism fully recovered, implying a tremendous economic loss by the country.

As a response to the Asian financial crisis in October 1997, and to prevent any additional negative pressure on the industry, the Fijian dollar was devaluated by 20% in 1998. This improved international competitiveness and resulted in an increase in visitor arrivals by 10% in that year (see Jayaraman and Choong, 2008).

However, the Fijian tourism sector took another hit from the 2000 coup. International visitor arrivals fell by circa 30% in that year and revenues

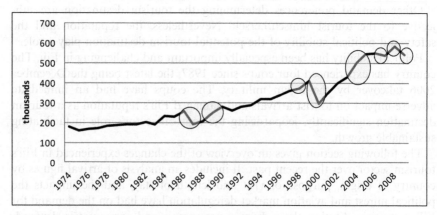

Figure 12.1 Fiji international tourist arrivals, 1974–2009
Source: Fiji Islands Bureau of Statistics, various years

generated dropped by more than 30%. The tourism sector did not recover to the pre-2000 coup level until 2003.

In 2004 the Fiji government deregulated the international aviation market, which resulted in strong growth when the NZ-based carrier Pacific Blue commenced flights between Fiji and the major cities of ANZ, increasing the demand from these two countries significantly.

Over the past five years, two major events have caused a decline in tourist arrivals in Fiji: the December 2006 coup and the 2008/09 global financial crisis (GFC). Interestingly, the latter had a more adverse effect, indicating how dependent Fiji's tourism sector is on international economic conditions.

According to figures from the Fiji Islands Bureau of Statistics (for various years), the political tensions that resulted from the December 2006 coup caused visitor arrivals to fall by only 1.6%; however, revenues generated from tourism increased by more than 5% in that year. Likely as a result of the GFC, over the period 2008–09 visitor arrivals declined by more than 7%, with tourist earnings dropping by 4.3%. Considering that the Fiji government devalued the Fiji dollar by 20% in April 2009, these figures likely understate the potential impact of the GFC. If there had not been a devaluation, the real decline of tourism might have been around 20%, showing the enormous pressure of the GFC on the Fijian tourism sector. Of course, the negative effect of the GFC was felt not only in Fiji but also in other major tourism destinations around the world in 2008 and 2009.

A detailed analysis of international visitor arrivals shows that more than 75% of all international visitors to Fiji are holiday seekers. This proportion has been steady over time. However, as Figure 12.2 presents, this was not the case for other visiting groups. Since the deregulation of the aviation market, visitors arriving in Fiji to visit friends and family have more than doubled. Their share as a percentage of total visitors increased from around 5% to

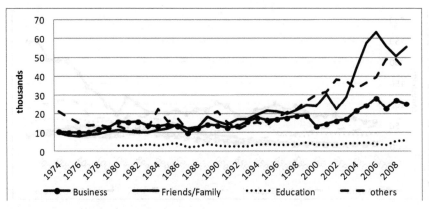

Figure 12.2 Fiji international tourist arrivals by purpose of visit, 1974–2009
Source: Fiji Islands Bureau of Statistics, various years

more than 10%. The data also show the impact of the political instability caused by the 2006 coup, as visitors arriving in Fiji to visit friends and family significantly dipped in 2007 and 2008.

Business arrivals and official conference participants have remained constant at 5% and 2% of total visitors, respectively. Arrivals for business have increased since the deregulation of the aviation market, but declined in 2007 (immediately after the December 2006 coup) and in 2009 due to the GFC. A similar effect was observed for the category of visitors for official conferences.

Considering that Fiji has faced two major crises in recent years, the relative stability in visitor arrival data is surprising. A closer look at country-of-origin figures reveals that this is mostly due to the stability in holiday seekers from Australia. Figure 12.3 shows that of all major tourism source countries, Australia is the only country where visitors to Fiji have not been declining since the 2006 coup. Figure 12.3 also indicates how significant the deregulation of the aviation market was for visitor arrivals from ANZ, as visitors from these two countries increased from around 200,000 in 2003 to about 350,000 in 2008. However, the effects of the overall deregulation process are much larger. In 1998, the first talks to deregulate Fijian international airspace took place. These were driven by the Pacific Forum Secretariat's Pacific Islands Air Services Agreement (PIASA) initiative seeking a liberalised and single Pacific aviation market. This initiative put price and cost pressures on the then Fiji-Australia-New Zealand routes carriers Air Pacific, Air New Zealand and Qantas Airways.

Prior to the entry of Pacific Blue, competition pressure led to an offering of additional flights and reduced prices, which increased the demand for Fijian tourism. According to figures from the Fiji Islands Bureau of Statistics (various years), between 2002 and 2003 available flight kilometres to and from

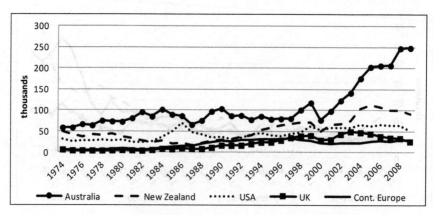

Figure 12.3 Fiji international tourist arrivals by country of origin, 1974–2009
Source: Fiji Islands Bureau of Statistics, various years

Fiji increased by more than 287%. Even though this number has declined slightly since the entry of Pacific Blue, mainly because of the restructuring of international offerings to Fiji by Air Pacific and Qantas Airways, available flight kilometres are still more than 285% higher than before the deregulation talks began in 1998.

Also, according to the Asian Development Bank (2007) and McNamara (2008), since 2004 air fares have dropped by as much as 40%. Additionally, several factors have helped in attracting short-term and budget visitors/ backpackers from Australia and in slowing the decline of arrivals from other countries of origin. These are the strong marketing focus by the tourism industry on the Australian market, the devaluation of the Fijian dollar by 20% in April 2009, and the reduction of tariff rates on tourism-related items. These factors have helped to convince many tourists to switch holiday destinations to Fiji from somewhere else because of Fiji's price competitiveness.

The deregulation of Fijian airspace for incoming flights from ANZ has also resulted in a shift in tourism market shares of country of origin. Before the deregulation, about 45% of total visitors came from the ANZ region. In 2009 this figure increased to more than 62%, with more than 45% of all visitors coming from Australia. The tourism industry has reacted to the increase in tourism demand by almost doubling the availability of rooms per night from 5,700 in 1998 to 9,800 in 2009. Over the same timeframe, the average length of stay increased from about eight days to ten days,[2] and tourism earnings grew by 69% to more than FJ$815 million.

Other major countries of origin are the USA, the United Kingdom and countries of continental Europe. Although their tourist numbers have mostly remained stable, there has been a slight decline in visitor arrivals from all of the countries since 2006 (see Figure 12.3). Furthermore, due to the strong increase in visitor arrivals from ANZ, the shares of other major countries as percentages of total visitor arrivals have also declined. Before the aviation market deregulation, 13% of all visitor arrivals were from the USA and this figure declined to only 9% in 2009. The UK and continental Europe both contributed 9% of total visitor arrivals, respectively, before the deregulation and only 5% each in 2009.

It appears that developments in the aviation market and flight availability play a vital role in the tourism development of a market. Evidence for this also comes from the development of Japanese and Korean tourist arrivals (see Figure 12.4). After suspending flights to Fiji due to the coups in 1987, Japan Airlines (JAL) began servicing Fiji again in 1989. This led to an increase in visitor arrivals from Japan from fewer than 3,500 in 1988 to more than 13,800 in 1989. This figure grew to 45,300 in 1995. The strong surge in Japanese tourist arrivals can also be explained by a 'mini boom' in special tours from Japan to Fiji, including Japanese honeymooners who celebrated their second marriage ceremonies in a white chapel on a beautiful beach. However, with the 2000 coup, JAL suspended its flights to Fiji indefinitely, reducing the available number of flights sharply (Japanese tourist demand had already

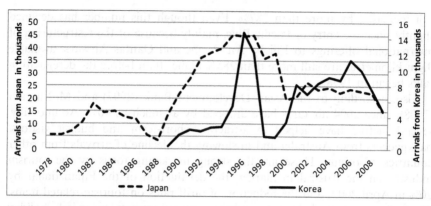

Figure 12.4 Fiji international tourist arrivals from Japan and Korea, 1978/1989–2009
Source: Fiji Islands Bureau of Statistics, various years

weakened before the 2000 coup because of the political instability preceding the coup). Even though Air Pacific also provided flights to Japan, the loss in available flights and the political tensions led to a significant decline in Japanese demand for Fijian tourism; in the following years, only about 20,000 visitors annually arrived from Japan. According to the *Fiji Times* (2008), 'Air Pacific's Japan sector has accounted for losses of $8million a year'. Together with the declining demand for tourism in Japan due to its slow economic growth, Air Pacific decided to withdraw from the Japanese market, leading to a further decline in tourist arrivals (to fewer than 15,000 in 2009) from that country.

Regular direct flights between Fiji and South Korea were introduced in 1995 and visitor arrivals from that country almost doubled immediately. Following a strong marketing campaign for Fijian tourism, visitor arrivals from Korea increased by another 170% to almost 15,000 in the following year. With the Asian financial crisis (AFC) of October 1997 impacting the Korean economy and tourism from that country, Korean Airlines suspended flights to Fiji because of a steep decline in tourism demand. Additionally, the 2000 coup significantly limited the recovery from the AFC in respect of visitor numbers from Korea. Since 2001, Korean Air has offered direct flights between Nadi and Seoul. Visitor arrivals increased to about 11,000 in 2006; however, the December 2006 coup and the GFC reduced arrivals from that country to fewer than 7,000.

Nevertheless, Korean Air's Seoul-Nadi route is important for other countries and may play an important role in the future development of tourism in Fiji because of the increasing importance of the international hub capacity of Seoul (Incheon) International Airport. For example, a majority of Japanese tourists are now using Korean Air to visit Fiji after Air Pacific withdrew the direct flights between Nadi and Narita. Also, despite the fact that Air Pacific now offers direct flights between Nadi and Hong Kong, a substantial number of Chinese nationals are travelling with Korean Air.

These examples show that whether it is Fijian political unrest (e.g. coups), aviation market developments (deregulation of the aviation market), or foreign economic shocks (the AFC and GFC), the Fijian tourism industry and therefore the Fijian economy will be affected by domestic and foreign economic developments. Therefore, to overcome and lessen the impact of these shocks, the Fijian government needs to act in a business- and tourism-friendly way and increase political stability. One of the ways to determine the right policies is to investigate further the demand for tourism with the help of econometric tools. The next section gives an overview of past studies and techniques, before section four investigates the demand for tourism econometrically.

Discussion of economic and econometric models

As Morley (1992) pointed out, 'tourism' is not a homogenous single product or service but a combination or bundle of various goods and services related to the provision of tourism services. These include transportation and accommodation services, services provided by tourism agents such as tourism attractions, as well as restaurant and catering services. The tourism demand of a host country is a reasonably well-researched area and generally a simple demand for goods (or services) model derived from basic demand theory is adopted or assumed. Schulmeister (1979) noted that similar to other services provision, most tourism services are produced and consumed simultaneously. Of course, some of the facilities necessary to provide these services, for example tourist resorts and hotels, have to be constructed well before the tourists consume the service.

There have been empirical studies covering almost all international tourism markets, in both developed and developing countries. To proxy the demand for tourism, the number of visitor arrivals or tourist expenditure data are often used. Other studies, such as Kim (1988), have applied tourism income, the length of stay and distance travelled as dependent variables.

The explanatory variables used in this area vary widely. These include most of the 'usual suspects' such as prices or relative prices of 'tourism' between the tourism-supplying host country and the country of origin of the tourism seeker, the real exchange rate, the (relative) prices of substitute destinations, and the income of tourists in the form of per capita GDP. Other independent variables used are expenditure and cost data for advertisements and marketing, transportation costs and capacity constraints. It is also common to include various dummy variables to capture the effects of infrequent events that may affect tourism demand – for example, natural disasters (floods, cyclones, earthquakes and tsunamis), epidemics (e.g. SARS), and political unrest or conflicts (riots, coups and wars) (see Song *et al.*, 2010).

In a review of econometric estimation techniques applied to tourism demand, Morley (2009) finds these mostly to vary around dynamic elements of time series econometrics. The author observes that these have been applied to avoid common problems of static models, including structural instability

204 Uwe Kaufmann and Haruo Nakagawa

which may imply that the estimation model is spurious (see also Song and Turner, 2006).

Narayan (2003) concludes that after 1995 many empirical tourism demand studies used standardised time series econometric procedures such as unit root tests and cointegration tests before estimating the main regressions. Additionally, in many studies, including Narayan (2002, 2004), various diagnostic test statistics have been reported. These are, for example, tests for autocorrelation, normally distributed residuals, specification errors, structural instability and heteroscedasticity.

Morley (2009) justifies the inclusion of dynamic elements in tourism demand analyses by pointing to the following:

- lags in implementing a decision to travel (for example, deciding in one year to travel in the next)
- information lags (for example, being influenced by hotel prices from last year in deciding between destinations this year)
- as a way of recognizing supply rigidities
- to account for long-term adjustment dynamics
- word-of-mouth recommendations (whereby a previous visitor influences a new visitor), and
- repeat visitors.

(Morley, 2009: 24)

The advancements in time series techniques, including Vector Autoregression (VAR) and Error Correction Modelling (ECM) have been the main driver of econometric methods applied in the estimation of tourism demand over the past 15 years. To implement VAR, the methodologies used include the General to Specific (GETS), Phillips and Hansen Fully Modified OLS (FMOLS), Johansen Maximum Likelihood (JML), and Autoregressive Distributed Lag (ARDL) or 'Bounds Test' approaches.

Table 12.1 Methodology and independent variables in Narayan (2002, 2004) and Katafono and Gounder (2004)

	Method	Period	Income	Relative price	Substitute price	Travel cost	Dummy VARs
Narayan (2002)	JML & ECM	1970–2000	RGDP per capita	Source and Fiji, CPI	Bali and Fiji	Air fares	Coups
Narayan (2004)	Bounds Test & ECM	1970–2000	RGDP per capita	Source and Fiji, CPI	Bali and Fiji	Air fares	Coups
Katafono and Gounder (2004)	JML & ECM	1974–2003	TWRGDP	TW REER	–	–	Coups, cyclones

Source: Narayan, 2002, 2004; Katafono and Gounder, 2004

There have been few empirical studies analysing Fiji's tourism demand. In two papers, Narayan (2002, 2004) uses visitor arrivals from Fiji's top three tourism source countries, namely Australia, New Zealand and the USA, as dependent variables to proxy the demand for Fijian tourism. Katafono and Gounder (2004) investigate Fijian tourism demand using total visitor arrivals. The estimation methodologies and independent variables used in these three studies are summarised in the Table 12.1.

Table 12.1 shows that all studies are based on the ARDL framework. Narayan (2002) and Katafono and Gounder (2004) utilise the JML methodology and Narayan (2004) the 'Bounds Test' approach advocated by Pesaran *et al.* (2001). To proxy a tourist's average disposable income, Narayan (2002) and Narayan (2004) apply the log of real GDP (RGDP) and the log of real gross domestic income (RGDI), both in per capita terms, respectively. Katafono and Gounder (2004) make use of the trade-weighted real GDP (TWRGDP).

In these papers three different internationally accepted approaches are used to measure the relative price difference between the tourist's host and home countries. The log of the trade-weighted real effective exchange rate (TW REER) is applied by Katafono and Gounder (2004) and the log of the exchange rate adjusted relative consumer price index is used by Narayan (2002). In his 2004 study, Narayan employs the log of relative hotel price indices. In addition to relative prices, Narayan (2002, 2004) includes a substitute destination analysis. The author assumes for potential tourists from Australia, New Zealand and the USA, that Bali, Indonesia, is Fiji's closest tourism substitute; his assumption had been supported by the World Bank (1995) and the Fiji Ministry of Tourism (1997).

In his 2004 article, Narayan uses the log of the exchange rate adjusted relative consumer price index between Bali and Fiji to construct a relative substitute price index from 'the cost of travel to the country plus the cost of accommodation and food in the country for a tourist from any one of Fiji's main tourist source markets' (Narayan, 2004: 204).

To estimate the impact that air fare price changes have on Fijian tourism demand, Narayan (2002, 2004) makes use of real air fare prices of one-way economy-class air tickets between the main tourism sources of Sydney, Auckland and Los Angeles, and the tourism host destination of Nadi, Fiji. Although air fare and travel cost proxies (e.g. the real crude oil price) are widely used as independent variables in the estimation of tourism demand, Katafono and Gounder (2004) assume that the REER variable captures the changes in travel cost and their impacts.

Table 12.2 summarises the estimation results of the three studies. Because the papers are based on slightly different timeframes and methodologies, a direct comparison of their results is difficult. The income elasticity estimates in both Narayan (2002, 2004) studies indicate relatively high results for Fiji's tourism demand compared with the estimates of Katafono and Gounder (2004). Narayan (2002) reports income elasticities varying between 2.2 for

Table 12.2 Long-run elasticity estimates in Narayan (2002, 2004) and Katafono and Gounder (2004)

Sources		Income	Relative price	Substitute price	Travel costs
Narayan (2002)	Australia	3.346 (0.498)	-0.379 (0.149)	-0.182 (0.132)	-0.806 (0.130)
	New Zealand	2.164 (0.541)	-2.847 (0.376)	-1.130 (0.306)	-2.875 (0.414)
	USA	3.207 (0.352)	-3.116 (0.696)	-2.898 (0.509)	-0.404 (0.305)
Narayan (2004)	Australia	3.590	-2.007	-2.494	-1.137
	New Zealand	3.071	-0.596	-2.405	-3.415
	USA	4.356	-0.898	-5.058	-1.978
Katafono and Gounder (2004)	World	1.105	0.101	–	–

Notes: The numbers in parentheses are standard errors; not provided in Narayan (2004) and Katafono and Gounder (2004).
Sources: Narayan, 2002, 2004; Katafono and Gounder, 2004

New Zealand, and 3.2 and 3.3 for the USA and Australia, respectively. These results imply that a 1% increase in tourist income in these countries increases their demand for Fijian tourism by between 2.2% and 3.3%. With income elasticities of 3.1 to 4.4, Narayan (2004) estimates an even higher impact of foreign income on Fijian tourism, as compared to the close to unity income elasticity reported by Katafono and Gounder (2004).

An increase in Fijian prices should have a negative effect on the demand for tourism. Therefore, a negative relative price elasticity is expected. The exchange rate-adjusted relative consumer price index applied by Narayan (2002) reports the highest negative price elasticities for the sample, except for Australia. Accordingly, a relative change in Fijian prices has the largest effect on tourists from the USA and the smallest for Australian holiday seekers. The application of the relative hotel price indices of host and home countries leads to different results. Narayan (2004) reports that the Australian market will be the most affected by a change in relative hotel prices. The TW REER used by Katafono and Gounder (2004) reports results with an incorrect sign, indicating that an increase in Fijian prices, in this case its TW REER, would increase the demand for Fijian tourism.

Narayan (2004) also reports the highest estimates for the substitution prices and travel costs. This researcher finds that a 1% relative price increase in Fijian prices compared to Bali will lead to a more than 5% decline in US visitors. Narayan (2002, 2004) also finds that a change in real air fares has the largest effect on tourism demand from New Zealand.

Table 12.3 provides an overview of the estimates for the 'coup dummy variable' (Coups) and the error correction terms (EC). Relative to the long-run estimates reported in Table 12.3, the short-run dynamics estimated, which are part of the EC model, are presented in Table 12.5. The EC term in the estimation shows how fast the relationship will recover from a shock back to the long-run equilibrium, and it is assumed to be negative (a positive sign means the ECM may not be applicable). A one-off event such as a coup, or a

Table 12.3 Coups and error correction terms in ECM in Narayan (2002, 2004) and Katafono and Gounder (2004)

	Sources	Coups	EC
Narayan (2002)	Australia	-0.345 (4.674)	-0.537 (2.934)
	New Zealand	-0.436 (5.419)	-0.128 (4.673)
	USA	-0.466 (3.331)	-0.089 (0.878)
Narayan (2004)	Australia	-0.195 (3.008)	-0.273 (4.031)
	New Zealand	-0.254 (3.837)	-0.289 (6.759)
	USA	-0.472 (5.492)	-0.166 (5.538)
Katafono and Gounder (2004)	World	-0.323 (10.712)	-0.499 (6.074)

Notes: The numbers in parentheses are T-statistics.
Sources: Narayan, 2002, 2004; Katafono and Gounder, 2004

natural disaster such as a big cyclone is included in this short-run analysis or the ECM. Coups were found to be statistically significant in all three studies reviewed and showed a clear negative impact on the demand for Fijian tourism; the coups reduced tourism demand by between 19.5% and 47.2%.[3] Other than the estimation equation for the USA in Narayan (2002), all EC terms were found to be statistically significant.

Specification, estimation and results

Our analysis of Fiji's tourism demand focuses on the timeframe 1974 to 2009. We generally follow Narayan (2002, 2004) in estimating the demand for tourism for Fiji's three main source markets, namely, Australia, New Zealand and the USA. Visitor arrival figures from these countries are used to proxy the countries' demand for Fijian tourism. The exchange rate-adjusted relative consumer price index of Fiji to the specific source country,[4] the relative price index of possible substitute destinations for potential tourists from these three countries, and a travel cost proxy are used as explanatory variables.

Our study adds value to previous studies as we take the increasing capacity and competitiveness of other tourism destinations within the Pacific into account. This is especially the case for ANZ tourists, who nowadays have a relatively large choice of competing tourism countries. Therefore, additional to Bali, which we see as Fiji's strongest competitor for visitors from the USA, we also include a Pacific price index. This index is a combination of the exchange rate-adjusted consumer price indices for the Cook Islands, Samoa, Tonga and Vanuatu, weighted by the number of visitor arrivals.

Where international air fare data are unavailable, a proxy commonly used to measure the cost of travel is the price of crude oil (see Garin-Munoz, 2006, 2007; Salleh *et al.*, 2008; and Habibi and Rahim, 2009).[5] The study follows this approach; however, instead of crude oil, it constructs a proxy of travel cost variables from kerosene prices.

Therefore, the long-run model estimated is as follows:

$$ln\ VA_{i,t} = \alpha_0 + \alpha_1 ln Y_{i,t} + \alpha_2 ln RP_{ij,t} + \alpha_3 ln SPB_t + \alpha_4 ln SPP_t + \alpha_5 ln TC_{ij,t}$$
$$+ \alpha_6 Coup_t + \varepsilon_t \rightarrow (4\text{--}1)$$

Where:

- i = Australia, New Zealand and the USA, j = Fiji;
- $ln VA_{i,t}$ is the log of visitor arrivals in Fiji from source i in year t;
- $ln Y_{i,t}$ is the log of per capita RGDP of the source in year t;
- $ln RP_{ij,t}$ is the log of exchange rate-adjusted relative price index of Fiji to the source i in year t;
- $ln SPB_t$ is the log of substitute price index of Fiji to Bali in year t;
- $ln SPP_t$ is the log of substitute price index of Fiji to the Pacific in year t (omitted for the analysis of US visitors); and
- $Coup_t$ is a dummy variable for coups in Fiji, and
- ε_t is the error term.

Unit root tests using the Augmented Dicky Fuller (ADF) test of individual variables were estimated prior to the test for cointegration. To preserve space, the test results are presented in the appendix to this chapter. Following the standard JML procedure, the variables were then tested for cointegration using the Johansen Cointegration Test. We determined that the number of cointegration relationships among the variables considered for these three source markets is one. Details of the cointegration tests are also presented in the appendix.

Table 12.4 summarises the long-run elasticities of Fiji's tourism demand for the three source countries, derived by normalising visitor arrivals in the cointegration or long-run equilibrium relationship. Most of our results are consistent with previous studies, as shown in Table 12.2. We found high income elasticities, with a similar range to those estimated by Narayan (2002, 2004); the only exception is the result for Australia.

Table 12.4 Long-run elasticities of Fiji's tourism demand, 1974–2009

Source country	In Y	lnRP	lnSPB	lnSPP	lnTC
Australia	3.641	-0.271	-0.173	-2.218	0.965
	(0.637)	(0.561)	(0.226)	(0.855)	(0.134)
New Zealand	4.822	-2.203	-3.488	-2.083	-1.268
	(0.404)	(0.678)	(0.465)	(0.874)	(0.278)
USA	4.478	-3.191	-4.080	–	-0.072
	(1.067)	(0.573)	(0.790)	–	(0.239)

Note: The numbers in parentheses are standard errors.
Source: Authors' estimates

Our results for substitute tourism destinations confirm that other Pacific islands such as Vanuatu and the Cook Islands are indeed considered as substitutes by ANZ holiday seekers.

The results for the travel cost proxy, the real kerosene price index, is the only drawback in the estimates. The long-run cointegration relationship of the travel cost proxy only gives the 'correct' sign for tourism demand for New Zealand where the travel cost elasticity is estimated at around -1.27. Even though the travel cost coefficient for the USA is negative 0.072, with the expected sign, it is rather low, implying that a change in air fares would have little effect on the demand for Fijian tourism. However, for Australian tourists, the result is a positive 0.97. While the coefficient is statistically significant, this result contradicts theory – indicating that the higher the travel costs, the higher visitor arrivals.[6]

The JML procedure also provides the short-run effects as an ECM equation (see Table 12.5). The magnitude of error correction is found to range from a relatively large 0.42 for Australia to a relatively small 0.023 for the USA. The latter result is not statistically significant. Nevertheless, our findings are very similar to Narayan (2002). He also reports a relatively small, statistically insignificant EC effect for the USA. The short-run effects of the coups show up as strongly negative and statistically significant in all estimations. These results imply that, on average, coups reduce visitor arrivals by between 22% and 26%.

Other variables in the short-run analyses were not found to be strong, and the bulk of fluctuations in the dependent variables are explained by the ECM and the coups. Additional diagnostic tests are presented in the appendix.

Table 12.5 ECMs of Fiji's tourism demand, 1974–2009

	Australia	New Zealand	USA
D(lnVA(-1))	-0.1494	-0.2504	0.1665
	(0.1182)	(0.1720)	(0.1895)
D(lnY(-1))	1.1542	1.7092	1.9045
	(1.3450)	(1.1139)	(1.670)
D(lnRP(-1))	-0.1741	0.1029	-0.1661
	(0.2533)	(0.2862)	(0.3199)
D(lnSPB(-1))	0.2610	0.4094	0.09282
	(0.1408)	(0.2347)	(0.2783)
D(lnSPP(-1))	0.3955	0.0109	
	(0.4546)	(0.4847)	
D(lnTC(-1))	-0.3685	0.0735	-0.1122
	(0.1411)	(0.1252)	(0.1419)
COUP	-0.2637	-0.2187	-0.2626
	(0.0695)	(0.0884)	(0.1163)
ECM(-1)	-0.4197	-0.1855	-0.0225
	(0.0865)	(0.0502)	(0.0649)

Note: The numbers in parentheses are standard errors.
Source: Authors' estimations

Further research and travel costs

As outlined above, the crude oil price is generally accepted as a proxy for international travel costs by the tourism demand literature (see Garin-Munoz, 2006, 2007; Salleh *et al.*, 2008; and Habibi and Rahim, 2009). However, the inconsistency of the air fare coefficients, especially the incorrect sign for Australia, led us to further the investigation of the issue of travel costs.

Figure 12.5 presents the history of the kerosene price index adjusted for inflation using the source country's consumer price index. The first thing that came to our attention was the contradiction between the history of air fares and the kerosene proxy. As stated by the Asian Development Bank (2007) and McNamara (2008), since 2004, air fares to Fiji have declined by as much as 40%. However, according to the real kerosene price index, travel costs would have increased significantly during this time. Considering that over the same time period especially tourist arrivals from Australia have increased, the results of a positive air travel coefficient can be explained.

Investigating the development of the real kerosene proxy also indicates that throughout the timeframe, the travel costs for all countries are strongly correlated and, at times, is the highest for New Zealand and the lowest for the USA. On the one hand, the strong correlation can easily be explained with the kerosene price. On the other hand, the difference in distance is clearly ignored by the kerosene price index. Naturally, the longer the time and distance one needs to travel, the relatively more expensive the trip becomes. Figure 12.6 summarises the average distance from the major source countries to the final destination of Fiji. The figure shows that the average distance travelled from the USA to Fiji is 7,345 miles, compared to only 1,587 miles from New Zealand. However, the distance is not only the factor to determine air fares and this is quite clearly shown in Table 12.6.

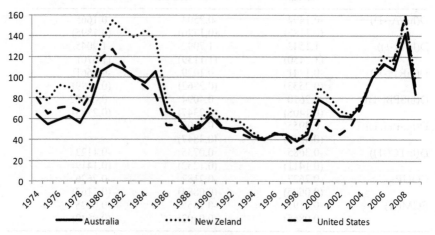

Figure 12.5 Real kerosene price index, 1974–2009
Source: Fiji Islands Bureau of Statistics, various years

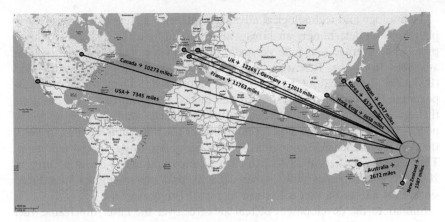

Figure 12.6 Average air flight distance to Fiji
Source: Google Maps, maps.google.com.au; distances are calculated by the authors
with the help of available flights from Webjet.com, 2011

Table 12.6 presents the lowest possible air fares for the travel period of
November 2011. The table indicates that for New Zealand the average actual
air fare to Fiji is $373.56, as expected the lowest of the three countries of
interest. However, the average air fare for Australia is $375.50, not much
more expensive, even though the average trip is 2,672 miles – about 1,100
miles longer than the average trip from New Zealand.

These surprising results led us to investigate the average costs per mile.
Simple maths show that the actual average cost per mile at 23.50 cents is
highest for New Zealand and the lowest for the USA at only 12.36 cents. The
average cost per mile for Australia is found to be 14.03 cents, indicating the
longer the trip takes, the relatively lower the average cost per mile.

Table 12.6 One-way economy air fare prices for November 2011 (US$)

	Air Pacific	Qantas	JetStar	Pacific Blue	Air New Zealand	Average price
Australia						
– Brisbane	358	412	–	314	428	375.50
– Melbourne	310	487	365	377	501	
– Sydney	310	419	235	314	427	
New Zealand						
– Auckland	296	446	–	–	310	373.56
– Christchurch	338	421	–	–	344	
– Wellington	454	409	–	–	344	
United States						
– Los Angeles	749	1,099	–	–	878	908.67

Notes: The prices show the lowest possible air fare and were derived on 2 September
2011.
Source: Webjet.com, 2 September 2011

Technology and technological advancements such as fuel efficiencies clearly play a role in determining air fares – also ignored by using a simple crude oil proxy. The average seat mile per gallon (ASMPG) calculated from the data available from the Research and Innovation Technology Administration (RITA) of the Bureau of Transportation Statistics, US Department of Transportation (for various years) showed that indeed the aviation market has gone through several stages of increasing fuel efficiencies and capacity over the period 1974 to 2009. The data reveal that over the timeframe of 1974 to 1980, the ASMPG increased from circa 30 miles per gallon (mpg) to about 50 mpg. The ASMPG peaked in 1994 with circa 51 mpg and fell to about 43 mpg in 2003. New aeroplanes with higher capacity and newer engines introduced since 2004 allowed a gradual return to circa 51 mpg per seat.

Similar to the development of real air fares over the latter timeframe, fuel and capacity efficiencies contradict the development of the crude oil price index. Last but not least, capacity in regards to actual flights offered also play a vital role. As outlined and discussed in the statistical overview of this chapter, there was a huge surge in flight kilometres offered over the timeframe of deregulation. This increased competition among the airlines and led to additional price pressures. Therefore, probably the most important factor, namely the competition effects on travel cost, are also ignored by a simple crude oil price index and lead to the conclusion that further research in a good valid air travel proxy is necessary.

Conclusion

The Fijian tourism industry is now the most important earner of foreign exchange and has become the backbone of Fiji's economy. While other major foreign exchange earners, namely the sugar and garment industries, have been struggling, the tourism industry has experienced a large increase in visitor numbers and revenues generated over the past decade.

Other than tourism, Fiji has become increasingly reliant on natural resources and remittances. Although these three sources of foreign exchange can easily be affected by economic and natural shocks, no other viable candidate can be seen on the horizon to carry Fiji's economy successfully into the twenty-first century. Therefore, a healthy tourism sector could be the key for sustainable growth of Fiji's economy.

However, our review of recent developments in the Fijian tourism sector shows that domestic (e.g. coups) and external shocks (the AFC and GFC) have adversely affected the industry. One of the most promising source markets, namely Japan, has almost been lost, likely a result of the political uncertainty in Fiji.

On the other hand, positive developments as a direct result of proactive policy decisions by the Fiji government were also noted. Devaluations of the Fiji dollar have made tourism internationally more competitive. Targeted policies such as the deregulation of Fiji's aviation market in 2004 also promoted particular tourism source markets. In particular, as shown with the statistical analysis, deregulation led to significant declines in air fares and increases in visitor arrivals from Australia and New Zealand.

To investigate further the potential impacts of foreign and domestic shocks on the tourism sector, we undertake econometric analyses on the demand for Fijian tourism from the top three tourist source countries: namely, Australia, New Zealand and the USA. We confirm findings of previous studies and show that changes in a tourist's income and costs of tourism strongly affect the demand for Fiji as a holiday destination. We further find that for Australian and New Zealand tourists, other Pacific island countries such as Cook Islands, Samoa, Tonga and Vanuatu are viable vacation alternatives to Fiji.

Thus, adverse domestic and foreign shocks highly influence the development of the Fijian tourism sector. To overcome and lessen the impact of these shocks, the Fiji government needs to act in a business- and tourism-friendly way and increase political stability.

We also point out that common travel cost proxies such as a real crude oil or kerosene price index ignore important factors that determine the final price of air fares. We suggest that distance, capacity increases, fuel efficiencies and competition effects are also strongly related to the development of air fares. Therefore, we conclude that a simple crude oil or kerosene price index is an inadequate air fare proxy and that the topic of air fares deserves further research.

Appendix

Unit root test of individual variables

For all the level variables, the lag length of ADF statistics chosen by the Schwarz Information Criterion (SIC) did not exceed the 5% critical value and thus a unit root was not rejected (see Table 12.7). The ADF statistics of the first differences of the variables exceed the 5% critical value except for the per capita RGDP for the USA. However, the ADF statistics (2.832) of the first difference of RGDP for the USA is found to be very close to the 5% critical value (2.954).[7] Therefore, this variable can be integrated of a higher order; however, we decide to proceed by assuming all of the variables used in the analyses are integrated in the order of one, or I(1).

Cointegration test results

Table 12.8 summarises the results of the Johansen Cointegration Tests for three groups of variables. For all the trace statistics indicate only one cointegrating relationship. However, the maximum eigenvalue (ME) statistics indicates no cointegrating vectors for the USA. Johansen and Juselius (1990), Kasa (1992), Serletis and King (1997) and Adefeso and Mobolaji (2010) point out that the trace statistic is the stronger of the two tests as it also takes

214   *Uwe Kaufmann and Haruo Nakagawa*

Table 12.7 Unit root test results

Country	Variables	Lag	ADF Stat	5% CV
Australia	lnVA	0	1.604	3.544
	lnY	0	2.282	3.544
	lnRP	0	3.455	3.544
	lnSPB	0	2.781	3.544
	lnSPP	1	3.213	3.548
	lnTC	0	1.765	3.544
	ΔlnVA	0	6.510	2.951
	ΔlnY	0	5.124	2.951
	ΔlnRP	0	5.920	2.951
	ΔlnSPB	1	5.954	2.954
	ΔlnSPP	0	4.477	2.951
	ΔlnTC	0	5.152	2.951
New Zealand	lnVA	0	2.161	3.544
	lnY	1	2.391	3.548
	lnRP	0	2.919	3.544
	lnSPB		Same as Australia	
	lnSPP		Same as Australia	
	lnTC	0	1.592	3.544
	ΔlnVA	0	6.174	2.951
	ΔlnY	0	4.034	2.951
	ΔlnRP	0	5.794	2.951
	ΔlnSPB		Same as Australia	
	ΔlnSPP		Same as Australia	
	ΔlnTC	0	4.595	2.951
USA	lnVA	0	2.161	3.544
	lnY	1	2.391	3.548
	lnRP	0	2.919	3.544
	lnSPB		Same as Australia	
	lnSPP		None	
	lnTC	0	1.592	3.544
	ΔlnVA	0	6.174	2.951
	ΔlnY	0	4.034	2.951
	ΔlnRP	0	5.794	2.951
	ΔlnSPB		Same as Australia	
	ΔlnSPP		None	
	ΔlnTC	0	4.595	2.951

Source: Authors' calculations

the smaller eigenvalues into account, which are ignored by the ME test statistic. Johansen and Juselius (1990) explain that in the case of contrary results between the two test statistics, the trace test statistic should be applied (see also Adefeso and Mobolaji, 2010). Therefore, we conclude with a single cointegrating vector for all of the three groups.

Table 12.8 Cointegration test results

	# of CVs	Trace stat	Trace 5% CV	ME Stat	ME 5% CV
Australia	None	132.037	117.708	48.274	44.497
	At most 1	83.763	88.804	35.853	38.331
	At most 2	47.910	63.876	21.225	32.118
	At most 3	26.685	42.915	15.150	25.823
	At most 4	11.535	25.872	7.546	19.387
New Zealand	None	108.325	83.937	51.686	36.630
	At most 1	56.639	60.061	21.981	30.440
	At most 2	34.659	40.175	19.117	24.159
	At most 3	15.542	24.276	11.003	17.797
	At most 4	4.539	12.321	4.139	11.225
USA	None	79.929	76.973	33.319	34.806
	At most 1	46.609	54.079	23.485	28.588
	At most 2	23.125	35.193	10.878	22.300
	At most 3	12.247	20.262	8.520	15.892
	At most 4	3.727	9.165	3.727	9.165

Source: Authors' calculations

Diagnostic tests

Table 12.9 summarises the results of the diagnostic tests for the three cointegration relationships as well as the corresponding error correction model. The goodness of fit statistics show a relatively poor fit of the estimation equation for the USA. The serial correlation is tested by the Lagrange multiplier test of residual correlation (*F* test version) and indicates a good result at the 5% level. The functional form is tested by the *F* test version of Ramsey's (1969) Regression Equation Specification Error Test (RESET), and the results for the USA indicate a specification error at the 1% level. Unfortunately, it was not possible to provide an alternative. The Jarque-Bera test is used to check for and confirm normality (Jarque and Bera, 1981). Heteroscedasticity (non-homogenous dispersion) is tested for by *F* version of Breusch and Pagan (1979). Both indicate good results.

Table 12.9 Diagnostic test results

	Australia	New Zealand	USA
Goodness of fit: adjusted R^2	0.606	0.442	0.148
Serial correlation: LM test of residual correction	$F(1,24) = 0.512$	$F(1,25) = 0.001$	$F(1,26) = 0.069$
Functional form: Ramsey's RESET test	$F(1,24) = 0.899$	$F(1,25) = 0.239$	$F(1,26) = 8.775$
Normality: Jarque-Bera's test	$X^2 (2) = 0.004$	$X^2 (2) = 0.734$	$X^2 (2) = 1.005$
Heteroscedasticity: Breusch-Pagan test	$F(1,32) = 1.972$	$F(1,32) = 1.413$	$F(1,32) = 1.852$

Source: Authors' calculations

Notes

1 Lim (1997) surveyed 100 empirical tourism demand studies and found that the income of a tourist's home country is, together with prices, the most often used explanatory variable; see also Narayan (2004).
2 Throughout the sample period of 1974 to 2009, the average length of stay remained mostly between eight and nine days.
3 Katafono and Gounder (2004) also include a dummy variable for large cyclones; however, as inclusion of this variable did not return statistically significant results it was not reported in Table 12.3.
4 Data limitations did not permit use of the hotel price index as applied by Narayan (2004).
5 We tried to obtain travel cost data similar to Narayan (2002, 2004), which is the real price of one-way economy-class tickets from Sydney, Auckland and Los Angeles to Nadi. These could be derived from the actual economy-class air fare data. Unfortunately, we could not access a similar kind of database or publication to that used in Narayan (2002, 2004).
6 The reasons for our contradictory results of air travel estimates are that even though internationally accepted and widely used, a simple proxy such as real crude oil or kerosene prices ignores important factors that contribute to air fares. The next section discusses in more detail the travel cost derivations and important factors ignored by crude oil or kerosene price proxies.
7 The MacKinnon (1996) one-sided p-value is 0.065.

References

Adefeso, H.A. and Mobolaji, H.I. (2010) 'The Fiscal-monetary Policy and Economic Growth in Nigeria: Further Empirical Evidence.' *Pakistan Journal of Social Sciences* 7(2): 137–42.
Asian Development Bank (2007) 'Oceanic Voyages – Aviation in the Pacific.' Manila: ADB Pacific Studies Series.
Australian Bureau of Statistics (2010) *Australian Social Trends, September 2010: Holidaying Abroad*. No. 4102.0. Canberra: ABS.
Breusch, T.S. and Pagan, A.R. (1979) 'Simple Test for Heteroscedasticity and Random Coefficient Variation.' *Econometrica* 47(5): 1287–94.
Fiji Bureau of Statistics (various years) *Visitor Arrivals Statistics*. Suva, Fiji: FBS.
Fiji Times (2008) 'HK Flights Provide Link.' 6 November. www.fijitimes.com/story. aspx?id=105390 (accessed 7 October 2014).
Garin-Munoz, T. (2006) 'Inbound International Tourism to Canary Islands: A Dynamic Panel Data Approach.' *Tourism Management* 27(2): 281–91.
——(2007) 'German Demand for Tourism in Spain.' *Tourism Management* 28(1): 12–22.
Habibi, F. and Rahim, K.A. (2009) 'A Bound Test Approach to Cointegration of Tourism Demand.' *American Journal of Applied Sciences* 6(11): 1925–32.
Jarque, C.M. and Bera, A.K. (1981) 'Efficient Tests for Normality, Homoscedasticity and Serial Independence of Regression Residuals: Monte Carlo Evidence.' *Economics Letters* 7(4): 313–18.
Jayaraman, T.K. and Choong, C.-K. (2008) 'Monetary Policy Transmission Mechanism in Fiji: An Empirical Analysis of – The Quarterly Model.' *International Journal of Business and Management* 3(11): 11–26.

Johansen, S. and Juselius, K. (1990) 'Maximum Likelihood Estimation and Inference on Cointegration with Applications to the Demand for Money.' *Oxford Bulletin of Economics and Statistics* 52(2): 169–209.

Kasa, K. (1992) 'Common Stochastic Trends in International Stock Markets.' *Journal of Monetary Economics* 29(1): 95–124.

Katafono, R. and Gounder, A. (2004) 'Modelling Tourism Demand in Fiji.' *Reserve Bank of Fiji Working Paper Series* 2004–1, RBF, Suva.

Kim, S.H. (1988) *The Demand for International Travel and Tourism to South Korea: An Econometric Evaluation of Major Economic Factors*. PhD thesis. University of Santo Tomas, Manila.

Lim, C. (1997) 'An Econometric Classification and Review of International Tourism Demand Models.' *Tourism Economics* 3(1): 69–81.

MacKinnon, J. (1996) 'Numerical Distribution Functions for Unit Foot and Cointegration Tests.' *Journal of Applied Econometrics* 11(6): 601–18.

McNamara, K.E. (2008) 'Pragmatic Discourses and Alternative Resistance: Responses to Climate Change in the Pacific.' *Graduate Journal of Asia-Pacific Studies* 6(2): 33–54.

Ministry of Tourism (1997) *Fiji Tourism Development Plan 1998–2005*. Suva, Fiji: Ministry of Tourism.

Morley, C.L. (1992) 'A Micro-economic Theory of International Tourism Demand.' *Annals of Tourism Research* 19(2): 250–67.

——(2009) 'Dynamics in the Specification of Tourism Demand Models.' *Tourism Economics* 15(1): 25–39.

Narayan, P.K. (2002) 'A Tourism Demand Model for Fiji, 1970–2000.' *Pacific Economic Bulletin* 17(2): 103–16.

——(2003) 'Tourism Demand Modelling: Some Issues Regarding Unit Roots, Cointegration and Diagnostic Tests.' *International Journal of Tourism Research* 5: 369–80.

——(2004) 'Economic Impact of Tourism on Fiji's Economy: Empirical Evidence from a CGE Model.' *Tourism Economics* 10(4): 419–33.

Pesaran, M.H., Shin, Y. and Smith, R.J. (2001) 'Bounds Testing Approaches to the Analysis of Level Relationships.' *Journal of Applied Econometrics* 16(3): 289–326.

Ramsey, J.B. (1969) 'Tests for Specification Errors in Classical Linear Least Squares Regression Analysis.' *Journal of the Royal Statistical Society, Series B* 31(2): 350–71.

RITA (various years) 'T1: U.S. Air Carrier Traffic and Capacity Summary by Service Class.' Washington, DC: RITA, BTS, USDOT.

Salleh, N.H., Siong-Hook, L., Ramachandran, S., Shuib, A. and Noor, Z.M. (2008) 'Asian Tourism Demand for Malaysia: A Bound Test Approach.' *Contemporary Management Research* 4(4): 351–68.

Schulmeister, S. (1979) *Tourism and Business Cycle*. Vienna: Austrian Institute of Economic Research.

Serletis, A. and King, M. (1997) 'Common Stochastic Trends and Convergence of European Union Stock Markets.' *Manchester School of Economic & Social Studies* 65(1): 44–57.

Song, H., Kim, J.H. and Yang, S. (2010) 'Confidence Intervals for Tourism Demand Elasticity.' *Annals of Tourism Research* 37(2): 377–96.

Song, H. and Turner, L. (2006) 'Tourism Demand Forecasting.' In L. Dwyer and P. Forsyth (eds) *International Handbook on the Economics of Tourism*. Cheltenham: Edward Elgar.

World Bank (1995) *Fiji: Resolving Growth in a Changing Global Environment*. Washington, DC: World Bank.

13 Hosting bluewater sailors
A destination model for the Pacific islands

Barbara Koth

Introduction

Travelling by sail across oceans for leisure, whether for personal mobility and/ or tourist sightseeing motivations, is perceived in the twenty-first century as a pleasurable lifestyle pursuit. Research on international arrivals of small sailing vessels is scarce, but the number of 'bluewater' sailors on ocean-going sailboats is thought to be increasing, even in polar regions (Hall and Wilson, 2010; Bergmann and Klages, 2012; Cater, 2013). Bluewater or offshore sailing – that is, oceanic non-motorised voyaging away from continental coastlines – has certainly been spurred by popular literature that romanticised ocean sailing in fiction (*Treasure Island* by Stevenson, 1883; *Moby Dick* by Melville, 1851), history (Charles Darwin's *The Voyage of the Beagle* (1839), *Mutiny on the Bounty* by Nordhoff and Hall, 1932), and biography (*Kontiki* by Heyerdahl, 1948; Shackleton's Antarctic journeys, by Lansing, 1959). However, over the last four decades, technological advances in navigation, forecasting and communications have been the primary drivers of this burgeoning transglobal movement of small boats. Global positioning has replaced the sextant and chronometer, mid-ocean weather forecasts received through email now supplement barometer readings, satellite communications are now the norm, the latest generation of affordable collision-avoidance radar for small ships increases safety margins, and innovations in food supplies and personal equipment all make onboard life more comfortable. One can speculate that the global financial situation may have slowed the entry of the middle class into ocean sailing; however, sectoral experts estimate that at any one time several thousand small yachts are traversing the world's oceans, with the busiest traffic in the Mediterranean and the Atlantic (Cornell, 2008).

Bluewater sailing is a phenomenon that spans both tourism and lifestyle dimensions. A standard westbound 10,000-nautical mile 'Milk Run' traverses the Pacific, with landfall from North America or the Panama Canal at the Marquesas Islands of French Polynesia, continuing through Tahiti and the Society Islands, to the Cook Islands, Tonga, Fiji, Vanuatu, and perhaps New Caledonia. New Zealand is a popular summering ground during the cyclone season (November through April). The crossing may be carried out in one rushed six- to eight-month season in the March to November window, or over several years, typically returning to New Zealand (or the Marshall Islands) when the season ends. For tropical Pacific destinations, hosting these ocean-going boats, along with their captains and crews, is a form of niche tourism that brings economic and other benefits to communities.

The distribution of boat expenditures in capital city ports will differ from remote anchorages, but payments for maintenance and repair, food and fuel, entertainment, and for other everyday living costs will be distributed more widely across the destination, and certainly span a wider retail range than traditional sun-and-sand visitors. As bluewater boats are often at sea for years at a time, lengths of stay at destinations are longer, including repeat visits for more supplies, possibly lasting several months in higher latitudes or protected 'hurricane holes' while riding out the cyclone season. As with other forms of tourism, satisfaction with the destination experience promotes positive word of mouth within the yachting community, and leads to repeat visits in subsequent seasons.

There is a strong economic rationale in destination areas for developing the bluewater market, and there are also social advantages to be gained by the host community through positive host-guest relations and an emerging market segment with potentially low impact. Oceanic sailing is about more than seeing diverse Pacific locales; rather, sailing is also a lifestyle choice that simultaneously promotes personal well-being and promotes civic involvement, and bluewater sailors in the Pacific have the opportunity to engage with host communities through volunteer activities, cultural reciprocity and resource sharing. Indeed, as bluewater sailing is a possible exemplar of a form of 'slow tourism' that values authentic cultural and natural attributes of place (Dickinson et al., 2010), it is useful to gain a deeper understanding of how cruisers can interact with Pacific island residents in a sustainable, low-impact manner as part of the sailing way of life. By contrast, such considerations as the commercialisation of culture and demonstration effects (Smith, 2009) and the biological dispersal of invasive species (Floerl et al., 2009; Hall et al., 2010), may also be foremost among the impacts of hosting international boats and their crew. While this chapter does not directly address the potentially negative influences of an increase in foreign vessels in rural or remote areas, it does highlight their minimal demands for physical resources and infrastructure. Apart from marina development/haul out facilities, the infrastructural requirements for bluewater boats are relatively low. However, sustainability is not guaranteed, and destination planning authorities need to be aware of water pollution and contamination, the sailors' need to dispose of solid waste, the possible inflation of retail goods, and exacerbation of crowded port conditions that arise as this niche market develops.

Statistics on yacht arrivals in Pacific countries are not widely available, and insofar as immigration figures are publicly accessible online, incoming small boats are likely to be placed in such imprecise categories such as 'via seaports' and 'other'. One exception is the annual immigration report from Tonga

(Kingdom of Tonga Statistics Department, 2012), showing 1,849 yachts arriving in 2011, an 11% increase from the previous year. This number will include super- or megayachts (greater than 30 metres), an expanding market in some locales (for example, Society Islands). Two additional major sub-groups exist within this statistic: bluewater boats crossing the Pacific from east to west, and New Zealand boats travelling north-east to visit for a season. Infrequent reports in Vanuatu show 924 international yacht arrivals to Vanuatu in 2007 (TRIP Consultants, 2008), while Samoan sources aggregate traffic data from competitors, noting that 'estimates indicated about 800 yachts a year visit Tonga, mainly Vava'u, under 1,000 yachts visit Fiji, and about 200 yachts to Niue' (Samoa Tourism Authority, 2009: 60). In 2006, Samoa recorded 200 yacht arrivals, reflecting its positioning off the primary Milk Run route. Alternatively, a proxy measure is private sailboat transits through the Panama Canal, of which there were 1,177 in 2010, with two thirds bound in the Pacific direction (Cornell, 2011). Only an unknown portion of these would continue oceanic passaging directly westward, as North American east-to-west coast boat deliveries are common (a 'right turn'), as is continued pleasure exploration of the coast in both the North and South (a 'left turn') hemispheres. The South Pacific Tourism Organisation considers yacht arrivals 'generally small', and claims that since 2008 specific statistics have been collected and published by only five of the 22 Pacific countries (SPTO, 2013).

This study attempts to address the current knowledge gap in formal study of bluewater sailors by reporting on a survey administered to yacht owners in the southern Pacific. This involved a quantitative analysis of lifestyle patterns, motivations and service expectations at destinations, along with a content analysis of cruiser responses, which together enabled the construction of a tourism planning model for Pacific ports of call. In addition, the author's on-board experience over several years facilitates a deeper insight into operation of the sailing community through case study examples.

On the assumption that after assessing the trade-offs of hosting the blue-water market, tourism officials and the business community will want to encourage independent yachts to visit, at the end of this chapter there are recommendations as to how this might be achieved.

A rich 'man's' pastime or a way of life?

There is a paucity of research on oceanic sailing, and the economic literature tends to be proprietary (e.g. Northland Marine Development Group, 2008). With no comparative expenditure data available, such proxy variables as skill specialisation, gender and the social world of sailing can provide insight into the functioning of this unique tourism and leisure community. Certainly, the skill set required places bluewater sailing in the expert category of recreation specialisation, as boats are comparatively large and the challenges (weather, collision, equipment failure, stress) ubiquitous in offshore sailing when contrasted with coastal or inland sailing. At a minimum, a boat moored in the Pacific represents a significant investment in skill building as well as 'equipment', and sailors clearly want to protect their marine assets.

Whether or not bluewater sailing is 'a rich man's sport' is arguable. A study by Kuentzel and Heberlein (1997), albeit of inland sailors, did not find income differences, irrespective of whether the point of entry for sailing was boat shows, sailing schools or yacht clubs. Coastal and offshore sailing generally require more financial investment due to maintenance issues and additional equipment, but boats varying dramatically by age, length overall, cachet of the manufacturer, and the extent to which advanced technology is used, cross oceans. When Lusby and Anderson (2008, 2010) asked members of the ocean sailing community to reflect on their own characteristics, they frequently described themselves as 'egalitarian'. However, because it violates the community's norms to seek details of personal income or purchase prices, researchers have to examine indirect evidence (for example, employment and sources of funding) to obtain further information about sailors' finances.

Another important area of inquiry focuses on gender roles and the stereotype that sailing is, in essence, a man's world. Arguing that it should be normal for women to captain boats, Porter (1999) suggests that for this to occur, several barriers must be overcome. These include the predominant male control of family leisure expenses, marine design requiring male upper-body strength (which can be compensated for by technology), the extensive time away from home that is required, and less familiarity with the repair of technical systems. Nevertheless, she notes the prevalence of women on boats as crew, and provides evidence of expanded roles, including skippering, that women increasingly occupy. Similarly, Burgh-Woodman and Brace-Govan (2008) consider offshore sailing culture more conducive to female participation than ocean racing, which is characterised by male hegemony, because of the opportunities in the former for women to build community, create a home and gain pride through enhanced boat skills (e.g. navigation, communication), while seeing the world. However, the author's observation confirmed much of the gender stereotyping found ashore, for example, women's role in cooking and cleaning, and the tendency to leave complex repair and maintenance tasks to men is also found, even though sailing couples emphasise the equal importance of these seemingly traditional roles. Similarly, Jennings (2005) asserts the marginalisation of female gendered roles in sailing, but highlights the importance of negotiated role complexity among couples who choose the sailing lifestyle.

The small number of researchers studying long-distance ocean sailors focus on the social world of long-distance sailing. Macbeth (1985, 1992) wrote the first PhD thesis on the bluewater sailing subculture in the Pacific, utilising an ethnographic approach to understand lifestyle choice and the rewards of moving outside the mainstream of Western society. He depicted cruisers as satisfied deviants who meet aspirational life goals and build community through participation in ever more immersive sailing experiences, where subculture norms are internalised. He embeds the whole-of-life activity into the concept of flow experience, whereby normal conceptions of life as a series of discrete events are altered in such a way that complete absorption occurs, challenges are met by a commensurate skill level, and the meaning and enactment of sailing become intrinsically rewarding (Macbeth, 1988). He went on to view bluewater sailing as incorporating the notion of a utopian way of life, with an implied critique of postmodern society (Macbeth, 2000), while Koth (2013) links the mobility of bluewater sailors to their need to create their desired lifestyle through cruising, and Jennings (1999), a colleague of Macbeth, focuses on 'empowered connectivity' in the sail yachting world, which involves negotiating and exerting influence on how to engage with the sailing milieu, shore-based externalities and intimate others in a perpetually transitory setting.

Other researchers target the communitarian nature of sailing and attendant life satisfaction. Lusby and Anderson (2008, 2010), for instance, interviewed cruisers in Florida and the Bahamas to build motivational profiles of ocean sailors. One prominent theme that emerged was their perception that freedom was a function of self-determination, requiring independent response to challenges, removal from societal stress, arising partially from the slower pace of life, and extensive travel in contrast to brief holidays. The relationship with the marine environment also emerged as critical: the ocean and its vagaries were held in respect, honoured for their beauty, and were a source of healing and spirituality (especially for women). Community is thus built around camaraderie and trust among sailors holding similar values, and high social capital is evident in a strong culture of mutual assistance and strong association (Lusby and Anderson, 2010). Most recently, ocean cruisers have been shown to score higher on a standard scale of life satisfaction than most respondents in economically advanced nations. This finding was linked to enhanced community relations; the centrality of cruising to lifestyle, advanced skill attainment and yacht club membership were all cited to explain statistically significant differences (Lusby, Autry and Anderson, 2012).

Although there is a basis for understanding why offshore sailing for extended periods is a lifestyle choice with strong community bonds, there is less literature on behaviour and decision making once at sea. However, there is evidence of contributions made by cruisers at their destinations, and stories of sailors with medical training providing health care and emergency services to remote local residents and within the sailing community are legion (Davies, 1984). On Maewo Island, Vanuatu, AusAID, the Australian aid organisation, built a community hall that also serves visiting yachts, cruisers placed buoys to protect coral and provide a local income stream through payment of mooring fees, and helped construct and maintain a small-scale hydropower system (Island Cruising Association, 2009). Indeed, the aid-volunteer partnership has matured to the point where some cruisers also pay part of children's annual school fees in the village, and bring household and fishing supplies (hooks, line, lures) for gifts or trade in remote anchorages. Similarly, on request, the New Zealand-based, non-profit OceansWatch (2013) harnesses its three-vessel fleet and 100 member cruising yachts to take volunteers, scientists, equipment and goods to work with communities in Vanuatu, Solomon Islands and Papua New Guinea, to help manage marine resources, overcome food and water shortages, and develop sustainable livelihoods. Elsewhere, in a form of citizen science, a communiqué from a web-based list for ocean sailors asked volunteer cruising yachts to assist climate change researchers from a British university in studying marine plankton by using a downloadable phone application (Pacificpuddlejump, 2014). Private sailing vessels have even enabled artists to sail to regions heavily impacted by climate change, after which their work has been exhibited at public exhibitions (Giannachi, 2012).

More broadly, the author suggests cruisers in port exhibit more intensive interaction patterns with local communities, in a wider range of (often remote) settings than mainstream tourists. Indeed, because many members of this market segment seek to create a unique relationship with the host community, attracting bluewater boats may demand a different service strategy.

Survey methodology

During the 2009 and 2010 seasons, a survey of two subsets of bluewater sailors, all of whom were native English speakers, was carried out. The first subset was from a population of sailors in the harbour of Whangarei, New Zealand, over a two-week sampling period.[1] Study periods were chosen when the boat crew would be most likely to be onboard having just completed the crossing from Tonga or Fiji (November), or preparing for the next season's departure (April/May). Forty-three boats with persons living onboard were located in the two marinas (Town Basin, Riverside), and there were no refusals for face-to-face surveys. Typically the author went on board and interviewed the captain, although crew members often added observations to open-ended queries. The survey addressed, *inter alia*, lifestyle profile, motivations, itineraries and decision-making context regarding choice of destinations, degrees of integration with land, and evaluation of New Zealand's cruising services and infrastructure.

The second subset of respondents was taken from a population of bluewater sailors who were members of two internet user groups devoted to bluewater sailing, namely Pacificpuddlejump (1,071 registrants), and Circumnavigation (166 registrants). Group members were contacted by email and those with Pacific experience were asked to complete a questionnaire identical to that used for the first subset, except for the exclusion of questions specific to New Zealand. A total of 21 boat owners responded. The disparate memberships of the lists is evident in that many 'volunteered' internet survey responses were eliminated because respondents did not meet conditions of current boat ownership, the southern Pacific as a geographic region of sailing focus, and at least six months' experience sailing offshore in the Pacific.

The small number of responses from each subgroup (43 and 21, respectively) can be attributed, at least in part, to the fiercely independent and transient nature of cruisers. Undoubtedly the sample is small, but as a boat owner with long affiliation with the sailing community, the author considers the responses appropriate and notes, too, that no other research has been based on such an intensive contact with offshore sailors, or has involved such a broad coverage of the academic literature.

Not all the research findings are reported in this chapter, as many have been presented elsewhere, especially those that relate to motivations for cruising (with gender-specific distinctions), decisions about destinations to be visited, which varied according to family circumstances (e.g. single-handers, part-time families), the extent cruisers retain contact home country employment, and levels of travel generated by crew changes and hosting international visitors on board (Koth, 2013). By contrast, in this chapter, focus is on recommendations for service improvement at the destination level. Ocean-crossing sailors were asked three open-ended questions:

1 What do you look for when you decide to stop and stay for a while in an overseas port in a non-rural community, specifically in towns of moderate size and services, rather than remote anchorages?
2 What services do you most often find missing?
3 What recommendations would you often make to communities that want to attract and provide high-quality service to trans-Pacific yachties?

Content analysis was used to analyse responses, with text counts performed by the author, who also provides illustrative examples from participant observation and case study destinations over a two-year period.

Cruiser profiles

In all, 19 countries were represented among the respondents. Citizens of the USA dominated the profile (46%), and Canadians accounted for another 10%. Europeans comprised 28% of respondents, and the largest generating European countries were the United Kingdom, Germany and Sweden. Some 75% of the respondents were captains, of whom five were female, and there were four cases of co-captaining. Couples were the most common sailing social unit (72%), and there were also solo single-handers (16%, all of whom were male), families with children (8%), and unrelated friends (4%). This is comparable with a study by Lusby, Autry and Anderson (2012), in which 82% of the boats were made up of a captain and one crew member, and where the average age was 58 years and 68% had retired. By contrast, in the study reported here, 63 of the respondents had retired, and 24% had sold a home residence to finance their sailing.

Other details also emerged from the survey. Some 84% of the respondents were sailing on monohulls, while the remainder had multihull catamarans, and the average boat length was 13 metres (43 feet), ranging from 9–25m. Only the offshore subsample was asked about travel mileage, and averaged

19,400 nautical miles on the present voyage. Sailors were absent from home for an average of almost five years (59.3 months), with a modal response of 4.2 years. However, the range is extremely variable, from six months to 20 years, and 10% had been away for over ten years. Indeed, 42% intend to circumnavigate the globe, despite ongoing incidents of piracy. Why do they do it? Respondents largely echoed, and then expanded on Lusby and Anderson's (2010) summary of motivational research that ocean cruisers sail because of freedom and an independent life, and love of the sea. There were gender differences, however, and Likert scale findings showed men were driven more by independence and a satisfying way of life, while women's connection to nature and the sailing community were essential to pleasure gained from the lifestyle.

Desirable features of port of call

For the remainder of this chapter, focus will be on the perceptions and expectations of bluewater sailors on destinations they visit. Table 13.1 displays responses to an open-ended survey question about desirable attributes of a port where the sailboat was moored or anchored for a lengthy stay of at least one week. The numbers represent rank order of topics based on frequencies (and word count in the case of ties), and responses were later clustered into several themes, centring on service availability, sailing infrastructure, 'feel' of the community, value for money, and tourism and

Table 13.1 Rank order of open-ended responses regarding desirable port attributes

Rank	Topic	Rank	Topic
Food service/entertainment		**Local community**	
1	Grocery stores nearby/varied provisioning	5	Connect with local community
6	Good restaurants		
18	Good pubs	9	Cost/value for money
		20	Affordable moorage
2	Marine services for repair and maintenance		
8	Chandlery/boat parts available	10	Accessible basic amenities: water, laundry, neat town centre
16	Skilled labour services		
		Recreation and tourism	
Boat facilities		11	Fun things to do when not on boat
3	Secure, safe, comfortable anchorage	12	Outdoor recreation
15	Safe, secure marina	14	Exploring the country
Other services			
4	Internet access onboard		
13	Shipping/import services		
21	Cheap labour to help with simple boat chores		

recreation options. It is considered that, in such a small sample, the relative order of the preferences is more important in the analysis than the absolute numbers. The top-ranked item was volunteered in an open-ended response by 14 individuals (21%), and the last item (ranked 20th) was cited by three respondents (5%). A question on service gaps was eliminated from discussion because of a low response rate and some duplication of the list of desirable attributes in port.

Further details of responses are recorded, but they should be interpreted with caution. One response to the query about desired services in ports of call, for example, was 'What an odd question! If I wanted a lot of stuff, I would have stayed in the First World. I am happy with what shows up!' Along with several similar reactions, this evidences a spirit of discovery and ingenuity in remote destinations that is part of the ethos of long-distance cruising. In such circumstances, formulaic offerings and characterless development are unlikely be appreciated by the sailing community.

Food provisioning

While travelling across the South Pacific, sailors normally eat simple and/or pre-packaged meals, especially during periods of rough weather. Therefore, on arrival in a port of call, special food items are more likely to be purchased, and quality restaurants (the sixth-ranked feature) will be patronised. It is also noteworthy that many sailors spend a significant amount of time in port socialising on other boats, so food purchases are especially important. Not surprisingly, then, the most desirable feature of ports for respondents was a nearby grocery store that offered opportunities to replenish provisions, and this was mentioned by 13 (21%) of respondents. Because of prevailing trade wind directions, trans-Pacific sailors generally cross from west to east, and so most will have stocked the boat with consumables from shops and markets on the west coast of Mexico, the USA or Panama in their first year, or New Zealand, if over summering during cyclone season. Indeed, consistent with an ethic of self-sufficiency and the desire for flexibility, many will have non-perishable food stocks lasting for one or two years, allowing for maximum mobility. However, fruit and vegetables do not store for extended periods and are thus at a premium when sailors reach the South Pacific. Similarly, cryovaced meats have a short shelf life. As a consequence, with spoilage in the tropical heat, limited on-board resources for cooling/freezing, and customs restrictions on the importation of many fresh foodstuffs, sailors often arrive at a port of call with depleted and monotonous food stocks. A United Nations Food and Agriculture Organization (FAO) report seeking to expand the linkages between tourism and local agricultural production, cites the case of Utukalongalu Market in Neiafu (Vava'u), where fresh produce vendors report that personal and charter yachts are the biggest customers, and place sizeable orders.

After an 18–35-day ocean passage from North America to the Marquesas Islands, for example, sailors may trade specially earmarked items (fishing gear, toiletries, cosmetics, tools, books and educational material) for fresh food, or (with local permission) may themselves harvest a variety of crops, for example, limes, mangos and guava. As local shops cater primarily for island residents, and thus carry only limited supplies of processed rice, tuna, cooking oil and local drinks, most boats wait until reaching Tahiti and its super-markets to replenish more commonly utilised foods and to buy 'treats' – that is, relatively expensive and favoured imported items not normally obtainable elsewhere on the trip. Pago Pago, in American Samoa, is another significant resupply location, with an extensive range of products from New Zealand or North America (which are duty free to some nationalities).

Although these preferences relate to non-remote anchorages, the impor-tance of food to sailors brings with it opportunities for local entrepreneurship both at ports and in more isolated villages. In isolated Asanvari on Maewo Island, Vanuatu, for example, the 'Bread Man' visits moored sailboats in a local canoe every morning with fresh bread, and does a brisk business as sailors take a break from baking bread onboard during their trans-oceanic passages. In addition, a local Asanvari woman has opened a small hut selling fruit and vegetables, along with local crafts. On a grander scale, the sole family at Toau Atoll, in Tuamotus, French Polynesia, offers cruisers a secure mooring buoy, a local coconut- and fish-themed meal served on the beach twice a week, informal lessons in making French bread over a barrel stove, and immersion in the local culture by helping with the copra harvest.

Marine services

The item ranked second (n = nine, or 14%) was the availability of marine services for repair and maintenance of sailboats. The corrosive marine envir-onment and constant motion of ocean passaging place heavy stress on hard-ware and running rigging (hence the popular adage 'sailing is fixing your boat in exotic locales'). This preferred destination attribute is a function of the existence of a chandlery, where boat parts, equipment and supplies are sold (the eighth preference), and good-quality labour (the 16th preference). The marine services required range from sail makers and diesel engine repair, to electronics/IT and navigation, pipefitting, and the stress-inducing hauling of boats out of the water. Although most boats carry extensive spare parts (another example of the desire for independence), a 'good' chandlery is valued for items required for regular maintenance and parts that commonly fail or are lost overboard.

Needed marine parts are often old or unique to the boat systems and so have to be imported from the USA, Europe, Australia or New Zealand. This explains why 'a rational policy for shipping and import' is ranked 13th among desirable port attributes. Time constraints in the trans-Pacific sailing season are common: sailors have to avoid cyclones and wait for good sailing condi-tions, for parts to arrive or for customs clearance. Delays can be frustrating, and might even put the safety of both boat and crew at risk. Furthermore, import duties can be high, which helps explain why many sailors prefer to have extensive repair work and retrofits in New Zealand, where most marine equipment is tax free.

Some respondents criticised the lack of a customer service ethic in the marine trades overseas:

> The only time I long for home is when I think of my relationship with my marine mechanic. These so-called tradespeople could learn a lot from his honesty and doing the job with excellence, but at a fair price. I feel cheated.

Such negative experience is widely reported and accounts for many contributions to sailing-related internet sites, where requests for recommendations of tradespeople in island destinations are common. At a minimum, a comprehensive list of marine service providers – such as Whangarei's popular brochure in New Zealand – should be provided for every port of call, distributed across the Pacific and on international arrival.

Unskilled as well as skilled labour is required by sailors in port. The 20th (and last) requirement of sailors was for inexpensive labour to help with routine boat tasks – for example, cleaning the hull, washing the decks and rigging, and varnishing. It seems appropriate here to note, from anecdotal evidence, that many sailors save for decades to purchase a used boat, which may be at least 25 years old. Indeed, despite outward appearances, many sailors are on a budget and sail 'until the kitty runs out'. As a consequence, boats departing westward from Mexico utilise such unskilled services, and workers with a good reputation are in high demand and 'passed' from boat to boat.

Anchorages and marinas

There are as many patterns of arrangements for staying in port as there are sailboats: some captains head directly for the comfort and service of a marina dock, other boats always anchor (or moor when available) for budgetary reasons or lifestyle objectives (for example, more privacy or independence), and many cruisers utilise both the mooring and anchoring modes at different times or places. Respondents in this survey showed a strong preference for 'secure', 'safe' and 'comfortable' anchorages, where the boat physically 'puts the hook (anchor) down' – a requirement that ranked third of their desired features of a destination. Security here refers to good underwater holding ground where the anchor will not drag with a strong wind or direction shift, and being 'in the anchorage' can also refer to mooring, whereby boats in deeper water are 'moored' by holding lines to a chain or float attached to a heavy concrete block on the bottom. Secure mooring is critical, and captains seek advice on the adequacy of moorings from other sailors, often diving or snorkelling personally to check for appropriate design and construction materials. By contrast, safety refers to personal and physical security from theft and injury. Crews often leave boats for day trips or extended excursions, and face such hazards as coral heads or subsurface debris (which, for example, are notoriously found in the harbour of Pago Pago, American Samoa). Finally, 'comfort' is typically experienced as protection from currents and rough surface water in all wind directions, so there is minimal motion of the boat while at anchor, along with freedom from constant and intrusive boat traffic. A safe and secure marina ranked 15th in expressed preferences, indicating that when sailors purchase a berth in a marina, their primary concerns are for personal security and controlled access so opportunities for theft are reduced. At the same time, however, this requirement may conflict with the interests of tourists who are not sailors, whose satisfaction with destinations seems to be reduced when confronted by locked gates and docks that are off-limits to the public (Russell, 2012), irrespective of the attractiveness of the public marine setting.

There are effort and cost considerations in each option for a stay in port. Anchoring is typically free, but can be easy or hard depending on holding ground. Anchoring and mid-priced moorings are more work in that the dinghy may be raised and lowered for each trip to shore. Marinas command the highest fees and are 'easy' once a boat is securely docked. Good anchoring options (free, easy) were mentioned most frequently by sample respondents, making this option imperative in all sailing locales. The availability of marinas (cost, easy) was less commonly mentioned, and might be thought of as complementary or less urgent development in that the marina infrastructure and services can enhance the destination appeal, as well as offer a small business opportunity. However, some sailors will not stop at a destination if there is not adequate anchoring, although they may use marina services regardless of whether anchored, moored or docked.

Internet access

Most modern sailors are networked with friends and family worldwide. They expect to be able to access weather bureaux websites, to communicate with a wide variety of others, perhaps including marine insurance agents, their children's teachers, or business associates (Koth, 2013; Dyer, 2006). At sea, Sail-Mail, a radio-based internet service, provides forecasts and emergency information, and the requirement for connectedness continues in port. This explains why on-board internet access is ranked fourth in their preferences, and in some of the most remote parts of the world sailors are observed in the cockpit of their boats blogging about the latest passage or downloading new recipes on ubiquitous laptops (which may contain navigation software). The decreasing cost of satellite phones is certainly an influence, but most still rely on shore-side internet providers that charge by the hour, day or week. One sailor remarked:

> There are crappy anchorages all over Mexico with mediocre beaches, jet skis whizzing past and booming discos at night, but if there is onboard

internet access, it's a magnet for bluewater sailors! At least for a night or two.

Connection to local community

Adventure and newness were secondary drivers for sailing offshore, and connecting with the local community is fifth in the list of preferences. Examples given in the survey include participation in local cultural events and wanting to interact with residents. When away for extended periods, sailors take their home with them, and expect to continue their hobbies and interests. As one woman remarked, 'I do crafts, and my husband is a musician, so we both like to meet local people similarly engaged'. In addition, many sailors seek involvement in local cultures – for example, in the South Pacific, they may attend church services, irrespective of their own religion, because of the island hospitality, distinctive regional singing, and the insight they obtain into local culture that such attendance affords.

Small rallies where sailboats sail in a group are popular because those on board can gain community access at a very personal level. A trip from Fiji to less-visited Vanuatu can be given as an example. On arrival at a remote island, the crew of every boat is partnered with a host family. Such rallies, called 'cruising in company', occur infrequently in the Pacific (perhaps fewer than ten a year), and are arranged by organisations such as the Island Cruising Association (New Zealand based) and the World Cruising Club (United Kingdom). Benefits include local customs and immigration clearance and a longer stay at the destination. Furthermore, the personal links can lead to volunteerism – for example, working with schools or disadvantaged groups, and restoring habitats. The Clean Wake Projects (Seven Seas Cruising Association, 2010) and Sailors Without Borders (Sailblogs, 2011) enable private yachts and especially targeted excursions to promote environmental and humanitarian assistance – for example, literacy and infrastructure projects – to disadvantaged communities. Otherwise, though, many sailors want to have a minimal impact on communities they visit – a value perhaps arising from their respect for the sea. They have a preference (ranked seventh) for places inhabited by nice and honest people, and avoid destinations where interaction with local residents is fraught, and/or where the destination has a reputation for criminal activity.

Costs

The ninth preference of respondents, for anchorages that were of 'reasonable' cost and good value for money, somewhat belies the stereotype that sailing as a leisure activity is dominated by wealthy elites (as is the case of megayacht tourism). In fact, many trans-oceanic sailors are solidly middle class. They have saved for many years to buy their boat and finance their trips, and continuously have to budget to finance their travelling lifestyle. As one respondent noted, 'We aren't poor cruisers, but we certainly aren't rich. Local people always think yachties are wealthy. Most aren't'. On internet lists, reaction to the 90-day visa imposed in French Polynesia centred on its cost, with a common view that 'it's probably long enough given exorbitant prices'. In like manner, radio chat groups in Mexico regularly share information about weekly restaurant specials, reduced attraction entrance fees or retail discounts. In circumstances where costs of boat maintenance and repairs expenses are typically high, and funds are needed for the air fare home in the cyclone season, sailors may have an occasional spending spree but, generally speaking, they are on tight budgets and search for the best value.

Basic amenities

Fresh potable water (to replenish tanks) and laundry facilities are also deemed important, and together were the tenth preference expressed by respondents. The ready availability of petrol and diesel are also likely to increase a destination's attractiveness, and location near a town and its services is also valued, especially as most cruisers lack motorised transport and have to walk, cycle (either using their own collapsible bicycles or those available locally), or take whatever public transport is on offer (if any).

Recreation and tourism

Lastly, preferences 11, 12 and 14 relate to recreational possibilities at destinations. When not working on the boat, cruisers value the availability of entertaining activities (11th preference), and are eager to learn of local recreation opportunities (12th preference), in some cases joining local hiking groups (for example, at Whangarei in New Zealand) and meeting residents. In port, they often engage in such water sports as sail boarding, kayaking and diving, thus demonstrating the level of physical fitness necessary for bluewater sailing, and they appreciate information about the destination (their 14th preference), so they can explore it, often with crew members of other boats or, alternatively, with family and friends who are visiting them from overseas. Indeed, 45% of the survey's respondents had taken such a trip in the last two years.

Bluewater yachties were also asked which attributes and services were most often missing in Pacific ports of call. Their responses mostly echoed answers to questions already discussed, but some raised the need for better communications to and among sailors. It was suggested, for example, that destinations provide meeting places for yachties to post notices, exchange information and books, and to socialise. As one respondent remarked, 'we are generally independent so we can make it work; we just need a location!' In addition, a daily radio network for cruisers in port, common at departure points in Mexico, would be appreciated in the Pacific. Finally, clear and consistent advance information on border check-in and official entry requirements, currently considered inadequate and inconsistent in the region, was deemed necessary.

Conclusion

In selecting a destination and length of stay, captains must first decide whether or not safe mooring and anchoring can be provided. As with land-based tourism, adequate accommodation is important. The two major activities in port are boat maintenance and repair, and sightseeing, so the availability of marine services availability and attractions are carefully assessed. Like other visitor segments, sailors need food and transport, albeit sometimes of a specialised nature, and they also want a good social life and community engagement. Destinations will be selected according to their assessment of whether or not these requirements can be met, and Pacific island countries able to meet these requirements will be successful in developing this bluewater niche market.

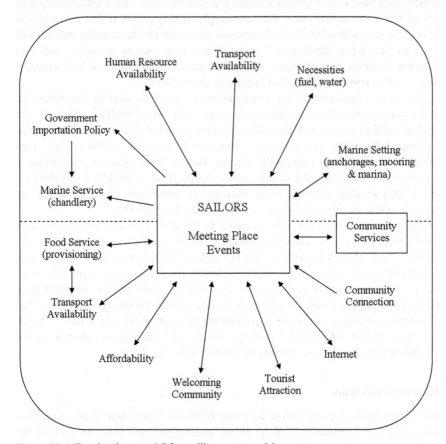

Figure 13.1 Destination model for sailing communities

The destination attributes previously discussed can be summarised and integrated into a destination model (Figure 13.1). The upper section defines the destination attributes that are unique to bluewater cruising, while the lower section portrays linkages with existing community tourism structures and resources. The sailor and the sailing community are at the centre of the model. Social connections are a defining characteristic of this market segment. During the season, sailors gather at key destinations, ports and anchorages, scatter for individual itineraries, and re-gather, building friendships and loyalties as they exchange information and recommendations (Koth, 2013). Such social activities can be supported by providing meeting places, a daily radio network in the harbour, and special events for sailors (e.g. the long-running Tahiti-Moorea Sailing Rendez-vous, which encourages interaction among residents, sailors and tourists).

Anchoring, mooring and docking at a marina are distinct and separate styles, and no one method is better or worse than another. The basic requirements are safety and security. Continued westward progress and the sailing lifestyle require that boats are regularly maintained and repaired, and a satisfactory port of call will have marine stores that can supply quality goods and an efficient and liberal import policy. Similarly, businesses that cater for the cruising market will need to develop a reputation for excellence. Easy access to water, fuel and laundry facilities is imperative, and a labour force of highly skilled workers, along with a supply of unskilled labour, is also valued.

The basic requirements for a destination to be successful in the bluewater sailor market are a host community that is perceived to be both friendly and safe, and affordability. Some of the sailors' requirements at destinations are similar to those when they are at home – more so than other tourists. They need health care, schools (especially during the cyclone season), hairdressers, seamstresses, cinemas and travel agents. As *de facto* residents, dependent on the length of stay, meeting local residents is important, as is an appealing lifestyle while in port, including restaurants and attractions.

The host community will be assessed by its ability to provide sailors with food through various outlets, including local markets, supermarkets and farmers, and also in providing internet access. Sailors are closely linked and constantly trade information about destinations, seasonality, reputable businesses, and tips about maintenance and repairs. Transport is important to them. Indeed, it is positioned in both sections of the model to emphasise that destinations need to meet the requirements of visitors who lack cars – hence the importance of shuttle services, buses and minivans, special rental arrangements, and direct delivery of products to the boats.

Recommendations

On the traditional Pacific crossing route from the west coast of the Americas to summering grounds in New Zealand, most boats will continue to visit the major capital cities and commercial centres of Tahiti, Nukualofa, Vava'u,

Lautoka, and often Pago Pago and Port Vila. These communities would benefit from strengthening the overall services for bluewater sailors, either by attracting more such visitors or maintaining their current market position. At the same time, smaller, less-frequented island groups and ports of call, where lengths of stay are shorter, for example, the Marquesas, Rarotonga and the Cook Islands (e.g. Aitutaki), Niue, Apia, Suva and Savusavu, could note the recommendations made in this chapter and develop strategies and policies to emphasise their relative strengths. For example, islands in the Marquesas might improve local sightseeing options, and Rarotonga could do more to separate cruising boats from commercial traffic. These improvements could be carried out in consultation with destination residents to develop a form of bluewater cruising tourism that is compatible with more traditional 'sun, sea and sand' markets, and yet recognises the potential for entrepreneurial development and economic growth.

A final caution is required in relating the findings of the survey reported in this chapter to remote anchorages and smaller villages in Pacific island countries. Fundamental to the offshore lifestyle is an underlying sense of discovery and independence – indeed, a mythology of place – and if destinations are over-planned or artificial, or the corporate sector and bureaucrats formalise or block authentic, serendipitous interaction with local residents, the reputation of ports is likely to decline (Laurier, 1999). The sailor operates at two social extremes: independently managing a vulnerable boat across thousands of miles of open ocean but then seeking out authentic experiences with fellow sailors and host community members while in port. This is not an easy balance to achieve. Indeed, for bluewater sailors, serendipity is potentially as important as formal destination planning.

This study primarily represents one type of cruiser, the sailing couple roughly following the standard Milk Run route across the Pacific. Many others avoid the well-trodden path and the company of other cruisers, going beyond the cruising guides to discover unspoiled cruising grounds. Sailing families certainly have different shore-side demands from solo sailors (Werth, 1987). More generally, perhaps, it is necessary for government officials and businesses, and all stakeholders that deal with sailors, to recognise the evolving onboard role of women, who are increasingly decision-making captains, as well as visitors with unique and differentiated shipboard experiences. Similarly, stereotypical treatment of members of the sailing subculture as wealthy is unwarranted, for the socio-economic status of many sailors is such that they, too, seek value for money.

New bluewater market opportunities for the Pacific region may be emerging. Most round-the-world sailors originating in Europe and the Americas move east to west with the prevailing trade winds. The increased problem of piracy in places like the Gulf of Aden, western Indian Ocean, Malacca Straits and Indonesia (Murphy, 2010; Coggins, 2012) is compounded by other risks – for example, as shown in the death of sailors onboard small yachts in the Middle East (Nagourney and Gettleman, 2011; Burke, 2009) and by hostage taking. Such developments could result in New Zealand and Australia (and South-East Asia) becoming more prominent turnaround points or sail centres, where (new) owners re-cross the Pacific by different routes. At the time of writing, there was a warning against Middle East transit in place (International Naval Counter Piracy Forces, 2013), and more sailors may choose to return to the Americas via the Line Islands and Hawai'i, moving west to east, or to visit lesser-known destinations on a return journey. Successful planning in such less well-known destinations will depend on resident opinion, governments' tourism policies, the costs of stopovers and word-of-mouth reports from sailors.

Findings reported in this chapter suggest that bluewater sailors and sailboats constitute a niche market of sustainable tourism development, interested in supporting and experiencing local communities, with little impact on local resources and infrastructures. With careful planning, hosting ocean-going sailboats and their captain and crew can make a valuable contribution to the region's development.

Notes

1 New Zealand immigration officials estimate that approximately 1,000 foreign sailboats enter their waters annually (personal communication, November 2011).

References

Bergmann, M. and Klages, M. (2012) 'Increase of Litter at the Arctic Deep-sea Observatory Hausgarten.' *Marine Pollution Bulletin* 64(12): 2734–41.

Burgh-Woodman, H. and Brace-Govan, J. (2008) 'Marketing and the Other: A Study of Women in the Sailing Marketplace and its Implication for Marketing Discourse.' *European Advances in Consumer Discourse* 8: 189–95.

Burke, J. (2009) 'How Somali Pirates Hijacked the Lemacon's Sailing Trip of a Lifetime.' *The Guardian*, 4 October.

Cater, C. (2013) 'Nature Bites Back: Impacts of the Environment on Tourism.' In A. Holden and D. Fennell (eds) *The Routledge Handbook of Tourism and the Environment*. Routledge, 119–29.

Circumnavigation and Ocean Crossing (formerly Circumnavigation) (2010) *Yahoo list*. groups.yahoo.com/neo/groups/circumnavigation/info.

Coggins, B. (2012) 'Global Patterns of Maritime Piracy 2000–2009: Introducing a New Data Set.' *Journal of Peace Research* 49(4): 605–17.

Cornell, J. (2008) *World Cruising Routes*. Camden, Maine: International Marine/McGraw-Hill.

——(2011) *Cornell's Survey of Global Cruising Yacht Movements*. www.cornellsailing.com/resources/survey-of-global-cruising-yacht-movements-jimmy-cornell/3/ (accessed 9 May 2014).

Darwin, C. (2010 [1839]) *The Voyage of the Beagle*. Seattle: Pacific Publishing Studio.

Davies, S. (1984) 'In a Small Boat Round the World.' *British Medical Journal* 289: 1780–81.

Dickinson, J., Robbins, D. and Lumsdon, L. (2010) 'Holiday Travel Discourses and Climate Change.' *Journal of Transport Geography* 18: 482–89.

Dyer, J. (2006) 'Bluewater Sailors in the Information Age.' *Margins: A Journal of Exploratory Research.* Turlock: California State University Stanislaus Honours Program, 47–52. www.csustan.edu/honors/documents/journals/margins/Dyer.pdf.

Floerl, O., Inglis, G.J., Dey, K. and Smith, A. (2009) 'The Importance of Transport Hubs in Stepping-stone Invasions.' *Journal of Applied Ecology* 46(1): 37–45.

Food and Agriculture Organization (2012) *Report on a Scoping Mission in Samoa and Tonga: Agriculture and Tourism Linkages in Pacific Island Countries.* www.fao.org/docrep/015/an476e/an476e00.pdf 49pp (accessed 1 May 2014).

Giannachi, G. (2012) 'Representing, Performing and Mitigating Climate Change in Contemporary Art Practice.' *Leonardo* 45(2): 124–31.

Hall, C.M., James, M. and Wilson, S. (2010) 'Biodiversity, Biosecurity, and Cruising in the Arctic and Sub-Arctic.' *Journal of Heritage Tourism* 5(4): 351–64.

Hall, C.M. and Wilson, S. (2010) 'Tourism, Conservation and Visitor Management in the Sub-arctic Islands.' In M.C. Hall and J. Saarinen (eds) *Tourism and Change in Polar Regions: Climate, Environments and Experiences.* New York: Routledge, 263–87.

Heyerdahl, T. (1984 [1948]). *Kon-Tiki: Across the Pacific in a Raft.* New York: Pocket.

International Naval Counter Piracy Forces (2013) *Somali Piracy Warning for Yachts.* October. www.mschoa.org/docs/public-documents/yachting-piracy-bulletin-final-version.pdf?sfvrsn=2 (accessed 9 May 2014).

Island Cruising Association (2009) *Asanvari Conservation Area Pledge.* secure.marketing.co.nz/ic/asanvari_pledge.php (accessed 5 January 2014).

Jennings, G. (1999) *Voyages from the Centre to the Margins: An Ethnography of Long Term Ocean Cruisers.* PhD thesis. Murdoch University.

——(2005) 'Caught in the Irons: One of the Lived Experiences of Long-term Ocean Cruising Women.' *Tourism Review International* 9(2): 177–93.

Kingdom of Tonga Statistics Department (2012) *Statistical Bulletin on International Arrivals, Departures and Migration 2011.* Series SDT 38–13, Nukua'lofa. 17pp.

Koth, B. (2013) 'Trans-Pacific Bluewater Sailors – Exemplar of a Mobile Lifestyle Community.' In T. Duncan, S. Cohen and M. Thulemark (eds) *Lifestyle Mobilities and Corporealities.* Ashgate: GLTRG (Geography of Leisure and Tourism Research Group) of the RGS-IBG.

Kuentzel, W. and Heberlein, T. (1997) 'Social Status, Self-development and the Process of Sailing Specialization.' *Journal of Leisure Research* 29(3): 300–19.

Lansing, A. (2014 [1959]) *Endurance: Shackleton's Incredible Voyage.* New York: Basic.

Laurier, E. (1999) 'That Sinking Feeling: Elitism, Working Leisure and Yachting.' In D. Crouch (ed.) *Leisure/Tourism Geographies.* London: Routledge, 195–212.

Lusby, C.M. and Anderson, S. (2008) 'Community and Quality of Life – The Case of Ocean Cruising.' *World Leisure* 4: 232–42.

——(2010) 'Ocean Cruising: A Lifestyle Process.' *Leisure/Loisir* 34(1): 85–105.

Lusby, C.M., Autry, C. and Anderson, S. (2012) 'Community, Life Satisfaction and Motivation in Ocean Cruising: Comparative Findings.' *World Leisure Journal* 54(4): 310–21.

Macbeth, J. (1985) *Ocean Cruising: A Study of Affirmative Deviance.* PhD thesis. Murdoch University.

——(1988) 'Ocean Cruising.' In M. Csikszentmihalyi and I.S. Csikszentmihalyi (eds) *Optimal Experience: Psychological Studies of Flow in Consciousness.* Cambridge: Cambridge University Press, 214–31.

——(1992) 'Ocean Cruising: A Sailing Subculture.' *Sociological Review* 40(2): 319–43.

——(2000) 'Utopian Tourists – Cruising is Not Just About Sailing.' *Current Issues in Tourism* 3(1): 20–33.

Melville, H. (1999 [1851]) *Moby Dick*. New York: Washington Square.

Murphy, M. (2010) *Small Boats, Weak States, Dirty Money: Piracy and Maritime Terrorism in the Modern World*. New York: Columbia University Press.

Nagourney, A. and Gettleman, J. (2011) 'Pirates Brutally End Yachting Dream.' *The New York Times*, 22 February. www.nytimes.com/2011/02/23/world/africa/23pirates. html?pagewanted=all&_r=0 (accessed 8 May 2014).

Nordhoff, C. and Hall, J.N. (1999 [1932]) *Mutiny on the Bounty*. New York: Back Bay.

Northland Marine Development Group (2008) *International Visiting Yachties Survey – Whangarei and Opua*. Whangarei, New Zealand. May 2008.

OceansWatch (2013) *What We Do*. www.oceanswatch.org (accessed 5 January 2014).

Pacificpuddlejump (2014) *Yahoo list*. groups.yahoo.com/neo/groups/pacificpuddleju mp/info?referrer=SanFranciscoSailing (accessed 10 October 2014).

Porter, M. (1999) 'The Mermaids are Out there so Why aren't We? Women and Sailing.' *Canadian Women's Studies* 15(4): 102–5.

Russell, D. (2012) *Are they Happy Now? An Evaluation of the Public Participation Process, Public Satisfaction and Physical Activity Outcomes Associated with the Queenscliff Harbour Redevelopment, Victoria*. Honours thesis submitted to School of Natural and Built Environments, University of South Australia, Adelaide.

Sailblogs (2011) *Sailors Without Borders*. www.sailblogs.com/member/transmarine/ (accessed 8 May 2014).

Samoa Tourism Authority (2009) *Samoa Tourism Development Plan 2009–13*. www. preventionweb.net/files/27077_samoatourismdevelopmentplan20092013.pdf (accessed 5 May 2014).

Seven Seas Cruising Association (2010) *Clean Wake Projects*. www.ssca.org/cgi-bin/ pagegen.pl?pg=links_human&title=Clean%20Wake%20Projects (accessed 8 May 2014).

Smith, M. (2009) *Issues in Cultural Tourism Studies*. Routledge.

SPTO (South Pacific Tourism Organisation) (2013) *Tourism Statistics in the Pacific: An Assessment*.

Stevenson, R.L. (2010 [1883]) *Treasure Island*. New York: SoHo.

TRIP Consultants (2008) *MCA Vanuatu Tourism Survey Baseline Study*. mcavanua tu.gov.vu/MCA%20CONTENTS/MCA%20Environment%20and%20Social%20Ass esment/MCA%20Vanuatu%20Tourism%20Survey%20Baseline%20Study.pdf (accessed 5 May 2014).

Werth, L.F. (1987) 'The Paradox of Single-handed Sailing – Case Studies in Existentialism.' *Journal of American Culture* 10(1): 65–78.

14 Understanding climate change vulnerability and resilience of tourism destinations

An example of community-based tourism in Samoa

Min Jiang, Emma Calgaro,
Louise Munk Klint, Dale Dominey-Howes,
Terry DeLacy and Steve Noakes

Introduction

Samoa, a Pacific small island developing state and territory (SIDST) (Figure 14.1) has been identified as a 'climate-tourism hotspot' where climate change is projected to have a major adverse effect on tourism (Becken and Hay, 2007; Scott *et al.*, 2008). As Samoa's leading foreign exchange earner, tourism accounts for over 20% of gross domestic product (GDP) (Samoa Ministry of Finance, 2012) and is a major employer, representing 10% of direct employment (Samoa Tourism Authority, 2009). Unlike Pacific destinations such as Fiji and New Caledonia, where large resorts are numerous, Samoa's tourism is dominated by small-scale operations owned and run by local people and communities (Harrison and Prasad, 2013; Scheyvens, 2005). Consequently, tourism makes a significant direct contribution to the social and economic development of Samoa.

Samoan tourism suffers from a range of difficulties associated with its location and size as a SIDST, including isolation from major markets, small population, limited transportation links, lack of local technical skills and inadequate levels of local capital. This in turn leads to lower resilience to external risks (Scheyvens and Momsen, 2008). Furthermore, it is expected to experience a range of climate change-related impacts similar to those forecast for the central Pacific region (AGBOM and CSIRO, 2011; AusAID *et al.*, 2011). Therefore, concerted efforts are needed to protect and strengthen the resilience of the tourism sector to the challenges and risks resulting from future climate change.

In order to maintain and enhance tourism's resilience at a time of continuing rapid change (caused by nature as well as human activities), it is vital to have a sophisticated understanding of the factors that contribute to the underlying vulnerability of an affected destination (Calgaro and Lloyd, 2008; Calgaro *et al.*, 2013a, 2013b). From this understanding, appropriate adaptation strategies

240   *Min Jiang* et al.

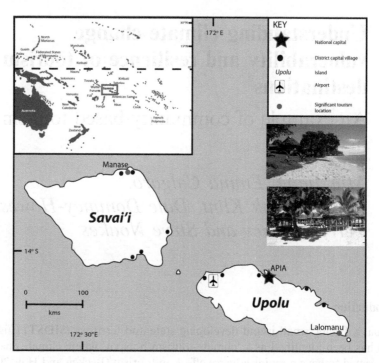

Figure 14.1 Map of Samoa

may be proposed to reduce vulnerability and protect and enhance resilience. There has been a recent emergence of interest in tourism adaptation to climate change (Becken and Hay, 2012, 2007; Scott *et al.*, 2012; Scott *et al.*, 2009; Simpson *et al.*, 2008), although knowledge about tourism vulnerability and adaptation, especially at the destination level, remains limited (Becken and Hay, 2012; Calgaro and Lloyd, 2008; Scott *et al.*, 2009). Similarly, tourism climate adaptation policies and strategies remain underdeveloped in most destinations, resulting in a lack of incentives and/or directives to encourage and support the sector to adapt.

To improve our understanding of some of the issues, this research focuses on community-based tourism in Samoa and examines how economic, social, environmental and governance factors influence the vulnerability and resilience levels of the tourism system to climate change. Here we present the key findings of a vulnerability assessment of Samoa's community-based tourism to climate change. This assessment was guided by a modified version of the Destination Sustainability Framework (DSF) developed by Calgaro (2010). The second and third sections present the modified DSF (our conceptual framework) and outline our methodology. The chapter then discusses the key components of the vulnerability assessment – namely, the tourism system's exposure, the shocks and stressors to which it is exposed, and its vulnerability and resilience to those shocks and stressors. The chapter concludes with recommendations for Samoa's community-based tourism to enhance its resilience. Implications of the application of the modified DSF for future research will also be discussed.

Our conceptual framework

Whilst the concept is contested, for us vulnerability is 'the degree to which a system is susceptible to, or unable to cope with, adverse effects of climate change, including climate variability and extremes' (IPCC, 2007: 883). It is 'a function of the character, magnitude, and rate of climate variation to which a system is exposed, its sensitivity, and its adaptive capacity' (IPCC, 2007: 883). Similarly contested, for us resilience is 'the ability of a social or ecological system to absorb disturbances while retaining the same basic structure and ways of functioning, the capacity for self-organisation, and the capacity to adapt to stress and change' (IPCC, 2007: 880), and is a direct expression of the strength of a coupled human-environment system (Carpenter *et al.*, 2001). Adaptation reflects the process of adjustment to actual or expected climate and involves countering the effects of moderate harm and exploiting beneficial opportunities that arise from change (IPCC, 2011). In doing so, it focuses on reducing exposure and sensitivity levels and increasing resilience of a system to climate change impacts (IPCC, 2011).

We identified and reviewed a number of theoretical models to assess the multiple causal factors and processes contributing to tourism vulnerability and resilience. Calgaro's DSF was considered to be the most comprehensive framework for understanding tourism vulnerability and resilience (see Calgaro, 2010; and Calgaro *et al.*, 2013b for more detail). The DSF is a holistic systems framework that is designed to guide the examination of the multiple socio-ecological factors and processes that may influence the co-constitution of vulnerability (weaknesses) and resilience (strengths) in a chosen system (household, community, population) at a given time and place. However, some modifications were needed better to understand vulnerability and resilience in the context of Pacific tourism and climate change (Figure 14.2). These included: first, the expansion of the tourism system component (adapted from Gunn, 1994; Leiper, 2004); second, the inclusion of an overview of the range of shocks and stressors (trigger events that destabilise the system and expose existing system strengths and weaknesses) that may affect South Pacific SIDSTs (detailed in the extended box in Figure 14.2); and third, the addition of Scott *et al.*'s (2009) climate adaptation portfolio for the tourism-recreation sector to the longer-term Adjustments and Adaptations box under System Adaptiveness. In line with Scott *et al.*'s (2009) Climate Adaptation Portfolio, the possible types of adaptation responses are grouped under six categories: behavioural and social; technical and structural; business management; policy; research; and education.

Research methods

Vulnerability and resilience are constant and place-specific conditions of coupled human-environment systems. To understand better the complex and place-based phenomena, the vulnerability assessment of Samoa's community-based tourism was designed as an instrumental case study, for which the case itself is of secondary interest (Hancock and Algozzine, 2006; Stake, 2005). While the case is still investigated in depth, the aim was to facilitate our understanding and insight into another theoretical question (Hancock and Algozzine, 2006; Stake, 2005): how do place-specific conditions of the tourism system contribute to its vulnerability and resilience?

Community-based tourism was chosen because of its dominant role in Samoa's tourism sector, and Lalomanu (Figure 14.1) was chosen because it was the top tourist destination in Samoa when this study commenced in June 2009 (Wong *et al.*, 2012). On 29 September 2009, a tsunami struck the south-east of Upolu and destroyed most of the coastal tourism infrastructure in this area, including 20%–25% of the tourism accommodation capacity of Samoa (Wong *et al.*, 2012). Given the destruction, it was no longer appropriate to conduct research in Lalomanu. Consequently, Manase in Savai'i (Figure 14.1) was chosen as the case study destination. The scope of the study was not

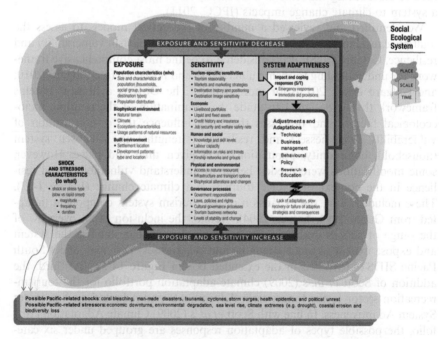

Figure 14.2 The modified Climate Change DSF for the Pacific tourism islands
Source: Calgaro et al., 2013b

limited only to Manase, but covered tourism stakeholders in other areas of Samoa, including Apia (Samoa's capital), the south-east of Upolu, and other areas of Savai'i where community-based tourism actively takes place (see Figure 14.1). By broadening the scope, we were able to obtain a better understanding of the community-based tourism system and its vulnerability and resilience to the 2009 tsunami.

Primary data collection was conducted in Samoa in November and December 2010 utilising multiple methods. These included secondary data analysis, participant observation recorded in field diaries, semi-structured interviews and focus group discussions (FGDs) – all approved to meet the requirements of the human research ethics clearance through the lead author's university (Berg, 2007; Krueger and Casey, 2009; Patton, 2002). Using multiple complementary methods (method triangulation) creates a body of overlapping data which ensures scientific rigour where the research question is addressed through multiple sources of data (Phillimore and Goodson, 2004).

A total of 24 interviews (representing 26 individuals) and two FGDs were conducted. A question outline was used to guide the interviews and FGDs, which reflected the key components of the modified DSF (Table 14.1). Despite the structured question outline, the interviews allowed flexibility for the researchers to seek clarification or elaboration on specific topics, as well as for interviewees to tell their stories without being interrupted. Interview participants included government officers, non-governmental organisation

Table 14.1 Interview and FGD question examples

Theme of questions	Examples
Shocks and stressors	– Have you noticed any change in tourism development/the environment/climate in Samoa in the past 15 years? What kind of changes are they? And what do you think have caused the changes? – What is the most concerning shock/stressor for you? And why?
Exposure	– What are the key players of the community-based tourism system in Samoa? – What are the main tourist attractions?
Sensitivity	– Which country do your guests mainly come from? What type of tourists are they? How do you market your business? – Do you have insurance for your business/property? – What skills and training/education opportunities are available for the locals to draw upon to set up tourism-related businesses? – Do the current policies and plans include building standards and/or development regulations (including coastal set-backs)?
System adaptiveness	– How would you comment on the emergency management system? – Are you aware of any existing/planned government policies that are designed to assist the tourism industry and your communities to respond to climate change? – How have these policies been implemented? – What can be done to assist tourism to respond to the shock/stressor that is concerning to you?

(NGO) representatives, tourism industry representatives and members of local villages. The two FGDs were held with tourism industry representatives including beach *fale* owners and managers, hotel managers, tourism attraction managers and tourism industry employees.

The data were analysed using a thematic analysis approach in the NVivo nine software (Patton, 2002). Through the identification of categorical themes (Patton, 2002), the central themes were identified to reflect primarily the detailed components featured in the modified Climate Change DSF.

Community-based tourism in Samoa: identifying *who* is vulnerable

Community-based tourism in Samoa, which features unique small-scale beach *fale* accommodation, differentiates Samoa from its neighbours. Ranging from basic, open-sided huts with thatched roofs and traditional woven blinds in the place of walls, to walled bungalows with small verandas with access to shared bathrooms and dining facilities (Scheyvens, 2005), beach *fales* provide affordable accommodation and meals to international tourists as well as Samoans living overseas who return for short visits. In recent years, the style of beach *fales* has evolved to cater for tourists who want more than basic comfort and security, such as permanent walls, lockable doors and air-conditioning (interview notes). Beach *fales* are symbolic to the traditional Samoan lifestyle referred to as *FaaSamoa* and contribute to the authenticity of the tourist experience (Wong *et al.*, 2010). Tourists are regularly included in traditional events and family celebrations of the village where they are staying, and many offer communal, local traditional meals (Hall and Boyd, 2005).

Manase (see Figure 14.1) offers tourists one of the country's finest white sandy beaches. It is home to five locally owned beach *fale* operations, namely Jane's, Regina's, Tailua, Tanu (the first beach *fale* operation in Samoa) and Vacation's, as well as an operation by New Zealand investors (Stevenson's at Manase), and a water sports operation owned by a Swiss couple (Raci's Beach Club), who also run an internet café attached to the local petrol station. These beach *fales* not only provide accommodation, but also operate on-site restaurants, bars and tourism activities.

Shocks and stressors: to *what* is the system vulnerable and/or resilient?

A scoping of past shocks and stressors that have impacted the community-based tourism system in Samoa revealed that tsunamis and tropical cyclones are the two major shocks that concern tourism stakeholders. Sea-level rise, changed patterns in rainfall/seasons, economic downturns and coastal erosion are the top four stressors that concern tourism stakeholders. This suggests that Samoa's tourism community faces the threat of multiple and often compounding events, some of which are not related to climate change. Therefore, whilst our focus is on identifying the major shocks and stressors that are specifically related to weather patterns and climate change – tropical cyclones, sea-level rise, changed patterns in rainfall/seasons, and coastal erosion – and exploring how these have affected the tourism system in Samoa, we have included tsunamis in our analysis of shocks and stressors and the community's various responses to these risks.

Tsunamis. In September 2009, an unprecedented earthquake doublet (averaging M_W 8.0) generated a tsunami that caused substantial damage and loss of life in Samoa, American Samoa and Tonga (Goff and Dominey-Howes, 2011). Data from recent tsunami events, coupled with palaeotsunami research, suggest that Samoa and the wider Pacific region are subject to regular tsunami events (Goff *et al.*, 2011; Okal *et al.*, 2011). Samoa recorded SAT$310.11 million (US$131.4 million) in damages from the event, equating to 22% of Samoa's GDP (Government of Samoa, 2009). Samoa's tourism sector was greatly affected, including the south-east coast of Upolu Island, one of Samoa's most popular tourist destinations. Damages to physical assets and knock-on losses from the loss of these assets were estimated at SAT$79.1 million (US$33.5 million) (Government of Samoa, 2009). All private-sector participants reported decreases in tourist arrivals: 'it affected the whole of Samoa and tourism wise ... and I felt that time to be the lowest season ever ... ' (interview notes). The media's misinformation of the tsunami negatively impacted tourism demand; Samoa was no longer seen as a safe and enjoyable destination. This created a widespread feeling of fear and helplessness among tourism community members. According to one community member, 'that is the biggest worry for us. Like I said – tsunami, it is fresh on our minds. Each and every Samoan that is what we [have] seen. And we never think this would happen to us ... it can happen overnight, within minutes, you have no time for anything; that is the worrisome ... '

Tropical cyclones. Samoa is located in the tropical cyclone belt of the South Pacific and, as a consequence, is regularly affected by tropical cyclones (SPREP, 2009; Sutherland *et al.*, 2005). The country also experiences long dry spells that coincide with the El Niño Southern Oscillation (ENSO) phenomenon (SPREP, 2009). Tropical cyclones most often occur between the summer months of December to February (SPREP, 2009). Eight major storms affected Samoa between 1980 and 2001 (McKenzie *et al.*, 2005) and Cyclones Ofa (1990) and Val (1991) caused widespread destruction (Fairbairn, 1997; SPREP, 2009). An accommodation representative observed that 'there was one year after the other ... and it affected the whole of Samoa ... ' The effects were not only limited in the economic damages and losses but also included environmental erosion, biodiversity loss and invasive species. One source described that ' ... it eroded the beach, took a lot of the white sand ... ' A focus group commented of Cyclone Heta (December 2003– January 2004) that ' ... a couple of invasive species of vines that are destroying all the rainforest. That came out after the last cyclone actually ... ' Changes in the frequency and intensity of tropical cyclones are anticipated to be a major effect of climate change (SPREP, 2009). While a decrease in tropical cyclone frequency for the Pacific is forecast (Emanuel, 2013), increasing intensity may have major implications for tourism in Samoa, including beach *fale* tourism.

Sea-level rise. Samoa's sea level has risen by about 4 mm per year since 1993, which is slightly higher than the global average of 2.8–3.6 mm per year (AusAID *et al.*, 2011). Sea-level rise is expected to continue in Samoa, up to 5–15 cm by 2030 under a high emissions scenario (AusAID *et al.*, 2011). Sea-level rise is a real concern for Samoa's community-based tourism as most of its infrastructure is located in the low-lying coastal areas. With the exception of one single participant, all accommodation business representatives identified sea-level rise as a main stressor. One participant observed: 'The sea level comes up quite high near the *fales*.' Another participant also said that 'Being near the sea does bring to mind if the sea rises a bit ... there could be a danger ... '

Changed patterns in rainfall/seasons. Being a typical tropical island country, Samoa's rainfall and humidity are usually defined by distinctive wet and dry seasons on the leeward (north-western) sides of its main islands, Savai'i and Upolu (SPREP, 2009). November to April is the wet season in Samoa, when 75% of its total annual rainfall occurs (AusAID *et al.*, 2011). Rainfall patterns in Samoa are projected to change with more extreme rainfall days expected (AusAID *et al.*, 2011), which may affect tourism experiences, particularly when tourists seek to undertake outdoor activities (Moreno, 2007). Changes in rainfall were identified as being a key stressor to tourism (based on past experiences) by almost one third of all participants. Some islanders observed that the weather has become unpredictable, limiting tourists' ability to engage in mostly outdoor tourism activities and therefore negatively affects customer satisfaction: 'This is a big worry. Sometimes, it rains for days without any season – this puts off our guests as they are unable to engage in any activities.'

Coastal erosion. Samoa is faced with serious coastal erosion problems caused by storm surges and coastal flooding related to tropical cyclones (SPREP, 2009). This may be exacerbated by climate change (AusAID *et al.*, 2011). Participants commented that 'there is a lot of wash out, coastal wash out'. The development of sea walls helped redress the coastal erosion problem, but the erection of these walls caused other problems for tourism. For example, a waterfront hotel business was grateful for the government-funded sea wall project, which helps alleviate land loss, but they had to build a jetty for their visitors to access the water for snorkelling and kayaking (interview notes).

Vulnerability: *why* is the system vulnerable?

Identification, analysis and assessment of Samoa's community-based tourism revealed that the principal factor contributing to exposure levels to the risks associated with climate change is *extensive coastal settlement and development.* About 70% of Samoa's population and infrastructure are located in the coastal zone (SPREP, 2009). Most tourism developments are also located on the coast, making its community-based tourism more exposed to tropical cyclones, tsunamis, storm surges and flooding. As a participant observed on the post-tsunami rebuilding, 'our telephone lines, our hospitals and our schools are all down on the coast so now we are moving them all inland … ' However, 'retreating the (tourism) industry inlands won't be a very viable option', and therefore 'the big *fales* for visitors are still at the waterfront because if they are not there then they lose their value in beauty and nature'. Beach *fales* are usually open-sided huts made from wooden timber with thatched roofs held up by poles. This type and style of construction is easy and cheap to build and repair when necessary, but it also makes them vulnerable to the effects of damaging natural hazard events (e.g. tsunamis and strong wind damage associated with tropical cyclones). Accommodation businesses are now increasingly building more permanent structures with steel and concrete (interview notes).

Pre-existing economic, social, political and environmental conditions within a given system not only have the propensity to influence the form shocks and stressors take in the tourism system, but also determine its response capabilities to destabilising events (Calgaro, 2010; Calgaro *et al.*, 2013b). The vulnerability assessment identified seven main factors that increase the vulnerability of the community-based tourism system in Samoa to shocks and stressors.

Limited local marketing resources. Marketing of the community-based tourism sector depends heavily on foreign resources and the industry expects more proactive local marketing support. Word of mouth was indicated as the most common and effective means of marketing, while other marketing tools include internet marketing, travel wholesalers, newspapers and magazines. Some businesses, especially those in Savai'i, are constrained by very limited access to the internet, and another constraint is heavy dependence in marketing on foreign resources, particularly the widely used Jason's visitor guide developed by a New Zealand company. Although the Samoa Tourism Authority has been making an effort to promote Samoa overseas as a destination, some tourism representatives were unsure how they benefit from such efforts and expected the government agency to be more proactive in local marketing for individual tourism businesses.

Limited access to economic capital and insurance. Although most community-based tourism businesses in Samoa are operated by local families on their own land, it was commonly felt that a lack of financial resources made it difficult for business to start. Some programmes, primarily sponsored by such international donors as AusAID, NZAid and the World Bank/International Finance Corporation (through the Samoan government), are available to finance tourism. These financing programmes are difficult for the communities to access due to limited business skills and access to information. Therefore tourism businesses have few financial resources to cope with and respond to shocks and stressors. A FGD highlighted that ' ... they make the criteria for people to access it too complicated ... Sometimes you don't actually even understand how to fill out the forms ... ' Again, due to the limited access to economic capital, the owners of most tourism businesses and beach front developments cannot afford to insure their properties, even though they are aware of the importance: 'probably most businesses should have insurance for these sorts of things (natural disaster) ... But ... you have to have the means to afford such things.'

Insecure employment for both businesses and employees. Staffing tends to be a big challenge for tourism businesses, partly due to the lack of skilled hospitality manpower. The majority of workers in the industry do not receive formal training. Instead, people are trained on the job, as they usually come from the extended family or the village of the business owner (interview notes). With regards to the availability of human capital, Savai'i is more disadvantaged than Upolu because it has only limited access to formal training opportunities. Furthermore, as perceived by some private-sector sources, staff 'do not take their jobs seriously'. Instead of having to work for food, they work only for cash to meet such expenses as school fees, school uniforms for their children and church donations. As a result, businesses can easily lose their staff. For the employees, on the other hand, tourism is not a very secure industry. 'There are fluctuations ... They [businesses in the tsunami affected area] still haven't rebuilt, so of course there is a workforce there out of work.' Beach *fale* workers are rarely covered by superannuation schemes for formally employed workers in Samoa, 'because they are mainly family owned, [they probably] don't go through the proper channels ... Some would just pay cash ... Usually it wouldn't even be an hourly or daily rate ... give them an allowance I suppose for doing chores ... '

Lack of basic infrastructure and transport. The existing road infrastructure in Samoa was heavily damaged by the 2009 tsunami and at the time of writing was being reconstructed. Tourism businesses in Savai'i and Manase, in particular, are faced with more challenges in persuading tourists to travel a long way with limited transport options. Changes in transport options that have negatively affected tourist arrivals also include the withdrawal of domestic flights between Upolu and Savai'i and the termination of an international flight connection to the USA through Honolulu by Air New Zealand in 2010. After Upolu–Savai'i flight services were terminated, the ferry became the only option between the two islands. As one industry representative stated, 'a major drawback is the distance – we are far away from the rest of the world ... If Savai'i also gets connected with air, it will help in bringing tourists'.

Constraining governance processes. Government achievements in providing infrastructure, marketing, financing and training have not met the private sector's expectations. One industry representative commented that 'if you look at the assistance extended to beach *fale* operators, government has not given financial assistance of their own. It has always been money from other countries ... ' It was also felt that communication with and involvement of community and industry is less than private-sector representatives expected: 'it would be very beneficial for us if we are given that chance to elaborate on things, and try and share, and be able to participate in a lot of things.'

Weaknesses in disaster preparedness. Even though some emergency procedures are in place (mainly under the Disaster Management and Emergency Act 2007), Samoa needs to enhance its natural disaster preparedness significantly. An effective early warning system was not in place at the time the research was undertaken. Communication barriers, such as limited information dissemination channels and lack of constant radio reception, prevented access to timely information for communities and tourism businesses, especially those based in Savai'i. Commenting on the 2009 tsunami event, an accommodation representative stated that 'our warning systems were totally ill-equipped. It was something like 45 minutes from when it happened when we got the official warning text from disaster management'.

Slow recovery and lack/failure of adaptation. Reflecting the emerging integration of disaster risk reduction and climate change adaptation in the Pacific (Gero *et al.*, 2011), adaptation measures were embedded in Samoa's post-tsunami recovery efforts. However, the country relies primarily on international funding and aid (Daly *et al.*, 2010). Tourism businesses and communities in the affected area recovered only slowly because of a lack of financial assistance in providing basic evacuation and recovery materials: 'there were 20 restaurants in Lalomanu before the tsunami, but only two reopened after more than one year of recovery.' Previously established developmental practices that made the system highly vulnerable to climate change risks remain in place at both government and industry levels. FGD participants commented that, 'the government is constructing [an] office building just next to the coastline. What will happen if there is a big storm or tsunami? What if the foundation is eroded?' Similarly, beach *fale* businesses 'still build the *fales* exactly at the same place where they were after the tsunami'. Tourist preferences are, in part, to blame for this choice. They want to be close to the beach. As a consequence, tourism facilities are provided in a style and location to meet their expectations (Calgaro and Lloyd, 2008; Calgaro *et al.*, 2013a). Some adaptation projects are not well coordinated, failing to enhance adaptive capacity. Instead, exposure to risk and sensitivity levels are increased (interview notes). As a participant observed, 'they even put seawalls in villages that already have planted mangroves. This is mad because you are starting a project and devastating another project!'

Resilience: *why* is the system resilient?

Small island communities have shown resilience to social and environmental change in the past (Barnett, 2001; Tompkins, 2005). A major component of the resilience of local communities in Pacific Islands is their traditional values and knowledge and social cohesion (IPCC, 2007). However, the tourism system links the local communities of the country to the rest of the world, where its resilience may be undermined by external events and wider economic, political and environmental factors. In order to adapt to the various changes, it is crucial to focus on both reduction of vulnerability and enhancement of resilience (IPCC, 2007). The vulnerability assessment of Samoa's community-based tourism provided an insight into how these traditionally resilient factors strengthen the tourism destination system in Samoa.

Strong family and kinship connections. Although Samoa has a history of European colonial influence from the 1800s, the country maintains a distinctive Polynesian culture and social system (Crocombe, 2008). *FaaSamoa*, a strong force in life and politics, has three key elements: *Matai* (chief), *Aiga* (extended family) and church (Samoa Tourism Authority, 2009). *Matais* are the heads of *Aiga* (including parents and children, brothers, sisters and cousins, grandparents and grandchildren, nephews and nieces). As a Samoan, it is one's duty to be of service to one's *Aiga* for life (Samoa Tourism Authority, 2009). The strong family and kinship ties ensure that community-based tourism businesses in Samoa support one another by providing basic needs, business finance, labour and marketing. Businesses use local food supplies, employ staff from the neighbourhood, and make contributions to various activities of the church, the village and the school. As a beach *fale* manager commented, 'I think there is a big future in beach *fales*, especially when you have the community work[ing] together ... '

Diverse livelihood portfolios. In addition to running an accommodation business, beach *fale* owners, who are often *Matais* of their extended family, usually have a range of such livelihood options as agribusiness, vegetable and fruit plantations, and fishing, as a result of customary land ownership. The *Matai* title is strongly tied to the family lands (Meleisea, 1997), which provide high-level security of the livelihoods. As one beach *fale* owner commented, 'Because we own the land ... everyone has private land ... That is where we are safe ... If we don't have tourism, we will go back to the land'. Having a range of income sources outside tourism lowers vulnerability levels to any disruptions in tourist flows.

Low tourism seasonality levels. The tourism markets of Samoa consist primarily of New Zealand, Australia and American Samoa, which together represent over 80% of international arrivals (SBS, 2011). Tourism numbers increase from May through to October, which is winter time in New Zealand and Australia. During the low season of international arrivals, community-based tourism businesses keep receiving domestic visitors 'coming from the town' to have family reunions or other community gatherings. As one beach *fale* operator commented, 'it's difficult for us to say high season because we are always full ... but I would say the highest season is the months of September and October, that's when we turn down a lot of reservations ... '

Strong remittance support. During the 1970s and 1980s, around one third of the Samoan population moved overseas and formed communities in Australia, New Zealand and the USA (Meleisea, 2005). As a result, a significant amount of remittances flow back to Samoa which may be used to facilitate tourism development and climate change adaptation. Samoa is one of the highest recipients of remittances in the world, and in 2009 they amounted to 22% of GDP (World Bank, 2011). As a consequence, owners of tourism businesses commonly receive help from family members overseas. Such support helped stabilise households and communities in the direct aftermath of the 2009 tsunami, and helped fund the longer-term recovery. Access to this external resource greatly improves household and community resilience levels to natural disasters. Tourists who had experienced the engaging style of Samoa's community-based tourism were also key contributors to the post-tsunami recovery in 2009. As a beach *fale* owner who recovered relatively quickly from the tsunami commented, guests 'have provided us with both cash and in kind. It is because of the help from our guests we have been able to rebuild so quickly ... And now once we have rebuilt, they are all coming back ... '

Effective community governance. Power at village and family levels is strong in Samoa, and Matais' roles encompass family, civic and political duties in their village. Strongly tied to the family lands (Meleisea, 1997), the Matai title has played a significant role in the development of beach *fale* tourism. The first beach *fale* business in Manase Tanu was indeed started by the Matai of the village (interview notes). The 1990 Village Fono Act strengthened the position of Matai to rule their village, and deal with health and social issues as well as local civil and criminal matters (Wong *et al.*, 2010). In Manase, for example, dogs are forbidden in order to create a safer and more enjoyable environment for tourists. According to a Manase-based beach *fale* representative, 'our village keeps us safe ... we have laws and order in each village ... So as the tourist comes in, they feel safe ... '

Enhanced natural disaster preparedness and climate change adaptation. The 2009 tsunami event highlighted Samoa's exposure to destabilising events and reaffirmed the need for proactive and targeted adaptation and resilience-building measures to a wide range of possible shocks and stressors. Evidence shows that the community-based tourism system of Samoa has been undertaking a range of adaptations. The most noticeable behavioural and social change was people moving inland from the coast. For beach *fale* businesses that need to stay by the waterfront to keep their appeal for tourists, alternative houses have been built inland. Structural and technical adaptations include building sea walls to protect the coastal infrastructure, replanting mangroves to prevent the coastline from erosion, and enforcing stricter building standards for new, post-tsunami constructions. Businesses started diversifying their tourism products and markets, for example, extending accommodation uphill and providing bush ecotourism tours. Research, education and awareness programmes specifically committed to climate change adaptation were also put in place, as when the Ministry of Agriculture and Fisheries ran workshops to educate communities about climate change impacts on crops and climate-resilient alternatives.

Conclusion

This research has undertaken an in-depth, systematic vulnerability assessment of a tourism system by examining how community-based tourism in Samoa is affected by and responds to climate change risks. Four climate change-related risks – namely, tropical cyclones, sea-level rise, changes in wet seasons, and coastal erosion – were those identified as having a critical impact on the tourism system and tourism flows. The application of the modified DSF framework in Samoa suggested that the vulnerability level of Samoa's community-based tourism is shaped by a range of human and natural factors of the system which collectively contribute to its exposure, sensitivity and adaptiveness. On the positive side, Samoan industry stakeholders have demonstrated resilience to such disruptive events as the 2009 tsunami. However, it can be concluded that the tourism system's vulnerability to climate change remains high. Some critical adaptation issues have not yet been addressed. Furthermore, some activities designed to increase resilience and assist adaptation actually resulted in maladaptation and created new vulnerabilities – the exact opposite outcome to what authorities were trying to achieve. The post-tsunami recovery process exposed some of these issues, such as a return to previous development patterns, lack of access to resources for recovery, and slow development of early warning systems.

It is suggested that the additional adaptation measures are required to assist the community-based tourism system in Samoa to reduce vulnerability and enhance resilience. Priorities could be given to: 1 improving disaster preparedness measures and build capacity in emergency responses at government, industry and community levels; 2 encouraging industry engagement in climate change issues and providing better climate change and environmental education; 3 providing better infrastructure and making financial resources more accessible for tourism-related communities; 4 strengthening public-private partnership in tourism development as well as in climate change adaptation; 5 ensuring integrated governance of government and the Matai system; and 6 enhancing the implementation and enforcement of environmental and climate change regulations.

The theoretical implications of the modified DSF framework are relevant not only to community-based tourism in Samoa, but also to tourism communities elsewhere, especially those 'climate-tourism hotspots' that face the challenge of climate change. The framework provides tourism destinations, policy makers and individual businesses with a comprehensive assessment tool to break down the components of the tourism system, identify the risks that may affect it, analyse its dimensional conditions which shape its vulnerability and resilience, and ultimately inform adaptation processes to climate change. Climate change adaptation involves tourism stakeholders at all levels, from the individual to the organisation, from public to private sectors, and from households to communities (Simpson *et al.*, 2008). To optimise the applicability of the framework, more research is needed to develop, refine and test it further within the tourism sector in different tourism destinations.

References

AGBOM and CSIRO (2011) 'Projections Based on Global Climate Models.' In AusAID, AGBOM, AGDCCEE, CSIRO and Vanuatu Meteorology and Geo-Hazard Department (eds) *Climate Change in the Pacific: Scientific Assessment and New Research (Volume 1: Regional Overview)*. Aspendale: Pacific Climate Change Science Program, 145–79.

AusAID, Australian Government Bureau of Meteorology (AGBOM), Australian Government Department of Climate Change and Energy Efficiency, Commonwealth Scientific and Industrial Research Organisation (CSIRO) and Samoa Meteorology Division, Ministry of Natural Resources and Environment (2011) 'Current and Future Climate of Samoa.' Aspendale: Pacific Climate Change Science Program.

Barnett, J. (2001) 'Adapting to Climate Change in Pacific Island Countries: The Problem of Uncertainty.' *World Development* 29: 977–93.

Becken, S. and Hay, J.E. (2007) *Tourism and Climate Change – Risks and Opportunities.* Clevedon: Channel View Publications.

——(2012) *Climate Change and Tourism: From Policy to Practice.* New York: Routledge (Earthscan).

Berg, B.L. (2007) *Qualitative Research Methods for the Social Sciences.* Sixth edn. Boston: Pearson Education, Inc.

Calgaro, E. (2010) 'Building Resilient Tourism Destination Futures in a World of Uncertainty: Assessing Destination Vulnerability in Khao Lak, Patong and Phi Phi Don, Thailand to the 2004 Tsunami.' Department of Environment and Geography, Sydney: Macquarie University.

Calgaro, E., Dominey-Howes, D. and Lloyd, K. (2013a) 'Application of the Destination Sustainability Framework (DSF) to Explore the Drivers of Vulnerability in Thailand following the 2004 Indian Ocean Tsunami.' *Journal of Sustainable Tourism*, DOI: 10.1080/09669582.2013.826231.

Calgaro, E. and Lloyd, K. (2008) 'Sun, Sea, Sand and Tsunami: Examining Disaster Vulnerability in the Tourism Community of Khao Lak, Thailand.' *Singapore Journal of Tropical Geography* 29: 288–306.

Calgaro, E., Lloyd, K. and Dominey-Howes, D. (2013b) 'From Vulnerability to Transformation: A Framework for Assessing the Vulnerability and Resilience of Tourism Destinations in a World of Uncertainty.' *Journal of Sustainable Tourism*, DOI:10.1080/09669582.2013.826229.

Carpenter, S., Walker, B., Anderies, J.M. and Abel, N. (2001) 'From Metaphor to Measurement: Resilience of What to What?' *Ecosystems* 4(8): 765–81.

Central Intelligence Agency (CIA) (2012) *World Factbook: Samoa.* www.cia.gov/library/publications/the-world-factbook/geos/ws.html (accessed 16 June 2013).

Crocombe, R. (2008) *The South Pacific.* Seventh edn. Suva: IPS Publications, University of the South Pacific.

Daly, M., Poutasi, N., Nelson, F. and Kohlhase, J. (2010) 'Reducing the Climate Vulnerability of Coastal Communities in Samoa.' *Journal of International Development* 22: 265–81.

Emanuel, K. (2013) 'Downscaling CMIP5 Climate Models Shows Increased Tropical Cyclone Activity Over the 21st Century.' *Proceedings of the National Academy of Sciences* 110(30): 12219–24.

Fairbairn, T.I.J. (1997) 'The Economic Impact of Natural Disasters in the South Pacific with Special Reference to Fiji, Western Samoa, Niue and Papua New Guinea', Suva: South Pacific Disaster Reduction Programme.

Gero, A., Méheux, K. and Dominey-Howes, D. (2011) 'Integrating Community Based Disaster Risk Reduction and Climate Change Adaptation: Examples from the Pacific.' *Natural Hazards and Earth System Science* 11; 101–13. Doi:10.5194/nhess-11-101-2011.

Goff, J., Chagué-Goff, C., Dominey-Howes, D., Mcadoo, B., Cronin, S., Bonté-Grapetin, M., Nichol, S., Horrocks, M., Cisternas, M., Lamarche, G., Pelletier, B., Jaffe, B. and Dudley, W. (2011) 'Palaeotsunamis in the Pacific Islands.' *Earth-Science Reviews* 107: 141–46.

Goff, J. and Dominey-Howes, D. (2011) 'The 2009 South Pacific Tsunami.' *Earth-Science Reviews* 107: v–vii.

Government of Samoa (2009) 'Samoa Post-Disaster Needs Assessment: Following the Earthquake and Tsunami of 29th September 2009.' Washington, DC: Global Facility for Disaster Reduction and Recovery.

Gunn, C.A. (1994) *Tourism Planning: Basics, Concepts, Cases.* Third edn. Washington, DC: Taylor & Francis.

Hall, C.M. and Boyd, S.W. (2005) *Nature-based Tourism in Peripheral Areas: Development or Disaster?* Great Britain: Channel View Publications.

Hancock, D.R. and Algozzine, B. (2006) *Doing Case Study Research: A Practical Guide for Beginners.* New York: Teachers College, Columbia University.

Harrison, D. and Prasad, B. (2013) 'The Contribution of Tourism to the Development of Fiji and Other Pacific Island Countries.' In C.A. Tisdell (eds) *Handbook of Tourism Economics: Analysis, New Applications and Case Studies.* New Jersey: World Scientific, 741–61.

IPCC (Intergovernmental Panel on Climate Change) (2011) 'Special Report on Managing the Risks of Extreme Events and Disasters to Advance Climate Change Adaptation (SREX) – Summary for Policy Makers.' Geneva, Switzerland: Intergovernmental Panel on Climate Change (IPCC).

——(2007) 'Climate Change 2007: Impacts, Adaptation and Vulnerability.' Contribution of Working Group II to the Fourth Assessment Report of the Intergovernmental Panel on Climate Change. New York: IPCC.

Krueger, R.A. and Casey, M.A. (2009) *Focus Groups: A Practical Guide for Applied Research.* Fourth edn. Thousand Oaks: Sage Publications Inc.

Leiper, N. (2004) *Tourism Management.* Frenchs Forest: Pearson Education Australia.

McKenzie, E., Prasad, B. and Kaloumaira, A. (2005) 'Economic Impact of Natural Disasters on Development in the Pacific.' Suva: University of South Pacific (USP) and Pacific Islands Applied Geoscience Commission (SOPAC).

Meleisea, M. (1997) 'The Making of Modern Samoa: Traditional Authority and Colonial Administration in the Modern History of Western Samoa.' Fiji: Institute of Pacific Studies.

——(2005) 'Governance, Developments and Leadership in Polynesia: A Microstudy from Samoa.' In A. Hooper (eds) *Culture and Sustainable Development in the Pacific.* Canberra: ANU E Press and Asia Pacific Press.

Moreno, A. (2007) 'The Role of Weather in Beach Recreation – A Case Study Using Webcam Images.' In A. Matzarakis, C.R. de Freitas and D. Scott (eds) *Development in Tourism Climatology*. Freiburg: Commission on Climate, Tourism, and Recreation, International Society of Biometeorology, 80–86.

Okal, E.A., Borrero, J.C. and Chagué-Goff, C. (2011) 'Tsunamigenic Predecessors to the 2009 Samoa Earthquake.' *Earth-Science Reviews* 107: 128–40.

Patton, M.Q. (2002) *Qualitative Research & Evaluation Methods*. Third edn. Thousand Oaks: Sage Publications, Inc.

Phillimore, J. and Goodson, L. (eds) (2004) *Qualitative Research in Tourism: Ontologies, Epistemologies and Methodologies*. London: Routledge.

Samoa Bureau of Statistics (SBS) (2011) 'Annual International Migration Statistics.' www.sbs.gov.ws (accessed 16 November 2011).

Samoa Ministry of Finance (2012) 'Strategy for the Development of Samoa 2012–16.' Apia: Samoa Ministry of Finance.

Samoa Tourism Authority (2009) *Samoa Tourism Development Plan: 2009–13*. Apia: Samoa Tourism Authority.

Scheyvens, R. (2005) 'The Growth of Beach Fale Tourism in Samoa: Doing Tourism the Samoan Way.' *CIGAD Working Paper Series*. Working Paper Number 3/2005. Palmerston North, New Zealand: Centre for Indigenous Governance and Development, Massey University.

Scheyvens, R. and Momsen, J. (2008) 'Tourism in Small Island States: From Vulnerability to Strengths.' *Journal of Sustainable Tourism* 16(5): 491–510.

Scott, D., Amelung, B., Becken, S., Ceron, J.-P., Dubois, G., Gössling, S., Peeters, P., Murray, C. and Simpson, M.C. (2008) *Climate Change and Tourism – Responding to Global Challenges*. Madrid and Paris: WMO and UNEP.

Scott, D., de Freitas, C. and Matzarakis, A. (2009) 'Adaptation in the Tourism and Recreation Sector.' In K.L. Ebi, I. Burton and G.R. McGregor (eds) *Biometeorology for Adaptation to Climate Variability and Change*. New York: Springer.

Scott, D., Hall, M. and Gossling, S. (2012) *Tourism and Climate Change: Impacts, Adaptation, and Mitigation*. New York: Routledge.

Simpson, M.C., Gössling, S., Scott, D., Hall, C.M. and Gladin, E. (2008) 'Climate Change Adaptation and Mitigation in the Tourism Sector: Frameworks, Tools and Practices.' Paris: UNEP, University of Oxford, UNWTO and WMO.

SPREP (South Pacific Regional Environmental Program) (2009) 'Pacific Adaptation to Climate Change Samoa Report of In-Country Consultation.' Apia: SPREP.

Stake, R.E. (2005) 'Qualitative Case Studies.' In N.K. Denzin and Y.S. Lincoln (eds) *The Sage Handbook of Qualitative Research*. Third edn. Thousand Oaks, CA: Sage Publications Inc., 443–66.

Sutherland, K., Smit, B., Wulf, V. and Nakalevu, T. (2005) 'Vulnerability in Samoa.' *Tiempo* 54: 11–15.

Tompkins, E.L. (2005) 'Planning for Climate Change in Small Islands: Insights from National Hurricane Preparedness in the Cayman Islands.' *Global Environmental Change* 15: 139–49.

United Nations (UN) (2009) '2009 UNISDR Terminology on Disaster Risk Reduction.' Geneva: UN.

Wong, E., Jiang, M., Klint, L., DeLacy, T., Dominey-Howes, D. and Harrison, D. (2010) 'Policy Analysis for Samoa.' A technical report for the AusAID Pacific Tourism – Climate Adaptation Project. Melbourne: Centre for Tourism and Services Research, Victoria University.

Wong, E., Jiang, M., Klint, L., DeLacy, T., Harrison, D. and Dominey-Howes, D. (2012) 'Policy Environment for the Tourism Sector's Adaptation to Climate Change in the South Pacific – The Case of Samoa.' *Asia Pacific Journal of Tourism Research.* DOI: 10.1080/10941665.2012.688511.

World Bank (2011) 'Migration and Remittances Factbook 2011.' Washington, DC: World Bank.

15 Climate change and island tourism

Louise Munk Klint, Terry DeLacy,
Sebastian Filep and Dale Dominey-Howes

Introduction

Climate change is real (IPCC, 2007a). The climate varies naturally, but the rate of change has increased, driven by anthropogenic interferences. Over the last 100 years, 11 of the 12 warmest years occurred in the period from 1995 to 2006. Atmospheric water vapour has increased in the last three decades; a warming of the ocean has occurred causing sea-level rise; westerly winds in mid-latitudes are greater than before; droughts have become longer and more intense; widespread changes have been observed in weather extremes; heavier precipitation is occurring and the intensity of cyclone activity has increased (IPCC, 2007a: 5–9). The Intergovernmental Panel on Climate Change (IPCC, 2007a) highlighted in their Fourth Assessment Report (FAR) that even with greenhouse gas[1] (GHG) concentrations stabilised, a general warming of the Earth resulting in sea-level rise will continue due to the so called 'lag effect'.

Climate change is a threat to physical, biological and social systems, and one of the greatest challenges faced by humanity (Beatley, 2009; Hall and Higham, 2005; IPCC, 2007a; Pearman, 2008; Rechkemmer and von Falkenhayn, 2009; Schnellnhuber *et al.*, 2010; World Bank, 2010). Through its impacts, climate change poses several challenges to the tourism sector that will have significant repercussions, in particular, for small island states (Reddy and Wilkes, 2013). The tourism sector is highly climate sensitive (Becken and Hay, 2007), and as such climate change will influence tourism systems. Different facets of the climate, including aesthetic, physical and thermal, may impact on tourists (Becken and Hay, 2007). For example, changes to the aesthetic facet may affect the attractiveness of a tourist site, while severe weather events may have an effect on the safety of people and places and could influence the level of participation in activities (Becken and Hay, 2007; Scott, Hall and Gössling, 2012). Extreme events will have a greater impact on tourism and other economic sectors closely connected to climate (e.g. forestry, agriculture and health) than sectors not directly connected to the climate (IPCC, 2012). Nevertheless, the effects of climate change may create both risks (e.g. reduced destination attractiveness) and opportunities (e.g. decreased seasonality) (Becken and Hay, 2007; Jopp, DeLacy and Mair, 2010).

This chapter will provide a general explanation of the definition of climate and climate change followed by an exploration of the likely effects of such climate change to small island developing states and territories (SIDSTs). The chapter then focuses on what climate change projections have been made for the Pacific in three island nations (Kiribati, Samoa and Vanuatu) and what general observations support the notion of a changing environment in this region. We shall also discuss how a changing climate may affect tourism systems both directly and indirectly, and then provide examples from the three SIDSTs to illustrate this point. The chapter concludes with some recommendations for how the tourism sector could be further involved in addressing climate change. A detailed discussion of climate change adaptation and mitigation is outside the scope of this chapter.

Climate change

A simple definition of climate is the average weather that is 'described in terms of the mean and range of variability of natural factors such as temperature, rainfall and wind speed' (Garnaut, 2008: 27). More broadly, however, it is a complex system involving living organisms and environments, such as the atmosphere, land and water (Schnellnhuber *et al.*, 2010; World Bank, 2010). It is primarily determined by incoming and outgoing energy (World Bank, 2010), and is caused by a number of interlinked processes, including physical, bio-physical and chemical, the timescale of these processes and of these processes' reactions to change (Pearman, 2008; World Bank, 2010). All of these interactions have an influence on the global climate (IPCC, 2007a).

The IPCC (2012: 29) has defined climate change as 'an alteration in the state of the climate that can be identified by changes in the mean and/or the variability of its properties, and that persists for an extended period, typically decades or longer'. The Earth has experienced a general warming, an increase in extreme events and changes to precipitation patterns (IPCC, 2007a, 2012; Preston *et al.*, 2006; Scott *et al.*, 2008). In the latest IPCC (2007a) assessment report and the recent IPCC (2012) special report on extreme events and disasters, it was confirmed that it is extremely unlikely that global warming in the past 50 years has been caused by natural forcing factors alone and that extreme events have been changed by anthropogenic causes. The Earth's increasing population, our technological advancement and our desires and needs are causing significant heat – a heat that McEwan (cited in Schnellnhuber *et al.*, 2010: xviii) termed 'the hot breath of our civilization'. In other words, anthropogenic causes, such as the burning of fossil fuels and land changes, have caused an increase in GHG emissions and concentration in the atmosphere, which in turn play a major role in driving enhanced climate change (IPCC, 2007a, 2012; Preston *et al.*, 2006).

The Earth will continue to experience changes to its physical and biological environment as a result of the Earth's warming. Even if GHG concentrations were to be stabilised, global warming will continue due to the timescales of past emissions and the oceans' thermal inertia (IPCC, 2007a; Scott *et al.*, 2008). The IPCC (2007a) has indicated that there will be increases to the global average surface air temperature, sea levels, and the intensity and frequency of heat waves and cyclones, changes in evaporation and precipitation, and a decrease in the number of frost days, snow cover and sea ice. It is further projected that climate change will impact heavily on coral reefs, fisheries, coastal conditions, freshwater resources and climate-sensitive diseases (NIWAR, 2007; Mataki, Koshy and Nair, 2006; Pelling and Uitto, 2001; UNESCAP, 2000; UNWTO, 2003). It is, however, important to recognise that the rates and intensities of such changes will vary spatially and temporally across the globe. Consequently, climate change is a global phenomenon with local consequences which requires a collective approach to address (Stern, 2006).

With a natural variability in the climate system, gaps in our knowledge about the global climate system and the difficulty in forecasting future GHG emissions, the science community can only provide educated guesses about what will happen in the future in the form of projections and scenarios (Preston *et al.*, 2006). Consequently, uncertainty is a key aspect of the global climate system (Zillman, McKibbin and Kellow, 2005). Uncertainty – not comprehending all elements of a system – does not represent a valid excuse not to act on climate change because we know more than enough to understand the consequences if we do not act now. UNESCAP (2000: n.p.) highlighted that 'it will require at least 50 years before any reduction [in GHG emissions] begins to reverse predicted climate change and sea level rise'. Consequently, today we know for certain that we need to act urgently to reduce the risks and limit the costs of climate change (Stern, 2006; UNWTO *et al.*, 2003). With this in mind, an understanding of the uncertainties of climate change is vital to ensure an appropriate response to climate change at national and international levels (Zillman *et al.*, 2005).

Although no place will be untouched by climate change (Green, 2008), some nations, regions and sectors are particularly vulnerable to its effects, and will be affected worst and first. Highly climate-sensitive sectors include agriculture, energy, food security, health, insurance, transportation, water and tourism (IPCC, 2007b, 2012; Simpson *et al.*, 2008). In terms of nations and whole regions, the IPCC (2007b: 689) stated with very high confidence – at least 90% chance of being correct – that SIDSTs are 'especially vulnerable to the effects of climate change, sea-level rise, and extreme events', due to a number of country characteristics.

Small island developing states and territories (SIDSTs) and least developed countries (LDCs)

Although an officially accepted definition of SIDSTs does not exist, SIDSTs generally refer to the United Nations (UN) member states that are 'listed on the website of the [United Nations] Office of the High Representative of the Least Developed Countries, Landlocked Developing Countries and Small Island Developing States [UN-OHRLLS]' (United Nations General Assembly, 2010: 4). As outlined in Table 15.1, there are currently 38 SIDSTs that are members of the UN and another 14 SIDSTS that are non-members of the UN (UN OHRLLS, 2013a). These nations have many similar characteristics to other developing countries,[2] but face unique, widely recognised challenges (United Nations General Assembly, 2010).

The challenges faced by most SIDSTs include but are not limited to: their small physical size and isolation; limited natural resources; a proneness to natural hazards and climate extremes; poorly developed infrastructure (Lück, 2008); limited freshwater resources; high population density and growth rates; limited economic and human resources; and a low economic resilience due to the high sensitivity to changes in external markets (IPCC, 2007b; Méheux *et al.*, 2007; Sem and Moore, 2009; United Nations, 2010). In IPCC's (2007b: 689) FAR, it was stated that these specific characteristics 'make them especially vulnerable to the effects of climate change, sea-level rise and extreme events'. SIDSTs' vulnerability to climate change is echoed by the current literature (Attzs, 2009; Méheux *et al.*, 2007; United Nations, 2010).

Further to the classification of some Pacific island countries and territories (PICTs) as SIDSTs is the designation of some as least developed countries (LDCs) (Table 15.1). To qualify as LDCs, nations must satisfy all of the following: a low income criterion; a human resource weakness criterion; and an economic vulnerability criterion (for further details of the criteria, see UN-OHRLLS, 2013b). In other words, SIDSTs that are also LDCs face even further challenges with additional limited economic resources, significantly lower human and economic development and a high proportion of rural populations that depend on the natural environment for income creation and sustenance (Sem and Moore, 2009). Six PICTs (Kiribati, Samoa, Solomon Islands, Timor-Leste, Tuvalu and Vanuatu) are considered both SIDSTs and LDCs, making them particularly vulnerable to climate change (see Table 15.1). Consequently, SIDSTs and LDCs will be hit harder by the effects of climate change than other regions, nations and sectors.

Climate change in SIDSTs in the Pacific

This section will explore the effects of climate change on SIDSTs and provide particular climate change projections for the Pacific and for three specific island nations (Kiribati, Samoa and Vanuatu). It will highlight what general observations in these three case study nations support the notion of a changing environment in this region.

Scott *et al.* (2008) undertook a qualitative assessment[3] of the tourism destinations most at risk to the effects of climate change by the mid- to end of the twenty-first century. They identified the key climate change vulnerability hotspots for tourism and a general distribution of climate change impacts that

Table 15.1 Overview of SIDSTs, LDCs and PICTs

Small island developing states and territories (SIDSTs)	Least developed countries (LDCs)	Pacific Island countries and territories (PICTs)
American Samoa		
Anguilla		
Antigua and Barbuda*		
Aruba		
Bahamas*		
Barbados*		
Belize*		
British Virgin Islands		
Cape Verde*	✓	
Commonwealth of Northern Marianas		✓
Comoros*	✓	
Cook Islands		
Cuba*		
Dominica*		
Dominican Republic*		
Fiji*		✓
Federated States of Micronesia*		✓
French Polynesia		✓
Grenada*		✓
Guam		✓
Guinea-Bissau*	✓	
Guyana*		
Haiti*	✓	
Jamaica*		
Kiribati*	✓	
Maldives*	✓	
Marshall Islands*		✓
Mauritius*		
Montserrat		
Nauru*		✓
Netherlands Antilles		
New Caledonia		✓
Niue		✓
Palau*		✓
Papua New Guinea*		✓
Samoa*	✓	✓
Puerto Rico		
Sao Tome and Principe*	✓	
Seychelles*		
Singapore*		
Solomon Islands	✓	✓
St Kitts and Nevis*		
St Lucia*		
St Vincent and the Grenadines*		
Suriname*		
Timor-Leste*	✓	✓
Tonga*		✓
Trinidad and Tobago*		
Tuvalu*	✓	✓
Vanuatu*	✓	✓
US Virgin Islands		

Note: *UN members. Pitcairn, Tokelau, and Wallis and Fortuna are also PICTs, but are not recognised on the official list of SIDSTs.

affect tourism. Figure 15.1 highlights the serious implications of climate change that SIDSTs regions like the Caribbean, the Mediterranean, the Indian Ocean and the Pacific Ocean will face.

Climate change in the Pacific

The Pacific is the world's largest ocean and covers an area of 156 million km², or one third of the Earth's surface (Luhr, 2003). While an ocean, it also comprises many smaller, regional seas. It extends some 15,000 kilometres from the Bering Sea in the north to the northern extent of the Southern Ocean at 60° S. Its greatest east-west width occurs at approximately 5° N latitude, where it spans almost 20,000 km from Indonesia to Colombia – halfway across the world. Its average depth is a little over 4,000 metres, with a maximum depth of 10,924 m (Luhr, 2003). The equator divides the basin into the North Pacific and South Pacific. Since the basin crosses the 180th meridian, the West Pacific or western Pacific closer to Asia is located within the Eastern Hemisphere, while the East Pacific or eastern Pacific closer to the Americas lies within the Western Hemisphere.

Twenty-two PICTs are dotted throughout the area. Of the 22 PICTs, 20 are classified by the UN as SIDSTs (Table 15.1 and Figure 15.2).

Table 15.2 presents an overview of climate change projections for the Pacific and observed changes and climate change projections for the case study nations identified in five studies. Common across the studies, projections

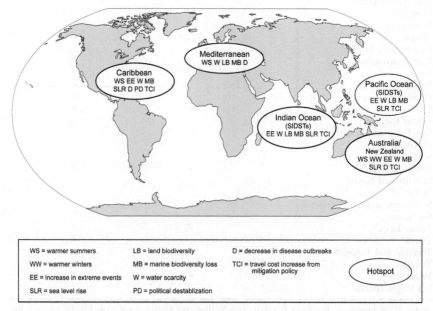

Figure 15.1 Hotspots of major climate change impacts affecting tourism destinations
Source: Adapted from Scott et al., 2008

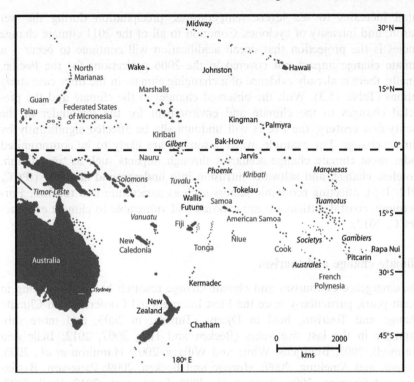

Figure 15.2 Pacific island countries and territories (PICTs)

Table 15.2 Quick facts for the three case studies: Vanuatu, Kiribati and Samoa

Key facts	Vanuatu	Kiribati	Samoa
Land area (sq km)	12,189	811	2,831
Coast line (km)	2,528	1,143	403
Population (rural/urban (%))	261,565[E] (74/26)	103,248[E](56/44)	195,476[E] (80/20)
GDP per capita (US$)	5,000[E]	6,200[E]	6,300
GDP composition by sector (%)	Services (67.6[E])	Services (67.8)	Services (64.1[E])
	Agriculture (20.6)	Agriculture (24.3)	Industry (26.5)
	Industry (11.7)	Industry (7.9)	Agriculture (9.4)
Economic importance of tourism:			
% of GDP direct/indirect tourism	19.4/37.7*	5.1/15.1*	19.7**
arrivals*** (2010)	97,180	4,701	129,487

Source: Adapted from Central Intelligence Agency, 2013; WTTC, 2011; and Harrison and Prasad, 2013
Notes: [E] Estimate; * 2011 figures based on World Travel & Tourism Council (WTTC 2011); ** 2007 figure based on Harrison and Prasad 2013; *** Excludes international arrivals from cruise ships.

entail increases to sea levels, temperatures, precipitation during the wet season, and intensity of cyclones. Common to all of the 2011 climate change studies is the projection that ocean acidification will continue to occur – a climate change impact not covered in the 2006 projections for the Pacific. Finally, there is already evidence of a changing climate in the three case study nations (Table 15.3). With the observed changes in the climate and the predicted changes to the climate and environment for the remainder of the twenty-first century, the PICTs will undoubtedly be affected significantly by climate change. For example, water resources are likely to be compromised under most climate change scenarios through impacts such as 'inundation, shoreline change, and saltwater intrusion into underground aquifers' (IPCC, 2012: 185), affecting economic sectors such as agriculture and tourism. Furthermore, coastal settlements are exposed and vulnerable to climate extremes (IPCC, 2012).

Climate change and tourism

The emergence of tourism and climate change research has been growing in recent years, particularly since the First International Conference on Climate Change and Tourism, held in Djerba, Tunisia, in 2003, and more substantially in the last five years (Becken and Hay, 2007, 2012; Belle and Bramwell, 2005; Buultjens, White and Willacy, 2007; Hamilton *et al.*, 2005; Moreno and Amelung, 2009; Moreno and Becken, 2009; Patterson, Bastianoni and Simpson, 2006; Scott *et al.*, 2008; Scott *et al.*, 2012; Wall, 2007; Wall and Badke, 1994; Zeppel, 2012). The UN World Tourism Organization (UNWTO, 2003)-convened conference brought together 140 delegates from 45 countries. The outcome – the Djerba Declaration – encouraged further 'research of the reciprocal implications between tourism and climate change' (UNWTO *et al.*, 2003: 14), placing climate change on the international tourism sector agenda. This section discusses the interconnectedness of climate change and tourism.

Tourism can cause changes to the climate system. Tourism affects natural resources, including air, land, water, flora and fauna (Douglas, Douglas and Derrett, 2001). It impacts on natural resources through land use changes and emissions of GHGs (Becken and Hay, 2007). Tourism contributes between 3.9% and 6.0% of global CO_2 emissions (Scott *et al.*, 2008).[4] Although tourism impacts on the climate through the emission of GHGs, climate change will also impact tourism in a number of ways (Becken and Hay, 2007, 2012; Scott *et al.*, 2012). The natural environment plays an important role in the tourism sector (Moreno and Becken, 2009; Scott *et al.*, 2008; UNWTO *et al.*, 2007) and climate is a key driver of international tourism (Becken and Hay, 2007; Hall and Higham, 2005; Hamilton *et al.*, 2005; Payet, 2008). Accordingly, a changing climate and consequently a change in the natural environment can and will have a substantial impact on tourism (Becken and Hay, 2007; Hamilton *et al.*, 2005; Scott *et al.*, 2008; UNWTO *et al.*, 2007; Uyarra

Table 15.3 Overview of climate change projections for the Pacific, observations and projections for Vanuatu, Kiribati and Samoa

Impact	2006 Pacific projections[1]	2011 Pacific projections[2]	Observations in Vanuatu[3]	2011 Vanuatu projections[3]	Observations in Kiribati[4]	2011 Kiribati projections[4]	Observations in Samoa[5]	2011 Samoa projections[5]
Sea-level rise	Regional sea variability will occur. Global scale predictions are: 2030: 3–16cm 2070: 7–50cm	Improved understanding required; sea level rise of 0.55 to 1.1m by 2100 is possible, but a more plausible estimate is at around 80cm by 2100	Since 1993 the sea level has risen by approximately 6mm per year across Vanuatu	2030: 3–17cm 2055: 7–31cm 2090: 17–63cm	Since 1993 the sea level has risen by 1–4mm per year across Kiribati	2030: 4–14cm 2055: 9–29cm 2090: 16–58cm	Since 1993 the sea level has risen by about 4mm per year across Samoa	2030: 5–15cm 2055: 10–30cm 2090: 17–59cm
Ocean acidification	n/a	Further ocean acidification expected to occur	Acidification has slowly increased in the waters of Vanuatu since the eighteenth century	Ocean acidification increases will continue	Acidification has slowly increased in the waters of Kiribati since the eighteenth century	Ocean acidification increases will continue	Acidification has slowly increased in the waters of Samoa since the eighteenth century	Ocean acidification increases will continue
Temperature increases	Air temperatures: 2030: 0.5–2°C 2070: 1–7°C	Air temperatures/ sea surface temperatures: 2030: 0.5–1.0°C/ 0.7–1.4°C 2055: 1.0–1.5°C/ 0.8–2.2°C 2090: 1.5–3.0°C/ 0.6–2.6°C	Maximum temperatures have increased at a rate of 0.17°C/0.18°C per decade in Port Vila/Aneityum. Minimum temperatures have also increased on average	Air temperatures: 2030: 0.2–1.0°C 2055: 0.5–2.0°C 2090: 0.7–3.2°C	Maximum temperatures have increased at a rate of 0.18°C per decade. Minimum temperatures have also increased on average	Air temperatures: 2030: 0.2–1.4°C 2055: 0.6–2.3°C 2090: 1.0–3.8°C	Maximum temperatures have increased at a rate of 0.22°C per decade in Apia	Air temperatures: 2030: 0.2–1.2°C 2055: 0.6–1.9°C 2090: 0.8–3.3°C

Table 15.3 (continued)

Impact	2006 Pacific projections[1]	2011 Pacific projections[2]	Observations in Vanuatu[3]	2011 Vanuatu projections[3]	Observations in Kiribati[4]	2011 Kiribati projections[4]	Observations in Samoa[5]	2011 Samoa projections[5]
Precipitation changes	Increased rainfall during summer monsoon season in decades ahead (some uncertainty related to the regional distribution of this)	Increases in annual mean rainfall for some countries, annual number of rain days will increase for some countries, widespread increase in days of heavy rainfall, droughts expected to occur less often	Wet season rainfall has been decreasing on average since 1950 in some areas of Vanuatu (e.g. Port Vila), but no clear trend can be detracted for other areas of Vanuatu or for dry season or annual rainfall	Rainfall decrease in dry season and increase in wet season (although some uncertainty as climate change framework results inconsistent)	A clear increasing trend has been observed from 1950 in annual and wet season rainfall, but no clear trend can detracted for the dry season	Reduced frequency of droughts. Increase in rainfall with intensified frequency of more extreme rainfall days (although some uncertainty in rainfall projections, as climate change model results inconsistent)	Data since 1950 show no clear trends in annual or seasonal rainfall, but there is substantial variation in rainfall from year to year	Rainfall decrease in dry season and increase in wet season (although some uncertainty as climate change model results inconsistent)
Cyclone intensity increases	More intense tropical cyclones and changes to the El Niño–Southern Oscillation (ENSO)	More intense tropical cyclones. Possible decrease in number of cyclones.		Average wind speed increase of 2–11% and rainfall intensity increase of 20% in a 100km radius of the cyclone centre. Frequency of tropical cyclones to decrease by end of twenty-first century		n/a		Average wind speed increase of 2–11% and rainfall intensity increase of 20% a 100km radius of the cyclone centre. Frequency of tropical cyclones to decrease by end of twenty-first century

Notes: [1] Preston et al., 2006; [2] AGBOM and CSIRO, 2011; [3] AusAID, AGBOM, AGDCCEE, CSIRO and Vanuatu Meteorology and Geo-Hazard Department, 2011; [4] AusAID, AGBOM, AGDCCEE, CSIRO and Kiribati Meteorology Service, 2011; [5] AusAID, AGBOM, AGDCCEE, CSIRO and Samoa Meteorology Division, Ministry of Natural Resources and Environment, 2011.

et al., 2005), although the impact will range from positive to negative depending on where one considers the impact. Marshall *et al.* (2011: 509) propose five categories of climate change impacts on tourism: 'direct climatic impacts, indirect environmental change impacts, impacts of mitigation[5] policies on tourist mobility, indirect societal change impacts and attitudinal and behavioural change impacts'.

The direct climatic impacts will influence tourism in a range of ways. 'The physical impacts include sea-level rise, beach erosion, increased frequency and intensity of extreme events, droughts, floods and changes in ecosystems' structures and biodiversity' (Moreno and Amelung, 2009: 1143). Destination appeal will be affected by the direct climatic impacts through changes to the climate, the natural resources upon which the destination is based (Marshall *et al.*, 2011) or the overall destination image (Hall and Higham, 2005). Changes to the climate may also affect the suitability of some activities (Hall and Higham, 2005), such as beach tourism and winter tourism (Scott *et al.*, 2008). Studies have predicted that popular tourist destinations will gradually change to countries near the poles and to mountainous areas (Hamilton *et al.*, 2005). The seasonality of tourism may also change due to direct climatic impacts (Hall and Higham, 2005). With a dependency on environmental conditions, input/operating costs will also be affected (Marshall *et al.*, 2011; Scott *et al.*, 2008). For example, increasing temperatures will affect tourists' comfort levels (Hall and Higham, 2005) and could cause increases to cooling costs (Scott *et al.*, 2008), such as the running of air conditioners. Consequently, the tourism industry needs to prepare itself to monitor the developments and ensure that any planning reflects changes to the environment (UNWTO, 2003) and tourism demand.

A number of indirect environmental change impacts may also occur. These may present themselves as risks or opportunities (Moreno and Amelung, 2009; Pacific Islands Regional Assessment Group, 2001; Scott *et al.*, 2008; Jopp *et al.*, 2010). Climate change may negatively influence biodiversity, coral cover, reef aesthetics, fishery production or ecosystem services (e.g. coastal protection and beach replenishment) (Marshall *et al.*, 2011). Conversely, positive changes may include increases in visitation to certain destinations due to improved climatic conditions (Scott *et al.*, 2008). For example, in Northern Europe, countries may see an increase in visitation during their summer due to the Mediterranean being too hot during the peak of that season (Hall and Higham, 2005).

Tourist mobility may also be impacted by the implementation of mitigation policies. As tourism relies heavily upon transportation, the sector will be sensitive to any future transport policies that aim to mitigate GHG emissions by increasing the price of carbon (Hall and Higham, 2005). As Burns and Vishan (2010) highlight, energy costs present a major element of tourism operations due to the high reliance on fossil fuels. Consequently, mitigation policies may also affect the competitiveness of nations by affecting the relative costs of energy (Becken and Hay, 2007). A number of studies have highlighted that mitigation policies may influence the flow of travel by affecting the pre-ferences and attitudes of tourists (Cohen and Higham, 2011; DeLacy and Lipman, 2010; Forsyth *et al.*, 2007; Marshall *et al.*, 2011).

Climate change will cause various societal changes (Green, 2008; World Bank, 2010) that may impact the tourism sector. Climatic extremes may affect food security (Pacific Institute of Public Policy, 2009) through inundation and drought, which can cause significant social disruption (Passioura, 2005), as past famines in Africa have shown. The Pacific region has been impacted by tropical cyclones in the past, affecting food supply and creating substantial financial losses (Barnett, 2001). Consequently, climate change, with its pre-dicted increases in drought and cyclone intensity, may create social upheaval and present significant security risks. Such societal changes may influence tourists' perceived attractiveness and/or safety of a destination. Academics are increasingly acknowledging the importance of understanding tourist's per-ceived risk (Baker and Coulter, 2007; Floyd and Pennington-Gray, 2004; Henderson, 2003; Hitchcock and Putra, 2005; Ritchie, 2009) and with climate change-exacerbated incidents, the awareness of such will be crucial to the tourism sector's adaptation[6] and mitigation to climate change.

As the awareness of the effects of climate change spreads, attitudinal and behavioural impacts will occur. Marshall *et al.* (2011) suggest that climate change policies may encourage carbon off-setting in tourism. Furthermore, as suggested by Yeoman and McMahon-Beattie (2006), climate change can become a major driver in consumer demand. In relation to these impacts, greener destinations may have an advantage over less sustainable destinations. Consequently, it is apparent that climate change and tourism are interconnected, influencing each other in a range of ways via complex feedback mechanisms.

The effects of climate change on Pacific tourism

This section discusses the possible effects of climate change on Pacific tourism by providing evidence from the three case study nations. A focus will be given to the effects of sea-level rise, extreme weather events such as cyclones, sea surface warming and coral bleaching.

Sea-level rise

Sea levels have been rising in all three case study countries and are projected to continue to rise. Sea-level rise is a real concern, particularly for the lower lying PICTs of which Kiribati is one. Others include Tuvalu, Tonga, the Marshall Islands and Tokelau (Kelman and West, 2009). The concern for these nations – and even nations in the Pacific that have more land well above any potential sea-level rise, such as Samoa, Vanuatu and Fiji – relates to the large percentage and high exposure of coastal populations, and the con-sequent high level of infrastructure in coastal zones (Kelman and West, 2009; World Bank, 2010).

Take the example of the capital and hub of the Republic of Kiribati: South Tarawa. It has been reported that South Tarawa will face some significant issues from climate change, including coastal erosion, depletion of marine resources, overcrowding, and lack of water and poor water quality, although many other issues (e.g. environmental degradation and sanitation) are more pressing at present ((Office of Te Beretitenti and T'Makei Services, 2012). The current population (based on the 2010 census) of South Tarawa is just over 50,000 and the island is showing a trend of rapid growth in its population. South Tarawa has an official land area of 15.76 km^2; and the vast majority of the island is less than 3 metres above sea level and is on average 450 metres wide (Office of Te Beretitenti and T'Makei Services, 2012). South Tarawa is also home to one of Kiribati's international airports, which not surprisingly is located close to the coast. The following quote highlights the risk of rising sea levels and the consequent threat of coastal erosion, coastal inundation and flooding:

> There are parts of Kiribati where you can't see the water, most notably in the southern Tarawa hub of Betio, but the threat of climate change is consistently there. The first thing you see when you land are the sandbags that try, and fail, to stop spring tides from flooding the only airstrip. If you are forced to go to hospital, you may get your feet wet. It is regularly inundated.
>
> (Government of Kiribati, n.d.)

Kiribati is already facing serious concerns related to potable, good-quality water. More than two decades ago, the School of Travel Industry Management (1990) at the University of Hawai'i at Manoa highlighted the issue of limited water supplies in South Tarawa and the need to consider ways to upgrade water infrastructure to support future growth in tourism. Since then both the population and tourism numbers have seen an increase. Combined with the effects of climate change (e.g. sea-level rise and changes to precipitation) which have the ability to change the nature of the availability and quality of fresh water (Kelman and West, 2009), there will be some real challenges ahead to meet tourists' water expectations (Graci and Dodds, 2010), as well as meeting the need for potable water for local residents.

Adaptation measures that could help address the effects of sea-level rise include mangrove planting to create a natural buffer (soft coastal protection) (Becken and Hay, 2007; UNEP-WCMC, 2006; McLeod and Salm, 2006); establishment and enforcement of protected areas thereby ensuring the healthy reef systems that act as natural buffers in surge and wave events (IPCC, 2012); installation of sea walls (hard coastal protection); installation of desalination plants; installation of rainwater tanks with filters; and building of (tourism) infrastructure further away from the coast (Becken and Hay, 2007).

Impacts of extreme events

Samoa has suffered serious economic shocks from both cyclones and tsunamis in the last couple of decades (World Bank *et al.*, 2010). In December 2012, Cyclone Evan hit Samoa and caused significant damage to its productive sectors, social sectors, infrastructure and environment. The total damage of Cyclone Evan was estimated at US$203.9 million,[7] of which 10.73% represents the total damage and losses affecting tourism (Government of Samoa *et al.*, 2013). The total tourism damage and losses covered total or partial destruction of 267 hotel rooms, the loss of 974 jobs, and loss of revenue during the reconstruction period, with knock-on effects on other aspects of the Samoan economy. The 2009 tsunami affected primarily beach *fales* and budget and standard accommodation in terms of damaged properties (Wong *et al.*, 2013), but Cyclone Evan affected mainly deluxe and superior accommodation (Government of Samoa *et al.*, 2013; Dominey-Howes and Thaman, 2009), and water and electricity supply to the tourism sector were also affected.

A key adaptation to more intense cyclones and extreme events is 'to ensure that buildings and other assets are designed to standards that enable them to cope with the greater wind stresses and more intense precipitation associated with storms' (World Bank *et al.*, 2010: 1). Other adaptation options worth considering include stimulation of tourism demand, and diversification of tourism markets and products (Government of Samoa *et al.*, 2013); coastal protection and/or relocation of assets away from coastal areas (World Bank *et al.*, 2010).

Impacts of sea surface warming and coral bleaching

With projected sea surface temperature increases ranging from 0.2°C to 3.8°C across the three case study nations, coral bleaching could potentially become a real stressor affecting the tourism destinations in these PICTs. Even modest ocean warming can cause coral bleaching (Riegl *et al.*, 2009). Furthermore, increases in sea-level rise and changes to sea-water chemistry (e.g. acidification) may lead to additional stress on coral reefs (Garrod and Gössling, 2008; Lück, 2008), which could lead to coral bleaching and biodiversity loss (Lück, 2008).

The reputation of dive tourism[8] destinations has been impacted by the degradation of coral reefs in the past (Cesar, 2000). Although, as highlighted by Gössling *et al.* (2012), the impact of such may vary in extent depending on the level of specialisation and experience with diving. For example, highly specialised divers often travel for the sole purpose of diving and are well aware of what constitutes healthy coral reefs. However, this is often not the case for novice divers, who may also not engage in diving as their sole purpose of travel.

Dive tourism is important to Vanuatu (UNEP and UNWTO, 1995). Scuba diving (including wreck and reef diving) is one of the key tourism attractions in Vanuatu (Asian Development Bank, 2002; UNEP and UNWTO, 1995). Howard (1999) argued that 30% of the tourism expenditure comes from dive tourism and that just under half of international arrivals to Vanuatu participate in dive tourism. The significance of dive tourism to Vanuatu is confirmed by the more recent Vanuatu 2004 *Visitor Survey Report* (Vanuatu National Statistics Office, 2007: 26), which stated that 'snorkelling topped the list of activities engaged by visitor[s] while in Vanuatu'. Although it is not clear how tourism numbers in Vanuatu have been affected by coral bleaching alone in the past, research on the dive tourism system in Vanuatu has indicated that coral bleaching is a stressor that may be exacerbated by climate change in the future (Klint, 2013). According to this research, dive operators in Vanuatu currently see the threat of Crown-of-Thorn Starfish as more significant to the sustainability and health of the coral reefs than coral bleaching.

Conclusion and future directions

In this chapter, we have identified that observations of changing climate in the Pacific region have been made and include temperature increases, sea-level rise and ocean acidification. Precipitation changes have occurred, but clear trends are not detected for specific regions of the nations or for specific seasons (e.g. dry season). All of the Pacific including the three case study nations has been projected to experience, to varying degrees, sea-level rises, ocean acidification, temperature increases, precipitation changes and cyclone intensity increases in the years to come.[9] Tourism in the case study nations has already been affected by sea-level rise, coastal erosion, inundation, potable water issues and extreme weather events, and may experience significant impacts from coral bleaching events in the future as sea surface temperatures increase.

Some future directions include soft and hard coastal protection, installation of desalination plants and rainwater tanks with filters, moving (tourism) infrastructure away from the coastal zone, improving building standards to cope with more extreme events, stimulation of tourism demand, and diversification of tourism markets and/or products.

The World Bank (2010: 328) highlighted an important aspect of ensuring action is undertaken to address climate change in that '[h]ow an issue is framed – the words, metaphors, stories and images used to communicate information – determines the action'. Applying this approach, the way forward will be about our stewardship of the Earth, the recognition that adaptation and mitigation measures do exist and that humankind can make a difference through successfully implementing such measures, the need to start thinking innovatively, applying new technologies, planning ahead and acting now. The focus should not be on how vulnerable these SIDSTs and PICTS are, but on how their resilience and adaptive capacity can be preserved and enhanced so that they are better prepared for the effects of climate change that lie ahead.

Acknowledgements

Large sections of this chapter are based on components of the lead author's unpublished thesis.

The authors acknowledge and appreciate the financial support received by the AusAID International Development Research Award (ADRA0800029) and the lead author's PhD stipend, which made this research possible.

Notes

1 GHGs refer to 'those gaseous constituents of the atmosphere, both natural and anthropogenic, that absorb and emit radiation at specific wavelengths within the spectrum of thermal infrared radiation emitted by the Earth's surface, the atmosphere itself, and by clouds. This property causes the greenhouse effect. Water vapour (H_2O), carbon dioxide (CO_2), nitrous oxide (N_2O), methane (CH_4) and ozone (O_3) are the primary greenhouse gases in the Earth's atmosphere' (IPCC, 2007a: 947).
2 It should be noted that Trinidad and Tobago are now considered developed countries.
3 The assessment covered scientific evidence of climate change, the adaptive capacity of nations and/or regions, and the importance of tourism to the various nations and/or regions.
4 Air and car transport represent the largest sources of emissions for tourism.
5 Mitigation here refers to a deliberate measure that is implemented and sustained in advance to diminish further climate change (Haque and Burton, 2005; Smit *et al.*, 2000).
6 Adaptation in this chapter refers to the 'adjustment in natural or human systems in response to actual or expected climate stimuli or their effect, which moderates harm or exploits beneficial opportunities' (Haque and Burton, 2005: 342).
7 US$1 = SAT 2.281.
8 Dive tourism refers to 'individuals travelling from their usual place of residence, spending at least one night away, and actively participating in one or more diving activities, such as scuba diving, snorkelling, scuba or the use of rebreathing apparatus' (Garrod and Gössling, 2008: 7).
9 Please note that there were no projections made for Kiribati related to cyclone intensity increases, but that this was projected for the other nations and the Pacific region in general.

References

AGBOM (Australian Government Bureau of Meteorology) and CSIRO (Commonwealth Scientific and Industrial Research Organisation) (2011) 'Projections Based on Global Climate Models.' In AusAID, AGBOM, AGDCCEE, CSIRO and Vanuatu Meteorology and Geo-Hazard Department (eds) *Climate Change in the Pacific: Scientific Assessment and New Research (Volume 1: Regional Overview)*. Aspendale: Pacific Climate Change Science Program, 145–79.

Asian Development Bank (2002) *Vanuatu: Economic Performance and Challenges Ahead*. Manila: ADB.

Attzs, M. (2009) 'Preparing for a Rainy Day: Climate Change and Sustainable Tourism in Caribbean Small Island Developing States.' *Worldwide Hospitality and Tourism Themes* 1(3): 231–51.

AusAID, AGBOM, AGDCCEE (Australian Government Department of Climate Change and Energy Efficiency), CSIRO and Kiribati Meteorology Service (2011) *Current and Future Climate of Kiribati*. Aspendale: Pacific Climate Change Science Program.

AusAID, AGBOM, AGDCCEE, CSIRO and Samoa Meteorology Division, Ministry of Natural Resources and Environment (2011) *Current and Future Climate of Samoa*. Aspendale: Pacific Climate Change Science Program.

AusAID, AGBOM, AGDCCEE, CSIRO and Vanuatu Meteorology and Geo-Hazard Department (2011) *Current and Future Climate of Vanuatu*. Aspendale: Pacific Climate Change Science Program.

Baker, K. and Coulter, A. (2007) 'Terrorism and Tourism: The Vulnerability of Beach Vendors' Livelihoods in Bali.' *Journal of Sustainable Tourism* 15(3): 149–266.

Barnett, J. (2001) 'Adapting to Climate Change in Pacific Island Countries: The Problem of Uncertainty.' *World Development* 29(6): 977–93.

Beatley, T. (2009) *Planning for Coastal Resilience: Best Practices for Calamitous Times*. Washington, DC: Island Press.

Becken, S. and Hay, J.E. (2007) *Tourism and Climate Change: Risks and Opportunities*. Clevedon: Channel View Publications.

——(2012) *Climate Change and Tourism: From Policy to Practice*. Milton Park: Routledge.

Belle, N. and Bramwell, B. (2005) 'Climate Change and Small Island Tourism: Policy Maker and Industry Perspectives in Barbados.' *Journal of Travel Research* 44(1): 32–41.

Burns, P.M. and Vishan, I. (2010) 'The Changing Landscape of Climate Change: NAMAs, SIDS and Tourism.' *Tourism and Hospitality Planning & Development* 7 (3): 317–28.

Buultjens, J., White, N. and Willacy, S. (2007) *Climate Change and Australian Tourism: A Scoping Study*. Gold Coast, Qld: Sustainable Tourism Cooperative Research Centre (STCRC).

Central Intelligence Agency (2013) *The World Factbook*. Washington, DC: Central Intelligence Agency. www.cia.gov/library/publications/the-world-factbook/ (accessed 13 July 2013).

Cesar, H. (2000) *Impacts of the 1998 Coral Bleaching Event on Tourism in El Nido, Philippines*. Narragansett: Coral Resources Center, University of Rhode Island.

Cohen, S.A. and Higham, J.E.S. (2011) 'Eyes Wide Shut? UK Consumer Perceptions on Aviation Climate Impacts and Travel Decisions to New Zealand.' *Current Issues in Tourism* 14(4): 323–35.

DeLacy, T. and Lipman, G. (2010) 'GreenEarth. Travel: Moving to Carbon Clean Destinations.' In C. Scott (ed.) *Tourism and the Implications of Climate Change: Issues and Actions*. Bingley, UK: Emerald Group Publishing.

Dominey-Howes, D. and Thaman, R. (2009) 'UNESCO-IOC International Tsunami Survey Team Samoa (ITST Samoa).' In J. Goff (ed.) *Interim Report of Field Survey 14th–21st October 2009*. UNESCO-IOC and Australian Tsunami Research Centre Miscellaneous Report, No. 2.

Douglas, N., Douglas, N. and Derrett, R. (eds) (2001) *Special Interest Tourism: Context and Cases.* First edn. John Wiley & Sons Australia Ltd.

Floyd, M. and Pennington-Gray, L. (2004) 'Profiling Risk Perceptions of Tourists.' *Annals of Tourism Research* 31(4): 1051–54.

Forsyth, P., Dwyer, L. and Spurr, R. (2007) *Climate Change Policies and Australian Tourism: Scoping Study of the Economic Aspects.* Gold Coast, Qld: Sustainable Tourism Cooperative Research Centre (STCRC).

Garnaut, R. (2008) *The Garnaut Climate Change Review.* Port Melbourne: Cambridge University Press.

Garrod, B. and Gössling, S. (eds) (2008) *New Frontiers in Marine Tourism: Diving Experiences, Sustainability, Management.* First edn. Amsterdam: Elsevier Ltd.

Gössling, S., Scott, D., Hall, C.M., Ceron, J.-P. and Dubois, G. (2012) 'Consumer Behavior and Demand Response of Tourists to Climate Change.' *Annals of Tourism Research* 39(1): 36–58.

Government of Kiribati (n.d.) *Tarawa.* Bairiki: Office of Te Beretitenti. www.climate. gov.ki/case-studies/tarawa/ (accessed 13 July 2013).

Government of Samoa, ACP-EU Natural Disaster Risk Reduction Program, Australia AID, New Zealand Foreign Affairs and Trace Aid Programme and World Bank (2013) *SAMOA Post-disaster Needs Assessment Cyclone Evan 2012.* Apia: Government of Samoa.

Graci, S. and Dodds, R. (2010) *Sustainable Tourism in Island Destinations.* London: Earthscan.

Green, D. (2008) *From Poverty to Power: How Active Citizens and Effective States can Change the World.* Oxford: Oxfam International.

Hall, C.M. and Higham, J. (eds) (2005) *Tourism, Recreation and Climate Change.* Clevedon: Channel View Publications.

Hamilton, J.M., Maddison, D.J. and Tol, R.S.J. (2005) 'Effects of Climate Change on International Tourism.' *Climate Research* 29(3): 245–54.

Haque, C.E. and Burton, I. (2005) 'Adaptation Options Strategies for Hazards and Vulnerability Mitigation: An International Perspective.' *Mitigation and Adaptation Strategies for Global Change* 10(3): 335–53.

Harrison, D. and Prasad, B. (2013) 'The Contribution of Tourism to the Development of Fiji Islands and Other Pacific Island Countries.' In C. Tisdell (ed.) *Handbook of Tourism Economics.* Singapore: World Scientific Publishing Co., 741–61.

Henderson, J.C. (2003) 'Terrorism and Tourism: Managing the Consequences of the Bali Bombings.' *Journal of Travel & Tourism* 15(1): 41–58.

Hitchcock, M. and Putra, I.N.D. (2005) 'The Bali Bombings: Tourism Crisis Management and Conflict Avoidance.' *Current Issues in Tourism* 8(1): 62–76.

Howard, J.L. (1999) 'How do Scuba Diving Operations in Vanuatu Attempt to Minimize their Impact on the Environment.' *Pacific Tourism Review* 3(1): 61–69.

IPCC (Intergovernmental Panel on Climate Change) (2007a) *Climate Change 2007: The Physical Science Basis. Contribution of Working Group I to the Fourth Assessment Report of the Intergovernmental Panel on Climate Change.* New York: IPCC.

——(2007b) *Climate Change 2007: Impacts, Adaptation and Vulnerability. Contribution of Working Group II to the Fourth Assessment Report of the Intergovernmental Panel on Climate Change.* New York: IPCC.

——(2012) *Managing the Risks of Extreme Events and Disasters to Advance Climate Change Adaptation: Special Report of the Intergovernmental Panel on Climate Change.* Cambridge: Cambridge University Press.

Jopp, R., DeLacy, T. and Mair, J. (2010) 'Developing a Framework for Regional Destination Adaptation to Climate Change.' *Current Issues in Tourism* 13(6): 591–605.

Kelman, I. and West, J.J. (2009) 'Climate Change and Small Island Developing States: A Critical Review.' *Ecological and Environmental Anthropology* 5(1): 1–16.

Klint, L.M. (2013) *'Buoyancy – Bifo and Afta': A Climate Change Vulnerability/Resilience Framework for Tourism – The Case Study of Vanuatu Dive Tourism.* Unpublished PhD thesis. Footscray: Victoria University.

Lück, M. (ed.) (2008) *The Encyclopedia of Tourism and Recreation in Marine Environments.* Oxfordshire: CAB International.

Luhr, J.F. (ed.) (2003) *Earth.* New York: DK Publishing.

Marshall, N.A., Marshall, P.A., Abdulla, A., Rouphael, T. and Ali, A. (2011) 'Preparing for Climate Change: Recognising its Early Impacts through the Perceptions of Dive Tourists and Dive Operators in the Egyptian Red Sea.' *Current Issues in Tourism* 14(6): 507–18.

Mataki, M., Koshy, K. and Nair, V. (2006) 'Implementing Climate Change Adaptation in the Pacific Islands: Adapting to Present Climate Variability and Extreme Weather Events in Navua (Fiji).' *AISCC Working Papers,* 34: 1–30.

McLeod, E. and Salm, R.V. (2006) *Managing Mangroves for Resilience to Climate Change.* Gland, Switzerland: IUCN.

Méheux, K., Dominey-Howes, D. and Lloyd, K. (2007) 'Natural Hazard Impacts in Small Island Developing States: A Review of Current Knowledge and Future Research Needs.' *Natural Hazards* 40(2): 429–46.

Moreno, A. and Amelung, B. (2009) 'Climate Change and Coastal & Marine Tourism: Review and Analysis.' *Journal of Coastal Research* 56: 1140–44.

Moreno, A. and Becken, S. (2009) 'A Climate Change Vulnerability Assessment Methodology for Coast Tourism.' *Journal of Sustainable Tourism* 17(4): 473–88.

NIWAR (National Institute of Water and Atmospheric Research) (2007) 'Pacific Islands Suffer Signs of Climate Change.' *NIWA Science.* 11 April. www.sciencealert.com.au/news/20071104-14912.html (accessed 13 July 2013).

Office of Te Beretitenti and T'Makei Services (2012) *Republic of Kiribati Island Report Series: South Tarawa.* Bairiki: Government of Kiribati.

Pacific Institute of Public Policy (2009) 'Climate Countdown: Time to Address the Pacific's Development Challenges.' *Discussion Paper* 12. www.pacificpolicy.org/wp-content/uploads/2012/05/D12-PiPP.pdf (20 August 2013).

Pacific Islands Regional Assessment Group (2001) *Preparing for a Changing Climate: The Potential Consequences of Climate Variability and Change.* Honolulu: East West Center.

Passioura, J. (2005) 'The Drought Environment: Physical, Biological and Agricultural Perspectives.' *Journal of Experimental Botany* 58(2): 113–17.

Patterson, T., Bastianoni, S. and Simpson, M. (2006) 'Tourism and Climate Change: Two-way Street, or Vicious/Virtuous Circle?' *Journal of Sustainable Tourism* 14(4): 339–48.

Payet, R.A. (2008) 'Climate Change and the Tourism-Dependent Economy of the Seychelles.' In N. Leary, C. Conde, A. Nyong and J. Pulhin (eds) *Climate Change and Vulnerability.* London: Earthscan, 155–69.

Pearman, G. (2008) *Climate Change: Risk in Australia under Alternative Emissions Futures.* Parkes: Department of Treasury.

Pelling, M. and Uitto, J.I. (2001) 'Small Island Developing States: Natural Disaster Vulnerability and Global Change.' *Environmental Hazards* 3(2): 49–62.

Preston, B.L., Suppiah, R., Macadam, I. and Bathols, J. (2006) *Climate Change in the Asia/Pacific Region – A Consultancy Report Prepared for the Climate Change and Development Roundtable.* Clayton: CSIRO.

Rechkemmer, A. and von Falkenhayn, L. (2009) 'The Human Dimensions of Global Environmental Change: Ecosystem Services, Resilience, and Governance.' *The European Physical Journal Conferences* 1(1): 3–17.

Reddy, M.V. and Wilkes, K. (2013) 'Tourism and Sustainability: Transition to a Green Economy.' In M.J. Reddy and K. Wilkes, *Tourism, Climate Change and Sustainability.* Abingdon: Routledge, 3–23.

Riegl, B., Bruckner, A., Coles, S.L., Renaud, P. and Dodge, R.E. (2009) 'Coral Reefs – Threats and Conservation in an Era of Global Change.' In R.S. Ostfeld and W.H. Schlesinger (eds) *The Year in Ecology and Conservation Biology.* New York: New York Academy of Sciences, 36–186.

Ritchie, B. (2009) *Crisis and Disaster Management for Tourism.* Bristol: Channel View Publications.

Schnellnhuber, H.J., Molina, M., Stern, N., Huber, V. and Kadner, S. (eds) (2010) *Global Sustainability: A Nobel Cause.* Cambridge: Cambridge University Press.

School of Travel Industry Management (1990) *Tourism Development in the Republic of Kiribati.* Honolulu: School of Travel Industry Management, University of Hawaii at Manoa.

Scott, D., Amelung, B., Becken, S., Ceron, J.-P., Dubois, G., Gössling, S., *et al.* (2008) *Climate Change and Tourism – Responding to Global Challenges.* Madrid and Paris.

Scott, D., Hall, C.M.M. and Gössling, S. (2012) *Tourism and Climate Change: Impacts, Adaptation and Mitigation.* Vol. 10. London: Routledge.

Sem, G. and Moore, R. (2009) *The Impact of Climate Change on the Development Prospects of the Least Developed Countries and Small Island Developing States.* New York: UNOHRLLS.

Simpson, M.C., Gössling, S., Scott, D., Hall, C.M. and Gladin, E. (2008) *Climate Change Adaptation and Mitigation in the Tourism Sector: Frameworks, Tools and Practices.* Paris: UNEP, University of Oxford, UNWTO and WMO.

Smit, B., Burton, I., Klein, R.J.T. and Wandel, J. (2000) 'An Anatomy of Adaptation to Climate Change and Variability.' *Climatic Change* 45: 223–51.

Stern, N. (2006) *The Economics of Climate Change: The Stern Review.* Cambridge: Cambridge University Press.

United Nations (2010) *Trends in Sustainable Development: Small Island Developing States.* New York: United Nations Publications.

United Nations General Assembly (2010) *Five-year Review of the Mauritius Strategy for the Further Implementation of the Programme of Action for the Sustainable Development of Small Island Developing States: Report of the Secretary-General (A/ 65/115).* New York: United Nations General Assembly.

UN-OHRLLS (2013a) *List of Small Island Developing States.* New York: UN-OHRLLS. www.un.org/special-rep/ohrlls/sid/list.htm (accessed 6 July 2013).

——(2013b) *The Criteria for the Identification of the LDCs.* New York: UN-OHRLLS. www.un.org/special-rep/ohrlls/ldc/ldc%20criteria.htm (accessed 6 July 2013).

UNEP (United Nations Environment Programme) and UNWTO (1995) *Final Report: Vanuatu Tourism Development Master Plan.* Port Vila: Republic of Vanuatu.

UNEP-WCMC (2006) *In the Front Line: Shoreline Protection and Other Ecosystem Services from Mangroves and Coral Reefs.* Cambridge: UNEP-WCMC.

UNESCAP (United Nations Economic and Social Commission for Asia and the Pacific) (2000) *Climate Change and the Pacific Islands.* Paper presented at the Fourth Ministerial Conference on Environment and Development in Asia and the Pacific, 31 August–5 September 2000, Kitakyushu City.

UNWTO (United Nations World Tourism Organization) (2003) *Climate Change and Tourism.* Paper presented at the First International Conference on Climate Change and Tourism, Djerba, Tunisia.

UNWTO, UNEP, World Meteorological Organisation, World Economic Forum and Swiss Government (2007) *Davos Declaration: Climate Change and Tourism – Responding to Global Challenges.* Paper presented at the 2nd International Conference on Climate Change and Tourism, Davos, Switzerland.

UNWTO, United Nations Framework Convention on Climate Change, Intergovernmental Panel on Climate Change, World Meteorological Organisation, United Nations Environment Programme, United Nations Convention to Combat Desertification, *et al.* (2003) *Climate Change and Tourism.* Paper presented at the First International Conference on Climate Change and Tourism Djerba, Tunisia, 9–11 April.

Uyarra, M.C., Côte, I.M., Gill, J.A., Tinch, R.R.T., Viner, D. and Watkinson, A.R. (2005) 'Island-Specific Preferences of Tourists for Environmental Features: Implications of Climate Change for Tourism-Dependent States.' *Environmental Conservation* 32 (1): 11–19.

Vanuatu National Statistics Office (2007) *2004 Visitor Survey Report.* Port Vila: Vanuatu National Statistics Office.

Wall, G. (2007) 'The Tourism Industry and its Adaptability and Vulnerability to Climate Change.' In B. Amelung, K. Blazejczyk and A. Matzarakis (eds) *Climate Change and Tourism – Assessment and Coping Strategies.* Freiburg: Albert-Ludwig Universitaet Freiburg, 5–19.

Wall, G. and Badke, C. (1994) 'Tourism and Climate Change: An International Perspective.' *Journal of Sustainable Tourism* 2(4): 193–203.

Wong, E., Jiang, M., Klint, L., DeLacy, D., Harrison, D. and Dominey-Howes, D. (2013) 'Policy Environment for the Tourism Sector's Adaptation to Climate Change in the South Pacific – The Case of Samoa.' *Asia Pacific Journal of Tourism Research* 18(1–2): 52–71.

World Bank (2010) *World Development Report 2010: Development and Climate Change.* Washington: The International Bank for Reconstruction and Development/ World Bank.

World Bank, Ministry of Foreign Affairs Government of the Netherlands, Department for International Development United Kingdom and Swiss Agency for Development and Cooperation (2010) *Samoa: Economics of Adaptation to Climate Change.* Washington, DC: World Bank.

WTTC (World Travel and Tourism Council) (2011) *Country Reports.* wttc.org/eng. Tourism_Research/Economic_Research/Country_Reports (accessed 28 July 2011).

Yeoman, I. and McMahon-Beattie, U. (2006) 'Understanding the Impact of Climate Change on Scottish Tourism.' *Journal of Vacation Marketing* 12(4): 371–79.

Zeppel, H. (2012) 'Research Note: Climate Change and Tourism in the Great Barrier Reef Marine Park.' *Current Issues in Tourism* 15(3): 287–92.

Zillman, J.W., McKibbin, W.J. and Kellow, A. (2005) *Uncertainty and Climate Change: The Challenge for Policy.* Vol. 3. Academy of the Social Sciences in Australia.

Index

to reach out to 138; Poppy's on the Lagoon Resort in Vanuatu 143; practice of, examples of 139–43; pro-poor tourism (PPT) 135; procurement 142; reporting and practice, gap between 137–38; scale and scope, limits to 138; self-regulation, limits of 137; small island developing states (SIDS) 136–37; social and cultural audits 136–37; social and cultural benefits 140; social responsibility, pressures for 134, 136; Sonaisali Resort 141; stakeholders, legal and economic concerns of 138; sustainable development 135; Tearfund 136; tourism, new approaches to 135; tourism revenues, distribution of 142; training 142–43; Uprising Resort 141, 142; value of CSR in tourism 137–38

Cottom, S. 7

Crick, M. 127

Crocombe, R. 4, 85, 250

cruise tourism 142

cultural heritage 25, 31, 86, 88, 90, 92, 93, 94, 95, 121, 122

cultural imperialism 104

cultural tourism, development of 30–31

culture-related events, marketing and promotion of 172

customary land tenure 9–10

Dahles, H. and Meijl, T. 177

Daly, M., Poutasi, N., Nelson, F. and Kohlhase, J. 249

Dann, G.M.S. 41

dark tourism 86, 90–92, 94–95

Darwin, Charles 219

David, Abel 95

David, C. 23

Davies, S. 223

Davutukia, Tui 105

Daws, G. 85

Day, A.G. 39

de Blij, H.J. and Muller, P. 24

de Burlo, C.R. 11, 114

de Grosbois, D. 136, 138

de Kadt, E. 5, 103, 118

Dear, J. 42

decolonisation, period of 4

Defoe, Daniel 39

deforestation 128–29

DeLacy, T. and Lipman, G. 268

DeLacy, Terry xv, 239–56, 257–77

demand for tourism in Fiji, developments and changes in 196–216; air fare data 207; Asian Development Bank 201; Asian financial crisis (1997), response to 198; Augmented Dicky Fuller (ADF) test 208, 213, 214; Autoregressive Distributed Lag (ARDL) approach 204–5; aviation market, tourist development and 201–2; business tourist arrivals 200; cointegration test results 213–15; competitiveness, capacity and 207; conference participation 200; cost of tourism, cost of travel and 197; demand preferences 197; diagnostic tests (and results) 215; economic and econometric models 203–7; Error Correction Modelling (ECM) 204–5, 206–7, 209; estimations 203–4, 208; Fiji Islands Bureau of Statistics 198, 199, 200, 202, 210; General to Specific (GETS) 204–5; global financial crisis (GFC), effect of 196; hotel and restaurant industry 196; international aviation market, deregulation of 199, 201; international developments, link between demand and 196; international tourist arrivals (1974–2009) 198, 199–200; Johansen Maximum Likelihood (JML) procedure 204, 205, 208, 209; long-run cointegration relationship of travel cost proxy 209; long-run elasticities of demand 208; macroeconomic view on Fijian tourism 196; military coups (2000, 2006), fall in visitors resulting from 198–99; Pacific Forum Secretariat's Pacific Islands Air Services Agreement (PIASA) initiative 200; personal incomes and demand for tourism 196–97; Phillips and Hansen Fully Modified OLS (FMOLS) 204–5; political stability, importance of 197; proximity to Australia and New Zealand 197; Research and Innovation Technology Administration (RITA) of US Bureau of Transportation Statistics 212; Reserve Bank of Fiji 196, 198; Schwarz Information Criterion (SIC) 213; timeframe of analysis 207; tourism demand, dynamic elements in

288   *Index*